Crazy and In Charge

The Autobiography of

Abraham (Abe) Hirschfeld

As
Told to Mark Ribowsky

ISBN: 1-4107-8570-X (e-book)
ISBN: 1-4107-8571-8 (Paperback)
ISBN: 1-4107-8572-6 (Dust Jacket)

This book is printed on acid free paper.

1stBooks – rev. 10/08/03

Table Of Contents

In dedication to my wife of 60 years.
And in dedication to the public, that I may share with them
the secret to a long and happy marriage.

CRAZY AND IN CHARGE

THE AUTOBIOGRAPHY OF ABE HIRSCHFELD

As Told to Mark Ribowsky

In setting out to write the story of my rewarding and controversial life, I wanted to set something straight right away. As you probably know, I have been called crazy, a lot, and by many people—mainly by people in the media who I suppose get tired of calling me by the boring title of "real estate tycoon." In 1999, a *New York* magazine profile about me was titled "Crazy As He Wants To Be," in which they said I was "crude and irrational." Other publications have called me "a wrinkled, rumpled eccentric," "riddled with delusions," and "the millionaire New York crackpot." The *New York Post* in 1993 ran a story on me that asked in the headline, "Who Is This Nut?" And I happened to have owned the paper at the time!

Sometimes I think the media exists just so they can call me names. Even high and mighty *Time* magazine got in the act, calling me "fabulously loopy," and let me tell you, it's nice to be called fabulous in *Time*—but it's even nicer to be called a genius in *Time*. That happened in 2000 when in the *"Time 100"* issue they named me—a Polish immigrant with a fifth-grade education and a middling knowledge of the English language—as one of "the most influential business geniuses of the century." Yes, under "Builders and Titans" there I was. Of course, they put me into a section titled "Crazy and In Charge" with "Brilliant tycoons [who] have had a tendency to get eccentric or worse" and lumped me in with Howard Hughes, J. Paul Getty, and H.L. Hunt, which is a lot better company to keep than the ignorant, lying nobodies who have torn me up in the press. I thought that title was so perfect, especially as it applies to me, that I used it as the title of this book. So thank you, *Time*, again.

Still, I have been called crazy so many times and in so many ways that I figured it was my turn now to set everybody straight.

Yes, I am crazy, or *meshuga*, as my people say.

Everybody should be so crazy.

Only if they were, then I wouldn't be half as rich as I am, because then I wouldn't be so much smarter than everybody else.

Not that being meshuga is such a bad thing. I've been called much worse. And isn't everybody a little bit crazy? Sure, I am a little mad. That's where my ideas come from. That's how I am rich. I am a Polish peasant. How else would I have become an American millionaire if I wasn't just a little bit crazy. Another Polish peasant, Lech Walesa, overthrew Communism. Einstein was thrown out of high school! As I like to point out, only truly sane people are in insane asylums. With the rest of us, I believe the expression is "crazy like a fox."

For the record, I should point out that a few years ago, a court-ordered psychiatrist and psychologist found me legally sane—actually, they found me absolutely, perfectly sane, but why ruin the image, especially when being meshuga has served me so well? Without being meshuga, I wouldn't be the guy who brought to an end the biggest crisis in the history of the American presidency. That's right, without me, Bill Clinton would have had to go into court and talk about his private parts and the country would have been so paralyzed it would have fallen into a Depression. This, of course, was where things were headed when I got involved in the Paula Jones case.

Most people in America probably know me mainly as the schlemiel who gave Paula Jones $1 million to drop her sexual harassment lawsuit against Clinton. If you're a New Yorker, though, chances are you knew me a long time before that. I have, for many years, been what they call a New York gadfly—whatever that means. All I know is, I've been around the block and back in my adopted hometown. In New York, in fact, I'm probably much better known as the man who owned the *New York Post* for eighteen stormy days during the biggest newspaper crisis in the city's history. (I was branded as the villain in the story, but I actually saved a paper that had been completely mismanaged and was about to be buried. Not before or since have sales of that paper been as high as they were during those turbulent two weeks.)

They also know me as the guy who built the world's finest parking garages and the first and finest upscale health and fitness club, and as the guy who has run for office so much—eight times, twice for the U.S. Senate—and won a term as City Commissioner and Deputy Mayor in Miami Beach. But I'm also the guy who once held a building inspector "hostage" over a permit (that charge was a gross exaggeration) and who spit in the face of the New York State Assembly Leader—just like I spat in the face of a lying newspaper reporter in Miami Beach. (Both deserved every ounce of my saliva.) I was charged with 123 counts of tax evasion by the crooked District Attorney of New York City, the eminent and stupendously corrupt Robert Morgenthau, whereupon I represented myself and walked free because of a hung jury, only to be re-tried and railroaded to conviction.

Recently, you may have heard, I spent two years in prison—the same prison where David Berkowitz, aka "Son of Sam" makes his residence—after the vengeful Morgenthau brought me up on a ludicrous charge of trying to have my business partner killed. (I also gained a mistrial on that charge, only to be, once again, railroaded in the retrial.)

I also made headlines when I once paid jurors in my first tax trial $2,500 apiece after they found me not guilty. (This was completely legal at the time, and as you will see, it changed for the better the entire legal system in New York. Today, there is something on the books there called "Hirschfeld's Law." It is the only law in America named for a person, except for one other—Son of Sam.

Gadfly or whatever, I am somewhat unfazed by this history. After all, at last count, I have been accused of plotting to kill *eight* people, including a District Court Judge and *my own daughter!* On a more upbeat note, I have, at the very least, saved the economy of the United States three times. I have produced Broadway shows and movies. I have run with the rich and famous and directly taught the real estate game to Donald Trump and Leona Helmsley—and indirectly showed the way to build the best buildings to every other developer worth his salt. I have been responsible for creating a Renaissance in the culture of many places, including New York,

Miami Beach, Harlem, Albany, and Union City, New Jersey. But if not for me, the "chic" Tribeca area in lower Manhattan would be a row of dilapidated buildings instead of the upscale playground of Robert DeNiro and other big stars.

For some reason, people seem to think my life is very colorful.

At least I read that it is in the media, where despite all of the above, most everything I do is put down as a publicity stunt and circus sideshow. *New York,* for example, wrote that I am "the city's longest-running public nuisance." Well, I have to admit I am not averse to a little attention—who isn't? And I admit, I like circus sideshows. And having written 10,000 jokes myself, I absolutely love a good laugh, especially at my own expense. If I didn't, I couldn't have made it through what I have. Too often, however, the media miss the real story, such as why I wound up *not* giving Paula Jones that $1 million. Hint: It wasn't that the check bounced.

And so, that is the main purpose of this book. To tell you the real story of every famous thing I have done—and some not so famous things that are equally as important.

What really happened in the Paula Jones caper, for instance, was typical of so many other moments of triumph in my life: namely, that it was undermined and ruined by a man who once meant so much to me only to later decide to become my Judas and try to ruin me. That man's name is Stanley Stahl, and you will be reading a lot about him as you turn these pages. You will also read about how Stahl sat atop a Mafia-style mob that has pervaded all levels of government, the justice system, and the media nationwide.

This mob has cost me millions and had me incarcerated in the toughest prisons. They have kept me in virtual lockdown in courtrooms for over a decade, burdened me with crooked judges, slandered my name in the media, cost me millions in legal fees, and forced me to defend myself in court, literally. (They say only a man who represents himself has a fool for a client, yet I have been the best lawyer I've ever had. Indeed, one of the very worst lawyers I've had is arguably the most famous, Allan Dershowitz.)

Along the way, they have ruined my beloved wife's health with all the stress and strain of the last decade. They had me indicted; yet, for eight years the judge in the case didn't hold *a single* hearing in court. They got admitted into evidence testimony from a person they identified under oath as Mrs. Stanley Stahl—who *was not Mrs.*

Stanley Stahl! Ultimately, they threw me into jail, fully hoping that I would not come out alive. Little did they realize that I would not only survive prison but that it would be the best two years of my life. Everything that keeps me going today—including a re-dedication of my life according to the writs of the Five Books of Moses (and I don't mean Robert Moses)—I learned in prison.

It is my belief, backed by the supporting evidence in this book, that the tentacles of this conspiracy have touched and corrupted institutions that are supposed to serve and protect us: the law, the justice system, powerful politicians, banks, lawyers, and the media. Perhaps by revealing this, I can hopefully be responsible for ending their reign of terror.

The good news is that I am here, I am alive, I am strong, I am vital, and I am more energized than ever about accomplishing what I believe God put me on Earth to do: bring peace to the Middle East. Although many people have tried to stop this quest, I have tirelessly worked on this goal since 1974 when Yasser Arafat accepted the simple, beautiful premise of the treaty—a single, unified Israel-Palestine with free movement between these two ancient and brilliant peoples. The treaty holds all the keys to peace in the world, and it is more urgent now than ever in light of 9/11, the ongoing terrorist threat, and what I consider to be George W. Bush's insane colonialist moves that only exacerbate hatreds between us and the rest of the world.

I was, as you will learn, a major backstage player at the Camp David Accords of 1978 between Israel and Egypt. Recently, I offered my old friend Jimmy Carter, whom I single-handedly elected President in 1976, $1 million if he would come with me to the Middle East and try to have my peace treaty ratified—by the time you read this, my parole will be over, and I will again be free to travel to the Middle East. I believe he can again be the man who brings peace to that war-torn region, and I will again be content to be the backstage force that made it happen.

I cringe when I think that, because of my persecution by a sinister and corrupt network, killing and bloodshed still goes on.

I hope you will see me in these pages exactly as I am: a modest and humble man, not the comic-book caricature I have been made out to be. Because of my rather thick Yiddish accent—at least people tell me I have one—and old-world, homespun philosophy, my great friend, the late comedian Joey Adams, once remarked, "Abe Hirschfeld has been in America forty years and still sounds as if he's arriving next Tuesday." Yet, my Everyman style is not an act; it's not by choice but by nature. My origins are simple, and so are my goals and my idealism. Money just happened to come along as a reward for my visionary instincts, timing, and, yes, my genius.

There, I said it; I'm a genius. But before you think I'm bragging, let me add that it's not because I'm better than anyone or smarter than anyone. Or maybe I am. I like to ask people what their definition of smart is. (It's a lot harder to figure out than what the definition of "is" is, though Bill Clinton never did tell us what that was.) And after they stammer for five or six minutes trying to sound smart, I'll cut them off and say, "You don't have a clue." Then I'll tell them what smart is. It's simple. It's being smart enough to know what you *don't* know. For what I don't know, I can hire people who will tell me. (Such as the overly burdened fellow who is taking my scattered musings, polishing them up, and bundling them together for this book.) But what I do know, by instinct, just usually turns out to be a perfect solution to a problem or need. Because I think from the people's-eye view, whereas most "smart" people think from a position of arrogance, looking down at people.

It is still a marvel to me that I have accomplished what I have as a sixth-grade dropout back in Palestine, where my family emigrated to from my birthplace in Poland, and where I grew to manhood. My visionary qualities, handed down to me by my beloved mother, helped me combine hard business realities with the restless mind of a man whose first reaction to the phrase "You can't do this" has been to say, "Why not?" Saying why not made me "The Pots and Pans King" in Palestine, a metals entrepreneur when I arrived in America in the 1950s, the "Garage King" of America, and, well, everything else I have been called.

What I like to call myself is, "The Man from La Mancha." I know. The name has already been taken. But I'm sure Don Quixote won't mind if I appropriate it. In fact, the name ran a very close second as a prospective title for this book. As it is, it's already been used as a title of an article about me, in 1997, written for a Columbia University web site, Third Rail Underground. In it, the author, Shonquis Moreno, quoted me as saying: "I always work with my theory of practical solutions. Not every problem has a practical solution, but where you can apply it, it's good." And: "I learned a little bit from the Bible. The Bible said a person should divide his time in three parts: One part to family, one part to business, and one part to the community."

And there, my dear friends, in a few sentences, is the binary essence of Abe Hirschfeld. Yes, I, too, have tilted at a few windmills in my time. As a social liberal, my head has been in the clouds at times, and I more than fulfill Webster's definition of "quixotic" as, "Caught up in the romance of noble deeds or unreachable ideals; romantic without regard to practicality." Yet, as my first quote above indicates, as an economic conservative in the neo-Capitalist, Keynesian sense, I sharply depart from that definition in that my ideas and ideals are *always* reachable and practical. The problem in our society is that we have ceded far too much power to the intellectuals—those snooty people with no real vision and no practical way to achieve noble goals; it is they who have ruined the world.

Still, given that almost no one thought I was sane when I created the idea for open-air garages, "quixotic" may be a far more accurate description of me than the tepidly generic "real estate magnate" or "millionaire developer." Not that I needed to be reminded of how much resistance always seems to await my best ideas, but for many years I kept that "Man of La Mancha" name plate on my office, until one day I came to the office and found it had been stolen. Metaphorically, that is the story of my life.

When wealthy people write their autobiographies, readers pore through the pages to find out just how wealthy these people are. I will save you some time and toil by telling you right now that I have no idea how much money I have. There's an old adage, probably even older than me, that says if you know how much money you have, you're not rich. However, I will tell you that if I were smarter, I would be much richer because among my inventions is the magnetic strip that makes your refrigerator stay shut when you close the door. The problem was, I was a very young man in Palestine when I invented it, and knew nothing about patents, so some other guy I'm sure made the money on it. That taught me a lesson. In the ensuing years, I received a patent on my high-speed Bullet Train with rubber wheels, which will revolutionize our woefully outdated system of railroad travel. I am awaiting a patent now for an electric car engine that needs no recharging and, of course, no gas to run on. Remember that because I may not be around when the whole world is driving cars with that engine (although I'm planning to be), which will benefit mankind by saving thousands of dollars, easing pollution of our precious air, and breaking the chain of extortion the Arab oil countries have had on us for so long.

I will also say, at the risk of sounding insensitive, that the World Trade Center would never have come down after the terrorist attacks if those had been my buildings, built in the design of my open-air garages, and you will learn why in succeeding pages. I have presented plans to New York City for a new, open-air Trade Center that would be "airplane-proof," and I have submitted detailed plans for an Olympic Stadium for New York to use in 2012. My plan is the only one that can work, as you'll see, and I can build it as I built my garages: at one-third the cost and in one-half the time.

My own bottom line, then, isn't written on an asset sheet. It is written on the world. I consider it worth Fort Knox that I was among Robert Kennedy's inner circle, and one of his closest friends, when I served as the New York State Democratic Party's Treasurer in the 1960s, as well as his top fundraiser. I was one of the first to speak to Bobby after he won the California primary in June 1968, and I will tell you of our conversation, which still haunts me because I foresaw what would happen to him a few tragic minutes later when he took that fateful walk through the kitchen of the Ambassador Hotel. I think I lost a lot of my idealism on that night, and I still grieve because I believe Bobby would have been one of our greatest presidents, and that I would have elected him, as I elected Jimmy Carter, Ronald Reagan, and George W. Bush (though I now deeply regret the latter).

Contrary to what you may think, it hasn't been all serious for me. I have accomplished things that have helped people by simply giving them great entertainment. I've produced some of the finest, most well-reviewed theatrical productions, including *The Prince of Central Park* on Broadway (and later as a movie), and fourteen other shows at the Hirschfeld Theater (the *Al* Hirschfeld Theater, which was my homage to my grand old friend, the legendary *New York Times* theater alley caricaturist) in Miami Beach from 1989 to 1991. You probably don't know that I produced the second version of *Phantom of the Opera,* which received stupendous reviews, calling it better than the original, as well as Jackie Mason's most successful one-man Broadway show, *Love Thy Neighbor.*

I must be blessed by God that the brilliant Al Hirschfeld—who is not related to me even though many people seem to want to call me Al—before his death in 2002 at age 99, drew a marvelous caricature of Zipora and me ringed by some of the famous people we've known through the years, people like Jackie Kennedy, Anthony Quinn, Luciano Pavarotti, Jackie Gleason, Carol Channing, Jackie Mason, and even, believe it or not, Elvis Presley and Michael Jackson! I have put it in the book with the kind permission of his estate, and I hope you enjoy it as much as I do. I will also let you in on a little secret. Al Hirschfeld used to play a little game with his artwork. He would hide his daughter Nina's name within the thick ink lines he would commit to paper. It was always great sport among the New York "literati" to count the Ninas whenever Al unveiled his newest painting. Well, there has never been more than twelve "Ninas" in any of Mr. Hirschfeld's thousands of drawings.

None, that is, except for one drawing—the one of me, in which you can find no less than *thirty-three* "Ninas." Thank you, my great friend; may you rest in peace in your heavenly studio.

I suppose I should also say once more that I look with pride at my much-too-brief ownership of the *Post*. The one overriding image that persists of that interlude was when the paper's writers ran their "Who Is This Nut?" story. You may ask, how could a publisher allow such insubordination? Very simple. Because when I bought the paper from Rupert Murdoch, who had run it into the ground, nobody else wanted it. It was doomed. Say what you want about those turbulent eighteen days of firings, re-hirings, and guerilla warfare with editor Pete Hamill, but when I took over the *Post,* its circulation was 325,000. Under me, it was over 500,000. And its high point was that now-famous front page of Alexander Hamilton, the paper's founder, with a tear rolling down his cheek, which I suppose was meant to say that Abe Hirschfeld made Alexander Hamilton cry in despair. Only the real story is that I was the one who came up with the idea for that front page. And that front page is the only one in history that is a collector's item. I think Hamilton would pat me on the back if he were here.

So, that has been my life, at least so far. And I think I have a long way to go and a lot still to do, and with my knack for coming up with practical solutions, I can do them all. For example, I have very practical solutions for re-organizing Social Security so that no elderly

American need suffer from poverty or anxiety over access to top-quality medical care. (By the way, I strongly believe that wealthy Americans should not be eligible for Social Security; I myself tried to reject my Social Security checks only to be *ordered* by the IRS to keep them.) I also have the solution for full employment with full medical and pension benefits for all Americans and for raising perfect children. I can eliminate slums—and not with the usual poor-quality public housing. I can solve the problem of police brutality, drugs, and crime. I've even invented a diet on which a person can eat all they want and lose weight without cost, gimmicks, pills, or exercise.

You will be amazed at how easy these solutions are. But, to get them, you will have to keep reading.

I figure that since I've done most of the things I've set out to do, the only one left is to become President. People tell me, "Abe, this cannot happen because you are not a natural-born citizen of the United States, and you are a convicted felon." This to me is a small problem, a non-problem. All that I need to do is win, and then amend the constitution. I figure if I can change the world, I can change a constitution.

I trust that as you flip the pages of this book, you will be entertained, enlightened, thought-provoked, and possibly outraged. But you will not be bored. The chapters will take you from Poland to Palestine, and then from Israel to America. During the journey, you will run across some of the most powerful and colorful people in America over the last half-century, people I have known well and about whom I will tell never-told stories. People like Bobby Kennedy, Jimmy Carter, Ed Koch, Donald Trump, Jackie Mason, Shirley MacLaine, Louis Farrakhan, Menachem Begin, Yasser Arafat, Mario Cuomo, Al Sharpton, Ross Perot, George Pataki, Rudy Giuliani, Tony Blair, and Stephen Seagal, And, of course, Miss Paula Jones.

To all the many who I hope will read my story, I say, "Come with me; enjoy the ride." I promise that you will learn a lot, laugh a little, and cry a little. And in the end, maybe be a little better for it.

L'chaim.

CHAPTER ONE: NEVER A MARTYR

It was after midnight, the first minutes of December 10, 1998, when the intercom buzzer sounded, awakening me and my wife Zipora as we slept in our bed in our apartment at 825 Fifth Avenue. I climbed out of bed, stumbled into the living room, and picked up the house phone.

"Mr. Hirschfeld," came the voice of the concierge, "there are two police officers here. They want to come up and see you."

"What do they want?" I asked, bewildered and still half-asleep.

"They have to come up and see you."

A minute later, the elevator door opened and two plain-clothes men, who identified themselves as New York City police detectives, came out and pounded on my ninth-floor door. As soon as I opened it, wearing just my underwear, one of them sternly told me, "Mr. Hirschfeld, you're coming with us. We're taking you to jail."

I have had better greetings in my life.

This was the last thing I expected, but then again, I knew who had sent cops to arrest me in the middle of the night, and about that I was not surprised. After all, I had already become aware that Robert Morgenthau, the famous Manhattan District Attorney, had been trying to put me in jail any way he could for the last year. The first way he tried was by having me indicted in 1996 on 123 charges of state income tax evasion, something like $2 million—a totally false indictment that I had been fighting in court, and beating Morgenthau's brains out, for the past year.

Morgenthau and his assistant DAs had pulled out all the stops—including, I believe, replacing elected judges with acting judges they could control, judges who allowed the state to introduce into evidence all manner of false evidence. Yet, it was clear to everyone that there was no case, and it ended in a hung jury and a mistrial. Morgenthau, however, wouldn't accept this and was trying me again, though his case was so weak that the judge allowed me to travel to Israel even though I was on $1 million bail, something that would be unheard of had he believed I was guilty. (Eventually, I did take an Alford plea, paying a fine without admitting guilt, for reasons I will make clear.) I had also made my highly publicized $1 million offer to Paula Jones during this period.

1

But the truth was that Morgenthau had it in for me and would stop at nothing to put me away. The most egregious example of that had come earlier in the week, when this man, who would indict a ham sandwich if he wanted to, got another indictment against me, and this time for a far more serious crime: criminal solicitation—legal talk for trying to have someone murdered. In this case, my longtime real estate business partner Stanley Stahl.

When the grand jury met to hear the evidence, I was called to testify; I blew away everything Morgenthau threw against me, but still the indictment was brought, and I was due to be in court at 7:30 in the morning for my arraignment. I looked forward to standing up before a judge and declaring my innocence and my resolve to fight until my very last breath, if necessary, to defend myself. But I had no intention of cooperating voluntarily with Morgenthau, a man who I regard with the same frozen loathing I have for the image of Adolf Hitler. Morgenthau, after the indictment, told my lawyer, Charles Haydon, and me that he would allow me to surrender voluntarily that very day. Haydon advised me that I should do just that. On the spot, I fired him.

However, I had no objection to surrendering voluntarily, as long as I had a few days to retain another attorney and prepare a statement for the judge. Morgenthau agreed that I could come in on my own at 7 A.M. on the morning of the tenth, and that is when my new lawyer, Ted Kupferman, and I were due in Morgenthau's office at 110 Centre Street in lower Manhattan. I should have known that men like Morgenthau don't keep their word.

I assumed that this bogus arraignment would be conducted in a dignified, respectful manner, that it would be little more than a technicality, and that I would be released, hopefully with no bail. In fact, the court date wasn't even the most pressing engagement I would have that day. In the afternoon, I was going to do some campaigning, one of many steps on a path that I believed would lead me straight to the United States Senate.

Ten days before, I'd enjoyed one of the proudest moments of my life when I announced my candidacy on the Independent Party line for the senate seat being vacated by Daniel Patrick Moynihan. I was eager, ready, and confident to run against the putative candidates of the Democratic and Republican parties, First Lady Hillary Rodham Clinton and, as everyone believed at that point, Rudy Giuliani. Despite the star power of these people, I sensed New Yorkers were eager to find an alternative. I had ways to cut them both down to size. With Mrs. Clinton, for example, I had found my theme for the campaign. "If Hillary can't please one man," I was going to keep saying over and over, "how can she please a whole state?"

After many political campaigns, this was going to be my time to achieve my long-held goal of serving people by serving in high office.

"My reason for running," I had told the press when I announced my candidacy at the Park Avenue restaurant Le Cirque, "is I believe I am the best qualified person for that office in terms of what is needed for New York in the Twenty-first Century. I have a track record to prove it, and I am not a part of the dominant ruling class in America today—lawyers.

"By contrast, Hillary Clinton and Rudy Giuliani are both lawyers. I am a builder, a job creator, an inventor. The new millennium will call for new, innovative solutions to the major concerns of our time: universal health care, high quality education and housing for all Americans, and jobs, jobs, jobs for everyone who wants and needs employment."

And, of course, I was going to use the senate as a platform to achieve my fondest wish: achieving peace in the Middle East by getting Israel to finally ratify my long-standing peace treaty.

Those ideals were bubbling in my mind as I drifted off to sleep that night. At least until the sanctity of my property and my life were violated by Morgenthau's goons, whom I first tried to reason with.

"Officers," I said, "why can't you wait until seven o'clock? I'm supposed to be in the DA's office then. If I won't come at seven, you'll take me. You can stay here with me all night, then we'll go." I even offered them coffee and dessert.

"No," came the answer. "You're going now."

I tried another tack.

"Do you have a warrant for my arrest?" I asked.

"No."

Now I was becoming frightened. Could I even be sure that these were, in fact, officers of the law? Zipora was cowering in the door to the bedroom, and I could read her thoughts: were these men about to rob us, even kill us? And so, I picked up the phone and dialed 911.

3

"Operator," I said, "I have two robbers in my apartment."

As soon as I had gotten the words out, one cop took the phone out of my hand and the other ripped the phone line out of the wall.

That sent a chill down my back. The setting may have been Fifth Avenue in a so-called democratic country, but as a Polish Jew who'd lost nearly all of his family in the Holocaust, I could imagine at that moment what it must have been like during *Krystalnacht* in Warsaw, or the pogroms in Russia. The pity was that my people, who were victims of the kossacks and the Nazis, couldn't stand up to the oppression they faced. And so, I wasn't about to go quietly into the night.

As the cops grabbed my arms, sending Zipora into a state of shock from which she has not recovered to this day, they said they would give me a few minutes to get myself dressed.

"I'm not going anywhere," I barked. "You will have to drag me naked!" If this was the way they were going to treat one of the world's most honored men in his own home, I was going to show the world what they were doing to me.

And so, wearing nothing but my underwear, robe, and slippers, I was handcuffed and hustled to the door, as Zipora—who was told she couldn't come with me—stood there hysterical in the doorway watching her husband dragged away like a common thief.

I received a temporary reprieve when two uniformed cops suddenly showed up at the door as the result of my call to 911. I believed they would rescue me from whoever these thugs were.

It was, however, a brief reprieve. For a few minutes, the detectives huddled with the cops, with everyone speaking in hushed tones. Then the cops left, and the nightmare continued.

Shackled and threatened, I was led into the elevator. Once downstairs, I was shoved past the doormen, out into the cold street, and into a police car.

My head was spinning, but I knew my rights.

"You have to let me call my attorney," I said, as the car began moving through the night.

"You're not calling anyone," one cop said. But after a few minutes of more hushed talk, they relented by telling me they would take me to my lawyer's apartment.

When we got to the apartment house of the attorney, Ted Kupferman, one of the cops went into the lobby. Then he came back and got in the car.

"Is he home?" I asked.

"He's asleep."

I was about to say, "Wake him up," but we were moving again, not to stop until we reached Morgenthau's office at 110 Centre Street. But since Morgenthau and his people were all home sleeping comfortably at the time, there was no one for me to see. Instead, I was dumped into a jail cell, literally thrown into a six-by-eight foot space with a broken toilet and no bed. There I was left, with no food or drink, to sleep on a cold, cement floor. All of this had been done to a seventy-nine-year-old prominent, American citizen who was not even being allowed to talk to his lawyer. If they'd wanted to, they could have let me rot there.

Could this really be America, the country to which I'd come in 1955 because it offered so much promise of individual freedom?

After a fitful night on that cold floor, I was finally allowed to make phone calls. The first was to Zipora, who had been trying all night, futilely, to get in contact with Ted Kupferman. I assured her that I was all right and to stay put in the apartment, as I was deeply worried for her and what all this strain was going to do to her fragile health. Finally, I reached Kupferman, who was, by now, apparently awake and accepting phone calls. That was when I learned that my arraignment was going to be anything but dignified and respectful. In fact, before it even took place, Morgenthau was going to grandstand against me by having a press conference to announce the charges.

I asked if I could appear at that conference to tell my side. When I was rebuffed, I began calling reporters I knew from the New York papers, telling them of my demeaning treatment and stating the absolute truth: that the charges they were bringing against me were completely baseless and senseless; that I'd never given anyone any money to kill Stanley Stahl; and that the only time I had heard anyone mention murdering Stanley Stahl was when two employees of mine had called me and said that *they* were going to kill him. They wanted $500,000—and would frame me for proposing it if I didn't pay them.

"I won't give you a nickel," I told them. "I don't want Stahl killed."

I had fired both people (one of whom, my secretary for twenty-four years, wore a wire at Morgenthau's direction to try and get me to incriminate myself). I knew they were up to no good. Both were also in legal trouble of their own, which was what had prompted them to try and frame me. I did not, however, believe that they would actually murder Stahl, and thus I never went to the authorities with their threat. As it turned out, they *did* go through with their plot to frame me—a plot, I believe, that was hatched and nourished by people in high places.

I will go into greater detail about the particulars of the case—how at every turn I was abused and victimized, and how feeble was Morgenthau's case, right down to his Big Lie that I would reap a fortune if Stahl were not around because there was a "survivor take all" clause in our partnership agreement. Of course, no such clause exists, or ever did exist—quite the contrary. The partnership interests are owned by several of our family members. But truth was the biggest victim of my persecution.

Morgenthau's press conference, I now understood, had been planned for one reason: to keep me from winning the senate seat. In fact, this was not the first time Morgenthau had done such a thing to achieve that very purpose. That day carried a strong scent of *déjà vu*. Only the year before, on May 10, 1997, I had been scheduled to announce my candidacy for Manhattan Borough President, but at 10 A.M., an hour before the announcement, I was indicted on those bogus income tax evasion charges. As you will read, that indictment was based on banking records that had been seized illegally on the stated premise by Morgenthau that a criminal action was pending against me. Later, Morgenthau admitted that he had made a false statement, and remarkably, I was allowed by the judge in the case to sue Morgenthau's office. (Again, more on this later.)

Quite clearly, Morgenthau was hell-bent to get me any way he could, legally or otherwise. And at the heart of this new indictment was the desire to kill my senate run—which it did, as it required so much of my time that it was all but impossible for me to focus on the issues. Instead, I had to fight for my freedom.

I knew how difficult a task that would be when I was taken to Criminal Court for the arraignment late that morning. The charge was second-degree criminal solicitation. The punishment: up to seven years in prison. I was allowed to call my driver to bring me a suit to wear.

State Supreme Court Justice Laura E. Drager seemed to be as skeptical of the charges as I was. The assistant district attorney Gilda Mariani, who was going to prosecute me, asked for an exorbitantly high bail of $2.2 million. Judge Drager, knowing I was already on $1 million bail in the tax evasion case, set bail at $1 million. As it happened, I had in my wallet the $1 million bank check from the Israeli Discount Bank that I was going to give to Paula Jones, which she had turned down (although her ludicrous claim that I backed out has kept me tied up in court with *her* ever since). Half in jest, I took the check out and told Judge Drager she could have it to satisfy the bail.

After inspecting this artifact of history, she grinned. "Well, I did say the one million dollars should be in cash, Mr. Hirschfeld."

Knowing she was on my side—I knew because Mariani was doing a slow burn during this absurdist interlude—I grinned as well.

"It's a good check, Your Honor," I said, drawing laughter everywhere in the courtroom except from the prunish faces of the prosecutors.

In the end, Judge Drager simply let me go without having to pay a penny, contingent on me furnishing the million dollars within a week. And so, after a night and morning in hell, I finally went home to see my wife. But Morgenthau's damage was done. Seeking big headlines that would taint any jury, he got just what he wanted when the newspapers splashed the story of my indictment all over its pages. The *Daily News* blared: "ABE'S CAUGHT ON TAPE PLANNING KILL – SOURCE." The *Post,* in typical, heavy-breathing fashion, told of my "slay-bid bust." Even the staid *New York Times* sounded more like a tabloid, running a headline that screamed: "CASE AGAINST HIRSCHFELD PORTRAYS A THWARTED PLOT TO KILL A FORMER BUSINESS PARTNER." The *Times* also ran the mandatory rip job about me in a sidebar article titled, "A Publicity Hound Longing for Respect," citing my alleged "unpredictable, uncouth behavior and his eccentricity." Well, I'm used to that sort of thing. The important thing was that I get across in all these stories my innocence. And I was pleased that the *Post* reported the exact words I'd used in court when it came my turn to speak.

"Not guilty!" I had said as firmly as a man can say those words. "It's all lies!"

For me, the entire episode was like something out of a bad movie—or a re-rerun of a bad movie, given that it was the same script as the tax-evasion business a year ago—but it was all too real. Suddenly, Abe Hirschfeld, a man who had never gotten even a parking ticket, had a trial and a possible seven-year jail sentence staring him in the face. With drug-crazed killers waiting for months to be brought to trial, Morgenthau put mine on a fast-track, leaving me precious little time to prepare and, as I found out, get a lawyer to defend me who wasn't working as an *agent provocateur* for my enemies. As it happened, I had been fighting Stanley Stahl in lawsuits and countersuits since 1992—yet I had not been given a single hearing to state my case for eight years as my enemies looked for ways and for judges to do me in. In that time, I had been deprived of hundreds of millions of dollars I was due from the two management companies I owned with Stahl. These proceedings had moved at such a snail's pace, rife with so many improprieties and so many crooked lawyers, that Stahl would die in August 1999 still with no resolution of the original lawsuit I'd brought against him in 1992. As this is written, it is still unresolved.

But my criminal solicitation trial began in an eye blink in March of 1999. Still, even with this bum's rush, the prosecution had only the flimsiest of evidence against me. The trial ended with the jury hung, and a mistrial was declared. Jurors told of resenting what had been done to me. It was at the conclusion of the trial that I paid each juror $2,500, an absolutely legal and oft-practiced act. But because the politicians hate me so much, they immediately rewrote the law prohibiting such payments—the Abe Hirschfeld Law. The mistrial did not stop Morgenthau from trying me again, and yet *again,* after a second mistrial. You can imagine the pressure that was put on the jurors to return a guilty verdict in the third of those kangaroo trials. Remember, I had made a fool out of Morgenthau, and his reputation was now squarely on the line. He was not about to let a Polish immigrant with a fifth-grade education beat him.

How desperate must Morgenthau have been for a guilty verdict. During each of the trials, there was a revolving door of judges, with each new one being brought in to be more amenable to the prosecution. The last judge on the case, a man named Harold

Beeler, did all he could to poison the case against me. At one point, I placed an ad in the New York papers, which had witness testimony. I made no comment. I simply wanted the public to come to its own conclusion about this crusade against me. Again, I thought I was living in America, not Nazi Germany. But I must have been wrong because Judge Beeler threw me in jail for 90 days because of it, ludicrously calling it "contempt of court." Judge Beeler may have sensed that this jury, like the previous two, was going to toss this bogus case into the sewer where it came from and give Morgenthau another spanking because he told them that if they would return a guilty verdict, he would not sentence me to more than one year in prison. That seemed to turn the trick. The jury came back and said "guilty" on June 17, 2000. Now it was Beeler's turn.

He sentenced me to *two* years.

Take it from me. If you should ever find yourself in court before a judge, do not believe a word he or she tells you. Right after the verdict was read, I was taken away in handcuffs—without the courtesy of even being allowed to hug my wife goodbye. I was driven to the Tombs, the infamous prison in lower Manhattan, then shuffled around to four different prisons, all of them among the toughest prisons in New York State. And that is where my story should have ended; at least that's what the underground mob hunting me had hoped for and worked so hard to achieve. In fact, it was Stanley Stahl himself who once dropped the biggest hint about what would happen. In 1992, when I wanted to terminate our partnership, I suggested to him that he either buy me out for $9 million, or I would buy him out for $9 million.

"Abe," he said unctuously, "I'll make *you* an offer. I'll buy you out for $3 million -- or I'll put you in jail."

And now, six years later, here I was, in a police cruiser on the way to the Tombs, not knowing if I would ever breathe the air of freedom again.

I did know this, though: I had every intention of enduring the way Ghandi, Martin Luther King, Nelson Mandela, and Jesus Christ had endured their unjustified punishments. The only difference between them and me is that I refused to be a martyr.

I was *meshuga* enough to believe I would come through it even stronger.

As I sat in the cruiser that black day, I couldn't help but turn my thoughts to my childhood in Poland listening to my mother and father try to prepare me for the cruelties and raw deals of life—and how they make you stronger. Eight decades later, their advice was as wise and more relevant than it ever was. Whether I would live or die, whether I would preserve or lose my good humor and optimism, whether my mission to bring about world peace would endure or perish—all would be determined by what I had learned in a very different time and place.

That place was Tarnow.

CHAPTER TWO: TARNOW

Many years ago, when I was a rambunctiously fresh and ambitious teenager, my mother gave me a trenchant piece of advice. She was always giving me advice, usually in the form of a cryptic, pointed, and often whimsical parables. My mother was a great storyteller, and if I have a gift for weaving a good yarn, it comes straight from her. I owe a lot more than that to her. It was her wry and pungent sense of humor, especially when confronted by the endless snarls, mysteries, and contradictions of life, that illuminated and inspired me as I was growing up. As a result, I've been able to journey through my own life with a keen sense of humor and an ironic appreciation for the more ridiculous aspects of life and fate.

That piece of advice she gave me happened when I was dreaming aloud about some juvenile ambition or another for myself.

"Abe," she said, "you can send a donkey around the world. You can send it through many different countries and let it see many different people and cultures. You can let it hear dozens of different languages and have a million different experiences. But when the donkey comes back to where it started, it'll still be a donkey."

She was right. I've been around the world. I've been through many different countries and known many different people and cultures. I've heard dozens of different languages and had a million different experiences. And while I'm no donkey, I've come back to where I started, many times in my life. I'm still the Abe Hirschfeld I was when I listened to my mother's story.

That was eight decades ago, but to know who I am you must go back even further, around seventy-five years before that, when fate brought Sarah Simon and Simon Hirschfeld together in Tarnow, a small city not far from Cracow, in the shadow of the Carpathian Mountains of southern Poland. Both my parents came from old, distinguished, Jewish families in the region—my father's father was one of the biggest bankers and landowners in Poland.

The Hirschfelds had everything—several homes, sixty in help, even a good-sized yacht. As if to show that money isn't everything, though, that yacht eventually proved to be a source of deep misery to my grandfather and his family. One summer, around the start of the century, the family was sailing through the Baltic Sea. The yacht got caught in a terrible storm and sank. Among those who drowned were three of my grandfather's sons, my father's brothers. It was said that afterwards, my grandfather was never the same, that he lost interest in everything, even making money. The tragic event affected my father in similar ways. I suppose he felt an enormous amount of guilt for having survived. He became a much more contemplative and introspective young man. He grew into an intellectual rather than a "doer" and adventurer like the rest of the males in the family.

That was both a boon and a bane to my two brothers and me later on. He was a very smart man and often could figure things out long before others could. For instance, in the early 1930s, he sensed before anyone else what was going to happen in that part of Europe. So, he got us out, got us all to Palestine before it could happen. He saved our lives. A lot of his Jewish friends, who laughed at his concerns, ended up in the gas chambers of Dachau and Auschwitz.

On the other hand, he would agonize endlessly over the most mundane questions and never make up his mind about what he could do. That cost him dearly in business. Before he married my mother, he'd gone to the University of Vienna and gotten a doctorate in economics. So, he became an economist at heart, not a banker, not a businessman. He was the kind of man who, if another man came to him for practical business advice, would give him an economist's abstract answer.

When my parents were married in 1918 and settled in Tarnow, my father expected to take over his own recently deceased father's part in the Hirschfeld family banking and land business. In the same year, though, those enterprises were confiscated by the Polish government in the final chaos that came with the end of World War I. Suddenly, although he had inherited a comfortable sum of money, my father was without future business prospects. A year later, when I became Sarah and Simon's first-born, my father found a new business opportunity. Commercial scales for weighing goods that were sold by weight in shops and stores were just coming into commercial use in Poland. So, he opened a scale factory in Tarnow.

At first he did well, toiling hard throughout the 1920s to build up the business. It was the first time he'd ever really had to work, and he got a lot of assistance from my mother, who he found useful in helping him make practical business decisions. They became a team, after a fashion, although she always kept a low profile and made it seem that he was making his success all by himself.

By that time, I was old enough to begin growing aware of the world around me. It was about 1923, and I was four. In the meantime, my mother had given birth to another son—my brother Menasha. Growing up in the '20s, my father and I did not see very much of each other. He worked long hours at the factory, traveled a lot, and like many men, preferred to spend most of his leisure time with his business cronies. When he was at home, there wasn't much communication between us. Although he was now in business, my father still cultivated his intellectual pursuits, and at home, he usually had his nose in a book.

Since I was the oldest child, the first son, he expected a great deal from me in the way of obedience, self-discipline, and intellectual achievement. I'm afraid I disappointed him. I was an outgoing kid, full of enthusiasm and a certain amount of deviltry. My father was too gentle a man to try to beat or otherwise punish me into conformity to what he expected of me. Eventually he more-or-less gave up trying to shape me in his own image and left my upbringing largely in my mother's hands. And she was glad about that because my father was excessively idealistic and dreamy. She wanted me to have dreams, but she wanted me to have the practical sense and ability to realize them, too—the chutzpah to make them come true. So, I was brought up to think big and to value the imagination and hard work needed to transform my dreams into reality.

My mother seemed to know by intuition that I would do just that. "Leave him alone," she would tell my father when he became exasperated with me. "He will make you proud one day."

Home for us was a nice but not splendid house in the small Jewish section of Tarnow. My formal schooling in the late 1920s and early 1930s was achieved in the local Hebrew schools.

Although not excessively religious, my parents were Orthodox Jews through-and-through. The language we spoke at home was Yiddish, not Polish, and our entire cultural orientation and input were almost exclusively Jewish. Which is to say that growing up, I had hardly any direct exposure to life outside our fairly narrow Jewish social circle. Although we were not stetl Jews in the strict sense, for all practical purposes, I was fairly restricted as a child in my worldview. I knew little of the outside world beyond what I learned in schoolbooks.

As it happens, I was not the only over-achiever in my school. One of my third-grade classmates was a boy named Karol Wojtyla, although everyone called him "Lolek." He was the son of an Army officer who became a tailor and a Lithuanian mother who was a schoolteacher, and evidently, he spent a brief time in Tarnow during childhood and lived in various environs of Cracow. He wasn't a Jew—he was from a strict Catholic family—but he was fond of playing with the Jewish boys and learning our customs. He would also spend a good deal of time in the ten-room apartment of a Jewish boy named Jerzy Kluger listening to a string quartet made up of two Jews and two Catholics.

I had forgotten about Karol until he himself told me—around half a century later—when he made his first trip to America as Pope John Paul II.

I had been invited to meet him during his stay in New York, and when I told him I, too, had grown up in Poland, he asked me where I went to school. When I told him, he instantly remembered me. Imagine how flattered I felt. I later learned that his great Jewish friend from childhood, Jerzy Kluger, had acted as an intermediary when the Vatican extended a long-overdue diplomatic recognition of Israel. It's no secret that until Pope John Paul II, Popes were never friends of the Jewish people or of Israel. This Pope is. He is because he knew us, heard us, understood our ways. Ending the evil of anti-Semitism is just that simple. The pity throughout history is that so few people have taken that simple step.

Still, back in Tarnow, I knew little of the outside world and of the anti-Semitism that existed not only in Poland but throughout the rest of central and eastern Europe. The region in which we lived had seldom known peace, especially its considerable Jewish population. Indeed, the word "pogrom" originated in the region just east of Tarnow, and to its people it meant pretty much the same thing as the ones that replaced it—"holocaust" and "final solution." Both the Hirschfeld and Simon families, rooted for almost eight centuries in the Tarnow area, had survived more than a few pogroms. Some Jews had even prospered, though they were all forced to ghettoize themselves and had to live with the deeply ingrained anti-Semitic attitudes of their native Christian-dominated regions.

Still, at the end of the First World War, shared suffering seemed to join diverse people in common cause, and a breeze of optimism wafted across the Carpathians. It was hoped, possibly even believed by some Jews, that the war had brought an end to centuries of vicious anti-Semitism. It was a brave but naïve hope. Although there was a brief lull, anti-Semitism again began to rear its ugly head in Poland. By 1930, with the advent of Hitler and his Nazi Brownshirts in the west, it was once again considered acceptable social policy.

Being only twelve at the time, I was largely unaware of what was going on. Oh, I had learned something of the history, but up to that point, I remained blissfully in the dark about what it all really meant, or could mean. The first hint of change came a year or two later. It was at about the time Hitler was making his final push to achieve total power in Germany. I remember my father saying to my mother—it must have been around 1931—that Hitler's rantings were beginning to be praised by certain Polish people he knew.

But more than that, his scale business began to falter. There were only two scale-manufacturers in Poland then, my father and someone else. That someone else was a Christian, a Catholic. Until then, they had competed on fairly even terms. But now, at the beginning of the '30s, my father began to complain about how the rising anti-Semitism in Poland was affecting his business. For example, the scale business was closely regulated by the government. After a scale-maker sold a scale to a store or a warehouse, he was required to send a mechanic out once a year to recalibrate the device to make sure it remained accurate. Then a government inspector came around to test the scale. It was like a Bureau of Weights and Measures.

More and more, though, the inspectors refused to certify my father's scales. No matter how many times the mechanic adjusted it, the inspectors would declare it inaccurate and unfit, thereby causing it to be seized and removed from the store. The customer would need a new scale immediately, of course. And where would he go? Not to my father's factory but to my father's competition. This was just one subtle example of the anti-Semitic harassment my father was forced to endure. There was also a regular pattern of attempted extortion by government officials. If he didn't pass out bribes, they'd refuse to certify his scales. If he didn't pay protection, they'd foment work disruptions and other labor troubles at his factory.

15

It got worse and worse as time went on. And then the worldwide Depression began to be felt. By 1933, my father had grown depressed and defeated. And profoundly worried. With Hitler finally in power in Germany, he saw no hope for a Jewish future in Poland. That's when he began to think about Palestine.

Until then, my family had remained almost totally aloof from the Zionist movement that had spread across central and eastern Europe. Being an intellectual, and something of an idealist, my father tended to be critical of all narrow, nationalistic political doctrines. At first, he rejected Zionism, mainly because it seemed too close a cousin of Communism. But now he began to reconsider—not so much the merits of Zionism, per se, but of Palestine. Suddenly, compared to what he saw looming in his corner of the world—not just in the business sense but in his sense of a future filled with further anti-Jewish persecution—Palestine began to look like a viable alternative.

He made his decision one day in 1933. It was the Sabbath. My father took my brother and me to the synagogue. While we younger ones were having *shul* in the basement, he was upstairs with the men. After the service, there was a meeting and a speaker, a friend of my father's. He had just come back from a visit to Palestine. He spoke very highly of the quality of Jewish life there, the freedom and openness of the place.

I was there with my father, half-listening. It still didn't mean very much to me. But he listened very attentively as the man spoke. Then, later, as we were all walking home from the synagogue, he came out with it. He announced it to us like a bolt from the blue. He had decided, he said, to liquidate everything he owned in Tarnow, including the factory, and take us all to Palestine to live.

That spur-of-the-moment decision would, in time, save our lives.

CHAPTER THREE: PALESTINE

I've often been asked why my father chose Palestine rather than the United States to immigrate to. After all, hundreds of thousands of Jews had gone to America from *mittel* Europe during the previous fifty years or so, whereas only a relative handful had immigrated to Palestine. The answer was simple. The reason so many went to America was because they couldn't afford to go to Palestine. Under the British Mandate after the First World War, anyone who wanted to settle in Palestine could do so only if he brought with him 1,000 English pounds, which was the equivalent of $5,000 in those days. If a whole family wanted to go, it was 1,000 pounds for each member. That was to ensure they'd have sufficient capital to live on while getting settled.

Now, a lot of Jews wanted to go to Palestine but didn't have that kind of money. So, they had to settle for America, where there were no such restrictions. My father did have the money—$5,000 for each of us, $25,000 in all. Besides, he figured we'd be able to live much better in Palestine than in America because there would be no need to learn a new language.

My father was to go first and find a place to settle. We would follow as soon as he did. When the summons came, it was mid-1934. He said he'd bought some land near Tel Aviv, had made some friends, and was preparing to start up a new scale-manufacturing business. Everything looked rosy for the future, he said, and he promised that we'd love it. So, off to Palestine we went. I was fourteen, Menasha was twelve, and Meyer was four. My father had sent us boat tickets, and we had to travel down through Bucharest in Romania to the Black Sea. There we got on a passenger ship and set sail.

Despite the adventure of traveling for the first time in my life, I was still unhappy about leaving Tarnow. All I could imagine about Palestine was being forced to live in a desert, in a tent. That was the only concrete image I had of the place. However, a lot of my unhappiness was eased by something that happened on the ship as it made its way down the Black Sea and through the eastern Mediterranean toward Jaffa. On that voyage, sitting right there on the ship, were two men named Chaim Weizmann and Nahum Sokolov.

17

I met both of them, and they did much to boost the morale of Menasha and me. My mother must have told them about how miserable we were immigrating. They took us aside and started telling us stories about Palestine and the building of a Jewish homeland. They made it all seem very noble and brave. And they praised my father to the heavens, calling him a man of great courage and foresight to be doing what he was doing.

What I didn't know at the time was that these were two of the most noble and brave men of that time—Weizmann, as the great leader of Zionism and the Palestine settlement, and Sokolov, among the foremost Jewish writers of his generation.

I had never been so impressed by anyone in my life as I was by Weizmann. And once we disembarked and saw that there was this small city gleaming in the sun across the harbor—Tel Aviv—my fears about being forced to live in some harsh desert were erased. Eventually I came to love the desert of Palestine. And I would make my first real money toiling in the desert.

My father made that possible. He had bought land in Jaffa and on it had already built a small plant to manufacture scales. By then, most of the Jewish settlers had scales, either brought with them from Europe or acquired locally from British distributors. The only potential market for such mechanical devices in Palestine was among the Arab population. But the Arab merchants preferred their own long tradition of weighing things, usually with primitive handmade devices made of stakes, strings, plates, stones, and the like.

Try as he did, my father was unable to convince the Arabs to change their ways and buy his scales. Consequently, his first business venture in Palestine quickly failed, and we were faced, if not with poverty, with a much more modest standard of living. As a result, during our first two years in Palestine, we were forced to live in a cramped apartment in Jaffa, which was mostly Arab in population. Although I was still only fourteen, there was no further thought of any formal schooling for me. I had to become a breadwinner, along with my father, so I was sent to work in a Jewish factory that built truck and bus bodies, as well as commercial refrigerators.

This was the best thing that had ever happened to me. I had never had to do a stitch of work before. And although it was hard, sweaty work, it was from my point of view much more desirable than sitting in school. It also gave me a sense of exhilaration about being able to function independently of my family. Up to then, I had been a spoiled, coddled, over-protected kid. Now I felt almost like a man.

The truck-body and refrigerator factory was set on a hill near the Jaffa hospital, overlooking the sea. The labor force was a mixed bag of Jewish and Arab workers. Compared to Tarnow—in topography, climate, and vistas—the scene was idyllic, even though Jaffa was little more than a slum, and no one had much money. I started at the lowest rung as a general, unskilled helper and all-purpose utility boy doing the dirtiest, heaviest, most boring work. I became pretty popular with the other workers because I liked to talk, make friends, and horse around. I was probably a wise guy who pretended to be more grown-up than he really was. I prefer to think I was aggressive, but agreeable.

My job took me to different parts of the factory every day. For a while I'd work on trucks, then I'd work on buses, then be out in the loading yard, then back inside in the section that made refrigerators. It was there that I made my first big breakthrough and began to think I could make something of myself in the business world.

The refrigerators we built were actually big, insulated boxes that were sold to restaurants and food stores. The most complicated part of the job was making and fitting the airtight walk-indoors. The door was constructed so that it had a heavy, iron, self-locking outside handle and opening mechanism. There was no way the door could be opened from the inside.

By the time I went to work at the plant, there had already been several serious accidents in restaurants and food stores where people had suffocated or froze to death after walking into the refrigerators and inadvertently letting the doors slam shut behind them. The box was so well insulated that no one on the outside could hear his shouts for help. After a few hours, unless someone happened to come along and open the door, he was dead.

There had been several lawsuits against the factory. They thought they'd solved the problem by putting an alarm system inside their refrigerator boxes so that if someone got trapped inside, he could push a button and be rescued by someone else in the restaurant or store. But that wasn't much help. Just the year before two people had locked themselves in, one at a restaurant in Tel Aviv, another at a store in Haifa. On each occasion, it was early in the morning, before business hours, and there was no one else to hear the alarm. So, two more people died, and there were more lawsuits.

When I started at the factory, everyone was trying to figure out how to deal with this. After a while, when I was working in the refrigerator part of the plant, a light bulb went on in my brain. Why not use magnets, I thought, instead of an exterior-locking door handle? Magnets inserted in a strip around the doorframe, and matching magnets around the perimeter of the door itself. That way, the door wouldn't need to lock. It could be held tightly shut, but could be opened from either side with a good tug or push.

I brought the idea to the head of the company. He was impressed and wondered why no one had thought of it before. He ordered it tried out. It worked, and thereafter, all the refrigerator doors were fitted with magnets rather than locking handles. End of accidents, end of deaths, end of lawsuits!

My innovation was so successful that refrigerator manufacturers—yes, I'll say it, refrigerator magnates—came from all over the world to study and copy it. Naturally, being but a callow youth of fifteen, it never occurred to me to take a patent on it. I got nothing out of it but a modest promotion and a slight raise in pay. The company made a fortune. Today, it is almost impossible to buy a refrigerator or freezer without a magnetic door-sealer.

Live and learn. And I did.

I worked at the refrigerator factory for about a year and a half. Then, with my mother's help, my father found financial backing for a new manufacturing enterprise of his own. He built a small factory in an industrial district called Kiryat Shmuel, about ten miles north of Tel Aviv. On the top floor, he had an apartment included, and in 1936, we moved into it.

The idea was that this would become a family business, with my father running it, my mother advising in the background, and me being groomed to one day take it over, along with my younger brothers. My father was already fifty, my mother forty-six. But the plan was doomed from the start, mainly because of my father's continuing ineptitude in the dog-eat-dog business world. Perhaps it was also the new climate—warm climates do not inspire men given to abstract deliberation; it just slows them down.

Nevertheless, I quit my job at Jaffa and went to work in the new family enterprise in Kiryat Shmuel. Hyperactive, aggressive, full of energy and ideas, I was no match for my father's waffling style. Soon we were at each other's throats, figuratively speaking, and I decided it best to take my leave.

I could never work for such a man of such lofty theories and principles, I realized, even if he was my own flesh and blood. We were as different as night and day. Not that I didn't have principles. But in the survival-of-the-fittest atmosphere of 1930s Palestine, you couldn't put principles on your dinner table. We weren't in a Gary Cooper movie, after all.

Abraham (Abe) Hirschfeld

CHAPTER FOUR: FROM LAND MINES TO POTS AND PANS

When I left my father, I needed a new job and fast. I didn't have enough money to commute between our apartment on top of the factory and Jaffa, however, so I couldn't get my job at the refrigerator plant back. In those days, there was no such thing as commuting anyway. You worked near where you lived. There was nothing else in the way of factory work available around Kiryat Shmuel, though. So, on the theory that I could use the fresh air, and thinking that it would tide me over until I could find another "real" job, I got myself hired to work in a large, commercial orange grove within walking distance of Kiryat Shmuel.

The grove was owned and run by a Jewish family that had immigrated from Persia years before. My job was the same as that of the other workers. There were four of us in all. Each of us had to water about five hundred trees a day. The grove stretched out for acres and acres from a central well-head, which was actually a pipe with a faucet on top. There were no modern irrigation methods.

What each of us had to do was, first, fill up a pair of three-gallon pails of water at the faucet, then lug them hundreds of yards away to our respective sectors of the orchard. At the base of each tree, narrow holes were drilled in a circle around it. Once out there with the heavy pails, the job then was to pour a couple of cupfuls of water into each hole, tree by tree. With two pails, you could only do about twenty trees. Then you'd have to trudge all the way back to the faucet and repeat the process. It was exhausting work, especially in the summer when the temperatures got up into the hundreds. For all that, the pay was twenty piastres a day. That would be about two dollars a day today—twelve dollars for a six-day week.

It didn't take me long to figure out a better way to get the job done without so much effort—and make better money in the bargain. I went to a farmer and bought a donkey for ten piastres, plus four, five-gallon cans, like milk cans. I strapped the cans on the donkey, two to each side, and filled them from the faucet. Then I marched him out to my part of the grove. I had a spigot and hose coming out of each can. That way, I could water more than three times as many trees in the same amount of time, and I didn't have to kill myself carrying those heavy, sloshing pails and cups. Instead of working from sun-up to sundown, like the others, I was able to finish my daily allotment of trees before noon.

The next thing I did was go to the owner of the orange grove, which was on the land where Bar Ilan University stands today. I said to him, "Look, with my system, in a full day, not only can I do my daily allotment of trees but also those of two of your other workers. Get rid of them. You pay the wages of one; you keep the wage of the other. You pay me twenty piastres more each day, but you save twenty." He agreed. And so there I was, making twice the amount of money of a normal laborer and working only half as hard. No, not even that. The donkey did all the work. I was his human operator. All I had to do was turn the faucet on to fill the cans and flip the spigots to empty them.

It was a crude but handy form of automated irrigation long before the real thing came along. Soon, all the fruit groves in Palestine began to copy my system. Of course, that was something I couldn't patent. How do you patent a donkey?

The point of my story is that the experience of working on the land is what made me first realize that land is money. That has to be what got my "real estate blood" going at an early age—the idea of taking a piece of property and developing or improving it commercially and making money from it. There are only two kinds of people who do that. One is the farmer. The other is the builder. All my life until then, I had been mostly an indoor kid—first as a schoolboy in Tarnow, then as a factory worker in Jaffa, and for that brief time with my father in Kiryat Shmuel. Now I was working outdoors on the land, solving outdoor land problems and getting paid extra for it.

Land, problem solving, money—those three concepts became an equation in my subconscious. I only regret that I waited so long to exploit them the way I eventually did, which was not until well after I came to America. In the meantime, I continued working at the orange grove. A year later, the owner made me the foreman, or field manager, at another big raise in wages. My father still wasn't having any success at his factory, and I was the main breadwinner in the family.

My youngest brother, Meyer, had just started in school about then. So, to make us a little more money, my mother bought a donkey of her own. She would purchase vegetables at the local farms, stuff them into baskets strapped on the donkey's back, and sell them in the village of Kiryat Shmuel. Nevertheless, life had become hard for all of us, much harder than in Poland, much harder than we'd expected it to be, I suppose. But then, looking back on it, who were we to complain? It was now 1938, and already they were rounding up Jews in Poland. We didn't realize how good we had it. Most of my father's family, and most of my mother's, would perish in the Holocaust.

Now that I think back on it, I might well have made my career as a farmer or fruit-grower in Palestine—later to become Israel, of course—if it hadn't been for World War II. I might even have gone into partnership with my Persian employer at the Perchea Orange Groves Ltd., as the business was called. God knows, once I became manager, I began to feel that the huge grove was mine in a way. My semi-proprietary feeling derived from the fact that I was constantly improving it and making it more efficient and productive over the next two years.

The crowning highlight of my fruit-growing career was when I persuaded my boss to scrap the donkey-system of watering I'd introduced and allow me to install a full-scale pipe irrigation system. My brother Menasha was just getting out of school at the time, and I hired him to help me build the pipeline system, thereby adding a little more survival money to the family coffers.

It took more than a year to complete the system. But when it was finished, it was a masterpiece of design and function, and it became the model for the rest of agricultural Palestine. Soon, using pipeline irrigation, Jewish farmers and kibbutzniks would transform much of the desert-like interior of the coastal region into a huge, green, fertile oasis.

But if I thought my efforts and ingenuity would be rewarded by an offer of a partnership in the grove, and thus a piece of the profits, I was wrong. Despite all my pointed hints, no such offer came along during the next year. Not even a further increase in wages. I began to think that a career in fruit farming might not be in the cards for me after all.

In 1939, while I was still twenty and toiling in the Perchea orange groves, World War II broke out in Europe. The start of the war was to be my passport to a new career in Palestine—this one much more financially lucrative. Palestine was ruled by the British, as were other parts of the Middle East, including the vital Suez Canal. Until then, no one in my family had acquired any more interest in politics than they'd possessed in Poland. We all continued to copy my father's disdain for narrow ideologies. Although we'd been in Palestine for six years, not even the politics of Zionism interested us as much. Zionism was determined to oust the British and turn Palestine into a new, sovereign Jewish nation.

Certainly, we were in sympathy with that. But, we thought, perhaps the Zionists—especially their more militant leaders—were trying to rush things too fast. Their militancy had created increasing tensions between the expanding Jewish populace and the British administrative authorities. There had been increasing instances of violence between the two sides all through the 1930s, and by the time war in Europe erupted, the Jews and British in Palestine were in a permanent state of mutual antagonism. Just as Zionist nationalist militancy was to blame, so, too, was British reaction and overreaction. During my time there, I never had any unpleasant encounters with individual Britons on a personal level. In fact, I liked them. But I could also see that as a group, they were not exactly sympathetic to Zionist aspirations and would not hesitate to enforce their Mandate commission with impersonal ruthlessness.

That commission was to keep Palestine in a political and demographic limbo, to maintain it as a territory where no single group, Jewish or Arab, could gain political or nationalist ascendancy. Of course, the war in Europe, and the subsequent tide of history, changed all that. Soon after the war, the British would throw up their hands in despair and say, "We can no longer deal with Palestine—let somebody else do it."

In addition to the Jewish-British problem, there was the Jewish-Arab one, much of which had been brought about by the former. I'm often asked by American Jews brought up in the postwar era of Arab-Israeli strife, "Wasn't it terrible in Palestine before the war with all that Arab hatred and violence?" They are always surprised when I answer, "No."

True, there was hatred and violence between Arabs and Jews in the 1920s and 1930s. But most of that was due to the increasing political manipulation and antagonism between militant Zionist groups and their Palestinian Arab counterparts. To put it quite simply, both wanted the land for themselves, for different reasons.

26

Both had justifiable reasons, albeit reasons that had little in common. So, the strife and riots and other kinds of violence that occurred between the two were inevitable. The fact that such hatred eventually became institutionalized—a matter of nationalistic policy between the two sides—was unfortunate. It, too, I suppose, was inevitable.

But in those days, as I say, I was not really part of Zionist politics. Nor were most of the Jews I was friendly with. We just wanted to live in peace and make a decent future for ourselves.

Personally, I never had any problems with the Arabs in Palestine. As a people, they had their virtues and faults, just as we did. I didn't particularly seek out their company. But if I was living in the Appalachians of West Virginia, I don't expect that I'd seek out the company of a moonshiner, either. That doesn't mean I'd hate him or scorn him, or look down on him as my inferior. It's a simple matter of human nature, of being a realist. People tend to seek out the company of their "own kind," if you'll excuse that much-misinterpreted phrase. Maybe that's what's wrong with the world, but there it is.

To me, the Arabs of Palestine were just another group of people like us Jews, trying to get along in life in their own traditional fashion. That many Arabs were relatively backward compared to the Jewish settlers from Europe didn't make them less worthy or dignified in my eyes. To be sure, I knew there was a lot about them that I would never understand, or even care to understand, but I didn't blame them for that. If they wanted to get along with me, I was happy to get along with them. And as far as I was concerned, we did get along.

I made many Arab friends in the 1930s—friends in the sense that we could talk and joke and agree or disagree in an amicable manner. I could like an Arab as easily as I could dislike someone among my own "people," and there were few of those. To me it had nothing to do with race, religion, ethics, politics, or anything else of that ilk. It was pretty personal.

To a certain extent, the war in Europe changed all that. Everyone now was thinking of survival on a much larger scale. The Arab politicians and religious leaders in Palestine directed their sympathies toward the Nazis, and many even became Nazi agents. As we Jews, Zionist and non-Zionist alike, began to learn what the Nazis were doing to our kinsmen in Europe, we naturally suspended much of our anti-British feeling and aligned ourselves with the Allied cause against the Axis. And that's when my life took a sudden turn for the better.

At the start of the war, the British were the ones among the Allies to take charge of defending the Middle East and North Africa against the Germans and Italians. As the British sent more troops, armor, and ships into the region, Palestine became a vital, strategic area for them, especially for the production of munitions and ammunition—bullets, mortar and cannon shells, land mines, even bombs.

Forty years of Jewish settlement from Europe had brought with it a fairly sophisticated level of manufacturing expertise in iron, steel, and other metal products. There were several Jewish factories that specialized in making such products, and the British decided to start paying them to manufacture munitions to be used against the Axis armies in North Africa and elsewhere in the Mediterranean theatre. That way, they would eliminate a lot of their transportation problems.

I happened to pay a visit to the bus and refrigerator plant in Jaffa one day, early in the war. The plant was being converted to a munitions factory and I was looking for another job. While I was there talking to some of the people, I heard about a problem the British were having.

Back in England, someone had invented a land mine that operated on a principle of proximity pressure. Until then, every mine required that an enemy soldier step almost directly on top of it before it would go off; the same was true with an enemy vehicle, like a tank or a truck. That was because the triggering mechanism was a stalk that jutted from the top of the mine. When the mine was buried, the stalk jutted upward to just beneath the surface of the soil. Downward pressure on the stalk itself was needed to set the mine off. If a soldier's foot, or a tank tread, or a truck wheel, missed it by an inch or so, it would not explode.

The new British mine had no stalk. Instead, the triggering mechanism was built into the interior. The top of the mine was traversed by a very thin band of steel that would flex downward when any pressure was applied to it. The flexing action would activate the interior trigger and the mine would blow up. With this design, sufficient pressure from a meter away from a buried mine would cause it to explode. It increased the efficiency and deadliness of mine warfare enormously.

The only problem for the British was that they could find no one in Palestine with the capacity to manufacture the fine, flexible steel band needed to make the mine work. They could fabricate it in England and ship it down, but because of the large armada of German U-boats in the Mediterranean, the likelihood was that the steel would never arrive.

Hearing all this, I got an idea. My father's factory in Kiryat Shmuel was set up for making steel products. I went to see the local British munitions commander in Tel Aviv and said I could produce the thin steel they needed for their mines. Doubtful, he asked how.

To tell the truth, I didn't know. All I knew was that an opportunity had arisen, and I should seize it. I said, "Give me a few days, and I'll show you."

I went back to my father's factory. For forty-eight hours, I toiled ceaselessly at a drawing bench, calculating by guesswork and tedious trial-and-error the proper calibrations I would need to make in the shop's existing metal-shaping machinery to produce just the right thinness and flexibility of the steel that was required.

To this day, I don't know how I came up with the correct numbers, but finally I did. On the third day, using a handful of rigid, steel reinforcing rods normally employed in concrete construction, I fed them through the recalibrated machinery and managed, through patient trial-and-error, to shape a single, square-foot sample of thin, supple casing.

That afternoon, I bicycled back to Tel Aviv and presented myself to the munitions commander. "This is what I can manufacture," I said, handing him my sample.

He looked at one, felt it, flexed it, even smelled it. He called in some deputies, and they did the same thing. They asked me to leave the room. Ten minutes later, they called me back.

"Perfect," said the commander. He tossed a contract on the desk between us. "When can you start?"

When could I start? I hadn't even thought about that. But I didn't hesitate. "Right away," I said.

And so, just turned twenty-one, I was in the munitions business. Within six months, I'd completely taken over my father's factory and had thirty workers employed, all of them turning out flexible metal rods for British proximity mines. Indeed, by then even my father was working for me, along with my mother and brother Menasha. Never let it be said that the Hirschfeld family didn't do its part to contribute to the defeat of the Nazis.

Like so many people in the world, the Second World War—though I was not directly involved in it, not even really threatened by it—transformed my life. And in more ways than one.

First, it made me a modestly rich young man for my time and place. And independently so. By which I mean I was no longer dependent on my father or anyone else, either for money or for direction. Just the contrary, in fact. In many ways, he and the rest of the family were dependent on me. The failed factory of Simon Hirschfeld had now become the successful factory of twenty-three-year-old Abe Hirschfeld. True, it was a one-product business. But so long as the war lasted, the business would prosper. The British paid very well for my land-mine rods. And I was gaining invaluable experience in the art and craft of running a competitive manufacturing business. Remember, my formal education stopped after having received the equivalent of a fifth grade education.

Second, the war finally thrust me into political awareness and commitment. While my father continued to maintain his above-it-all attitude, I could no longer do so. To begin with, I had become a successful capitalist. To me, the great—the true—democracies of the world were the capitalist ones. So, I became a believer in the capitalist form of democracy, as opposed, say, to the socialist form.

But I had a problem there. Zionism, though democratic in its aspirations, was more socialist than capitalist in its practical orientation and expression. On the other hand, I was becoming a Zionist of sorts. Soon after the European war started, I was recruited into the Haganah—the Jewish defense militia of Palestine. I was happy to serve.

But the Haganah was not just a military organization. It was also highly political, an arm of the Zionist and Jewish statehood movement. As much as it existed to defend our British-Mandate homeland from hostile foreign predators, its function was also to assist in the push for a sovereign Jewish nation.

Thus, by its very nature, the Haganah was anti-British. Not as vehemently so as the more militant Zionist offshoots, like the Irgun and the Stern Gang, but anti-British nevertheless. Of course, I was doing business with the British; in fact, I was getting rich off them.

So, I found myself in a bit of a political quandary during the war years. I could not really hate the British the way many of my militant Jewish brethren did. I had known many of them on the local scene and liked them. On the other hand, I could not really quarrel with the increasing insistence on statehood of my more militant Zionist friends—especially after the news of what the Nazis were doing to the Jews in Europe began to reach Palestine. Thus, I became a Zionist in my own fashion, allied to no particular splinter group but approving of the movement's overall goal of a Jewish state. I only hoped that once such a state was achieved, as I was sure it would be, it would strike a proper balance between capitalist and socialist practices.

In the meantime, I did my Haganah service. That consisted of four or five hours of patrol duty every night after a full, twelve-hour day of work at our factory in Kiryat Shmuel. The primary purpose was to protect against acts of Arab terrorism directed at the Jewish population. Emboldened by the early Axis successes in the war, Arab militants, often trained, armed, and financed by German agents, attacked not only Jewish but British installations. They expected the Nazis to win the war and hoped to be rewarded by being given dominion over a Jewish-free Palestine.

For all practical purposes, the Middle Eastern-North African phase of the war was over by the end of 1943. By then, I was making a lot of money and could even afford to own a motorcycle. That led to the third radical change in my life.

I was getting on toward twenty-four. It's no secret that the summers in coastal Palestine, now Israel, were and are very hot. In 1943, there was no such thing as air conditioning. Summertime working conditions in the factory at Kiryat Shmuel were brutal. Yet, there could be no letup, since the British demand for our steel remained intense, as did my desire to keep making money. Nevertheless, between my work at the plant and my nightly Haganah duty, I was feeling drained. One particularly hot day, on a whim, I decided to get away for a few hours. A dip in the sea might refresh me, I thought. And there might be a few pretty girls on the beach I could ogle.

31

I climbed on my motorcycle and drove up the coast to Netanya. There were some pretty girls on the sand, several of whom I'd encountered before. But the prettiest, the most striking, was one I'd only seen once two years earlier. She was with a group of friends, one of whom I knew. By then, I was not so shy, maybe because I was doing so well in business, and girls had begun to look upon me differently. Whatever the case, the girl I knew beckoned me to join them. I went over and started talking. I couldn't take my eyes off the new girl, the one I'd seen only once before.

She remained quiet, a bit distant, a bit superior in attitude. Which, of course, made me all the more curious and interested. When she finally spoke, she was cool and regal, not at all like her chattering, giggling friends. A real woman, I thought, although she was obviously still just a girl. She told me her name: Zipora Teicher.

Needless to say, I fell instantly in love. She told me she was hoping to become a nun. I laughed, thinking she was making a joke. How could a Jewish girl like her become a nun? I asked.

She was offended by my sarcasm. "It has nothing to do with religion," she said. "If I want to become a nun, I will become a nun."

"No you won't," I answered, my attraction overcoming whatever shyness remained in me. "You know why?"

"Why?" she said, a challenge in her voice.

"Because you're going to marry me."

Her laugh was haughty and disdainful. But a year later, on July 4, we were married. Zipora Teicher, the daughter of Elimelech and Pesia Teicher, became Mrs. Abraham Hirschfeld.

It was 1943. By then, the war in Europe was largely over for the Middle East; only the postwar consequences remained to be settled. In the meantime, the Jews and Arabs of Palestine stepped up their jockeying for political dominion within the British Mandate, with the Jews getting much the better of the struggle.

But with the war gone, so, too, was the British need for locally manufactured munitions. Suddenly, the Hirschfeld factory at Kiryat Shmuel was without a customer. I began to look around for new ideas, new products, new markets. Nothing practical came readily to mind, though. That is, until Zipora and I were married.

As a wedding gift, my father gave us a two-burner electric stove for cooking in the apartment we planned to move into and two metal pots to go with it. After a few weeks, Zipora decided she needed a few more pots and pans, but you simply couldn't buy pots in 1944 Palestine, not even on the black market. Imports had been shut down since the beginning of the war, and no one made them domestically.

That became my new idea. I did some research and found that there was an acute shortage of pots and pans throughout Palestine. I decided immediately to turn the factory over to the manufacture of these products. But how? my father asked. There was still no metal available from which to make them. That was my father, always negative, always doubting, always skeptical when it came to business initiative.

I had already figured out the answer. Palestine and the lands around it were dotted with warplanes that had been shot down, crash-landed, otherwise damaged. I quickly arranged to acquire the aluminum fuselages of many of those aircraft and had them trucked to Kiryat Shmuel. They would be my raw material.

At the factory, I melted down the aluminum and poured it into molds shaped roughly like stove pots and frying pans. Once they cooled and hardened, the objects were extracted from the molds and sent to the factory's lathes and grinders, where they were further shaped into actual pots and pans, and then shined.

If I thought my land-mine idea for the British was the ultimate in spontaneous business ingenuity, I was wrong. My pots-and-pans brainstorm outdistanced it by miles. In a very short time, the demand for my new products climbed out of sight, and I could barely keep up with it. I could charge practically any price I wanted to on items that cost me only a few pennies to make, and get it.

It was in this way that I learned not only how to manufacture, but how to merchandise. Instead of selling my pots and pans through middlemen, I decided to open my own retail store on Herzl Street on the Tel Aviv-Jaffa border. I called it Hirschfeld Brothers. My whole family worked in the store, while I traipsed back and forth to the factory. It was an enormous success, some days with lines around the block waiting to get in.

I deliberately kept a rein on production in order to maintain the spiraling demand and obtain increasingly high retail, and I would have cornered the cooking-utensil market in the Middle East forever if it hadn't been for the 1947 Partition and the subsequent War of Independence. When it came along in 1948, it effectively put an end to the demand.   Then, after Independence, we started to get competition. By that time, I'd lost interest in pots and pans. Bigger things were on the horizon.

CHAPTER FIVE: THE CRUCIBLE

I often joked to Zipora that the reason she wanted to become a nun was because she knew she would never find a man who could measure up to her beloved father. I felt I had to prove myself to him, that I was capable of being a financial success like him and would look after his daughter in the same way he did. Today that sounds dreadfully old-fashioned. But that's how one thought in those days. Having long been the father of a daughter myself, and having experienced a few qualms about some of her romantic attachments when she was a teenager, I could later understand how Zipora's father felt about me.

Not that I was poor when I married Zipora in 1944. The only question was, would I be able to continue making good money after the British no longer needed my calibrated steel for their land mines? The pots-and-pans business had answered that question very nicely. But by then, I knew I had more in my future than pots and pans. Perhaps Zipora's father's career as a successful urban developer and builder was quietly inspiring me without me really knowing it.

After Zipora and I were married, I was able to settle us in a nice apartment in Bnei Brak, a town just off the road between Tel Aviv and Kiryat Shmuel. The only trouble with Bnei Brak was that it was a very Orthodox religious community. I had been brought up an Orthodox Jew, but by then, I'd become less religious. The town closed up tight for the Sabbath between Friday and Saturday nights. The main entry gate was blocked off by chains, and nobody was supposed to drive around or enter or leave.

I had acquired a Ford convertible in 1945. I was one of the few people in town who could afford a car. I paid no attention to the Sabbath rules. In addition to the main gate, there was a gate at the other side of Bnei Brak, which was also supposed to be chained on the Sabbath. I would often leave the chain off and drive in and out to our apartment. That gate came to be called, rather disparagingly by the townspeople, the "Hirschfeld Gate."

But despite my cavalier approach to the town's religious customs, I became popular there. In 1946, there was an election for mayor. Since I was still only twenty-seven, and the law said that a man under thirty could not be a mayor, I couldn't run for the top office. But I was elected deputy mayor. That was my introduction to everyday politics, and I must say I enjoyed it. Yet, I still had no great political ideology, aside from my commitment to the idea of capitalism and democracy operating in tandem.

The main political party in Bnei Brak was the Orthodox Religious Party, which was right-wing. Through my military duty in the Haganah, however, I had become a member of the General Zionist Organization, which was basically a middle-of-the-road political group. Being a member of the GZO at that time was like saying today in America that one is a Conservative Democrat. Or a Liberal Republican. Or, as I like to call such a person, a "Hippocrat."

In other words, the GZO tended to go with the political consensus while carefully maintaining a fence-sitting distance that would allow it to swing easily in whatever direction the consensus later pointed. The GZO was a party for those without doctrinaire political ideologies. Nevertheless, it served a useful purpose as a kind of institutional middleman and peacemaker among the more extremist parties of Palestine while it was still under British administration.

The GZO was a party of pragmatism and negotiation, which was why I was attracted to it. The two traits that dominated my personality by then, at least in business, were my ability to see opportunity ahead, and then to pragmatically negotiate my way to realizing the opportunity I perceived. Today, books and courses on management extol those qualities as "vision" and "salesmanship," and try to teach them. I'm not sure they can be taught; they must be learned through hard experience.

Hard experience is what I had. Like my father, I suppose, I was a dreamer. But from my mother I'd gotten a large genetic dose of sharp-edged realism, along with her caustic sense of humor and hard-nosed business sense.

I didn't get to enjoy it for very long, though. My practice was strictly on the local level. Immersed in my burgeoning pots-and-pans business, I didn't have time for anything beyond that. In the meantime, outside my fairly limited purview, international political currents were afoot that would soon turn Palestine into the independent state of Israel. Palestine would no longer be simply our "homeland." Under a new name, it would be our long sought-after sovereign nation.

Nationhood would not come easy, though, just as nothing good in this world comes easy. First, we were compelled to win a war of liberation from the hysterical political wrath of our neighboring countries. Our victory in the war secured Israel's independence and its rightful place in the international community of free nations. Sadly, it did not liberate it from Arab wrath.

Had Egypt, Syria, Iraq, Jordan, and the rest of the Arab world reacted to the United Nations' Partition of Palestine more rationally, and allowed us time to establish ourselves peacefully and work out a modus vivendi with the Arab inhabitants of the Palestinian region, I am certain the history of the Middle East since 1948 would have been radically different. I know that I had thousands of other newly minted Israelis, motivated by the traditions of fairness and justice that are at the core of our religious and cultural heritage, wanting to arrive at such a modus vivendi. But the combined Arab military attack on the fragile new nation made it impossible. By then we all knew—and all too well—about the European Holocaust. The rhetoric of the surrounding Arab nations often made Hitler's diatribes sound like nursery rhymes. The notion of "Never Again" was instilled in the modern Jewish soul long before the likes of the crazed Rabbi Meier Kahane made it the motto of his American Jewish Defense League.

Personally, I would have liked to have negotiated a resolution of the Arab threat in 1948. Between 1945 and 1948, I had done increasing amounts of business with merchandisers and manufacturers in neighboring Arab countries, gotten to know their people, and was friendly with many of them. On the personal level, there was no antagonism between most Arabs and Jews. One of the chief business principles I had learned was always to treat your customers with dignity, respect, and friendliness, for customers are the lifeblood of any business. I practiced that with my Arab customers as religiously as I did with my Jewish ones, and I never had any problems of consequence with either. Had it been left to the people of the two sides, there would never have been any need for an Israeli War of Independence in 1948.

But as I've said, I was and am a realist. I had also learned that one cannot negotiate from a position of weakness. That is why the Arab governments refused to talk and chose to wage war instead. They believed we were weak, that we had no strengths to negotiate from.

In a sense, they were right. Ironically, by opting to send their armies against us, they made it possible for us to gain the power we lacked.

The War of Independence brought another radical change to my life. Already Zipora had given birth to our first child, our beloved daughter Rachel. A second child, our cherished son Elie, would soon join us. Beyond that, pots and pans were no longer important. What was needed in Israel were the resources to repel the Arabs and ensure the nation's early survival.

That meant military arms, equipment, and other material. Most of them had to be imported, along with the vital raw materials that would allow us to begin making our own munitions and armaments. That was where I came in.

I had been working exclusively in metals for eight years at my Kiryat Shmuel factory. I knew as much about iron, steel, and other metals as just about anyone in Israel. There were still no steel mills or other metal-making plants in the country. Anything new that was fabricated of metal was done so either from existing scrap, melted down like my reinforcing rods and airplane fuselages, or from imported metal. By 1947, scrap metal was in short supply, most of it having been used up by entrepreneurs like me. It was imperative that we begin importing iron, steel, aluminum, and other alloys.

And so, I became a major metals importer, exempted by the governments from military service. Like a fisherman, I cast out my lines in the form of urgent cables and letters to various countries in Europe, and then reeled in shiploads of aluminum, brass, copper, and other vital, non-ferrous metals.

By the time the war was over, I was known as the "metals king" of Israel and had established many valuable source contacts abroad. The end of the war did not bring any reduction in the need for such products. It was only natural, then, that I should expand and capitalize on this new career. Which is what I did. I became one of Israel's leading post-Independence metal importers.

At that time, Zipora and I left Bnei Brak and moved into a much larger and nicer apartment on the most fashionable street in Tel Aviv. By then, I had become the sole support of my family—not only of Zipora and Rachel but also of my father, mother, and two brothers. My father was well into his sixties and had more-or-less given up any further attempts to be successful. He was content to work in my organization, although what work he did was of little consequence.

Yet, I was happy to provide for him. He had always tried his best to make a good life for us and really couldn't help that he'd failed since coming to Palestine. Anyway, as I've said, we all owed him a great deal for his foresight in making the move. Even my mother, who'd been miserable at the idea originally, now was eternally grateful.

My younger brother Menasha had grown up to be as different from me as night is from day. He had much more of my father in him and was cautious and meticulous in his approach to business. Yet, he became a valuable deputy to me in my importing enterprises. Where I aggressively rooted out the opportunities and made the big deals, innovating and improvising as I went along, he was the detail man, keeping the accounts, organizing the schedules, and attending to the paperwork.

In that sense, Menasha complemented me and was an asset to the business of Hirschfeld Brothers. But at the same time, we didn't really work well together. I was bold and daring in business; he was much more conservative. He preferred deals that entailed small volumes, produced small profits, and carried little risk. I was always compelled to go for the high-volume, high-profit, high-risk transaction. My theory was: Why waste your time and energy on trying to make hundreds when with the same time and energy, and a little more chutzpah, you can make thousands. Sure, I got burned once or twice. But most of the time, through raw determination and perseverance, I made the deal work.

As we grew older, the difference between our business styles became sharper, and eventually we agreed to disagree. We parted ways. My other brother, Meyer, who was ten years younger, was more like me, with an entrepreneurial flair. Rather than work for me, though, he wanted to be independent and go his own way. There came a time when he decided to start his own bus business. I got him started by financing it.

When I became the metals king of Israel following the War of Independence, I separated the business into two divisions. Menasha handled the smaller retail end of it, while I made the major wholesale deals, importing metals in great quantities to sell to the nation's burgeoning civilian and military manufacturing industries.

But while I continued to accumulate more and more money from this, I still continued to try to bring about a reconciliation between the Jews and Arabs of the region. I figured now that the war had been fought and the issues had more or less been settled, it was time to put our differences aside and exploit our similarities. After all, in the context of history and religion, the Jews and Arabs were cousins, each people deriving from the same patriarch—the Biblical Abraham. Even the Arabs acknowledged this.

No doubt, my hopes of achieving anything in this regard were naïve. The mutual hostility and suspicion engendered by the war were too powerful to be countered by rational discourse; indeed, in many quarters, rational discourse was impossible. The Arab governments, shamed by their failure to eradicate Israel, further inflamed Arab emotions with their rhetoric of future revenge. And the beleaguered government of Israel, responding, did little to discourage hatred of the Arabs, for it portended an endless future of war and death and deprivation in a land that had the potential of providing prosperity to everyone. Although I was a peaceful man, I would fight if attacked, and I would do so even today as I approach my nineties. But then, as now, I much preferred to talk, to discuss, to negotiate. In the Israel of the late 1940s, that instinct was not very fashionable. A warrior mentality was becoming embedded in the national consciousness, and I began to wonder if there would be a place for me in such a world. Not to mention for my family—Zipora, Rachel, and Elie, who was about to be born.

I didn't realize it at the time, but fate was preparing to step in and give me a new direction. It would provide the answers to the questions I was asking myself about my future. The year was 1949. Up to then, all the metals I imported came from Britain, Belgium, and Italy. But most of my trade had been done through cable and mail correspondence or on the telephone. Since arriving from Poland in 1934, I had not stepped out of the Middle East. I had met a few visiting Britons, Belgians, and Italians in the metal-producing industries of those countries, most of whom were my suppliers, but had never visited them or their factories and mills. And I had never encountered anyone from the United States. To put it bluntly, although I was becoming wealthy and prominent in Israel, I was fairly provincial in my attitudes and opinions. I had little curiosity about the rest of the world and certainly no desire to see it.

All that began to change in 1949, despite my continuing resistance. I suppose the initial phase occurred when I met my first American.

His name was Max Jacobs, and he was an American Jew in the metals business in Rahway, New Jersey. We were introduced when he traveled to Israel on a combined business-pleasure trip. He was full of stories about the glories of America, especially the metals industry there, and insisted I should visit. Rather cockily, I said, "Why? I've got my own America here in Israel." By his standards, though, my operation was relatively modest.

Throughout his stay in Israel, he continued to paint a rosy picture of America, both from a business and from a political and social point of view, with an emphasis on its material abundance and diversity. Although he'd finally gotten me curious, I was still content just to hear about it. I had no ambition to go and see it.

But then, a while later, I received an invitation from Imperial Chemical Industries, a company in England from which I imported some of my non-ferrous metals. The invitation was for me to go to England as their guest, and then to travel to the United States to attend an industry convention.

Although I did a lot of business with I.C.I., I had several other good suppliers in England. I feared that if I accepted the I.C.I. invitation, I would insult those other companies. Thus, I tore it up. Besides, I was still uninterested in traveling anywhere.

When I got home that night, I mentioned the invitation to Zipora, who was pregnant with our son, and said, "Who needs it?"

Disbelievingly, she said, "You threw it out! What, are you crazy?"

Fortunately, Zipora had much more education and culture than I did. She asked me how I could pass up such an opportunity. She told me that it was about time I saw something of the rest of the world, that it would help me in business to make new contacts, and so on. When she was finished, I had to admit she was right. I had to admit, too, that much of my reluctance to travel was due to my fear of not being able to make myself understood in the countries I did business with. I still spoke only Hebrew and Yiddish.

And so, I wrote back to I.C.I. and accepted their invitation.

Since I was going to England, I arranged to stop on the way in Italy to visit my suppliers there. Fortunately, a few people there spoke German, and between their German and my Yiddish, I managed to make myself understood. By the time I proceeded to England, I felt more comfortable about being abroad in foreign lands.

Arriving in London, I was put up by I.C.I. at the Grosvernor House Hotel on Park Lane and was treated with lavish hospitality. As a result, my first exposure to the English-speaking world was a most enjoyable one. I fell in love with London. Of course, it was totally different from the culture I was accustomed to. The cool politeness of its society was in distinct contrast to the casual freneticism of Israeli life, both in the business and in social realms. It was only later, when I began to understand the language, that I learned that the English could be as sharp-edged in business and social intercourse as any Mediterranean people. It was just that their style was different.

After a few days in England, I was very glad Zipora had talked me into going. I had always been comfortable with the English people I'd dealt with during the Palestine Mandate days, and I felt very much at home in London.

Naturally, I realized that that had much to do with the fact that I was getting such first-class treatment. To be sure, I was a good customer of I.C.I. But maybe the treatment also had something to do with a story some of my hosts knew about.

The story went back a few years, to when I was in the Haganah. One day, Menasha and I, and another Haganah member, were patrolling the road between Tel Aviv and Netanya. At the time, the British Mandate police were in constant battle with the Irgun, the Jewish underground in Palestine, which was trying to hasten the departure of the British. Unbeknownst to us, the day of our patrol, an Irgun squad had killed three British soldiers near Netanya. As we drove into Netanya in my Ford, we were seized by the British authorities and tossed into jail. There we were accused of being the killers and were interrogated under mild torture.

The episode was frightening at the time, but wryly amusing in retrospect. Of course, we were eventually cleared and released, but I never let an opportunity go by without telling my British friends about how my brother and I had been terrorized by their forces in Palestine. In London, they made it up to me with hospitality that was beyond the call of duty. You hear a lot about guilt being the engine of the Jewish soul. It was then that I learned that guilt is as powerful an emotion in the British.

From Britain, it was on to New York. Before I left Israel, a customer of mine had told me he was going to New York to start an automobile tour of the United States! Moishe Rubin had said, "Let's meet there."

I said, "How?"

Moishe had been there before. He said, "When you get to New York, go in from the airport and check into the Knickerbocker Hotel, which is near Times Square."

He went on to tell me about a sign in Times Square that was a great tourist attraction. The sign was a huge billboard, he said, that depicted a man smoking a Chesterfield cigarette—actually smoking and blowing smoke rings through his mouth, which was really a hole in the billboard.

"After you check into the Knickerbocker Hotel," Moishe said, "go out and stand beneath the Chesterfield sign. I'll find you."

Sure enough, he did. So, on my first trip to New York, I was with someone I knew, someone who was familiar with the city. To me, on first sight, it was the eighth wonder of the world.

Also, before leaving Israel, through my friend Max Jacobs of New Jersey, I had learned of a new metal technology that had been pioneered by the Jones & Laughlin Steel Corporation in America. It was a "continuous welding" mill that fabricated, all in one automated process, finished steel flexible tubing for electrical conduits and other commercial uses. I had decided to look into the process while I was in the United States, with the idea of importing such a mill to Israel. Accordingly, once the convention I had come to attend was over, I arranged to visit Jones & Laughlin's headquarters in Pittsburgh.

Moishe Rubin was about to set out on his automobile trip across America with two other friends from Israel. They rented a car, and I hitched a ride as far as Pittsburgh. There, with Max Jacob's letter of introduction, I was received by George Jones, the chairman of the Jones & Laughlin Steel Corporation, one of America's biggest steelmakers.

For some reason, Jones and I immediately took to each other. I was introduced to him as the metals king of Israel. To me, he was the steel monarch of America—this despite the fact that his company was only the third or fourth largest American steel producer after U.S. Steel, Bethlehem Steel, and possibly one other. Like mine, but in a much more significant way, his was a family business, whereas the others were vast public corporations run by hired executives.

Perhaps it was my personal business style that George Jones appreciated. Plus, his sympathy for my inability to speak English. Although I'd learned a few rudimentary English words and expressions by the time I'd arrived in Pittsburgh, I was still unable to communicate effectively. Yet, I did not stand on ceremony. I barged ahead in my inept fashion, and through the use of gesture and inflection, managed to make myself understood.

Somehow, I still do that, six decades later.

CHAPTER SIX: A BITE OF THE APPLE

My meetings with George Jones of Jones & Laughlin resulted in his agreement to sell me his continuous welding and tubing machine. My plan was to use the mill to start a whole new metals business in Israel—the supplying of domestically produced steel tubing to the construction industry there, which was just beginning to go into a boom period.

The deal I made with Jones was simple. The mill was easily worth $300,000. But since it was considered World War II surplus, he could not sell it within the United States. He was willing to give it away for practically nothing, just to be rid of it. Another attraction for him was that whomever bought it and shipped it abroad would have to use Jones & Laughlin steel if he intended to put it into profitable operation. The machine would produce a lucrative new foreign customer for the company.

Jones agreed to sell me the mill for $20,000. Included in the price was a shipment of free steel to get me started, plus the costs of dismantling and shipping the huge device to Israel. For someone who could barely speak English, I thought I'd done extremely well in my first English-language venture.

Even Jones was impressed. When he took me to lunch to celebrate our deal, he congratulated me on my ability to surmount the language barrier between us and conclude the transaction. I told him, still in my fractured English, that all it took was learning the important words. To illustrate, I related another of my mother's stories.

This one was about three Israeli friends of hers who had visited New York for the first time a few years earlier. None of the women spoke English when they left Tel Aviv, and none spoke it when they returned a month later.

"So, how did you manage all by yourselves, in such a big place like New York, without knowing the language?" my mother asked them.

"Who needed the language?" one of them replied. "We just learned the three most important phrases: Bergdorf-Goodman, Bonwit-Teller, and Saks Fifth Avenue. Those were all we needed to know."

45

George Jones got a laugh out of the story, mainly because he realized that it was exactly what I had done. I'd learned the English words, "buy," "sell," "contract," "deal," and "ship." They were all I needed to make myself clear to him. And they were all he'd required to make himself clear to me, he said later, chuckling over the way we'd negotiated in Pidgin English.

However, it would take a better knowledge of English on my part to explain to him, the following year, why I was unable to make good on the deal. It was that failure that brought me back to America for good.

As I've indicated, when I left on my trip, Zipora was pregnant. My stay in the United States lasted two months longer than I'd planned, and by the time I got back to Tel Aviv, at the end of December 1949, my son Elie had just been born. That was a wonderful return gift, but I also found a host of problems on my arrival.

First of all, having left Menasha in charge of the Hirschfeld Brothers organization, I was astonished to discover that he had allowed the business to drift close to the brink of collapse. In my absence, the new socialist Israeli government had imposed a harsh regimen of tariffs, taxes, and other economic controls on independent capitalist enterprises such as mine. Menasha had, for all practical purposes, ignored them.

The other major difficulty had to do with my intention of importing the tubing mill I'd agreed to buy from Jones & Laughlin. George Jones was awaiting my payment and shipping instructions so that he could dismantle the mill and send it on its way to me. But I now found myself in a financial Catch-22 situation.

The government had seized all my corporate assets, including my bank accounts, until I satisfied their tax and tariff demands. I had to go to the Bank Leumi and ask for a loan to pay the $20,000 I owed Jones & Laughlin. The bank said fine, we'll lend you the money, but first you must have certificates of approval from the government to import the mill.

I applied to the government for the appropriate certificates. "Sorry," the government said, "neither you nor anyone else in this country can run an independent capitalist business anymore. From now on, you must be in partnership with the government. You can only import your mill if you assign us 51 percent ownership of it."

I said, "Are you willing to pay 51 percent of the price I promised to Jones & Laughlin?"

"No," they said.

"Then, forget it," I said back. "Your socialist ideas are not to my liking. I want more than anyone for Israel to succeed financially. But it will not succeed if you stifle individual initiative. You will just create a welfare state that will produce a never-ending cycle of inflation and reduce every citizen to constant financial hardship."

I argued for weeks, but to no avail. The Labour government—Ben Gurion and his closest advisers—had long before formulated its Zionist-socialist plan for building the country. I could appreciate the plan's good intentions, which were to achieve an expanding economic, as well as political, democracy. But I believed such a scheme was too self-limiting. Israel should have been emulating the American economic system, not those of the European socialist states, which were little more than moderate forms of militant communism.

The trouble was that most of those in power in the newly established government of Israel, from Ben Gurion on down, came from the very countries in central and eastern Europe in which Marxism and socialism had flourished the most during the previous half-century. And that Zionism itself, at least in its practical organizational aspects, got its inspiration from the ideas of the political cooperative and economic collective. Ben Gurion and the rest of the Zionist leadership didn't want communism, exactly. But they didn't want capitalism, either. They wanted an amalgam of the two, a system that would produce an essentially classless society in which everyone would have a more-or-less equal slice of the pie.

Although commendably idealistic, the system was unrealistic, I thought. But as I've said, my arguments against it were unavailing. I could either accept the system, or I could think about moving elsewhere. The decision was almost made for me, as it was for many capitalist-minded Israelis in the early years of the nation's existence.

For me, the decision turned on my continuing desire to bring the tubing mill into the country. In the spring of 1950, I managed to come to terms with the government over the issue of Hirschfeld Brothers. The organization was permitted to resume business again, but only under the government's strict new anti-capitalist regulations and controls, which applied to all such business enterprises.

Still, I could not persuade the authorities to let me bring in the Jones & Laughlin tubing mill without giving a 51 percent share in the new manufacturing business I'd planned for it to the government. Unwilling to do so, I was prohibited from paying George Jones the $20,000 I owed for the mill. It was still sitting in Pittsburgh.

I had no choice but to travel back to Pennsylvania, explain my predicament personally to Jones, and try to make other arrangements to get him the money. He had been so fair with me, and had taken such a liking to me, that I was determined to show him I was not the deadbeat I was beginning to fear he thought I might be.

My return to the United States in the late summer of 1950 was for that purpose only. I had no intention of remaining there any longer than it took me to settle my account and, I believed, straighten my reputation with Jones. I must admit, though, that I was seriously pondering the question of my commercial future in Israel in the face of its increasingly more stringent socialist economic system. I was a dedicated Jew and a reasonably committed Zionist, and Israel was my country. That was not to say, however, that I should be blindly beholden to it.

I suppose what happened next could be compared to a man who has a longtime wife, yet is drawn away from her bed by the promise of a jazzier existence in the arms of a more sophisticated and understanding woman. For on my second trip to America, that's what I discovered: the business equivalent of a more sophisticated and understanding woman.

When I arrived in Pittsburgh, I found George Jones totally understanding. I told him I wanted to pay, even though I now could not bring his surplus mill into Israel without signing half my life away. He said, "Don't worry, Abe, I think I have a solution to your problem." And that's where the sophistication came in.

His solution was a small, steel-fabricating company in Philadelphia. "After I made the deal to sell the mill to you last year," Jones said, "they came to me dying to buy it. I had to tell them they were too late. Now, since you can't take it, I could easily cancel our contract, then turn around and sell it to them for much more than you agreed to pay. Right?"

I said, "Right," thinking that Jones was kindly letting me off the hook.

"But I like you, Abe," he went on. "I see you're honest, and you've suffered an unexpected setback with your government, and instead of writing me, you've come all this way again to try to make good on our deal. That means something to me. So why should I take advantage of your misfortune to make a greater profit? The Philadelphia people are still dying to have the mill. You go see them. Make your own deal with them; sell them the mill. They'll pay a lot more than $20,000. After you sell it, pay me the twenty and keep the difference for yourself. That way, you'll have fulfilled your contract with me and everybody'll be happy."

Jones was not only letting me off the hook, he was giving me a chance to make some money on my own out of our abortive deal. How could I ask for anything more of a man? An offer like that, from a business creditor, would never occur in Israel. I was almost delirious with gratitude and relief. That a man of Jones's keen, hard-nosed business sense would be so magnanimous was a phenomenon I had never imagined possible. If I had any doubts about the glories of America, they were erased by that single, simple gesture of business kindness on his part.

The next day, I took a train to Philadelphia to visit the Westmorland Metal Manufacturing Company, the organization that had approached Jones about buying the tubing mill. Jones called ahead to let them know I was coming and advised them to listen to me, despite my still-limited English. Sure enough, when I arrived they were extremely eager to acquire the mill, which was the last of its kind in the United States.

During the train ride, I'd had a brainstorm. Jones had talked about me offering the mill to Westmorland on a sale basis. But who said I had to sell it? So, when I met with Irving Kucher, the president of Westmorland, I offered to lease it: $20,000 in advance, plus $10,000 a year for ten years.

He commended me for my candor and agreed to the $20,000 in advance. With respect to the subsequent lease payments, we negotiated and settled at $6,000 a year, starting immediately. What it all amounted to was that I would be able to pay off George Jones straight away, still make $60,000 for myself in the long-term, and in the process, retain ownership of the mill. Thus, my first business transaction in America, despite its initial difficulties, was a signal success. And those difficulties had nothing to do with America; they were strictly Israeli in origin.

The experience was an eye-opener in two ways. To begin with, it showed me that it was a lot easier to do business in the United States than it was going to be in the future in an Israel saddled with increasingly restrictive economic controls. Second, pure money-making business opportunity was infinitely greater in America than it was in Israel, if only because of the former's vastness, its highly capitalistic orientation, and the willingness of its people to do business and solve problems fast and creatively. Those factors had a great appeal to my basic nature. I had taken a bite out of the seductive apple of America and found it delicious. I wanted more.

My impulse for more was shaped by the fact that as a result of my deal with Westmorland, I would be receiving $6,000 a year without having to do anything for it. In 1950, $6,000 a year, though by no means a fortune in America, was a very decent sum to be earning. Anyone could live fairly comfortably on it. And if I could make that amount so easily, why couldn't I make much more? How? By acquiring further income-producing assets like the tubing mill.

But first, I had to make an important decision. I was, after all, an Israeli, not an American. My emotional allegiance to Israel remained powerful, even though I had begun to doubt my ability to continue being successful in business there. At the same time, I was entranced by America. But was I fooling myself? Had my Westmorland transaction been nothing more than a happy fluke, a matter of beginner's luck? What should I do?

It was Zipora who, in a large way, made the decision for me. While waiting for the Westmorland transaction to close, I had written her to say that I'd have to remain in the United States longer than planned. She wrote back that she wanted to join me. I said fine, come. I figured she'd spend a week or two with me in Philadelphia and New York, and then we'd return together. The children, I assumed, she'd be leaving with my parents.

When I went to Idlewild Airport to meet her plane, I was astonished to see her come through Customs with four-year-old Rachel in tow and nine-month-old Elie in her arms.

"Why did you bring the children?" I said. "You're only here for a week or so."

"Abe," she answered, "my mother always told me, a woman never crosses an ocean without her children. Anyway, knowing you, I have a feeling we'll be staying for more than a week or two."

Zipora was right. Between the time I'd told her to come and the time she'd arrived with the kids, I had gone to see Max Jacobs in Rahway, New Jersey. I told him about my little coup with Westmorland and asked his advice about whether I should stay in America to seek more deals. He also prodded me toward my decision.

He said, "Abe, your main experience is importing steel and other metals."

"Yes," I replied, "but in Israel."

"Nevertheless, you're an expert. You know quality, you know price. You know all the sources of supply. You know the business like the back of your hand."

"What are you getting at?" I asked.

He explained. The Korean War was at its height. Although the United States was the biggest steel producer in the world, much of its domestic production was now being devoted to military manufacture. Steel shortages were beginning to show up in civilian manufacturing. A market for imported steel was growing.

"With your knowledge and experience," Max Jacobs said, "you could do very well here in the next few years as a steel importer."

Thinking about it, the idea appealed to me. "But Max," I said, "that would mean starting my own company. I'd need start-up capital in dollars. I can't take any money out of Israel to do that; the government won't allow it. And the $6,000 I'm getting from Westmoreland—well, that's to live on."

Max and I were reading each other's minds, of course. "I'll put up the money," he said. "You put up the brains. We'll start a business together."

It succeeded beyond my wildest dreams. Max Jacobs and I formed a fifty-fifty partnership called Jacobs Associates. Within the first year, between the fall of 1950 and the fall of 1951, I made more than $2,000,000 selling imported steel to warehouses and manufacturers all over the Northeast. We were the only importers in the New York region, and most of our product came from the same British, French, and Belgian suppliers I had developed in Israel.

51

The formula was simple. Quality European steel was still very cheap, about $55 a ton. In America, the situation was just the opposite. The domestic steel shortages caused by the Korean War, plus the continuing post-World War II boom in ordinary consumer-product manufacturing, had created high demand and very high prices, about $120 a ton.

Between shipping costs and duties, it cost us about eight dollars a ton to get our steel from Europe to ports in and around New York. That meant a total cost to us of $63 a ton. Selling at $120 gave us an almost 100% profit on every ton. It was, to use the first English-language slang expression I learned at the time, like taking candy from a baby. My future in the United States, if I wanted such a future, looked very rosy indeed. Much more than it had been in Israel.

The decision to stay—to settle permanently in New York—became inevitable the following year when we trebled our income. But it was not only that. My success in the steel business brought with it two additional things. The first was a rapidly increasing ease with the language, although I still spoke English with a heavy Israeli accent. The second was a fast-expanding circle of American friends in and out of the business.

Not only I, but Zipora was growing extremely comfortable and "at home" in New York. And the children were beginning to take on the coloration of natives as they became more and more exposed to New York playmates. Indeed, Rachel spoke English so well that it almost embarrassed me, on her behalf, to be her father.

The final decision came one beautiful day in the fall of 1952, when Zipora and I were walking the children in Central Park. We stopped and looked at one another, as if we'd had the identical idea simultaneously and the need to voice it in unison.

"We're staying," we said to each other.

CHAPTER SEVEN: A CANADIAN INTERLUDE

But then I found out we couldn't.

We had to come to the United States two years earlier on tourist visas. Our visas had expired long before. I had made numerous efforts to have them renewed, and I had also applied for resident visas. But the American immigration laws and quotas were so strict that no amount of persuasion succeeded. Technically, we were in the United States illegally.

That fact was vividly brought home to us one day, shortly after our Central Park experience, when a U.S. Marshall appeared at our door and handed me a document. It was a deportation order. We were given thirty days to get out of the country. Otherwise, we would be put on a plane or a ship and deported. Oddly, another stroke of fate intervened.

Unknown to me, back in 1964, Zipora had received, in the mail at Bnei Brak, a brochure from the British government inviting all Jewish inhabitants of Palestine to apply for permanent immigrant visas to Canada. That had been part of Britain's postwar attempt to solve its troublesome Palestine Mandate problem. Canada was a leading nation of the British Commonwealth. Britain thought that if it could induce enough Palestine Jews to immigrate to Canada, or to other Commonwealth countries like Australia, it would be able to defuse the increasingly fiery movement for Jewish statehood in Palestine and keep the peace there.

Also unknown to me—why she never told me abut it I'll never figure out—Zipora had sent in the application. A few months later, she received another document, this one from Canada. It was an immigrant visa to be used by her and her family at any time she chose.

It was only when our difficulties with the U.S. Immigration Service came to a boil that Zipora remembered her open Canadian visa and told me about it. "Where is it?" I asked, astonished.

It was in the personal belongings that she had left behind in Tel Aviv when she'd first come to New York, she said. She had stored those belongings in her mother's house.

We immediately wrote to her mother. We asked her mother to dig out the Canadian visa and send it to us. A few weeks later, a few days before we were due to be deported from the United States, it arrived. As a result, instead of been sent back to Israel, we "immigrated" to Montreal.

I found that I could do my Max Jacobs business as easily in Montreal as I could in New York—Canada, too, was suffering from Korean War steel shortages. So, business continued and thrived.

We were more or less resigned to settling permanently in Montreal, which wouldn't have been bad, since it was a beautiful city with excellent cuisine and a low-pressure ambiance. But it also had those long, exceedingly cold, snow-bound winters—a climate that people raised in the balmy temperatures of the Middle East found not very conducive to personal peace of mind. Zipora especially found it hard.

One evening in the fall of 1953, as our second winter in Montreal was about to set in, I took Zipora to the city's fanciest restaurant to cheer her up. Who did we discover sitting at the next table but the American consul and his wife. We got to talk, and in no time, I was telling him of our problem in trying to get back into his country.

To make a long story short, at the end of the evening, the consul invited me to go see him the next day at his office.

When I arrived, he asked me a few questions about my history and what I was doing for a living. When I finished telling him, he said, "Abe, I think the United States needs people like you and your charming wife. I shall be delighted to sponsor your application for a permanent-resident visa. Just fill out this form." As he passed the form across his desk, he gave me a knowing wink.

A few days later, he phoned. "Abe, I have your Green Card on my desk—Zipora's, too. You can pick them up at your convenience. As of today, you can return to the United States whenever you wish."

A few days after that, we were all back in New York. Now we were legal and authentic. And now Zipora was really intent on settling there permanently.

In the meantime, we moved out of the small, rented apartment we'd been occupying on New York's Central Park West and into a much larger residence on Riverside Drive, overlooking the Hudson. Unlike seven or eight years later, when there would begin a large-sale immigration of Israelis to New York and its environs—most of them driven out by the continuing economics hardships and dizzying inflation caused by the country's socialist system—there were very few of my countrymen in the city. I was a "pioneer" for the second time in my life.

Still, I wasn't sure I liked the idea of being a double immigrant. It would be carrying the myth of the "Wandering Jew" a little too far, I thought.

Nonetheless, I had to face reality, and the reality was that I was thriving beyond belief. Max Jacobs and I established offices at Seventh Avenue and 27th Street. There the business continued to bring in tons of money during 1953 and 1954. Before forming his steel-importing partnership with me, Max had been an exporter of non-ferrous metals. He continued to look after that part of the business, while I continued to do all the importing.

Sure enough, the bubble eventually burst. One of the key talents of any successful entrepreneur is his ability to recognize trend and business cycles and to know how to deal with them without their having an appreciably negative effect on his business. No one is infallible in that regard. But the ones who make the fewest misjudgments are those who are burned the least. I had that talent more so than Max Jacobs did, and soon the difference between us led to a falling out.

The first sign of trouble began to raise its head late in 1954. Our steel-importing success had produced several competitors the year before. They began to undercut us—that is, they began to offer higher prices for steel from our foreign suppliers and sell it at lower prices to domestic customers.

Then there was the fact that the Korean War had been formally suspended, reducing the demand for steel in the United States. Finally, there was the fact that the demand for steel in Europe, and therefore the price, started to rise as the European industrial nations began to undergo their own post-World War, all domestic, consumer-product booms.

Over the period of a year, our profit margins on imported steel began to shrink, from nearly 100% to 75%, then to 50%, then lower. By mid-1955, we were operating on 30% profit margins. After the heady years of 1952–54, this development was a rather radical comedown.

To take up the slack, we intensified the non-ferrous metal-exporting side of the business. For a while, we did well at it, for there was a rising demand for American metal—tin plate, brass, copper, and the like—among the developing Third World countries such as India and Pakistan. But exporting didn't excite me very much. By then, our competitors were many, and profit margins were nothing like those we'd enjoyed in the first three years of our steel-importing enterprise.

In addition to all that, Max Jacobs was becoming distracted by other ventures, as well as by personal problems. Max and I had become good friends, as well as solid business partners. But we were as different in nature and temperamental as my brother Menasha and I were. Not in the same way, though. As Max grew more prosperous, he became more of a compulsive gambler with the investment funds he had at his disposal.   I, on the other hand, although I was certainly a risk-taker, preferred the logical investment.

The seeds of our parting were planted in 1955. He had some friends who persuaded him to make a major cash investment in an apartment complex in Houston, Texas. At first, he wanted me to join him, using our partnership funds to make the investment. I'll concede that for various reasons, I was contemplating real estate myself. But up to then, I knew very little about it.

Max thought he knew everything there was to know about it. Given what I was beginning to see as his over-ambitious and basically ignorant bravado, I decided not to go in with him. I said, more out of instinct than knowledge, "Max, why should I become a landlord in Houston, Texas? If you want to be a landlord, why not do it here in New York? At least that way, if one of your tenants has a problem, he doesn't have to call you long-distance."

Of course, I knew nothing about real estate investment syndicates in those days. That was what Max was getting into. To me, commercial real estate was a very personal affair. For example, ten years before, I had bought my mother a small apartment house in Bnei Brak. She and my father had moved into one of the apartments from their top-floor flat in the factory at Karat Shmuel. She took over the building and rented out the rest of its apartment.

Later, she obtained a mortgage to finance a two-floor addition on top so that she'd have more apartments to rent. She became a regular landlord, collecting rents, looking after the building's maintenance, and having daily contact with her tenants.

That's what I thought someone did who invested in apartment housing. I didn't trust Max Jacobs's idea of becoming a landlord in absentia, his Houston apartment complex managed by some New York real estate syndicator who probably didn't know a boiler valve from a gas line.

Next, Max came up with a proposal for us to buy several hundred thousand dollars worth of Canadian government bonds. His sales pitch was that he could get them cheap, through friends he had on Wall Street, and then turn around and sell them at a good profit.

"I smell a rat," I told Max. I didn't believe in trying to get something for nothing. I said that if he wanted to buy the bonds with his own money, fine—but leave me out of the deal.

He called me crazy to pass up the opportunity. But sadly, I was right. A few month after he'd bought the bonds, it was discovered that they were stolen and, basically, worthless. Max got into no ends of trouble with the American and Canadians authorities as a result, and in addition, was out a couple of hundred thousand dollars.

It was while trying to sort out those problems that he pulled a stunt that finally made it clear to me we could no longer work productively together as partners. Desperate for money to make up his bond losses, and without telling me, he committed us to a huge purchase of European black-market steel, 100 tons, just at the time when the demand for imported steel in the United States had dropped practically to nil. His purchase was at a price much higher than I would have paid. Just to recover our outlay and expense, we'd have to sell it in America at a figure far beyond what anyone was paying.

I was livid with Max when I found out about his foolhardy deal. He said not to worry; if we couldn't sell the steel in the U.S. at a good price, he knew of people in Argentina who'd take it off our hands at a cost.

Well, as I anticipated, no one in America would buy at a price remotely close to that which would enable us to recover our cost; forget about profit. The steel sat in a warehouse in New Jersey for months, piling up further cost in the storage charges we were forced to pay. Our only choice was to discount the stock at a huge loss or try his Argentina connection.

It was left to me to fly to Argentina and meet with Max's "savior," a firm of metal brokers in Buenos Aires. There I made a deal, whereby they agreed to buy the steel at a price that would help us come at least close to recouping. By then, I would have been happy to recover half of what Max had spent.

There was a fly in the ointment, though, and it pertained to what I wrote earlier about being forced to negotiate from a position of weakness. Whether you're a government, a business, or an individual, if you are making a deal without the wherewithal to enforce it, you're bound to come out the loser.

The Argentinians knew about out problems before I arrived in Buenos Aries; no doubt, Max, in his desperation, had let the cat out of the bag. They were willing to buy the steel all right, but only on their terms. Which meant a small down payment, about $10,000, with the balance of $442,000 to be paid upon their receipt of the steel. They explained that they would have to take a bank loan to pay the $442,000 and that no Argentinian bank would lend them the money until the steel was actually in Buenos Aries.

Since I had no bargaining chips, I was forced to accept the terms and fly back to New York with my finger crossed. For the first time since my arrival in America, luck deserted me. We duly shipped the steel C.O.D. to our new Argentinian "customers." We never heard from them again, and we never saw a cent of the $442,000. We were out nearly half-a million dollars, no small sum in the mid-1950s. Despite another trip to Argentina to try to collect, all I got out of it was that: another trip to Argentina. We could not acquire legal jurisdiction.

That disaster was the straw that finally broke the camel's back. I could not be too angry with him, though, since it was he who'd originally put me in a position to make all the money I had in New York—more than $7 million in four years, including my share of the Argentinian loss. Yet, I knew I could no longer trust him in any important business deal. He'd become a quick-buck gambler. I knew that such a psychological cycle was like an addiction, and once embarked upon, it was almost impossible to stop. I was happy to engage in business risk. But what Max Jacobs was caught up in was a form of reckless personal gambling.

All this came at a time when the outlook for the future of our steel-importing and metal-exporting business was not all that bright anyway. As I've said, the imported-steel boom in America had already ended by 1956. And the postwar export of metal was coming more under the control of the big producing companies as they realized how increasingly lucrative the foreign markets were. As a result of that, and my disillusionment with Max Jacobs, I knew it was time, once again, to make some hard decisions about the future.

With that hurdle passed, there only remained the question of what I would do in terms of my career. We made a decision to stay in New York and bring up our children here. By now, I had enough money to coast for a while. I could simply invest my capital and live comfortable off the income it produced.

But that was not me. I still had to be working at something demanding and challenging to give my life meaning. What was left of Hirschfeld Brothers in Israel I had turned over completely to Menasha. I still had another year or so of commitment to my partnership with Max Jacobs, and I was willing to continue to work at that if only to ensure its smooth and profitable liquidation. But I retained little further interest in the metals import-export business. I intended to wave it goodbye as soon as I could.

But what could I replace it with? Here again, my wife, whose physical and spiritual beauty remained undimmed by the passage of the almost fifteen years since I'd met her, was my inspiration.

"Abe," Zipora said to me one night in 1956, "all this talk about assets and leasing and steady income. All this talk about how you admired my father in his big business way and your mother in her small business way. What is it all saying to you?"

It had already occurred to me. What my subconscious had been saying all those years: Real Estate.

Abraham (Abe) Hirschfeld

CHAPTER EIGHT: LEARNING TO WALK

Totally ignorant about commercial real estate, but knowing that I was a fast learner and that direct, hands-on experience is the best teacher, I decided to school myself by plunging straight into the business. What I found myself plunging into in New York was a forest of gold, but one that was laced with barbed wire and planted with minefields.

Luckily, although I had a lot of money to invest, I started small. That was thanks to Zipora. She said, "Abe, learn to walk before you run."

"What do you mean?" I said.

"Buy a small building somewhere, like your mother's in Bnei Brak. See what it's like."

This was at the time when New York's Third Avenue El had just been torn down. Until then, real estate to the west of Third Avenue on the upper East Side of Manhattan was considered more valuable than that to the east of it. With the El gone, there was bound to be an upgrading east of Third Avenue, with a rise in the value of real estate. That's all I knew. And the only reason I knew it was because I'd heard somebody talking about it in a restaurant.

On Sunday, I looked in *The New York Times* real estate section and saw that a five-story walk-up tenement-type building was for sale on East 76th Street, between First and York Avenue. It contained ten large, cheap rental apartments and was located right in the midst of the dingy East Side area that I'd heard was due to be upgraded. The owner was asking $12,000 for it. The next day I called and arranged to see the building. It was old and forlorn-looking, but no different from the rest of the buildings on the street. I thought, Well, Abe, you've got to start somewhere, why not here? I offered the seller $8,000. We shook hands on $10,000, and I gave him a $1,000 down payment. There remained the details of the closing to be attended to. Later that day, I said to Max Jacobs, "Max, I've just agreed to buy a building I know nothing about it. What do I do NOW?"

He said, "Get yourself a lawyer."

Max sent me to see Harry Ostrow, a prominent real estate lawyer in New York and the head of the Masons in the state—he was the Grand Mason.

I told Ostrow I'd just contracted to buy my first building and would like him to represent me at the closing. He agreed and said, "How much are you paying?"

I told him. Then he said, "And how much is the mortgage?"

"Mortgage?" I said. "What's mortgage?" Until then, I'd never heard of such a thing.

Looking at me a little dubiously, he explain what a mortgage was. He said I shouldn't be buying a building without a large mortgage, seventy to eighty percent. That's the way it was done in New York.

It wasn't the way I wanted to do it, though. Ostrow was being rather patronizing with me, so I thought I'd better establish myself with him straight away. I said, Mr. Ostrow, do you want to change seats with me?"

"What do you mean?" he answered.

"What I meant is this. I didn't ask you how I should buy the building. I'm telling you how I intended to buy it—all cash. If you want to be my lawyer, then you just go ahead and buy it the way I say. If not, I'll get another lawyer."

He was a bit nonplussed. But after a moment's thought, he said, "Fine, we'll do it your way." Ostrow arranged on the phone with the seller and his lawyer to have the closing the following week. We arrived at the closing, and all the necessary papers were passed around. One sheaf of papers seemed particularly to bother Ostrow. He frowned and asked to see me privately outside the room.

When I followed him out, he said, "Abe, you can't buy this building; it's got dozens of violations against it."

"Violations?" I said. "What are violations?"

He explained, again somewhat impatiently, what violations were—defects in a residential rental building's structure and systems that were "in violation" of the city's housing codes and statutes. Showing me the sheaf of papers, he pointed out all the violations that had been lodged against the building by city housing inspectors— holes in the walls, dripping water pipes, loose masonry, flaking paint, frayed wires, things of that sort.

"I can't let you buy the building in this condition," he insisted. "Anybody would be crazy to buy it."

I said, "I came here to buy it. I don't care what's wrong with it, as long as it isn't going to collapse tomorrow. I'm doing this to learn the business. You've told me what is wrong with it, but it's my decision to buy the building despite all that. So, are you going to help me buy it or not?"

Grudgingly, he agreed to complete the closing. But before he did, he had me sign a legal waiver absolving him of any responsibility for the consequences of my decision. At the end of it all, I owned my first building. I was in the New York real estate business.

It would be an exaggeration to say that I enjoyed my first few months in the trade. The building proved to be every bit as much of a headache as Harry Ostrow had suggested by his warnings. Dealing with grumpy, late-paying tenants; dealing with the city's housing authorities and red tape bureaucrats; and dealing with undependable plumbers, electricians, and other tradesmen needed to keep the building and its apartments in reasonable working order all constituted a whole new realm of business that I was neither used to nor sure I wanted to become used to. Who knows, after several months I might have thrown up my hands and said, "This is not for me."

But then I received a phone call.

The call was from a real estate broker named Mike Garimoni. He said he'd learn that I'd bought the building at 420 East 76th Street for $10,000. "I've got a client who'd be very interested in buying it from you now for $15,000. Would you be interested in making a $5,000 profit, Mr. Hirschfeld?"

"I am always interest in making a profit," I replied. "Although in the business I used to be in, I was accustomed to much greater profits than that."

"What, greater than 50 percent in a few months?" Garimoni exclaimed.

"You better believe it," I said.

"Well, anyway, what do you have to say?"

I thought about it for a second. "I'll tell you what," I answered. "Tell your client I'll sell him the building for $18,000, not $15,000."

"I can guarantee you fifteen," Mike Garimoni said. "I'm not sure he'll go to eighteen. Why do you pick that figure? Why not twenty?"

I said, "Tell me, is your client Jewish?"

"Well yes, I think so."

"Tell him I'm a Jew, too," I said. "He'll understand why."

"So, can't you tell me?"

"It's hard to explain to someone who is not a Jew," I said. "But in the Jew tradition, chia, eighteen, is considered a very good number. Like twelve. Twenty is not a good number. Neither is seventeen or nineteen. If your client knows his Jewish folklore, he'll know why I insist on $18,000."

Garimoni called me back the next day. "Okay," he said. "My client will buy your building for $18,000."

So, I had made a profit of $8,000 in a few month's time.

Maybe there was something to this real estate business after all, I thought.

What really convinced me of this was when I met the buyer at the closing. He was not some small-fry tyro like me. Instead, he was one of the city's most experienced and prominent property wheeler-dealers. He told me he was buying the building only for the purpose of turning around and selling it to a developer for $40,000. "Do you mind?" he asked me.

"Why should I mind?" I said. "I get my profit, you get yours."

Secretly, though, I did mind. While I was earning an 80 percent profit over a period of several months, he'd be making 115 percent in a few days on the same property. That, I realized, was the part of the business I wanted to be in. After the closing, I said to Mike, "Let's do some more business."

A few days later, he phoned me. "Abe, I've got two adjoining buildings for sale on the northeast corner of Third Avenue and 64th Street."

"How much?"

"Seventy-five thousand."

"I'll buy at sixty-eight."

"It's a deal."

"Wait," I said. "I've only got $8,000 to invest—my profit from 76th Street. Can I get one of those things—what do you call them?"

"A mortgage?"

"Yes, a mortgage."

"No problem."

"Good," I said. "So, here's what we do. I'll pay $8,000 in cash and take a mortgage for $60,000."

The deal was made immediately, with me signing the contract on a Tuesday. The next day was the closing. I brought Harry Ostrow as my lawyer, and he did a repeat of his first performance.

"Abe," he said, "you can't buy these buildings. They have a bathroom violation. There's only one bathroom to a floor. You're going to have to put a bathroom in each apartment, or else the building will be closed down by the city. You'll be fined. I must advise you against going through with the deal."

"Harry," I said, "I want these building. I don't care about the violation. Go into that room and complete the closing."

"Okay," he said, "but not until you sign another waiver."

So, I signed another waiver letting Harry Ostrow off the hook for any problems I encountered after I took possession of the building. What he didn't know was that I had no intention of taking possession.

Just before the closing, Mike Garimoni had phoned me again. In the wake of the removal of the Third Avenue El, the market in real estate all along the avenue and its side street had become volatile, with everyone looking toward future upgrading development opportunities. (Today, forty years later, Third Avenue on the Upper East Side is among Manhattan's most expensive commercial and residential stretches.)

Garimoni had said, "Abe, I've just found someone who wants the two buildings you're buying for development. He'll buy from you for $25,000 over what you're paying."

That represented a $25,000 profit in a mere 24 hours, more than a thousand dollars an hour. "Make the deal," I said. So, a few hours after I closed on the two buildings that Wednesday, I resold them at a $25,000 profit. I didn't even have to pay a penny on the mortgage I'd taken out.

Within the next week, Mike Garimoni found me another building on 63rd Street between Third and Lexington Avenue. I did the same kind of deal, "turning it over" quickly at a major profit.

From that point on, there was no stopping me. I closed out what remained of my partnership with Max Jacobs. I started my own close corporation to deal exclusively in real estate buying and selling, with Zipora as my vice president. We moved from Riverside Drive into an even more spacious apartment on West 96th Street, near the Hudson. I opened an office on the East Side under the name of my corporation, Hirschfeld Realty. And I started buying and selling buildings left and right. As my reputation spread, dozen of other brokers came knocking at my door with profitable deals.

Hardly a week went by that I didn't clear $50,000. It was almost like playing Monopoly. I was a speculator, but I was always speculating on what were virtually sure things in the rapidly expanding East Side building market. I was content to be just that at the beginning, to let the ultimate buyers take on the headaches of actually improving or developing the properties they got from me. With the Third Avenue El gone, that section of Manhattan's East Side, east of Tony Park Avenue from 34th Street north to 96th Street, was in for a major developmental transformation. It was a transformation that has since turned it into the commercial gold coast it is today.

Nine months after I started, I knew something about how to do business in real estate. And as with the steel-importing business of a few years before, I knew that the lucrative market in small-building transaction on the East Side could not last forever. It was time to start doing some developing myself. But again, how?

Like most of my answers, this one came through serendipity. When Zipora and I and the children moved from Riverside Drive to 96th Street, it was going to take a couple of weeks to get the new apartment repainted and decorated. Although I was "playing Monopoly," I don't mean to suggest that it was all fun and games. In fact, I was having to work harder than I'd ever had—long hours spent scouting properties, negotiating buyers and sales, dealing with lawyers, bankers, title searchers, insurance agents, brokers, and city housing officials, that sort of thing.

By the end of nine months, I was richer than ever, but exhausted. Zipora said, "Abe, you need a vacation. I don't want a rich husband who dies before he's forty. (I was thirty-eight at the time.) It's going to take a few weeks to get the new apartment ready."

I agreed, so we packed up the children and took off for Miami Beach. We stayed at a new hotel called the Seville, whose owner we knew from my days in the steel-importing business. While we were there, the word got around that I was in real estate in New York.

Next thing I knew, I received a call from a local Miami lawyer. "Mr. Hirschfeld," he said, "I hear you're in the business of buying and selling property in New York."

He went on to explain that he had a client in Miami who owned six apartment buildings in Manhattan and one in the Bronx. "To be frank about it, my client has had some problems in New York with the housing authorities. He can't go back without risking prosecution. He's fed up with New York and wants to get rid of his properties. He needs money to settle himself here in Miami. He's willing to sell his New York buildings at a very favorable price to the first taker. But time is of essence. He wants out now."

After days of back-and-forth phone calls, I agreed to buy the buildings—sight unseen. I paid $10,000 cash over a $40,000 mortgage for the Bronx building. The six Manhattan buildings together cost me $30,000 up from mortgages totaling over $270,000. For $40,000 in cash, in other words, I owned seven new apartment houses. Now it was time to return to New York to see what I'd gotten. And to decide what I'd do with them.

All things considered, it was a dumb deal on my part. Yet, in the end, it gave me my new direction.

Abraham (Abe) Hirschfeld

CHAPTER NINE: A LITTLE HELP FROM ABOVE

Zipora and I returned to New York from Miami to find no disaster, but no triumph either. The six Manhattan buildings were in areas below 34th Street that I was not familiar with. The Bronx building was in a neighborhood that was well on its way to becoming a slum.

Had I been in the city when the package deal was proposed, had I had a chance to see the buildings beforehand, I most likely would have passed it up. It was too late for self-recrimination though. So, I set out to make the best I could of the situation.

The Bronx building soon proved to be beyond redemption. A pity, too, for it had once been a beautiful structure. Because of its architectural quality, it might have achieved landmark status in another part of the city. But it had been sorely neglected for two decades, as had all the other buildings in the fast-decaying neighborhood. With neglect had come a radical downscale in the quality of its tenants, most of whom were protected by rent control and had no regards for their surroundings.

When I first went to see the building, I found hallways piled with garbage, graffiti all over the walls, overcrowded apartments that resembled pigsties, and a general aura of human rot and stench throughout.

Zipora and I spent several arduous months valiantly trying to rescue the building; it became clear that financially, it was a lost cause and would remain so for as long as all its apartment were rent-controlled.

The money we collected in rents each month was about a quarter of what was needed simply to begin putting it back in reasonably livable shape. Even at that, we might have made the long-term effort. But would it have been worth it—if not financially, morally? Our beginning endeavors were met with nothing but indifference and contempt on the part of the tenants we'd inherited. No sooner did I have all the hallways replastered and painted than they were covered again with graffiti and garbage stains.

No sooner did I fix clogged toilets than they were clogged again. No sooner did I put in new windows than they were smashed. And so on, and so on.

There was a derogatory term that was just coming into vogue those days to describe landlords who operated in neighborhoods like the one in the Bronx where I had bought my building. The term was "slumlord."

Although occasionally accurate, the word was often unfairly applied to landlords who were simply trying to make the best of it in the increasing number of poor neighborhoods in the city. I say "unfairly" because those landlords didn't create the slums; if anyone, it was the city and state that created them through their expanding welfare housing and tenant-subsidy law.

I had no intention of becoming a slumlord. In the real estate business barely a year, I had quickly learned about all the pitfalls. The Bronx building was sure to be a major pitfall for me, I realized, if I continued to operate it as a landlord.

No matter how hard I tried to rescue it, success would still leave me in a no win situation. So, a few months later, I decided that wisdom was the better part of valor. I found a buyer for the building and sold it at a $4,000 loss. It was loss well worth taking, at least from the building point of view. If the neighborhood was crumbling then, it grew unspeakably worse in the years to come. Eventually, it would become a desolate wasteland, with practically all of the buildings in it torn down.

But it was a sad and costly lesson in human nature all the same.

In spite of my feelings against rent control early in my real estate career, I have come around to the conviction that because the laws have been so long and well-entrenched, it would be a disaster to do away with them today.

New York is the largest and most ruthless "manufacturer" of homeless people in the United States. To repeal rent controls now would be to throw countless additional citizens into the street, creating a further vast drain on the city's resources. The real estate community must learn to accept and live with residential rent regulations.

I have thrived, notwithstanding the fact that many of my buildings were and are rent-controlled and rent-stabilized. Any other competent landlord can thrive, too, so long as he puts his mind to it instead of using the laws as an excuse for failure.

The six Manhattan properties I'd acquired were collectively not much more promising that the Bronx building. Two were in reasonably good shape, and I could keep them going, making an improvement here, an improvement there. I was able to realize a modest profit from them after about two years.

A third I had to close down completely, refurbish and improve at great expense, and then re-open. Eventually, notwithstanding the rent-regulation laws, it also became marginally profitable.

What this all meant was that in addition to buying and selling buildings, Hirschfeld Realty was now permanently in the business of being a rental landlord in New York City.

It was the other buildings, though, that gave me the new direction I was really looking for. That was to become an urban real estate developer, just as Zipora's father had been. Development was where the greatest potential long-term profits lay. By its very dynamic, kaleidoscopic nature, New York had always been a changing landscape of replacement renewal.

The three remaining buildings were on East 30th Street, which was a real estate disaster area at the time. The reason was Robert Moses, the autocratic New York highway czar. He planned to construct a crosstown, elevated expressway along the length of 30th Street from the Hudson to the East River, linking the Lincoln Tunnel to and from New Jersey with the Midtown Tunnel to and from the borough of Queens. Its purpose was to relieve the traffic congestion of the local midtown streets.

Moses' plan had been in the works for years, but he had not yet succeeded in getting it approved or funded. As a result, 30th Street remained in a state of commercial limbo. The three buildings I had bought adjoined each other on the block between Fifth and Madison Avenue.

The neighborhood was one of light industry, low-rent offices, cheap hotels, and cheap apartments. It was just south of the much more fashionable Murray Hill area.

My three buildings had little if any resale value. Nor could I refurbish and redevelop them as apartment or office buildings so long as it remain likely that the entire street would become a noisy truck-and-car thruway.

In a sense, I had been stuck with them by the man in Miami. Despite the fact that I'd paid well under market for them, I was still stuck—still paying taxes, maintenance, and mortgage installments on three buildings from which I was receiving barely any income. If I allowed the situation to go on too long, it could wipe out all the gains I had made in my first year in New York real estate.

I thought long and hard about what to do with the buildings. As I cogitated, I kept cursing Robert Moses and his career-long obsession with the movement of cars, trucks, and New York City traffic in general.

Then it hit me—another lightbulb! Cars, trucks, traffic. I'd walked the streets of midtown and seen it every day.

Much of the traffic congestion Moses was trying to solve was caused by cars either illegally parked on the narrow streets or roaming about the area looking for a place to park.

This was at a time when there were no tow trucks and few real parking enforcement rules beyond the issuance of tickets. Most drivers paid no attention to parking tickets, however, and it was practically impossible for the city to collect on unpaid fines.

But in 1957, the city was beginning to crack down on illegal parkers. Plans were in the works for police tow-trucks and new laws that would make it easier to collect fines. Soon, drivers would begin to think twice about parking illegally, especially after their cars got towed away or their registration renewals were blocked for failure to pay alleged parking fines.

They would start looking for an alternative. What the neighborhood needed, I concluded, was a large, off-street garage where the fee to park legally would be more attractive than the risk of parking illegally on the street.

Could my three adjoining buildings on East 30th Street be converted to fulfill such a need? I wondered.

I went to see an architect named Max Siegel, a man who had already designed several indoor garages in New York. He looked the building over with a team of engineers and concluded that my idea was feasible. But, he warned, the city would never allow it; Moses would never allow it.

"Why?" I said.

"Because," Siegel said, "when they get the okay to build the expressway, they'll have to tear down all the buildings along 30th Street to make room for it. They're talking about four lanes each way, plus side exit-and-entrance ramps. Thirtieth Street, as it exists today, is only wide enough for two lanes each way."

I said, "Max, you're an architect, right?"

He agreed.

"You're not in real estate."

"Well, only so far as I build buildings."

"So, I'm telling you," I said, "you don't know what you're talking about."

"What do you mean?"

"The city just got finished tearing down the Sixth Avenue El and the Third Avenue El. Elevated roadways through the city, whether for trains or cars, are out of date. No one here's going to allow Moses to build a new El across the city, cutting it in half. Mark my words."

As it turned out, my hunch was right. But Siegel wouldn't believe me.

"Never mind," I said. "Draw me up plans for converting my buildings into a parking garage. What will you charge?"

He named a price, at the same time warning that I was wasting my money.

"Here's my check," I said. He took it.

The plans Siegel drew up were for a conventional indoor garage, fully enclosed and with complicated heating and ventilating systems. When he showed them to me, I said, "No, this is too expensive. I'm not building a place for people to live. All I want is a multi-level parking lot for cars." I began to form my idea as I spoke.

He said, "But this is how all parking garages are built in the city."

I took Siegel to a regular, outdoor, street-level parking lot.

It was a winter's day, and all the cars were covered with snow.

"Look there," I said. "Do you think those cars are going to catch pneumonia?"

"No."

"So, I don't want to turn my building into a garage like every other garage in the city. All I want is a multi-level parking lot. Eight parking lots, vertical, one on top of the other. No walls, no windows, no insulation, no heating, no violation. Just open, one level on top of another. The cars aren't going to catch cold."

I sketched on a piece of paper what I meant—an eight-story, open-air garage. "You see?" I said. "At least the cars will have a roof over their heads. And it's much cheaper to build than a regular garage."

Siegel said he'd never seen anything like it before. I answered, "The pharaohs never saw anything like the pyramids before, but they built the pyramids."

Siegel went back to his drawing board and came up with new plans for what I had in mind.

"That's better," I said. "See how much cheaper it is? Why spend all that money just so cars can be warm in the winter? People don't care about that. They just want a cheap, convenient place to park off the street so they don't get a ticket. And instead of a single, open, ground-level lot that holds 50 cars, I'll have six vertical, semi-enclosed lots that hold 300. Drivers will be happy, and I'll be happy."

"You won't make money, Abe," Siegel said.

"You want to bet?" I said.

Soon, I began to be glad Siegel hadn't taken me up on the bet. He was right; the city wouldn't go for it. We took the plan and proposal to the New York City Planning and Department of Transportation, and we were turned down flat. I couldn't convert my buildings into any kind of garage, they said. All the buildings along 30th Street would soon be condemned for Moses' elevated expressway.

I argued that there would never be an expressway. They said maybe not, but until that decision was finally and officially made, there could be further development on 30th Street.

So then, out of the seven buildings I had bought from the man in Miami, I was left with two that were making any money. The building in the Bronx I'd had to unload at a loss. One of the buildings in Manhattan I'd had to close for extensive repairs, and the three on 30th Street I could do nothing with. I was beginning to feel like a helpless fool.

But then I thought: Wait a minute, since when does Abe Hirschfeld accept it when someone tells him it is impossible to do something? Remember the refrigerator door magnets? Remember the donkey in the orange grove?

I was still convinced that cheap, vertical, open-air parking garages were just what New York needed to alleviate all the illegal midtown parking that went on and the frustrating traffic congestion that resulted from it. So, I went back to the Planning Commission and Department of Transportation and argued common sense. They still turned me down.

"The only thing that can help me now," I said to Zipora, "is a little divine intervention. Otherwise, I'm stuck with three buildings I can't use and can't sell."

I spent the next week racking my brain over the question of how to solve the problem. At the end of the week, on a Sunday morning, I went to the property to pick up some papers I'd left there. Suddenly, I heard church bells. It was then, for the first time, that I realized that the buildings were just a few steps away from the rear of a church. The street was jammed with cars looking for places to park. That gave me another idea.

The church was called the Church of the Transfiguration but was better known by its popular name: "The little Church around the Corner." It had been built early in the nineteenth century when much of that section of Manhattan was still in fields and pasture. Then it had been a country church; now, still quaint and picturesque, it was shoe-horned into a densely packed, semi-industrial, metropolitan neighborhood—and a rundown one at that.

Nevertheless, it remained one of the most popular Protestant churches in New York and drew parishioners from all over the city to attend service each Sunday.

Monday morning, I phoned the church and asked to speak to the pastor, Reverend Charles Ray.

When he got on the line, I identified myself and told him I owned the three buildings directly behind the church property on 30th Street.

"Sorry," he said before I could another word out, "we're not interested in buying your buildings."

"But Reverend," I said, "I'm not calling to sell you the buildings."

"Then what can I do for you?"

I said, "Reverend, I have a problem, and I'm calling to see if I can discuss it with you."

There was a silence at the other end. I could imagine the pastor wondering what kind of problem this caller with a thick,

Jewish accent could possible want to discuss with him—a problem of religion?

"What is your problem then?" he finally said.

"Reverend," I answered, "the Bible said that when a man has a problem, he should take it to a person eye-to-eye, not through an intermediary. Even though there were no telephones in Biblical times, I consider a phone today an intermediary. So, if you would be kind enough to see me face-to-face, I'll be glad to tell you my problem. If not, then I'll have to take it to someone else."

So, I went to the church and met him in his office. I told him, "Reverend, what I'm here for is that I want to turn my buildings into a parking garage."

He barely let me finish. He leaped to his feet, a huge smile on his face, and said, "That's the best news I've heard in weeks. God bless you! It's been terrible here these thirty years—no place to park nearby. I've been loosing parishioners because of it. A garage just up the street will bring them all back." He put his hand on my shoulder. "You, Mr. Hirschfeld, have been sent from heaven."

"But wait a minute," I said. "I haven't told you my problem."

"What is it?"

"I want to build the garage, but the city won't let me. I need your help. Do you know Mayor Wagner?"

"I married Wagner," he said. "We're good friends."

"Do you know Robert Moses?"

"I married Moses, too. I know him well."

Reverend Ray went to his desk, picked up the phone, and called City Hall. When he got Mayor Wagner on the phone, he said, "Bob, I've got Abe Hirschfeld in my office. He tells me he's been trying to turn the buildings behind the church into a parking garage. He keeps getting turned down by your transportation commissioner, Wiley. Bob, I don't have to tell you how badly we need a garage near the church. I want you to get behind Hirschfeld."

The mayor said something I couldn't hear. The reverend nodded, said, "Good" and "Thank you," and hung up.

He made a second call, this one to Robert Moses. After going through the same routine, he looked across his desk at me and smiled. "Abe," he said, "go file your plans again."

I filed my plans and a few weeks later, was called to another hearing before the Planning Commission. Robert Moses and Wiley showed up at the hearing "to have a look," as Moses said later, "at this guy Hirschfeld who suddenly had all this influence." Moses announced to the commission that he no longer had any objection to my building a garage on 30th Street, so long as it was understood that when the time came for him to build his expressway, the garage would come down.

I said, "Mr. Moses, you may be a smart man, but I'm telling you, I'm a little smarter. You'll build an expressway the day I grow hair on the palms of my hands. I'll be happy to accept your condition."

This time, my proposal was approved, with that condition.

My garage is still there on 30th Street. The expressway was never built.

Abraham (Abe) Hirschfeld

CHAPTER TEN: "THE GARAGE KING"

Not only was that garage an instant financial hit when it was completed and opened, but it also became both the foundation and fulfillment of my desire to expand my real estate activities into widescale building and development. Since then, I have built nearly thirty large, open-air garages in New York and elsewhere and have become known as the "Garage King."

My twofold rationale for going in that direction was simple. First, each garage did alleviate traffic problems. Moreover, built in neighborhoods that had become rundown and underutilized, they tended to encourage the rejuvenation and rehabilitation of the neighborhoods, attracting new commerce, creating new jobs, and providing new tax revenues to the city. So, my focusing on garage construction had clear social benefits.

The other part of my rationale had simply to do with the commercial benefits to my family and myself. When I started out in real estate with my first building on East 76th Street, I'd thought, "This is easy. You buy a building for $10,000, sell it a while later for $18,000, reinvest the profit in a second building, sell that at a similar profit, reinvest again, and then do the same thing over again."

But as I become more knowledgeable about the art and craft of the city real estate business, especially after I built the 30th Street garage, I realized that there was much more money to be made in buying and developing a piece of property than in quickly turning it over.

Let me use garage building as an example. A few years after my 30th Street experience, I bought a pair of old, tenement-style buildings on West 46th Street, near Rockefeller Center and Radio City, for $1 million. Tearing down the buildings cost $200,000. I then built a 350-car open-air garage on the site for $700,000. The entire project cost $1.9 million. At the very start, I was able to go to one of my banks and get a mortgage on the property for $2.9 million.

Thus, I took an immediate cash profit of $1 million. I then leased the garage to a regular parking garage operator and easily paid the annual mortgage and the tax payment out of the proceeds from the lease, which also gave me substantial additional income. Multiply $1 million cash profit by the nearly thirty garages I had built over a fifteen-year period, and you get nearly $30 million, or about $2

79

million a year in instant profits alone, not to mention the additional annual lease income from each.

This became my simple formula and the second part of my rationale for concentrating on garage building.

But another advantage, which I hadn't even thought about when I decided upon further garage building following the success of 30th Street, was the notoriety my reputation as the New York open-air "Garage King" would bring me. First of all, the 30th Street garage was hailed as a valuable new invention in the use of city space. It convinced New York, as well as other cities around the world, that the ground-level urban parking lot was obsolete, for it used up too much space compared to the revenue it produced. Additionally, the fully enclosed, multi-level indoor garages that had been built until then were now seen as wasteful in another sense—they simply cost too much to erect and maintain, and they required much higher parking fees to pay off and operate.

My idea was deemed by urban planners as a perfect compromise. As a result, 30th Street became the prototype of the new "open" urban garage, and officials came from cities all over the country to study and learn the details of its construction. Abe Hirschfeld was suddenly "the worlds leading expert" on solving big-city parking problems. The rallying cry of city officials throughout the United States, when addressing solutions to their traffic and parking difficulties, became, "Go see Hirschfeld."

Of course, I didn't tell them that the real reason I stumbled onto my open-air solution was that it was the cheapest form of construction; and that I didn't want to put a lot of money into converting my moribund 30th Street buildings into a garage only to see it torn down for an expressway.

So now, in 1957, I was in the real-estate development business, as well as in the business of buying and selling buildings at a profit. But was I going to be content to limit myself to parking garages? Not on your life. Development meant residential and commercial, or office, buildings as well. Until then, I had been dealing in small, residential buildings—walk-up tenements and brownstones containing a few apartments each. It was time to graduate to bigger properties. As I had learned at 30th Street, the bigger the building, the greater the potential profit—and the more credibility one had with bankers.

You'll recall I said earlier that among the buildings I'd acquired through my Miami deal was a small apartment house in Manhattan that I'd been immediately forced to close in the 30s, albeit in the slightly more upscale East 35th Street neighborhood of Murray Hill. To my uneducated eye, when I first saw it, it was nothing more than an ordinary, seven-story, street-corner apartment building that had fallen into neglect and decay—several steps up from a conventional tenement building, but in about the same sad condition. To my surprise, I learned that it was quite a bit more than that. It was a Stanford White Building!

Stanford White, for those who don't know, was a legendary architect of New York's turn-of-the-century Gilded Age, a time when the nouveau-riche big business Robber Barons were trying to transform the city visually into an imitation European capital like London, Paris, or Vienna. White was responsible for the design of dozens of new buildings that went up during the period, all of them dense with rich, architectural adornment and sophistication. His fame became even more widespread when he was revealed as a principal in a celebrated murder scandal involving his rival for the affections of a beautiful showgirl.

So revered was the memory of White the architect that, in the New York of the 1950s, to live in a Stanford White building was considered the epitome of taste and refinement. As is often the case in such matters, for every genuine White edifice that survived, ten others were claimed to be his. Ersatz Stanford White buildings—especially apartments and town-homes—were as numerous as the farmhouses and mansions that George Washington was alleged to have slept in.

Nevertheless, in my modest-size East 35th Street apartment building, I had unwittingly acquired a genuine Stanford White creation. I learned of this from Max Siegel, my garage architect, when he first came with me to check out my purchases. This was the genuine article, he insisted, and produced documents from the city's Hall of Records to prove it.

Of course, I didn't know Stanford White from Greta Garbo. All I knew—and this came from Max Siegel, an architectural professional and a student of the art—was that I had "lucked onto" a building by Stanford White, and that if I brought it back to something resembling its original condition, I could either operate it very profitably as a landlord or re-sell it at a huge profit.

I took Siegel's advice. Thus, at the same time I was building my 30th Street garage, I gutted and restored the Murray Hill apartment house to its former grandeur and added a penthouse floor in the process. He was absolutely right. When I was finished, I operated it at a nice profit. Years later, I sold it at huge one.

In that way, I quickly doubled my new role as a New York City property developer, dealing in both garages and residential buildings. Over the next few years, I built ten more garages. I bought, rehabilitated, and held onto or sold twenty more apartment buildings. Then I moved on to office buildings and warehouses, doing essentially the same thing. Hirschfeld Realty was suddenly on its way, a fast-growing presence on Manhattan's commercial real estate scene. Once again, through a series of accidents, I found myself standing at the entrance to a gold mine.

If I had a fault, business-wise, it was that I tried to do everything myself and run the entire enterprise out of my pocket, with little help from anyone. It was what is called today an "inability to delegate." If I needed a lawyer to take care of the technical aspects of closing a deal, I hired a lawyer. If I needed an architect or an engineer to do a building, I hired them for that particular job. If I needed an accountant to put everything in order for the tax man, I hired him.

But beyond that, I ran my own show single-handedly. I sought out and made deals by myself, relying on brokers only occasionally. I visited my development sites every day, schmoozing with the foremen and laborers. I usually talked to bankers and city officials on my own. I avoided feasibility studies, market research investigations, and other forms of consultant advise, as if they were the plague, on the theory that I could tell better than anyone, just by the feel and sense of a prospective deal, whether it could work or not.

I ran a "seat of the pants" operation, as Bunny Lindenbaum, one of my lawyers, once described it. He was right. By 1958, I was turning over millions of dollars a year and had only two permanent employees. That had been my way of doing business since my beginning days in Palestine, and I saw no reason to change it. When I finally took small but fancy office facilities on Madison Avenue, mostly for appearance' sake, it was a major change in my style. Nevertheless, the offices remained sparsely populated and devoid of much paperwork. Unlike some of my more established colleagues and competitors in the business, I preferred to run a lean, trim ship with minimum crew. It all derived from what my mother had drilled into me: Keep things plain and simple; reduce everything to its essentials.

That was easy to carry out with regards to the business side of my life, not so easy on the personal side. Zipora and I, each having grown up in the casual, outdoor environment of Palestine, were beginning to feel hemmed in by living in a New York apartment. No matter how spacious our dwelling, we tended to feel bound by and to it. So were the children. And so, we moved to a fine house in the leafy suburb of Great Neck, which was on the north shore of Long Island about fifteen miles from Manhattan and a few miles from my golf club. The only trouble was, instead of waiting for elevators and taxies, I now had to wait everyday for commuter trains, and when I drove to and from the city, I had to wait in rush-hour traffic jams.

Happily, though, I got to play more golf. It got me outdoors, and that's what was important. There is nothing more beautiful than an American golf course on a spring morning or golden autumn afternoon, even when it is laced with miniature deserts and seas. At my club, one big sand trap became known as the Hirschfeld Desert. That was because I spent so much time in it. And a pond was dubbed the Hirschfeld Sea, ditto.

Nevertheless, I found golf a great tonic and antidote to the daily hurly of the New York real estate business. Normally, I was a fairly excitable person. The frustration of golf tends to turn calm men frenetic with anger and despair. In my case, it had a calming, relaxing effect.

But with our move to Great Neck, my personal life became less simple—more complicated. Great Neck was a wealthy, manicured town with a large Jewish population. As Israelis, Zipora and I were objects of curiosity and fascination at first. To all the assimilated American Jewish living there—Jews to whom Israel was as Mecca is to Muslims, a place everyone must eventually make a pilgrimage to—we were the "real thing." Soon, we had a lot of friends and a very busy social life. And then there were civic responsibilities, synagogue responsibilities, school responsibilities, club responsibilities, and so on. Often, after a hectic weekend of responsibilities, I was happy to get back to the relative peace and calm of Hirschfeld Realty in Manhattan.

The children burst into full bloom in Great Neck, though, so our move there was worth it. Another reason for our choosing the suburbs was that it had the best public school systems in the area. I discovered that the biggest chunk of the property taxes one pays, wherever one lives in the United States is school taxes. It always bothered me that a lot of wealthy people in New York City paid huge school taxes for public education but sent their children to expensive private schools. Why live in a place where you can't trust the school system you're paying for to properly educate your children? No such problem existed in Great Neck. We enrolled Rachel and Elie in public school there, and they did fine.

Better than fine, in fact. Both became brilliant students. But beyond that, both were developing into terrific human beings, with a lot of help from Zipora. At ten, Rachel possessed her mother's slim beauty and my sense of independence and a drive to do things her own way. That did not always make for the most serene of households, but I believe in giving children the leeway to make their own mistakes and to learn from them!

The fair-haired, seven-year-old Elie was more like me in looks and more like his mother in his cool, wary temperament and passion for details. Where Rachel solved problems by rushing in and seizing them by the throat, Elie stood back and studied them calmly, experimented like a scientist with different possibilities, and then came up with the answer that worked best. It was not that he was less independent or creative than Rachel, it was just that he expressed those qualities in a different way.

With two such growing children in our house, Zipora and I had our hands wonderfully full. And because both were gregarious and outgoing, and therefore accumulated many friends among their schoolmates, our house became one of Great Neck's leading social centers.

Our move to Great Neck also brought about the climactic installment in the process of our permanent settlement in the United States. Since the time of our return from Canada, we had existed under the status of resident aliens. I'd remained content with that, since it gave us the option of one day resuming life in Israel. It was an option I had not entirely abandoned, although Zipora clearly had no interest in it—the children even less.

Great Neck forced me into a final decision. Because I had money, shortly after we moved there, I was approached by several local political organizations seeking financial support. When I was asked what my political affiliations were, I had to admit I had none. I knew nothing about American politics beyond the fact that Eisenhower was President. Moreover, as a resident alien, I was unable to vote. Hence, I could not become a registered voter.

Great Neck was largely Republican in its political orientation. It was under the new Republican Eisenhower administration in Washington that the State Department had allowed us back into the United States from our year-and-a-half exile in Canada. I had reason to be grateful to the Republican Party, then, and I was sympathetic to appeals for funds from its Great Neck branch. Furthermore, in light of my experience as deputy mayor in Bnei Brak ten years earlier, I began to think that one day I might want to get involved in Great Neck politics. But I would be barred from doing so as long as I remained a resident alien. I would have to become an American citizen.

And so, the decision was made. We would all become American citizens.

Abraham (Abe) Hirschfeld

CHAPTER ELEVEN: A THREE-CENT POSTCARD AND A PARTNER

Notwithstanding my success in my initial parking garage venture, and notwithstanding my awareness that it could lead to a very lucrative business in the building of future garages, I sensed that to put all my eggs in that single basket would be a mistake. Sure enough, years later, after I had built some 30 additional open-air garages in New York, the city (foolishly in my opinion) put an end to such construction on theory that it would bring too many more private automobiles into Manhattan, thereby compounding the traffic problem and robbing the mass-transit system of riders. Had I been content to remain in garages alone, I would have continued to do well to this day, but not anywhere near as well as I've done through the diversification of my real estate operations.

It was the instinctive need in 1957 to continue diversifying that led to the next profitable stage in my career. Again, it came about largely through a series of random events —linked accidents that had nothing to do with the kinds of things one learns in business school textbooks.

One day, as I was completing construction of the 30th Street garage and just beginning my makeover of the Stanford White apartment building, my eye happened to come across a small ad placed in the back pages of *The New York Times* by the New York Central Railroad System. What I gathered from it was that the railroad owned much of the real estate along Manhattan's Park Avenue between 46th and 59th Streets. The railroad's main-line tracks traveled northward out of New York's Grand Central Station beneath Park Avenue. Above, the broad avenue itself was lined on both sides by many mammoth, old, fifteen-story apartment buildings that were among the choicest residential addresses in the city. Those buildings, and the land on which they stood, had long been the property of the New York Central. Sprinkled among them were several elegant hotels, including the world-famous Waldorf–Astoria, the exclusive New York Racquet Club, and the landmark St. Bartholomew's Church.

At the time, the Central was suffering from the same disease that afflicted all railroads in America—severely declining revenues caused by the postwar growth of the airline, trucking, and interstate

Abraham (Abe) Hirschfeld

road systems throughout the country. In an attempt to offset its increasing deficits in freight and passenger revenue, it had decided to exploit its choicest New York real estate holdings. The ad was an invitation from the Central for inquiries from "interested parties" about development of its coveted Park Avenue properties.

I perused the ad with little more than casual interest at first. However, I had just moved into my office at 300 Madison Avenue, a block west of Park Avenue. At lunchtime that day, I walked over to Park and strolled along looking at the various residential buildings that flanked it between 46th and 50th Streets. One structure very soon caught my eye. It was a magnificent, block-long, block-deep rental apartment building between 47th and 48th Streets with its own private automobile entrance into a vast, central, gardened courtyard.

Having just gone into the parking garage business, I was struck by an idea. If someone could acquire the building, continue to operate it as a rental residence but turn the interior courtyard into a parking facility, he might find himself with a very successful venture on his hands.

Although I thought little more about it, the notion gestated in the back of my mind over the next few days. The reason I consciously thought so little about it was because the building was so big—a square block in size—that I was sure it would be beyond my means to acquire. And yet, the idea wouldn't go away.

The pivotal event came the following Sunday. I was reading *The New York Times* again. In it was an article on the difficulties being encountered by the American railroad industry and by the New York Central in particular. Reference was made to the Central's interest in capitalizing on its Park Avenue real estate. The inference was that the railroad was eager to cooperate in the "commercialization" of Park Avenue north of Grand Central Station. The article suggested that the stretch between the station and 59th Street was ripe to be the next area of modern, office building development in Manhattan. It envisioned a future Park Avenue lined with modernistic office towers rather than its present ornate apartment houses. Office building development! That was a field I had not yet seriously contemplated. As soon as I read about it, my pulse began to rise.

Here was a whole new course for the still relatively tiny Hirschfeld Realty to pursue. And why not? The economics were the same as those that pertained to the building of parking garages, albeit on a much larger scale. If it cost $2 million to create a garage out of an existing property, it might cost $30 million to create a substantial office building. But almost immediately, you would own a building worth twice or three times that, one that you could re-mortgage at a monumental profit.

The New York Central ad in the *Times* had said to write to a man named James Boise, the head of the railroad's real estate division. The day after reading the *Times* article, I went into my office with the intention of sending him a letter. I possessed no official Hirschfeld Realty stationery, however, and it would take several days to have some made up. Instead, I bought a plain, three-cent postcard, prestamped, at a nearby post office and mailed it off. On it, I handwrote in cryptic telegram style:

Am interested to talk to you about recent ad *New York Times* regarding properties Park Avenue, especially building No. 277. Please call me at (I included my telephone number).

(signed) Abraham Hirschfeld

If ever an opening gambit in a New York real estate transaction was doomed to fail, that was. People simply did not send the New York Central cheap postcards in order to make serious inquiries about any form of business. That I heard back from them, I learned years later from James Boise, was purely a matter of luck.

Boise told me my postcard was but one of fifty or so responses his ad had produced, all the others having been typed on conventional business letterheads. One morning, he said, he sat down at his desk at New York Central's headquarters above Grand Central Station and started to sort through the responses, dictating to his secretary his answering letters. About halfway through his task, he came to my postcard. He read it, then wondered who would have sent such a brief, casual, unbusiness-like inquiry. Certainly no one to be taken seriously, he concluded. With that, he recalled to me, he tossed the card into his wastebasket. He wouldn't bother answering it.

"I finished half the job by lunchtime and went out for a bite to eat," Boise once told me. "After lunch, I came back and dealt with the rest, working with my secretary until six or seven P.M. When everything was done, I closed up my office and headed down to the station to catch a train to my home in the suburbs."

"For some reason, though, your postcard had been sticking in the back of my mind all day. I guess I kept wondering about just what kind of real estate person could have sent it. Halfway down to the station, my curiosity got the better of me. I realized that if I went home without retrieving it, it would be gone by the time I got in the next morning—thrown out with the rest of the contents' of my wastebasket by the night cleaners.

"I had a few minutes to spare before my train was due to leave. So, I turned in my tracks, went back to my office, fished around in my wastebasket, and found your card. The next morning, still purely out of idle curiosity, I phoned the number you'd written on it."

When Boise's call did come, even I was a bit surprised, since I had practically forgotten about sending the postcard. But when he explained who he was, I immediately got myself into gear. I told him who I was and what I was doing in New York real estate. Then I asked if I could come see him about 277 Park Avenue. He said, "Sure."

When we met, he laid out the program the New York Central had in mind for its properties on Park Avenue. Put simply, the Central wanted to lease out all its buildings—twenty in all—in order to produce an immediate fusion of cash to offset its recent railroad operating losses.

"Why not sell the properties?" I asked. "You'll get much more money that way."

"We may well have to do that in another year or two if the railroad business continues to sag," Boise said. "But for now, we're interested in leasing. Of course, if and when we do sell, those who lease and run the buildings on their own will have the first option to buy, with their lease payments credited toward the purchase amount."

How much did he want to lease 277 Park, the courtyard building I had taken a shine to, I asked.

"A million dollars a year," he said.

That was my signal to start negotiating, for it was clear to me that the Central was in dire straits. Over a period of two days, Boise and I became Jim and Abe to each other as we hammered out an agreement. I finally got him to lease the building for $600,000 a year with an option to buy. At that rate, with the existing rental income and the conversion of the courtyard into a parking facility, I figured a profit could be made. What was more important, though, was my sense that within a year or two, the railroad would definitely have to start selling off its Park Avenue properties. The lease would give me an inside track.

Jim Boise and I shook hands on the deal and agreed to wrap it up formally a week later. The only trouble was that the $600,000 would have to be paid in one lump sum upon the execution of the lease, instead of in monthly installments throughout the year. I didn't have $600,000 in cash to spare or anything near it. Most of my funds and credit were tied up in the completion of the 30th Street garage and the rehabilitation of the Stanford White building. I was not yet well-known enough to the city's banking community to be able to command the kind of quick loan that would have enabled me to take on the 277 Park Avenue lease on such short notice. Had I gotten myself in over my head?

I put that question to Arthur "Bunny" Lindenbaum, a politically well-connected real estate lawyer whom I'd retained to help me in my initial hearings before the city's planning commission in connection with 30th Street. He said "Abe, what you need is a partner."

A partner. The last partner I'd had was Max Jacobs, my steel and metals cohort, and I wasn't sure I wanted to get back into the business of arguing with partners again.

"Nonsense," said Lindenbaum. "If you want to make it big in real estate in this town, you're going to need partners. Every time you take a mortgage, you take a partner—a bank. So, why not a private partner? You say you've got this deal set up with New York Central to acquire their Park Avenue building? I know someone who might want to go in with you."

"Who?"

"Stanley Stahl."

Stanley Stahl was a wealthy investor whose money had originally come from his immigrant father's successful real estate business. We met and I explained my problem. He agreed to provide the necessary $600,000 in exchange for a 50 percent partnership in the Park Avenue lease. I agreed to pay him back $300,000 out of my half of the building's profits.

On that basis, we acquired lease possession of 277 Park from Jim Boise and the New York Central. We quickly discovered that what we had on our hands was one of the city's most celebrated residential buildings, chock full of families straight out of the society, financial, and political pages of the city's newspapers.

One of our most famous tenants was Joseph P. Kennedy. He, I discovered, was the father of John F. Kennedy, a recent unsuccessful contender for the 1956 Democratic Vice-Presidential nomination and a man predicted to be a shoo-in, with the help of his father's money, for the presidential nomination in 1960. The elder Kennedy had long rented two big apartments in the building, one for him and his wife Rose (it was their New York residence) and another a few floors away for him and his mistress of the moment, whose name I shall keep to myself.

My involvement in the building was the beginning of a long and increasingly intimate relationship with the Kennedy family that has lasted to this day. My first encounter was with Joseph Kennedy himself. Stanley Stahl preferred to remain in the background, so I took over the daily management of 277 Park. One day, early in 1958, Joseph Kennedy paid me a visit and said he'd like to rent a pair of empty, ground-floor apartments as the New York headquarters for his son Jack's campaign for the 1960 Democratic nomination. During the course of our negotiations, he told me he was heavily into commercial real estate himself, with properties in several cities around the country. His negotiating style certainly lent credence to his claim, for he knew the jargon better than I did. Eventually, I learned that he wasn't kidding me. He owned, among other properties, the Chicago Merchandise Mart, the biggest building in the world in rentable square footage.

At the time Kennedy approached me, though, I was unaware of his and his family's notoriety. I found him brusque and condescending, preemptory and rude. To put it another way, he treated me like some two-bit building superintendent. I was constrained, through forceful language of my own, to disabuse him of his attitude. Once I did, he revised his behavior, and we reached an agreement on a lease for the campaign headquarters.

Later, I heard that he'd complained about me to someone at New York Central in words akin to the following: "Who's that Jew with the funny accent you've got running 277? Goddamn Jews—you give them an inch, they take a mile."

I did not hold their father's well-known anti-Semitism against his surviving sons when, later on, I met and got to know them. In fact, I believed that much of the humanism I perceived in them must have evolved in reaction to their having grown up in the shadow of the bigotry Kennedy Senior constantly displayed, not only about Jews but about every other ethnic and racial group that did not suit him. They very cleverly used his money to try to correct many of the social injustices in America, which he had believed in perpetuating. Even before he suffered the 1961 stroke that would eventually kill him, he was a confused, shunted-aside old man who felt that his archaic beliefs and principles had been betrayed by the sons whose political fortunes he'd so obsessively fostered.

The Kennedy campaign headquarters did not last long. Nor was there time to make good on my idea of using the building's courtyard as a commercial parking facility. For within a year, I heard from Jim Boise that the railroad intended to sell the building. Since Stanley Stahl and I had the option to buy, we immediately exercised it.

However, I had not yet been able to repay Stanley the $300,000 for my share in our leasing partnership. Nor was I able to come up with the additional millions I'd need for my 50 percent contribution to the building's purchase. So, I made a new deal with him. I offered to relinquish my half of the partnership in exchange for his cancellation of my debt and his payment to me of an additional consideration for my role in "finding" him the property.

By accepting my offer, Stanley was able to purchase the building on his own. The New York Central was already selling other apartment buildings along Park Avenue, and plans were being announced by developers for the razing of the buildings and their replacement by futuristic, glass-walled office towers. The controversial, forty-story Lever Brothers building would be the first to go up, followed by the spare, cool tower of the Seagram Building. The predicted transfiguration of Park Avenue from a residential to purely commercial boulevard was under way.

As the new owner of 277 Park, Stanley Stahl soon joined the parade, tearing down the old, low-rise, square-block apartment house and replacing it with what is today the modernistic and very profitable fifty-story Chemical Bank Building.

It was in that indirect fashion that I—still a relative newcomer to the New York development game, and still a relatively minor player—contributed to the renaissance of Park Avenue. Over the next ten years, the renaissance would provide the city with a new midtown corporate and financial core that began to rival, and in many ways exceed, the traditional Wall Street center in importance and vitality. Indeed, it encouraged and stimulated the commercial renewal of the entire width of midtown Manhattan between First and Eighth Avenues, and played a key role in making New York the modern-day financial capital of the world.

For me personally, my involvement in the first stages of the Park Avenue rebirth produced a palpable expansion of my reputation as a man who could make things happen in New York real estate. I was still somewhat of a "small fry" financially, but I was getting known in the big-bucks development arena as someone it paid to do business with.

I had, in a sense, "arrived." All thanks to a three-cent postcard.

CHAPTER TWELVE: "I PLEDGE ALLEGIANCE..."

It's conceivable that if I hadn't sent that postcard, and if Jim Boise hadn't been curious enough to retrieve it from his wastebasket, I might have remained a relative small-timer in New York real estate to this day—a man content with developing a few parking garages, with acquiring a small building here, a small building there, and with living a comfortable but not spectacular, event-filled life. The postcard changed all that. It changed it mainly by bringing me into contact with Stanley Stahl.

When Stanley and I dissolved our partnership in the 277 Park Avenue property, he said to me, "Abe, let's not let this be the last time we work together. You brought me a good deal with 277. Find me more good deals, and I'll go in with you again. You put up the know-how, I'll put up the money."

Thereafter, I began to work in two separate businesses. The first was for the account of Hirschfeld Realty alone, developing further garages and small apartment buildings. The second was for the joint account of Hirschfeld Realty and Stanley Stahl. Although the first was tracing a steadily rising profit curve, the second proved to be the source of periodic major profits.

By 1959, the commercial transformation of Park Avenue below 59th Street was well underway. North of 59th, the avenue was a continuation of what it had been to the south; that is, a wide boulevard separated by an "island" of greenery and lined on both sides with once luxurious but now slightly faded old apartment buildings, twelve stories in height on the average. Between 59th and 96th Streets, the avenue was the central residential artery of the wealthy Upper East Side.

But at the same time, the street had a slightly down-at-the-mouth look. Most of the buildings were rental apartment houses. In almost every building, the majority of the spacious apartments, one or two to a floor, had been leased by the same occupants for decades. Rent-control laws from the time of World War II had ensured that the income the buildings' owners received could not keep up with the rising costs of maintaining them.

As a result, a new strategy had developed in the 1950s. It was called "co-oping," which was short for a device whereby a building's owner sold the building to its tenants, and the tenants, instead of renting their individual apartments, "owned" them through their purchase of shares in a "cooperative corporation" formed to purchase the building. In that fashion, a building's owner could unload his property, usually at a profit, and rid himself of the financial headaches of landlordship.

Not every building owner on Park Avenue who wished to co-op his building could easily do so, however. Initially, there was a great deal of resistance to the idea among tenants, for it meant having to put up a lot of money all at once instead of paying a few hundred dollars each month in rent. It also meant a myriad of other problems, financial and otherwise, for tenants. First, their monthly living expenses might double or even treble as a consequence of co-oping, since each tenant in such a building was responsible for his or her share of the monthly mortgage and tax payments and, in addition, its monthly maintenance costs—doormen, elevator men, janitors, repairmen, the physical plant, and so on. For wealthy tenants, this was not a hardship, and it even had certain income-tax advantages. But for tenants who enjoyed only modest incomes, it was.

The co-op movement, then, was in a state of flux in 1959, not only on Park Avenue but also in other fashionable residential neighborhoods in Manhattan where costly-to-maintain apartment buildings were being fettered by rent control. Owners found that some buildings were easy to co-op; others were difficult, if not impossible. In the latter case, rather than struggle further, owners were offering their buildings for sale to private buyers at rock-bottom prices.

Two things occurred to me. The first was that co-oping was here to stay. Despite the difficulties facing some building transfiguration of Park Avenue south of 59th Street, a tremendous demand would quickly arise for residential apartments along the avenue directly north of it. And, so I immediately started to look for just such buildings there.

Within days, I found two buildings for sale at extremely low prices—903 and 929 Park. One I could get for a mere $700,000, the other for $75,000 more. The $700,000 building contained forty-eight apartments. If I could buy the building, then turn it around and co-op it at an average of $60,000 per apartment, I would gross more than $2.9 million. After expenses, my net profit would be $2 million. The other building, though slightly more expensive, would produce a similar profit.

I brought my idea to Stanley Stahl. He agreed to put up half the money for 929 Park, the $700,000 building. We succeeded in buying it, and the plan went like clockwork. I convinced a great majority of the tenants that if they agreed to purchase their apartments, they would be able to sell them a year or two later for three times the price they'd paid, if they wished. Stanley and I came out with a $1.9 million net profit, $100,000 less than I'd projected, or $950,000 respectively on an investment of $350,000 each.

I used my profit on 929 to buy, on my own account, the slightly more expensive building at 903 Park, which I maintained as a profitable rental property. Between my garage developments, my apartment-house rehabs, and my co-oping transactions, in 1959, I netted $4.7 million. This was after only three years spent in the real estate business full time, and at a time when much of the market was in a depressed state.

But with the market due to soon rise, the future seemed limitless. With that kind of profit, moreover, I was suddenly a highly credible credit risk in the eyes of New York's principal lending institutions. They began to beat down my door in their eagerness to finance my further acquisitions and developments. I had paved the road to future riches, and now the time had come to travel it.

But first, there was a loose end that needed to be tied up. My father had died in Israel the year before, and I was long overdue to return to help my mother reorganize her affairs.

The reason I say I was overdue is because I'd discovered, when my father died, that if I returned for his funeral, I would have been immediately conscripted into the Israeli Army. A new law, which had a retroactive effect, stated that for every year an Israeli male remained out of the country after 1952, he would have to serve for one month in the army upon his return. By 1958, I had been in America and Canada continuously for six years since 1952. Thus, if I'd returned for my father's funeral, I would have had to go straight into the Israeli army for six months.

About to turn forty, I felt that the law, which was enacted by the Knesset two years after my departure, was unfair—indeed, irrational. After all, it wasn't as if I'd fled the country to escape army duty. Just the opposite; I had done several years of Haganah service prior to the War of Independence and had been exempted from military duty in 1948 so that I could contribute to the war effort in other ways. Although I had long wanted to return to Israel during the mid-to-late 1950s, if only to visit my parents, I was blocked from doing so by the compulsory military duty law. The only way I could return without falling under the law's jurisdiction was if I did so as an American citizen.

Zipora and I had applied for American citizenship after our move to Great Neck, but we'd had to wait several years before our applications, and those of Rachel and Elie, were accepted. Finally, in 1959, we were sworn in as naturalized citizens. Soon thereafter, we returned to Israel for the first time in nine years. The trip was important to us not only because it allowed us to visit what was left of our respective families but also because it gave us the opportunity to show Rachel and Elie the land of their birth and heritage.

My return to Tel Aviv in 1959 was a source of both joy and dismay. My joy derived from seeing my mother again and from meeting old friends and visiting former haunts. The country had changed remarkably in nine years, with vast expanses of new development and a huge increase in the immigrant population.

My dismay was occasioned by my realization of how solidly entrenched the hatred had become, which was more a matter of official policy on both sides than a personal one between peoples. Although I did not sympathize with them, in a way, I could understand Arab attitudes. Among other things, Israel was a reflection of their own inability and failure to enter the modern world. Rather than look to themselves in assigning the blame for such shortcomings, they used Israel as their scapegoat. So long as they could focus their fury on Israel, they were able to divert it from themselves, where it really belonged. Such impulses were stupid and self-defeating of course, but they were very much part of human nature.

Israel was caught up in an emotional bind of its own. Under other circumstances, it might have expended much more energy than it did to seek reconciliation with its Arab neighbors. But the memory of the Holocaust, and the mass psychology that collective memory produced in the Israeli psychology, effectively barred such efforts. It was precisely because Jews the world over had decreed an end to being the scapegoats of other people's troubles that Israel had been established. Israelis, as a whole, were certainly in no mood to be conciliatory in the face of the often virulent Arab scapegoatism that bombarded them daily.

The real difficulty though, was that both sides were caught up in the larger ideological and real political global struggle between East and West, which made reconciliation virtually impossible. When I was growing up in Palestine, the Jewish population, even though most of it was European and Western in its outlook, was largely dependent on itself for its well-being, identity, and self-determination. Because of that, the population began naturally to mold itself into the local Arab culture—remaining distinct, to be sure, but seeing itself as an increasingly integral part of the wider Arab world in which it existed. This trend had gathered force over fifty years of Zionist immigration to Palestine. Except for occasional outbursts of violence between Arabs and Jews, occasioned mostly by clashing religious militancy's, the two peoples got on along amicably.

Of course, assimilation and integration were easier said than done, especially under the circumstances Israel faced early in its existence. It was easier preached, as well, particularly when such preaching came from a man like me who had left to become a citizen of another country—a Western country, in the bargain.

So, I thought these thoughts, but I didn't try to preach them. Instead, I simply resolved to do all I could to help Israel from my new base in the United States, most of it in the way of financial support. Yet, as time went on and increasing numbers of Israelis were killed in succeeding wars and border violence, I could not help but begin to urge, if not preach, that there was another, better way to resolve the problems between Arabs and Jews. What I urged was cooperation and integration.

How could the process be started? I said, "Let Israelis and Arabs begin doing business together." Commercial trade is the lifeblood of every society. My career in business had taught me that trade and commerce created understanding through a mutuality of interests. You didn't have to like people you did business with. You didn't have to socialize with them or subscribe to their personal views and prejudices. But as long as you could do business with them, there was no reason to fight. Doing business encouraged peaceful co-existence.

My prescriptions may have sounded simple. But as I've said more than once in these pages, I believe in reducing thorny matters to their plain essentials—without over-simplifying, of course. Living in the complex world we do, when confronted with the problem of solving problems, we often tend to be unable to see the forest for the trees. I have always found during my business career that the most effective solution is the simplest and most direct one.

I have always found, too, that every complex problem that seems firmly fixed in the glue of insolubility contains within it a loophole that not only makes possible its solution but also encourages it. It is simply a matter of looking for and putting your finger on the loophole.

As far as I was concerned, the loophole in the seemingly interminable and insoluble Arab-Israeli problem was the commencement of trade between the two mutually hostile sides. The road to reconciliation, I repeatedly insisted, was through commerce. Finally, in 1979, my unpopular position was vindicated to a certain extent. That was the year in which my old friend, Menachem Begin, Prime Minister of Israel, and Anwar Sadat, President of Egypt, signed the Camp David Agreement that had been hammered out with President Jimmy Carter's hands-on assistance. I'll have more to say about that later.

CHAPTER THIRTEEN: ADVENTURES (AND
MISADVENTURES) IN THE LANDLORD TRADE

When I returned to New York from Israel in 1959, I remained
totally innocent of any compelling interest in, or knowledge of, the
contemporary American political scene. Beyond my awareness that
Eisenhower was President, that Joseph Kennedy's son John was
hoping to succeed him, that Robert Wagner was the mayor of New
York, and that I'd registered to vote as a Republican in Great Neck, I
had paid no attention to American domestic politics. Aside from my
deep concern over the political fate of Israel, which was basically a
matter of international geopolitics, I was personally apolitical.

Well, perhaps I'd better qualify that. Having engaged in the
New York real estate business for four or five years, I had come to
learn how inextricably real estate development was tied up in the
machinery of the city's political bureaucracy, often to the detriment of
those like me who sought to exploit the industry to its fullest.
Nowhere in the free world, I thought, was a form of free enterprise
more fettered by politically inspired regulation and legal complexity
than the conduct of real estate. I often wanted to publicly condemn
the system. But since I was not a citizen, I kept my mouth shut.

Upon becoming naturalized in 1959, though, I felt I was
entitled. So, I began to speak out about the basic corruption I saw in
the umbilical relationship between real estate and politics and in the
even more corrupt dependence of both on the city's trade-union
establishment. It was virtually impossible to conduct creative,
efficient, and economical development in New York. The best one
could hope for was to be able to carry out a project with a minimum
of hassle and extortion from city government and the unions. The
hope was usually misplaced.

Although the unions played fast and loose with the law, the
ultimate culprit, in my eyes, was the municipal government. The
government of New York was firmly controlled and conducted by the
city's Democratic Party. The Democratic Party was, to a great extent,
beholden to the unions for its support, and many of the unions were
under the invisible rule of the most unscrupulous underworld
characters imaginable.

Despite it all, my business boomed in the early 1960s. During
that period, I built several more vertical, open-air garages, each of

which provided handsome profits both through my re-mortgaging formula and through the annual revenues they produced under my system of leasing them to independent garage operators. My most well-know garage after the East 30th Street facility was one I erected between Fifth and Sixth Avenues in the shadow of Rockefeller Center. The main attraction of Rockefeller Center was the Radio City Music Hall. Since there was already a Rockefeller Center Garage as part of the Rockefeller Center complex, I named my 320-car facility the Radio City Garage.

Thereafter, I formed all my garages into a separate division of Hirschfeld Realty called Radio City Parking Corporation. Likewise, I created a separate division to cover my residential building transactions and developments, and yet a third to handle the acquisition and management of commercial office, warehouse, and industrial properties.

My residential acquisitions multiplied considerably during the early 1960s. Most of them—there were twenty in all—were on the East Side of Manhattan, where real estate values were still waiting to explode. My formula remained simple. I bought old, rundown apartment buildings at rock-bottom prices, then rehabilitated and modernized them. In that way, I was able to establish new, higher rent rolls that would produce a profitable operating return. Then I either resold or retained and refinanced them to gain an immediate, large, cash profit.

As it happened, I retained quite a few more buildings than I sold. Thus, I also found myself moving more and more heavily into the "landlord business"—that is, running my own large rental buildings. This was undoubtedly the least pleasant aspect of dealing in New York real estate. All it took was one nasty tenant out of a thousand good ones to make your life miserable. I averaged about one a year who made it a practice to exploit the tenant-favoring housing laws to avoid paying rent to gain some other kind of shady advantage.

Maybe that's why I pursued the garage side of my business so vigorously over the years. Housing cars was much easier than housing people. Cars did not break leases, deface walls, let bathtubs overflow, fake injuries, and fail to pay rent. Eventually, I learned that the only way to function as a large-scale landlord and keep one's sanity was to grow a thick skin so that one became impervious to occasional tenant outrages. However, although I learned that rule in theory, it was not always easy to adhere to.

As time went on, and I acquired more buildings and tenants, that began to become impossible. In my previous years, I had grown accustomed to doing business on a one-to-one, face-to-face basis with those of whom I dealt with and negotiated contracts with. Although an apartment lease is a contract, in New York it was more of an adversarial contract than a cooperative one. The main reason for that was the plethora of rent and housing regulations, most of them designed to protect "tenants' rights," and the court system that supported them.

My simple credo in life, whether in the personal or business realm, was the same as the old Biblical injunction that said you should treat people just as you expect them to treat you and to do so for as long as you possibly can. In the adversarial context of the tenant-landlord relationship in New York, that mandate became harder and harder for me to follow, as I acquired more and more cynical, destructive, and venal tenants. Finally, I threw up my hands and said, whenever I encountered a particularly nasty situation, "Let the lawyers and courts handle it."

All in all, though, I think that as an increasingly major residential landlord in New York, I fared well under the adversarial system. Over the years, I got involved in relatively few landlord-tenant squabbles of the kind that end up in court. And those I did get involved in, I usually won, thereby vindicating my claim that I was always interested in doing the right thing by tenants as long as they acted decently.

I say all this because there were a few cases I did lose, and I would not be telling the whole truth in this book if I didn't disclose them. I believe the reason I lost them, however, was not because of any malevolence on my part as a real estate operator but because of my impulsive nature and the fact that some of the bureaucratic hurdles everyone in the business faces stretched my patience beyond the breaking point.

Two cases immediately come to mind, both of which occurred in the late 1970s. This first had to do with an apartment building I owned at 15 Park Avenue. In June of 1978, I leased a small apartment to a man who moved into it with his girlfriend. The lease had the usual provision whereunder the man agreed that the apartment would be occupied solely by him and immediate members of his family.

That provision, a standard one in residential leases, was designed to deter tenants from turning their apartments into communal crash pads, whorehouses, dormitories, and the like. Its purpose was also to prevent tenants from subletting apartments to third parties at rents greatly in excess of what they were paying, thereby making profits at a landlord's expense. Its ultimate purpose was to protect other tenants in a building from nuisances and to enable a landlord to retain control over the use of an apartment. There was a law on the books that enabled landlords to enforce the provision, although it was a law riddled with loopholes.

Fifteen Park Avenue was a nice building in a choice New York residential neighborhood, Murray Hill. It was the kind of building that cried out for the protection of the "immediate family" provision of the lease. A landlord really had no way of determining, when he leased an apartment, what the tenant's ultimate intention in leasing it was. To be sure, most tenants simply wanted a place to live. But it was not unusual for a tenant to rent for one or another of the purposes I've just outlined. At 15 Park Avenue, I certainly didn't want a lot of unauthorized strangers going in and out of the building, or living there, or carrying on some activity that had nothing to do with maintaining a home. To allow that would have justifiably brought the wrath of other tenants down on my head. "You're allowing tenant so-and-so to ruin the building," was a refrain landlords heard regularly from tenants.

Despite the fact that I'd rented the apartment at 15 Park to the man alone, and despite the "immediate family" provision of the lease, I made no objection when I learned that he'd brought a girl to live with him. That sort of thing happened all the time, especially in the 1970s age of the "live-in lover." It would have been churlish of me to make an issue of it, or to raise his rent by the five percent the law allowed in such circumstances. I was as much a romantic as anyone.

But soon, the situation changed. In September, the man—the tenant of record—abruptly moved out and left his former girlfriend in occupancy without informing me. This was a time when the regulated-apartment rental market had begun to tighten up in Manhattan. Legally, by vacating the apartment and leaving his former girlfriend as the only occupant, the male tenant was in violation of his lease.

Now the woman began to pay the rent. That posed a dilemma. Had I accepted her checks, I would, in effect, have waived the male tenant's breach and by implication, legally acknowledged the woman's right to occupy the apartment alone. This would have meant that I'd be obligated to give her a renewal lease when the lease in the former male tenant's name expired nine months later. The entire affair had every appearance of being a scam on the male tenant's part to get his female friend a nice Park Avenue apartment at a relatively low monthly rent.

Such ploys were not uncommon. And even though I felt my trust and good faith had been abused, I was tentatively prepared to go along with it as opposed to making trouble for the woman. But then she sought to stretch her advantage. I learned that she had brought in two female roommates to share the apartment with her. Suddenly, I'd lost complete control over the nature of the occupancy of my apartment. Moreover, I began to get complaints from other tenants about the daily traffic of strange men in and out of the building and about the general litter my "new tenants" were leaving in the hallways. The building was beginning to look like some cheap transient hotel, said one.

I offered the woman and her roommates a lease on their own, with a legally permissible rent increase if they wished to remain in the apartment. They refused in no uncertain terms. I then politely informed them that they would have to vacate the apartment, since they were not the legal tenants. Again, they refused, daring me to try and evict them. They gave me no choice but to take them up on their challenge.

In these particular circumstances, I could only sue the male leaseholder and hope that the court would eventually order him to remove the illegal occupants. The trouble was that my original male tenant had taken a powder, and you cannot sue whom you cannot find. My only option was to forcibly evict the recalcitrant women so that I could recover my "landlord rights" to re-lease the apartment under proper legal terms. I might add that insurance companies that insure apartment buildings do not look kindly on landlords who allow apartments to be occupied by illegal tenants—another reason why building owners must insist on formal leases.

One day, when the three women were away from the apartment, I had my building-management employees go in, remove their belongings to a safe place, and change the lock on the door. Attached to the door, I left a notice that said they were thereby officially evicted, explained why, and told them where they could recover their possessions. I was sure I had acted on proper legal and moral grounds.

They found a lawyer and sued me for nearly $10 million. The court agreed with my contention and dismissed the suit. When they appealed, the intermediate New York appellate court upheld the dismissal. It was only when the women—or their ambitious lawyer—appealed to the highest appellate court in the state that I ran into trouble.

Six years after the fact, the Court of Appeals decided that although my eviction may have been factually justified, in the light of recently enacted revisions of the housing and tenant laws, I had acted improperly from a procedural point of view. The high court remanded the case to the lower court for a trial to determine if I had inflicted any compensable damages on the women.

By then, I had lost all interest in the matter. Although I was sure a trial would find that the women suffered no damages, I simply didn't have the time to waste on further proceedings, which probably would have dragged on for another year or more. So, I paid the women a modest settlement to drop the case.

The other case would become one the most "infamous" incidents of my life. It did not involve a tenant. Nevertheless, my adversary was a woman, and I was on the receiving end of her lawsuit for $16 million. The incident that triggered her suit occurred in 1977. To me, it was a culmination of the frustrations and exasperation New York real estate developers are confronted with every day by the city's maze of regulations, and even more so by the army of petty political bureaucrats appointed to administer them.

Almost a year before, I had applied for permits to build another parking garage, this one next to the Empire State Building. Before I could take my plans to any other agency for the requisite permits, I had to submit them to the city's Office of Environmental Impact for approval. I did so.

But this time, rather than the normal six-week wait for the approval to come through, I noticed after two months that nothing had happened. I was waiting to sign contracts with construction crews, and my bank financing was pending. The official go-ahead, and dozens of other elements involved in such a venture, were in a state of ready suspension, including the weather. I had hoped to begin construction in the spring of 1977 so as to take advantage of the weather and suffer fewest delays. By spring, I still hadn't heard from the Office of Environmental Impact.

Finally, I wrote to the director of the office, one Dorothy Green, a middle-aged mother of three, and a long-time Democratic Party functionary, she had been appointed to her position by Democratic mayor, Abraham Beame, a bland clubhouse politician who was about to be voted out of office.

In my letter, I politely explained that her organization's unusual delay in responding to my construction plan was beginning to cause inconveniences with my banks and contractors. I said that if the OEI found any environmental defects in the plan, I would be happy to correct them, but that I was puzzled by the lack of any word at all, one way or the other, after two months. With equal politeness, I asked her to please expedite the matter and let me know if there were any difficulties.

I waited two weeks for an answer. I got none. By now, it was June, and all hopes of getting a head start on the weather were gone. In addition, I would have to re-arrange my financing and contractor commitments.

Finally, I telephoned Dorothy Green. I asked her what was happening and why everything was being delayed. She was polite but strangely evasive. She said she "hoped" to have a response to my submission in two or three weeks.

I said that I'd wait with utmost patience and wondered to myself if her evasiveness and delays were politically motivated. I was definitely not supporting the re-election of her boss, Abe Beame, as mayor. If he were to lose the coming fall's election, she would no doubt find herself out of a high-paying job. I wondered if that was what it was all about—a brand of petty political harassment. But I kept my musings to myself.

Three weeks passed, and I heard nothing further from Dorothy Green. I gave her another week's grace, then called once more. Now it was mid-July. She said, sorry, but they needed more time—there had been a heat wave, a blackout, riots, so on, and everyone's schedule was out of kilter. Two more weeks, she promised.

I waited three weeks, into mid-August. I phoned again. "Sorry," I was told, "Mrs. Green is on vacation. She won't be back till after Labor Day."

I was now beginning to get as hot under the collar as the August dog-day weather. But I held my tongue and waited for Labor Day to come and go. Another call to Green's office. She was "in a meeting" and would get back to me. Not only didn't she get back to me, she kept ducking my further calls over the next ten days. We were in mid-September. My financing and contracting arrangements were in disarray. On September 16, I tried calling her yet again. Same result, only this time I heard her voice in the background telling her secretary to say she was "out of the office."

I had reached the end of my tether. The time had come to take the bull by the horns. My son Elie had recently joined Hirschfeld Realty. I beckoned to him and two of my assistants in the office. "Come with me," I said.

We piled into a taxi and headed for the Municipal Building downtown. Once there, we clambered into an elevator and ascended to Dorothy Green's office. Trailed by my little entourage, I marched through the reception room to Green's inner office and flung open the door, ignoring the protests of her secretary. Green, sitting at her desk, looked up in surprise.

"Hello," I said. "Abe Hirschfeld."

I motioned Elie and the others into the office and shut the door.

"Mr. Hirschfeld, you can't just come barging in here like—" Green started to shout.

"Mrs. Green," I interjected, "that is exactly what I have done. You have left me no choice. I've come here to get an answer one way or another. You're not leaving this room until you give me one."

Her face flushed with fury. After further discussion, she sprang to her feet and started for the door. I beat her to it and blocked her exit. "An answer, Mrs. Green."

She scurried back to her desk and picked up the phone. Before she could speak into it, I took it away from her. "An answer, Mrs. Green."

She started screaming at the top of her lungs, "Help, come help me. I'm being imprisoned."

Soon, people were pounding at her door. She continued shouting for help. I signaled to Jack Thorp, one of the colleagues I had brought with me, to let them in. In came a security guard, her secretary, and several others, one of whom was Robert Low, the head of the city's Department of Environment and Green's immediate superior. Sobbing uncontrollably, she went flying into his arms.

Low asked what had happened. I told him I'd come to get a response to my garage application after six month's of irresponsible inaction and procrastination on Green's part. Low said he'd look into it, and the episode came to a close.

Within days, I heard directly from Low that my application was approved and received an apology from him for the delay. It seemed, he said, that Dorothy Green had been suffering from psychiatric problems and that practically every other builder in town had had the same difficulties with her that I had. Soon, he told me, she would be eased out of her job.

Out of her job, perhaps, but not out of my life. Not long after, she sued me for $16 million in damages, claiming that I had kidnapped, or "unlawfully imprisoned," her and submitted her to "outrageous abuse" resulting in her inability, among other things, to have sex with her husband.

After several years of procedural maneuvering by the lawyers for each side, that case did go to trial. Both fortunately and unfortunately for me, the jury learned that Mrs. Green indeed had a troubled psychiatric history. As a result, it discounted her claim that I had caused the crippling emotional difficulties she held herself out as suffering as a result of our encounter. But the jury also declared that I should have been more circumspect in confronting a woman in the thrall of psychiatric problems, even though I had not been aware of them. Given her six months' experience of inexplicably erratic behavior, the jury decided that I should have been alerted to the fact that I was not dealing with someone who was playing with a full deck.

The jury, then, found me liable for at least partially aggravating Dorothy Green's mental condition. The matter was concluded by my agreement to pay her a token sum, infinitely much less than what she'd hope to recover. To demonstrate my opinion of the frivolousness of the suit, I threw in a similar amount to be paid not to her, but to a Jewish charity. It was my way of saying that there are two kinds of charity in the world, the undeserving and the deserving.

My 1977 encounter with Dorothy Green was the climax of two decades of "fighting City Hall"—that is, of tying to deal even-temperedly with the sluggish and often inane bureaucracy of New York's municipal government.

CHAPTER FOURTEEN: ME AND BOBBY KENNEDY

By the early 1960s, I was heard to complain frequently to my friends and colleagues about the shortcomings of the system and the people who run it. "Abe," they would say, "couldn't agree more. Why don't you change it?"

"Me?" I'd answer. "How the hell can I change it?"

"Run for office. Get in there and clean it up. Make it operate as efficiently as you do our business."

"You've got to be kidding," I'd say. "Me, run for office? With my accent? Who'd vote for me? Anyway, I'm a Republican. A Republican gets nowhere in this city."

"So become a Democrat!" they'd say.

"What, and become part of a problem?"

So, although I complained, basically I continued to ignore politics, not just on the local but on the national level as well. It took my son Elie, then fifteen years old, to shake me out of my indifference. And even then, my actions were nothing more than an attempt to please him.

Elie was in high school in Great Neck by then. Like many teenagers, he had been devastated by the assassination of John F. Kennedy the year before. I must admit that I, not a native of the United States, and definitely not caught up in the glamorous aura that had surrounded J.F.K., was not as emotionally affected by his murder as most Americans were. Sure, I thought it was terrible. But having lost a large part of my extended family in the Holocaust, I had also lost my capacity to be stunned by such barbarities.

Once the national trauma was over, I thought little more about it. Younger people, though, were magnetized and politicized by it in a way previous generations of American youth had never been. The result was the increasing political turmoil fomented by the youth of the late 1960s and early 1970s. The "young" J.F.K. had been taken away from them and replaced, in their eyes, by a bunch of repulsive, old-fogy politicians of the past. I remain convinced today that the violent, social upheavals of the '60s were a direct result of Kennedy's assassination.

As a high school student, Elie's capacity for intellectual and scholarly achievement never ceased to amaze me. That was probably because I had never gone beyond receiving a fifth-grade education and even at that had never been much interested in formal learning. I suppose I expected my only son to have a similarly cavalier attitude towards school. On the contrary, he was an intrepid, high-achieving student. I can remember times when he would come home with report cards that had straight As on them except for one subject, in which he'd gotten an A-minus or B-plus. He was almost apologetic about that single glitch in his record. To me, the entire report card was a miracle.

In addition to being an outstanding student, Elie became very active in school politics as a fifteen-year-old, and he was elected president of his class. In 1964, Robert Kennedy, who had been the Attorney General in his assassinated brother's administration, decided to run for the United States Senate from New York. To many young people in the area, Kennedy's candidacy represented a rebirth of the heady Camelot days of J.F.K.

I didn't know Bobby Kennedy from Adam—had I passed him on the street, I wouldn't have recognized him. Elie, though, was very much a Bobby supporter in 1964, despite the fact that he was only fifteen and still years away from voting eligibility. As election day approached, Elie kept asking me who I intended to vote for. Although I had no personal preferences, my plan was to vote the straight Republican line, if only because that was what I believe a registered Republican did.

But Elie wouldn't stand for that. He hounded me for weeks before the election to cast my vote for Kennedy. And so, I did, solely as a favor for my son. The rest of the Republican candidates on that year's slate got my ballot.

Having voted for Kennedy, who won the contest for the senate, I still had little idea of who he was beyond the fact of his status as the younger brother of J.F.K. and son of Joseph Kennedy. And in the two years following, I paid no attention to his senate career. It was only in 1967 that Bobby, purely by accident, entered my life in a personal way. It was a way that would, once again, set me off on an entirely new path of endeavor.

It happened through, of all things, golf. One spring day, I was invited to play golf at an exclusive club in Westchester. When I arrived at the club, I learned that my host had had an emergency and would not be able to get there. Since I'd travel that far, I decided to hang around for a while and get in a little practice on the putting green. As I was stroking balls, three youngish men appeared and began practicing. Soon, they were making bets on their putts, and eventually, they drew me into their contest.

After ten or fifteen minutes of that, the three announced that they were off to play a round of golf. One of them asked if I was playing. I explained about having been stranded, and that I was about to return to New York. "Why don't you join us?" the fellow said. "We'll make a foursome."

Why not, I thought, and I accepted the invitation. The three seemed like good pals; they were friendly, jocular, and didn't appear to take golf too seriously. I introduced myself. The fellow who'd issued the invitation said his name was Steve. "This is Jim," he went on, introducing the second. "And this is Bob."

We all shook hands and made our way to the first tee. It was then that I learned that my three fellow-golfers were there for a Democratic Party golf outing.

We played, and since none of us were very good, we spent much of the round joking about our ineptitude. If there was anything unusual about our eighteen holes, it was my growing awareness that the slight fellow named Bob seemed to garner a lot of attention from the other golfers on the course.

After we finished, the three invited me into the clubhouse for drinks and a humorous post-mortem on our games. As we sat around a table, Bob kept getting more attention, with many other men drifting over to engage him in conversation. Each time, he'd introduce me to his friends. "John, Peter, Charley," he'd say, "meet my friend Abe."

Beyond their names, I still had no idea who Bob, Steve, and Jim were. Finally, my original host arrived at the club and found me at the table. I introduced him: "Mort, meet Bob, Jim, and Steve. They were kind enough to ask me to tag along when you were unable to make our game."

Mort joined us all for another round of drinks. Then Steve said to me, "You going back to the city tonight, Abe?"

I said I was.

"So are we," he went on. "We're going to have some dinner at Toots Shor's. We'd be honored if you'd join us as our guest."

"I'd be honored, too," I replied. "But only on one condition. Since you were good enough to ask me to play golf with you, you will be my guest at Toots Shor's."

As we were leaving to return to the city, I pulled my friend Mort aside. "By the way," I said, "who are those guys? The one called Bob seems to be important."

"You don't know?" Mort said, his eyes widening in amazement. "You mean you played three hours of golf with them? You sat around with them after, having drinks and telling jokes? And you don't know who they are?

"The one called Bob, or Bobby, is Senator Robert Kennedy. Steve is Steve Smith, his brother-in-law and the guy who runs the Kennedy family business. The third fellow, Jim, is James Foley. He's from Minnesota and a key aide to Vice President Hubert Humphrey."

The good fellowship I'd established with the three continued that night at Toots Shor's. When I confessed my ignorance of their identities, they were amused rather than offended, especially Bob Kennedy. He had, after all, been a household name and an instantly recognizable face in America for at least six years.

I defended myself by telling them of my lack of interest in politics. "Anyway," I added to Bob Kennedy, "I'm a Republican. Just to show you how little I know, I voted for you two years ago in spite of that." I told him how Elie had pestered me into casting my ballot for him.

"Well," quipped Kennedy, "I was brought up to believe that the father was the great fount of wisdom in any family. I guess in your case, it proves that it's not the father who's the wisest, but the son."

"Yes," I replied, "but remember what the Bible says. "Where does a son get the wisdom to choose the father he does?"

It had long been my style to cite sayings from the Bible, whether in a business or social milieu. That day, in fact, I had invoked several Biblical adages to explain the bad golf shots we had all periodically made.

"To tell you the truth," Steve Smith said later at Toots Shor's when we were sorting out our respective identities and occupations, "we thought you were a Rabbi. That's why we asked you to join us. None of us had played golf with a Rabbi before. With all that Biblical knowledge, you must have studied to be a Rabbi."

"No," I said, "it's just that my education never went much beyond the Bible. To tell you the truth, it's all I know."

That got us into a long, good-natured discussion about religion and its history. They were three Irish Catholics; I was a Polish Jew. I found Bobby Kennedy nothing as I might have imagined him to be, given my knowledge of his father. He seemed genuinely interested in Judaism, as did the other two.

"One thing I've never understood, Abe," said Bobby at one point. "If you Jews were correct back there in ancient times, if your God was the one and only God, and his law was the one and only law for mankind, why do you suppose He allowed others to come along and form other religions? Christianity, for example."

The answer was simple, I said. "The Jews needed someone to buy retail."

That got the usual laugh around the table. But then Bobby came back with an ad-riposte that, while just as funny, also gave me an insight into his quick, forensic wit.

"Well," he said, "in the retail business, the customer is always right, isn't he?"

"Bobby," I said, "you won't persuade me to become a Christian with that logic. But you could persuade me to become a Democrat."

And that's exactly what he did. A few days later, he phoned me. "Abe, were you serious when you said I could persuade you to become a Democrat?"

I answered that although my remark had been made in the jesting spirit of our evening together, I was open to anything.

"Well," he said, "I've been asking around about you. Everybody tells me you're not only as dynamic and honest a guy as you struck me as being, but that you're also a whiz at raising money for various causes."

"I do my best," I said.

"Can you keep a secret?"

"I can and will."

"I'm seriously thinking of running for the Presidency next year. I'm asking you now, if I do will you support me, help me?"

"Bob," I answered, "for you to have picked me—a total stranger with a strange accent—to play golf with you last week was the kind of thing that could only happen in America. I've been telling everybody I know about it and about what a terrific man I think you are. I'm sure I've already gotten you a few more supporters than you had before. If you want to run for President, I will go to the ends of the earth to help you."

115

From that point on, I became a committed Democrat, as well as a fervent backer and intimate friend of Bobby Kennedy. A close political adviser, too. On this point, I later said to him, "Bobby, why do you ask my advise when you can see how little I know about politics in America?"

"Because, Abe," he answered, "I know you'll talk straight to me. Do you remember the exchange we had when we first met—about fathers being wiser than sons?"

"Yes."

"Well, you've become like a surrogate father to me. I've decided that you were wiser than you knew when you allowed Elie to talk you into voting for me when I ran for the senate. When I ask your advice, I'm seeking specific political recommendations. What I'm not depending on you to do is to tell me I'm not trying to fool myself or the public."

"When Lyndon Johnson surprised the country by announcing that he wouldn't seek re-election in 1968, the decision for Bobby Kennedy to run for Democratic nomination was sealed. But he had determined to mount a challenge to Johnson even before that, mainly over the issue of the Vietnam war, and in the fall of 1967, I became an integral part of his campaign.

Steve Smith ran the effort out of the Kennedy family business office in the Pan Am building, while I organized business support and raised money from my new Hirschfeld Realty office on Fifth Avenue. With Johnson's announcement early in 1968, the campaign really picked up steam as Bobby prepared to battle for the nomination through the various state primary elections for that spring and early summer. Suddenly, I was hooked on politics.

One of the more curious features of the spring, at least for me, occurred when I was traveling on the stump with Bobby and his campaign entourage. We arrived in Chicago, where Bobby was to give a speech to a union convention. He already had many of America's younger voters in his camp, but the nation's union still leaned strongly towards his chief rival, Hubert Humphrey. It was to be a rival speech, a major effort on his part to persuade the older working class of the country that he could serve labor better than Humphrey in the years to come.

At a meeting with union leaders before the speech, one of them accused Bobby of being anti-labor and warned him that he was likely to be locked during his speech.

"Why?" he asked. "What have I done that's anti-labor?"

The union reminded him of his prosecution of Teamster Union leader Jimmy Hoffa and others when he was Attorney General during his brother's administration.

Bobby argued that his crusade against Hoffa and other crooked unionists had been for labor, not against it. I added my two-cents worth in support of him. To the union leader I said, "To claim what the senator did to Hoffa was anti-labor is like saying a doctor who removes a tumor from a sick man is anti-life."

Then another union leader piped up with a different objection to Kennedy. "In New York," he said, "you and your family own a building at Eight Avenue and 14th Street that housed the office of many of the city's union locals. We've been getting lots of complaints lately about how you, as a landlord, have been treating those locals."

Bobby was genuinely surprised by this. Although the bulk of the Kennedy family fortune came from his father's many real estate holdings around the country, he'd paid scant attention over the years to the actual properties—what they were and where they were located. That was the business of Steve Smith, who managed the family's portfolios. Upon hearing the union leader's accusation, Bobby turned to his brother-in-law and said, "Is this true? We own the building he's talking about?"

Steve conceded that they did and started to deny the union leader's charges. Before he got very far, Bobby interjected. "Get rid of it!" Then he turned to the union leader. "I'm sorry. I was not aware of that. As of now, the building no longer belongs to me and my family. My brother-in-law will be disposing of it immediately."

In light of Bobby's public commitment, Steve Smith had no choice but to unload the 14th Street office building. Later that night, after the speech, Steve came to me and said, "Abe, what'll I do? Can you find a buyer?"

I said, "What's the building worth?"

"It appraised at $2.2 million."

"What'll you sell it for?"

"To whom?"

"To me."

"To you, I'll sell it for $1.8 million.'

"Steve," I said, "you've got a buyer."

Within days, I took the title to the twenty-story Union Building for $1.8 million. Using my tried and tested formula, I immediately acquired a new mortgage on it for $2.6 million, giving me a cash profit of $800.00. Even my new involvement in politics was proving a boon to business.

Eventually, I became the main New York fundraiser for Bobby Kennedy's 1968 campaign. In the process, I began to get to know all the state's Democratic bigwigs, the politicians, and the behind-the-scene operators, and I was both repulsed and fascinated by what I saw. What I saw was an amalgam of petty bickering and lofty idealism, of personal ambition and selfless altruism, of insatiable power-hunger and unprincipled limelight-seeking. What I saw most of all, and at first-hand, was that most career politicians in New York—city and state—were hacks who were more interested in serving themselves, in protecting and preserving their jobs, than in serving the people.

Fortunately, Bobby Kennedy had no need to indulge in such self-protection. He wasn't even all that comfortable about chasing after the power his campaign sought to achieve. He had only real power-interest in seeking the Presidency, and that was the power to reverse the consistently escalating course of the Vietnam war and bring about a reconciliation in the country between its younger and older generations.

He once said to me, "Abe, my brother's murder started all the madness in America. If he hadn't been killed, he'd still be President today, and none of this would be happening. All I want to do is put a stop to it, and I think I can."

I agreed with him thoroughly, and that was the real reason I became such an ardent supporter. I believe today that had he won the Democrat nomination in 1968, he would have gone on to beat Richard Nixon handily in the election. In my view, the only reason Nixon defeated Hubert Humphrey was because Humphrey was perceived by so many to be a piece of dead wood, a relic of the discredited Johnson administration.

And once Bobby had won the White House, he would indeed have brought an end to the social upheaval that Nixon only succeeded in perpetuating, despite his promise to end the war.

The Bobby Kennedy of 1968 was radically different from the Bobby Kennedy of 1958, when he was seen, and rightly so, as an overweeningly ambitious and ruthless crusader who sometimes grossly abused his power. In the interim, he had watched his many children begin to grow. He had been transformed by the experience—from the aggressive warrior his own father had brought him up to be, into a much more temperate and conciliatory man. His intimate experience of the Cuban Missile Crisis of 1962 had also inspired the transformation, as had his brother's assassination.

Violence begat violence, he knew now, and he had became almost priestly in his abhorrence of it and of the conditions that promoted it, whether in an urban ghetto or on the international stage. "That's become by favorite song," he once said to me, as he heard the anthem of the young generation, "Give Peace a Chance," being sung at an antiwar rally in New York.

But Bobby had by no means become a shrinking violet in the process of his transformation. He understood politics on all its levels, from local to international. He remained well-skilled in its most fundamental thrust-and-party aspects. Yet, he had also begun to acquire the attitudes and instincts of a statesman.

He had just started to grow and in my opinion, would have been a far more effective President than his brother.

Of course, just when it appeared that Bobby would get his chance to prove my contention, he—and the United States—was robbed of it. On the day he won the all-important California primary in June of 1968, he himself was assassinated.

For the first time since I could remember, I wept.

My tears were made even more bitter by my knowledge that had Bobby listened to me, he would not have lost his life. Our original plan had been for him to fly back to New York the morning of the California primary so that he could reach the city in time to attend a large victory party I had arranged for that evening. More than four hundred New Yorkers had accepted invitations to the party, and just the day before the California primary, Bobby had assured me over the phone that he'd be there.

That morning, though, he called me from Los Angeles at about eleven New York time and said, "Abe, I'm sorry, I'm going to have to miss your party. I'm going to stay here so that I can make an appearance at a party tonight, after the polls close, and thank everyone who worked for me.

"Bobby," I said, "I understand your sense of obligation to your California workers, but I don't thing it's a good idea. I'll tell you what a lawyer friend of mine says. 'When you win a case in court, get out of the courtroom before the judge has a chance to change his mind.'"

He laughed but said he'd been persuaded by the California Democrat leaders that the right thing to do was to stay. It was when he was leaving the Los Angeles victory celebration, that night, that he was gunned down.

By not returning to New York as planned, Bobby Kennedy remained in California forever.

CHAPTER FIFTEEN: ABE FOR SENATOR

It was an awful time, and my memories of it are fragmented. Standing guard for hours on end at Kennedy's coffin in New York's St. Patrick's Cathedral as untold thousands of mourners filed slowly past. On board the funeral train as it made its agonizing way to Washington, the mood alternately despairing and brave. The funeral itself. The aftermath at the Kennedy house in McLean, Virginia—a macabre party. Ethel Kennedy, to whom I had become close, smiling through her grief and fury. The scores of famous faces.

There was no time for anyone connected with Bobby to indulge his or her agony, though. Within weeks of his murder, the 1968 Democratic Convention was gaveled to order in Chicago. I had become a New York delegate, and Elie, then nineteen and a politically active student at Brown University, had been appointed a page. We both went to Chicago to discover chaos in the streets and a Humphrey bandwagon in the convention hall. When it was all over, Humphrey was the candidate, and the surviving Kennedy forces, including me, swung their support to him in the coming campaign against Nixon.

Unfortunately, Nixon won by the slimmest of margins. This was due, I believe, to the fact that the large Kennedy element of the Democratic Party could not muster much enthusiasm for Humphrey, despite its nominal support of him. The Kennedyites, their political vigor sapped by Bobby's murder, their emotions drained, were simply unable to demonstrate to the electorate that Humphrey's election was imperative. Of course, Humphrey, stigmatized by his close involvement in the Johnson administration, and basing his campaign on stale liberal platitudes, did little to help his own cause.

Once again, the assassination of a Kennedy brought about another long-term disaster for the country. In this case, it enabled Richard Nixon to gain the Presidency, thereby producing a vast escalation of the war in Vietnam, the national shame of Watergate, and the further ugly polarization of the nation. It is sad to contemplate the number of young American lives that were lost or ruined, both at home and abroad, solely because of the irrational conduct of Nixon and his cohorts between 1969 and 1974.

I think it's fair to say that I was not among those in the Kennedy branch of the party who failed to get behind Humphrey during the 1968 presidential race. Beyond the emotional trauma of

121

Bobby's death, many longtime Kennedy loyalists felt that by supporting Humphrey, they would be betraying their slain leader's memory. Although I had been closely attached to Bobby, our relationship had spanned little more than a year, whereas many others' went back two decades or more with him. Thus, when I was asked to become treasurer of the New York State Democratic Party, I had no qualms about accepting the position.

The New York branch of the party was solidly behind Humphrey in 1968, as well as the local candidates for congress and important state offices. My new status as the party's treasurer brought me into the mainstream of political fundraising, and I found myself traveling endlessly throughout the state—giving speeches, meeting local and regional party leaders, and raising money out of rank-and-file Democrats. It was almost as if I was a candidate myself, and I found the experience immensely satisfying.

The fact that I spoke English with a heavy Jewish accent, rather than being a hindrance, worked in my favor. Since I'd come to the United States, I had always tried to offset the handicap of my accent with humor. In 1968, I found that humor was a fundraiser's most valuable weapon. Indeed, it was a politician's most valuable weapon—as John Kennedy had so amply demonstrated during his Presidency.

But my humor was not the patrician, ironic wit of a J.F.K. It was earthy and blunt, often anecdotal, frequently Biblical. I found that I could go into a political meeting in upstate Buffalo or Rochester and make people smile while they parted with their money. I could achieve the same results among farmers in a rural grange hall, many of whom had never encountered a Jew before, much less a Polish-Israeli Jew.

I don't believe I'm being immodest when I say that I was one of the most energetic and effective fundraisers the New York State Democratic Party ever had. And to be candid about it, my success in that role got me to thinking that I should eventually become a candidate for office myself. In a sense, the treasurer of any political party is the party's key functionary, the pivotal figure around whom the party succeeds or fails in every election. He not only plays a vital role in bringing in much-needed money but also has considerable say in how the money is spent. If I was able to persuade tens of thousands of New Yorkers to donate significant sums to the party, despite my accent and often freewheeling personal style of relating to people, why couldn't I use those talents to persuade them to support me if I ran for public office?

I'd found that it was not my accent that people ultimately judged. Once they were able to get beyond the novelty of my accent, they began to listen to what I had to say, and many responded positively to that.

What I had to say, basically, was a repeat of my erstwhile theme: that government had become too complex to be left to the politicians of this world. Politicians had done a very complete job of turning government on every level in America into labyrinthine bureaucracy. But having done so, they had proved in the process that they could not efficiently or effectively manage it. Instead, in the guise of managing it, they were simply exacerbating its inefficiency and fiscal wastefulness, not to mention its demoralizing effects on the average citizen. By seeking to please everyone, politicians pleased no one.

America was celebrated the world over for its industrial and technological sophistication and for the creative, dynamic business and management techniques that had produced that sophistication. What the United States needed now, especially on the state and local government levels, were experienced businessmen to enter politics and sort out, streamline, and make more efficient the bureaucratic messes created by generations of politicians.

The trouble with my idea was that most businessmen, no matter how talented they were at organization and management, were singularly lacking in the personal charm, charisma, and (if you'll forgive the crudity) bullshit that American voters seemed to require from their political candidates.

I continued to sound that dilemma-ridden theme throughout 1969, as I became more well-known in my role as treasurer of the New York State Democratic Party, as well as a member of the national Electoral College. It wasn't until the end of that year, though, that I began to think of myself as an appropriate example of what I was preaching—that is, that I should lead the way and become a candidate for public office. And even then, the idea was not one that sprang full-blown from my own mind. Rather, it was urged on me.

The occasion was my fiftieth birthday party in December of 1969. What had originally been planned as a relatively modest gathering for friends at my golf club near Great Neck soon turned into a much larger affair, one that had the overtones of a political rally. Once they heard about the party, many among the Kennedy brain trust requested invitations, as did countless other Democratic public officials on the city, state, and national levels. Suddenly, I was the subject of all sorts of testimonials. For instance, Theodore (Ted) Sorensen, one of John F. Kennedy's chief White House aides in the early '60s, and later a key adviser in Bobby's presidential campaign, recited the following self-authored poem:

THE SAGA OF HONEST ABE

Fifty years ago this week
In a part of the world then dark and bleak
The Hirschfelds hailed their new-born babe;
He looked so honest they named him Abe.

Young Abe was brilliant as a boy,
He got better marks than any goy;
He became a man, both wise and witty,
And made a pile of money right here in Fun City.

And now at fifty years of age,
He's a well-known businessman, philanthropist, sage;
A fabulous lover, an exuberant liver,
And he's known above all as a generous giver.

He contributes to Democrats at every layer
He even supported Mario for Mayor;
He donates so much to every cause
He's known as the Jewish Santa Claus.

To help the Israelis fighting Nasser
He's bought more of their bonds than all of Hadassah;
If he cashed them all in for a capital gain
They'd have to mortgage Golda to King Hussein.

Rejecting political labels pat,
He's a regular reform liberal Democrat;
And he perceives the voters as a whole
Considerably better that the Daily News Poll.

Today his friends are gathered here
To drink a cup of birthday cheer,
To honor Abe Hirschfeld's years of fame
And wish him fifty more of the same.

It was a memorable event. And it was nice to know that I, a political nobody two years earlier, had become the object of so many important people's affections. But what made the affair more memorable than anything else was when several of the celebrated political guests got me in a corner and urged me to think about running for office myself.

"Abe, you've talked a lot about the need for talented businessmen to get into the political process," said one. "Don't you think it's time you showed the way?"

"Me?" I said. "Who'd vote for me with this accent?"

"Wrong," answered another. "People vote for who they trust and feel comfortable with. We've watched you operate. We've seen how effectively you bring people into your personal orbit, despite your accent. Or maybe it's because of it. The next time I run, I'm thinking of putting on an accent like yours. It appeals to the underdog and outsider instincts in people. The way you talk, people sense they're not getting any fancy political rhetoric. They know that what they're hearing from you means exactly what you're saying. They see that you don't have the craftiness in English to trick them with words. You may not be precise in the way you talk. But you're direct."

Thus, the idea was planted, although for the next couple of years I continued to view it as far-fetched. Not because I didn't think I could be effective in public office but because, despite my friend's assurances, I felt that my accent and my grammatical deficits when speaking English would still be too much of a liability. I could only imagine some immigrant from America running for office in Israel and speaking Hebrew as poorly as I spoke English. No matter how well meaning he was, he would be laughed off the campaign trail.

As the 1970s dawned, more and more of my friends urged me to run for political office. I still wasn't sure. In my two years of intimate association with the Kennedy branch of the national Democratic Party, and through my continuing stint as treasurer of the New York State Democrats, I had learned first-hand how the American political system worked. Most successful candidates for office had to spend years working their way up the political ladder, acquiring both a name and a "power base" within their party and among other people. Although I had become well-known to the Democratic political establishment in New York via my work as the party's treasurer, I was virtually unknown to the voting public. To make a serious run for office, whether on the city, state, or federal level, I knew I would have to gain a lot more public visibility before I could put together a viable statewide organization.

The question was: Would the effort be worth it? My instinct was to answer it in the negative. But then there occurred a series of events that effectively countermanded my instincts.

The first had to do with what I perceived to be the gap between the lofty progressive ideals espoused by leaders and spokesmen of the New York Democratic Party and the reality of their personal practices. For example, in the early '70s, I bought an apartment building on West 79th Street, the geographical center of Manhattan's upper West Side. The building was inhabited mostly by people who were political liberals, and among them were several notable Democratic Party figures. When I co-oped the building a short while later, most of those tenants were happy to be able to buy their apartments at cheap "insider" prices.

But then came the trouble. I had a few apartments left over—apartments that were not going to be purchased by tenants and which I was able to offer to "outsiders." Among the outsiders who wished to buy was a black family. Without thinking twice about it, I agreed to sell the desired apartment to the family.

Within days, the news was all over the building. Soon after, I received a letter from a committee of tenants protesting my "decision to allow" blacks into the building. I was astounded, not only because I had no personal prejudices against blacks, but more so because the letter arrived with the signatures of several tenants who were active in the Democratic Party and enjoyed reputations as progressive liberals and public advocates of full civil rights for blacks and other minorities in America.

Such hypocrisy! I thought. I said as much to them. Indeed, I warned them that if they refused to accept the black family, who would be buying their apartment at the outsider, or open-market, price, I would withdraw my offer to sell to them at the well-below-market insider prices and charge them outsider prices as well.

That took care of that. They withdrew their protest, albeit solely because of economic coercion. But the entire incident got me to thinking seriously about the difference between word and deed among so-called Democratic luminaries in New York. Compounding my anger was the fact that in addition to being self-proclaimed liberals, most of the objectors were Jewish.

Another example pertained to the movement for equal rights for women, which was reaching its zenith in the New York of the early 1970s. A group of "progressive" women, led by Sarah Kovner—the wife of Victor Kovner, a well-known liberal lawyer—had received a charter to start a "woman's bank" in the city, a bank to be run primarily by and for women. The group was having difficulty completing its financing, despite the reams of favorable publicity it had received, and it desperately needed a final $150,000 to meet its required capitalization.

Because I'd spoken out many times in the previous few years in favor of the women's equality cause, Sarah Kovner came to me and asked that I put up the remaining $150,000 in the form of a stock purchase. Zipora tried to discourage me, suggesting that Kovner and her associates were biting off more than they could chew, that although they were competent political women, they knew next to nothing about the banking business.

I acknowledged the probable accuracy of Zipora's assessment, but I thought that the experiment—for that's what it was at the time—deserved support. Accordingly, I agreed to buy $100,000 in stock and persuaded a business colleague, Eric Spector, to take the remaining $50,000. My purchase made me the largest individual stockholder in the Women's Bank Corporation and entitled me to a seat on the board of directors. I figured that from this vantage point, I would be well positioned to advise Sarah Kovner and her team of female executives in getting the bank actually started. My impression was that Kovner and the others would welcome my input.

At first, they did. The initial problem was getting the bank located and opened. They had arranged to lease street-level quarters on Manhattan's East 57th Street at Park Avenue, one of the city's choicest business and residential crossroads. A great deal of architectural construction and contracting work had to be done to convert the quarters into a proper commercial banking facility. When I joined the board, I found that Kovner and her group were up to their knees in construction plans and proposals, the technical and financial details of which they barely comprehended. What they had in mind was, physically, more of a boutique than a bank.

I explained that they were going about it all wrong. Not only would the building plans they'd settled on take an inordinate amount of time to complete, as well as be ultra-expensive, but they would also create an atmosphere inconducive to serious banking. A bank for women was one thing. A bank for women that gave the appearance of being a frivolous female enterprise was another. Once the novelty wore off, I said, it would not be taken seriously, either by customers or by the financial community.

They heeded my advice and asked me to take charge of getting the physical plant completed and ready for opening. I did so—in half the time it would have taken otherwise, and at half the expense. But my success in that endeavor evidently sowed seeds of resentment in the minds of Kovner and her management colleagues. In a sense, I inadvertently reminded them that they were amateurs dabbling in a world of professionals, and they didn't like that. Thereafter, once the bank opened, they did everything they could to shut me out of any discussions about how best to run it—on the grounds, again, that it was designed to be a bank by women, for women.

As a consequence, they made many operational and planning mistakes. Instead of managing it like a business, they ran it more in the spirit of a coffee klatsch. Thus, instead of growing and expanding and thriving in the fashion it could have, the bank stumbled along, tripping over its management errors, getting caught up in interpersonal female politics, and barely surviving.

The experience was disillusioning for me only because Sarah Kovner and her colleagues represented themselves as examples of "the new woman" who could compete with men on their own terms. I wanted very much to see The Women's Bank succeed handsomely just to prove that assertion. That it didn't was evidence to me that these new women were fooling themselves. To be sure, they could mount and run a business that catered almost exclusively to women, but that was not unusual; thousands of other women had done so successfully before. The point was that banks in general, presumably run by men, did not limit their appeal or clientele to one sex. If the Kovners of the women's equality world were really to prove that they could compete with and even do better than men, they would have to test themselves in the broadest possible market place. Sarah Kovner and her friends didn't take up that challenge. In a way, their claims remained hollow.

There was also my longstanding exasperation over the wildly expanding bureaucracy and red tape of government. I simply began to believe that the average New York citizen, male and female, deserved better political representation than he or she was getting. And a lot of people convinced me that because of my ability in business to get things done simply and quickly despite the manifold obstacles placed in my way, I could have the same success in government. Notwithstanding my foreign origins, my accent, and my linguistic eccentricities.

But it was not until 1973 that I became finally convinced that I must put myself forward as an independent political voice. That year was a fateful and pivotal one, not just in my life but also in the life of the United States—indeed, in the life of the Free World. It brought with it the ugly revelations about Watergate and the Nixon administration. It brought the start of the catastrophic conclusion of the Vietnam War. It brought the fourth major war between Israel and its Arab neighbors and Nixon's ominous hesitation in sending the Israelis promised material assistance. Perhaps worst of all, it brought the first organized Arab oil boycott against the West and the economic recession and hyperinflation that would soon ensue throughout the industrialized world.

Inflation had already become a trend in the early stages of the Nixon administration. I had long worried about it getting out of hand, for those who would be hurt most by it would be the low-income classes. I had witnessed the dispiriting effects of the inflation that perennially afflicted Israel, and I could see only disaster ahead for great masses of people in the United States if something wasn't done by the government to reverse the trend. Now, with the Arab oil boycott, it was certain to become epidemic. The Nixonians, caught up in the Watergate nightmare, paid scant attention to the problem. Nor did Congress, which was also transfixed by Watergate.

I started to speak out in warning. Some people didn't believe me. Or they questioned my motives. "Abe," they said, "how can you complain about inflation when you're in the real estate business? If the inflation you talk about comes, it'll mean a tremendous increase in the value of your properties. A building you bought for a million will be worth ten million. You'll make a killing. So, what are you bitching about? Who loves a big profit better than you do?"

"Such a myopic view," I explained. I wasn't a trained economist, but I knew this much from experience. If an inflationary price-spiral were allowed to set in, people would find their income buying less and less. That would bring about a sharp reduction in the demand for consumer goods and services, which in turn would produce a much lower level of industrial output. The result of that would be economic recession and rising unemployment to go along with soaring prices. And the effect of that would be a greater reliance on borrowing, both public and private, which would send interest notes on an upward climb and eventually squeeze the average American out of all but the most elementary consumer marketplace.

"Sure," I said, "maybe my buildings will triple in value. But so will the cost of operating them. And who'll be left to rent or buy apartments in them? No thanks," I added. "I'd be very happy to do without inflation."

Of course, although my scenario turned out to be accurate, many of the dire predictions I drew from it would prove to be wrong. Throughout the later 1970s and into the '80s, the country would go through its worst recession-inflation cycle since the Great Depression. The value of real estate in New York, including my own, would indeed balloon upward, and my business and personal fortune would rise by leaps and bounds.

Yet, that did not belie the fact that many, many Americans were severely hurt by the chain of economic events and that a whole new economic order was created, which concentrated the nation's wealth in fewer and fewer hands and reduced the financial expectations of the vast majority of citizens.

Among those I spoke to about my concern over the then creeping inflation were New York's two senators in Washington— Jacob "Jack" Javits and James Buckley. Javits, a liberal Republican and a Jew, had been in the senate for eighteen years. We were friendly, largely because he had long been one of the government's most avid supporters of Israel and frequently appeared as a speaker at various fundraising events for Israel in which I was involved.

But in 1973, there was a "downside" to Javits, who was nearly seventy. He possessed an almost overwhelming pride in his position as the senior Senator from New York. He faced re-election without difficulty. But circumstances for any Republican were far from ordinary in the 1973–74 period. In the public mind, all Republicans had been tarred by the brush of the Nixon administration's Watergate sins. Javits had compounded his own problem by failing to disassociate himself from Nixon once it became clear that the much-reviled President was a goner.

It was in this context that I tried to alert Javits to my concerns about inflation and other probable consequences of the 1973 Arab-Israeli War. I found him totally oblivious to the problem. He was interested only in his own problem of getting re-elected in 1974 despite the onus of being a Republican in a state that had become vehemently anti-Nixon.

Suddenly, Jack Javits, who I liked, seemed to be in danger of losing his seat in the senate. As treasurer of the New York State Democratic Committee, I was well aware of those among the state's Democratic politicians who were gearing up to run against him. Probably the foremost name was Allard Lowenstein, an extremely liberal member of the House of Representatives from Long Island who had been a close adviser to Bobby Kennedy during his 1968 campaign for the Presidency. Another potential contender was Ramsey Clark, the son of the one-time Supreme Court Chief Justice Tom Clark and a man who, after serving as Attorney General in the Johnson administration, had become an outspoken anti-Vietnam War activist and had made several visits to North Vietnam to demonstrate his sympathy for the communists.

I knew Lowenstein well and liked him very much personally, but I thought that since Bobby Kennedy's death, he had become too left-leaning in his political agenda. I hardly knew Clark at all, but there was no doubt that he was even more to the left than Lowenstein. Despite Javits's precarious position, I did not view either Lowenstein or Clark as a serious threat to him, since the great majority of

131

Democratic voters in New York were moderate liberals and would not be inclined to support candidates with such radical backgrounds.

Nor would they receive enthusiastic support from the state's Democratic Committee, which was chaired by Joseph Crangle of upstate Buffalo and dominated by downstate county leaders who, for the most part, were middle-of-the-roaders. This was important, for the candidate who ultimately faced Javits in November would have to win a September Democratic primary election. There were only two ways to get one's name on the primary ballot. The first was to receive the endorsement of the Democratic Committee at its convention. The second was to file a petition containing the signatures of 20,000 registered Democrats.

Here's how I saw the prospects at the start of 1974. Javits would run for re-election on the Republican ticket. If he was faced in November by Lowenstein or Clark, he would probably win, notwithstanding his advanced age and Republican identity. That would not be good, since Javits, if returned to the senate, would largely be ineffective in dealing with the severe economic problems that lay ahead. He remained eminently beatable, but only if the Democrats came up with a more likely candidate than Lowenstein or Clark.

The only more likely candidate most Democratic Committee leaders could think of was a woman. That was solely because they believed that the novelty of running a woman against Javits, given the spreading influence of the women's movement, would give the Democratic Party in the state greater credibility with the female vote. No one believed that a woman could actually defeat Javits, however. So, the two women who were sounded out on the prospect—Mary Anne Krupsak and Bess Myerson—declined the invitation to become candidates, claiming that they would be served up as sacrificial lambs.

At the start of 1974, then, although it was widely agreed that Javits was extremely vulnerable to defeat in the November general election, the New York Democrats had no one with whom they could realistically hope to oust him. Other possible candidates were Hugh Carey and Ogden Reid, each a congressman. But they had decided to fight it out for that year's state Democratic gubernatorial nomination.

A frustrating political vacuum therefore remained. Javits could be beaten, but the Democratic Party had as yet found no one who could do the job. It was then that I decided to step into the breach. Although I realized that the possibility of my succeeding was remote, I had surmounted greater and more improbable obstacles in my life. Thus, I resolved to run for the senate seat held by Jack Javits.

Abraham (Abe) Hirschfeld

CHAPTER SIXTEEN: MAVERICK

I immediately discovered that although I was highly appreciated as the chief fundraiser and a heavy personal contributor to the Democrat Party, I would get little party support in a contest for the senate nomination. "Abe," more than one party leader said, "you're unknown; you don't have a chance. Stay and be treasurer; you'll serve us much better that way."

"No," I answered. "Maybe you're right, maybe I don't have a chance. But neither does Lowenstein or Clark, or anyone else you've mentioned, have a chance to beat Javits. Why should I raise money for a lost cause like them when I can raise it for a lost cause like myself? The majority of the voters of this state want Javits out—they can see he's old and tired and hanging in with Nixon. But you're not giving them a realistic alternative with left-wingers like Lowenstein and Clark, or some token woman candidate. At least if I run and get the nomination, I'll be a realistic alternative. I'll be seen as a younger, more vigorous version of Jack Javits, not some wild-eyed radical."

What I didn't say was that after five years in the highest echelons of the party, I was sick and tired of the way its internal politics and finances were handled. I had been drawn into the party by my admiration for Bobby Kennedy and had accepted the treasurer's job in the hopes of keeping alive the youthful reformist movement he had started. Five years later, though, that movement was dead, killed by a combination of disenchantment over Bobby's murder, apathy, and the resurgence of the party's big-city clubhouse powerbrokers.

During my tenure as treasurer, I had not exactly endeared myself to those characters, even though I had wiped out the party's perennial deficits. So, I was not surprised by their indifference to my senatorial aspirations once they realized I was serious. Nevertheless, I was not quite prepared for the concerted vehemence of their objections when I formally announced my candidacy in March 1974. Of all the regular party organization leaders, only Mathew "Matty" Troy, the Queens Country chairman, initially encouraged me. To the rest of the party hierarchy, I became a "maverick Democratic," a "rogue candidate," a "spoiler." For all practical purposes, I was "excommunicated" from the party. Although still nominally a Democrat, I was on my own in the run for the Democratic senatorial nomination.

I can honestly say that that disturbed me not at all. I had plenty of money to run without party funds—and plenty of moral support from the New York business community. So what if I didn't win? At least I would bring to the public's attention an issue that none of the other candidates seemed willing to tackle.

The issue, again, was inflation, recession, and rising interest rates. With New York City on the verge of bankruptcy as a result of the fiscal ineptitude of the consecutive mayoral administration of Robert Wagner and John Lindsay in the 1960s and early 1970s, New Yorkers needed to be told where they stood. And with the inflation effects of the Arab oil boycott beginning to take hold, Americans in general needed to be appraised of the future economic consequences—consequences that would bite them directly in their pocketbooks. Since New York and America had provided me with so much in the way of business opportunity and personal good fortune, I genuinely felt—as corny as it may sound—that I owed them something in return. The expenditure of two or three million dollars to bring my message to the people seemed a small price to pay.

But it was not just me who owed; my entire family was in America and New York's debt. So, my campaign became a family affair.

Essentially a reserved woman in public, Zipora pitched in with great enthusiasm and became a valuable asset. Elie, who at twenty-four had recently graduated with high honors from the New York University Law School and had joined the prestigious Wall Street law firm of Milbank, Tweed, Hadley & McCoy, became my campaign manager.

In contrast to me, and very much in the spirit of his mother, Elie had developed into a young man who could handle the myriad details of any complex and difficult transaction with cool efficiency and aplomb. There was no more complex and difficult transaction in life than a month-long, statewide political campaign, especially when the candidate had no formal, experienced organization and was actually disapproved of by most of his party's hierarchy. In the face of great obstacles, and despite his relative inexperience, Elie performed superbly.

So did Rachel, in her own way. Having "found" herself, Rachel had graduated from the leading school for chefs in Paris and was working long, arduous hours in a top French restaurant in New

York to complete her practical training. She planned eventually to open her own dining establishment and to start a culinary career as a food and restaurant consultant. She had also remarried and given birth to the first of our grandchildren. Yet, despite her grueling work schedule, she happily pitched in.

I opened my Manhattan campaign headquarters on April 17, 1974 with a press conference in which I sounded my main theme. I warned of the coming of a high inflation recessionary period in the United States and announced that, if elected, my first order of business would be to introduce federal legislation placing a six percent ceiling on the interest banks and other lending institutions could charge on loans.

My reason was simple. The only effective way government could control a nation's economy was by maintaining a cap on interest rates. All the other monetary theories, experiments, and tinkering of professional economics that had been tried in the past, and were being tried in 1974, had not only proved ineffective but had often exacerbated economic instability. On the other hand, history clearly demonstrated that every nation's economic health and prosperity was contingent upon low interest rates. In other words, when interest was low, economics thrived; when interest soared, they stagnated and crumbled.

Naturally, my proposal was questioned as being simplistic. I answered in my usual way, which was to distinguish between the simple and the simplistic. That which was simple was fundamental and direct—the Ten Commandments were simple. The simplistic, on the other hand, was native and circuitous.

"Do you like the bureaucracy of New York?" I asked one of the reporters at my press conference.

He admitted he didn't.

"Do you think it's necessary?"

Some of it probably was, he answered, but certainly not most of it.

"Would you call this bureaucratic labyrinth we all live under simple?" I went on.

"Of course not," he said. "It's the epitome of complexity."

"Aha," I shot back. "Then you are saying that complexity is the opposite of simple."

He nodded.

"But you've also distinguished between simplistic and simple. You've implied that simplistic is also the opposite of simple."

"Yes," he agreed.

"So then," I said, "something that's overly simplistic and something that's needlessly complex amounts to the same thing. They are both the opposite of the simple—of the plain, the direct, the fundamental."

"You could say that," the reporter responded.

"If you can say that, can you also say my plan for a government cap on interest rates is a complex plan? Can you claim that a plain, one-sentence law that says no loan in America may exceed six percent in interest is a complex law?"

"No."

"Well, then," I could concluded, "if it is not complex, how can you claim it's simplistic when you agree that the complex and the simplistic are more or less the same thing?"

That type of Socratic dialogue would become a hallmark of my campaign style as time went on. I found that in modern politics, the press conference, along with television and newspaper advertising, are the main channel of a candidate's communication with the public. Yet, I was astounded to find also that reporters and journalists are just as susceptible to swallowing unexamined and untested assumptions as anyone else. They distrust the simple, the direct, and the fundamental as being out of place in the "ultra-complex" world in which we live. Although they enjoy invoking the maxim that those who ignore history are bound to repeat its mistake, they merrily continue to do just that—ignore history. And what history teaches us is that the worst mistake of civilization occurred when they abandoned the simple for the simplistic and complex.

If modern journalists had been around to cover Moses' descent from the mount with the Ten Commandments, their first question would have been, "Moses, wouldn't you say these commandments are rather simplistic for the troubled times of today?" Of course, those "simplistic" ethical prescriptions have remained for five thousand years the rock-ribbed basis of Judeo-Christian-Islamic moral law, as well as of the statutory civil and criminal law of every advanced nation.

During my campaign, then, I made no apologies for my formulation of "simple solutions" to "complex problems." My whole career had been based on simple, common sense approaches to unraveling the sticky, complicated problems others had created. American government on every level—federal, state, and local—had become mired in a swampy, stagnant morass. The mindset of the political community was that complex problems required even more complex solutions. But history was proving that the more things changed in that fashion, the more they remained the same—only worse. "Catch 22" was no longer just a humorous concept. It was a cruel reality.

My senatorial campaign, alas, ran along two separate tracks from the start. The first track was the smooth one, the one that put me directly in touch with the people of New York State via my campaign trail appearance, speeches, and press conferences. Partly because of my label as a self-financed maverick, partly because of my accent and sometimes fractured English, and partly because of my irreverent common sense dialogues with journalists, I found myself becoming popular with the press. To use the journalistic phrase, I made "good copy," which is to say I was an entertaining candidate as compared to the earnest, humorless Ramsey Clark and the intellectually remote Allard Lowenstein.

I didn't kid myself, though. "Good copy" often translated into nothing more than opportunities for journalists to present me as a less than serious contender, as a rich man who was on an ego trip. Frequently, my dead-serious message about the damaging inflation and recession I saw ahead was obscured by journalists who used me to exercise their own egos, literary and otherwise.

But it was in my direct contact with voters that I found the real response I was looking for. This was especially true in the upstate urban and rural regions, as well as in the Jewish districts in and around New York City. In the latter, I could speak in Yiddish or Hebrew and make sense. Upstate, my style was different.

In Albany, I was already somewhat known. A few years earlier, I had rescued the Kennedy family again by buying a pair of failing buildings they'd owned on State Street, the capital's faded, main downtown thoroughfare, and turning them into a profitable combination parking garage and office complex. That conversion had been the first step in the revival of State Street, and in 1972, I had been given a Man-of-the-Year award by the Albany Chamber of Commerce. As a consequence, when I campaigned in and around the

Capital District in the spring of 1974, I was listened to with interest and respect.

Beyond Albany, though, were western and northern New York—collectively, in the eyes of many, almost a separate state unto itself and much less cosmopolitan in its values than the "downstate" precincts, where I encountered my most enthusiastic receptions. My earthy, shirtsleeve, plain-speaking style struck a responsive chord among many of the natives. Despite the forgiving nature of my persona, I could talk to farmers knowledgeably about tractor hitches and dairy prices, citing my own experience as an orchard tender and the son of a woman who had once sold farm produce from a donkey's back.

Similarly, in big cities like Syracuse and Rochester, I could talk in terms of my New York urban experience as a developer. And in Buffalo, which had a large Polish population, I could speak about my boyhood in the foothills of the Carpathians.

I found myself less an alien to voters upstate than to those in New York City and its environs. As one resident of the Finger Lakes area was quoted as saying in a Syracuse newspaper, "That Hirschfeld fella is my kind of people. He walks and talks like a man who cares. He's got my vote, for sure."

The campaign's more bumpy second track traveled through backstage corridors of the Democratic Party's organization hierarchy. Ironically, the root of my difficulties lay precisely in my success in convincing much of the party leadership that neither Lowenstein nor Clark, nor any of the state's foremost female politicians, was capable of beating Javits—that many Democrat voters would cross over to Javits rather than cast their ballot for such a radically òriented candidate, or they wouldn't vote at all. What was needed, I repeated, was a candidate who would reassure rather than frighten the vast, middle-of-the-road Democratic constituency of the state.

The leadership bought my argument, but then, instead of considering me as an appropriate alternative, proceeded to look around for someone else to fill the bill. That in itself did not bother me, for I was well aware that most party leaders thought that my accent and difficulties with the language were as much a liability as Lowenstein and Clark's histories of radicalism.

What bothered me was that the majority of the leadership claimed that Lowenstein and I were not suitable candidates because

140

we were Jews. It was decided that since Javits was a Jew, the only way to beat him would be to run a non-Jew against him. Accordingly, as the time for the June Democratic nomination convention approached, the leadership began to cast around for a non-Jew, male notable to put on the ticket.

The man the party came up with was Lee Alexander, the bland, journeyman mayor of Syracuse. Although I had nothing against Alexander personally, I was thoroughly disgusted by the leadership's racially motivated rationale for choosing him and became more determined that ever to contest him.

Sure enough, at the Democratic convention in Niagara Falls on June 15, the party nominated Alexander by an overwhelming majority, but they also gave Allard Lowenstein barely enough votes to put him in the September 10 primary runoff. Ramsey Clark and I, the only other two contestants, were roundly rejected.

The result did nothing to extinguish the flames of my desire to get onto the primary ballots; if anything, it fanned them. The only path left to me was to file a nominating petition signed by 20,000 registered Democrats—a device created by the state's election laws, but one that was costly, time-consuming, and bureaucratically exacting. Notwithstanding those hindrances, I set out to acquire the needed petition, as did Ramsey Clark, on his own account.

While busy campaigning for signatures late in June, I received a disturbing phone call from Allard Lowenstein. Although he had narrowly made the primary ballot as a result of the Niagara Falls convention, he told me that he was now being pressured by the party leadership to withdraw because of his Jewishness. He was getting ready to do so, he said, not for that reason but because his campaign funds were drying up.

I was livid. I told him that he could not give in to such pressure and offered him a campaign contribution of $10,000 to stay in the race. I added that I would make an identical donation to Ramsey Clark—to show that I was not playing favorites but was interested only in helping to ensure an open primary in September. My offer, made in the spirit of democratic principals, would soon come back to haunt me.

Clark accepted my contribution, but Lowenstein declined it on the grounds that he could not take money from an opponent, even though it was entirely legal to do so. A few days later, much to my dismay, he publicly announced that he was dropping out of the race and withdrawing his name from the September primary slate. He admitted that he was doing so largely because of the pressure that had been put on him with respect to the "Jewish issue." Shortly after, he said he would redirect his energies to running for a seat in the House of Representatives from his home district in Long Island's Nassau Country.

It was in that latter announcement that things began to get sticky for me. On July 15, I was able to file my 20,000-name nominating petition. Thus, the party had a Jew in the September primary after all, despite Lowenstein's withdrawal. Several party leaders urged me to drop out now that I'd made my point that a citizen could get on the ballot without being supported by the party machine.

I said, "No way, I'm in the election to stay."

What they were afraid of was that most voters who would have gone for Lowenstein would vote for me in September, especially if Lowenstein personally endorsed me. Clark had also filed a petition, and between us, we were likely to amass enough votes to take the primary away from Alexander, the party establishment's candidate.

The leaders threatened retribution, and it was not long in coming. They leaked word to the press of my offer of a $10,000 contribution to Lowenstein, claming that I had made the offer as a bribe to remove him from the primary. Lowenstein denied it. I denied it, responding that the truth was just the opposite, that I had been trying to help him stay in the race, especially since he'd conceded that his withdrawal was the result of the pressure he'd received over the matter of him being Jewish.

As usual, in such a case, the initial journalistic slur got much more attention than the replies of those who were slurred. Suddenly, my name was tarnished by the suggestion of bribery. I simply vowed to fight harder. And when the party leadership saw that I was not about to fold under such intimidation, it raised the ante.

Early in July, shortly before he announced that he was going to run for the House of Representatives, Lowenstein had phoned and asked for my support. He'd also said that since he was no longer opposing me in the senate primary, he'd have no ethical difficulties accepting a campaign contribution. Without thinking much about it, and since there was no law against a candidate for one office contributing to the campaign of a candidate for another, I sent a check for $5,000. I made it clear to him that I expected nothing in return for the money. If he wanted to endorse me in the senate primary, fine, but such an endorsement was not the purpose of my contribution. He concurred.

Soon, the Democratic leadership learned of my Lowenstein contribution. Anonymous "sources" within the leadership again leaked the story to the newspaper. In the process, my $5,000 contribution became a $50,000 one, and the charge that was made was that it was both a payoff for Lowenstein's withdrawal from the senate primary and a bribe for his endorsement of me.

To make a long story short, the entire matter was investigated by the New York State Board of Elections, and at the end of August, I was exonerated of any wrongdoing. Indeed, the board castigated those who had brought the charges against me for making "spurious claims of misconduct" solely to muddy my name with the electorate.

By then, it was too late. In the interim, Nixon had resigned as President and been succeeded by Gerald Ford. Ford had "pardoned" Nixon and named Nelson Rockefeller to be his Vice President. Except for voters' outrage in New York over those events, which Ramsey Clark was best able to exploit, political apathy set in the race. No one wanted to hear about economic problems, only about the Nixon-Ford-Rockefeller machinations in Washington. Although I struggled hard to revive my campaign in the wake of my exoneration, and I received endorsements from thirteen upstate Democratic county leaders, I could tell as September 10 approached that my chances were fading.

The September 10 primary confirmed that. In one of the smallest Democratic turnouts in history, Ramsey Clark was elected to run against Javits in November. No doubt, Clark's victory was a cynical voter reaction to the smarmy events in Washington. I drew 25 percent of the votes, but it was not nearly enough. Alexander, the bumbling machine candidate, was an even greater disaster.

As I'd predicted, though, the still intrepidly left-wing Clark was no match for Javits in November. Despite a Democratic sweep of many other key federal and state offices in the general election, including Hugh Carey's victory in the gubernatorial contest, Javits easily turned back Clark and was returned to the senate for another six years. There, resting on his aging laurels, he would do next to nothing to try to stem the nation's soaring inflation and deepening recession.

For me, the experience of running was at once exhilarating and disillusioning. The exhilaration came from my contact with the people and the positive responses I often got. The disillusionment came not from the fact that I'd lost but from my direct experience of the petty veniality and skullduggery of machine politics in New York and of the unwillingness—indeed, the inability—of the powers that be to confront the central domestic problem of the society they imagined themselves to represent and govern.

I had run on a clear-cut economic platform that offered incredible methods by which an increasingly unstable national economy could be stabilized. While Gerald Ford in Washington had began passing out inane WIN ("Whip Inflation Now") buttons, I had advanced hard, detailed solutions to the problem of inflation. I discovered that many American people, or at least many people in New York, were more interested in empty slogans than well thought out solutions.

However, as always, I was an optimist. My time, I was sure, would come. I immediately began to think about 1976, when the other New York seat in the United States Senate would come up for grabs. Ironically, it was the seat that Bobby Kennedy had left to seek the Presidency in 1968.

CHAPTER SEVENTEEN: MEETING ARAFAT

If my 1974 race for the senate had branded me as a maverick in the minds of the New York press and political establishment, what happened next would only etch the brand deeper and make it more permanent.

That was all right with me. The world, the country, the state, and the city were beset by profound political and economic problems in the mid-1970s. Conventional approaches had done nothing to ease any of them. Creative and responsibly unconventional approaches were needed. As far as I was concerned, to be called a maverick was a badge of distinction and honor. The only trouble was that most people were so hidebound by convention in economics and politics that it was almost impossible to stir them out of their lethargy. That didn't stop me from continuing to try, however. One of the marks of the political maverick is that he never stops trying.

The event that sharpened my reputation as a maverick was the highly controversial visit of Yasser Arafat to the United Nations in the fall of 1974. The only other problem that concerned me as much as America's gathering economic storm was the never-ending crisis in the Middle East between Israel and the Arab nations. Now the two problems were umbilically linked, for the American economy was being directly damaged by the actions of the Arab oil nations in the wake of the 1973 Arab-Israeli War. My position was that if we were to solve our domestic troubles, we must first solve the Arab-Israeli situation, which had only been aggravated by the 1973 war.

I believed that I enjoyed a somewhat unique perspective in America toward the Arab-Israeli conflict. Unlike most American Jews, I was an Israeli—if not by birth, by upbringing. I had spent my formative years in Palestine and had been involved first-hand, on the scene, in the birth of Israel as a sovereign state. I knew the region's Arabs—now the self-styled "Palestinians"—much better than most American Jews did. I was also much more familiar with the cultural, social, and political processes of Israel, and I was on a first name basis with practically everyone in the Israeli establishment.

A distinctive phenomenon of the American Jewish community was the vicarious pleasure it took in the exploits of Israel. This was understandable, since Israel gave American Jews a much more powerful sense of identity, cohesion, and self-worth than they'd ever had before. It was enormously beneficial to Israel in that it produced tens of millions of dollars in private and public financial support.

But the phenomenon had its dark and regressive side, too. Almost every American Jew I met, whether by virtue of brief visits to the Middle East or simply as a result of what he or she heard at a hometown synagogue or United Jewish Appeal rally, considered themselves experts on Israel. Much of that "expertise" was laden with myth, misapprehension, and wishful thinking.

The saddest part of it was that most Jews in America seemed to get a special thrill whenever war broke out between Israel and the Arab nations and the Israelis performed in their usual efficient and winning style. This, too, was understandable, since each new Israeli victory reinforced Jewish self-esteem in the United States. But it also struck me as perverse, for the sustenance of the American Jews' passionate support of Israel seemed to depend in large part on the prospect of future wars. Very subtly, Jewish Americans' hyper-interest in Israel appeared to me to encourage the extension of enmity and armed hostility between Arab and Jews in the Middle East.

Arafat's reception by the UN in 1974 provided the Jewish community in the United States with all sorts of opportunities to vent their passions anew. To American Jews, Arafat was just another tinhorn Hitler; his Palestine Liberation Organization, just another crypto-Nazi terrorist movement.

In many respects, they were right, of course. But what most Americans failed to perceive were the realities of the Middle East and its post-World War II political evolution. I had grown up with the Yasser Arafat of Palestine. As a member of the Haganah, I had been a freedom fighter for the establishment of the Jewish nation. I had been involved with members of the Irgun, the 1940s version of Arafat's guerilla group, al-Fatah. I knew that in desperate situations, desperate men do desperate things, even Jews. I also knew that outrageous public deeds and words are often secret cries for negotiation and conciliation.

I didn't approve of Arafat, certainly. But I understood "where he was coming from," as the saying goes. When he traveled to New York in 1974 to give his pistol-olive branch speech to the UN, I decided it would be worthwhile to meet with him—if for no other reason than to test my theory that as a popular leader among his own disenfranchised people, he could be won over to a more moderate approach to a solution of the Palestinian problem.

For my troubles, not only was my label as a political maverick further seared into the public's mind, but I also became somewhat of a pariah among my own people in America for "talking to the enemy." I reminded them of Abraham Lincoln's old saying: "The quickest way to make an enemy a friend is to get to know him and let him get to know you."

As a Jew, and as a onetime Palestinian, I did not see Arafat and his Arab constituency as enemies anyway. We were brothers who'd become alienated by certain cruel twists of historical circumstance, who were squabbling over our respective rights to conjugal property. I thought I might be able to convince him of that.

I had already convinced a number of other, less well-known, Palestinian Arab leaders of it, particularly those within Israel. Indeed, during the previous several years I had formulated an Arab-Israeli reconciliation plan that had gained the approval of many indigenous Arabs and Jews in Israel who were seeking "peace, at last." In its simple (but not simplistic) outline, the plan read as follows:

We believe that the road to peace in the Middle East is by mutual recognition of the right of equality and coexistence. The Palestinians' right to return to their land must be recognized. The coexistence of the Palestinians and the Jews in Palestine is the only path to peace in the area.

We call upon the Israelis and world Jewry, and upon the people of Palestine and the Arab world, to overlook the mistakes and problems of the past and to direct their attention solely to the establishment of a peaceful Middle East of the future.

The basic problem in the Middle East at present is the lack of cooperation, discussion, and negotiations between the Israelis and the Palestinians. In order to bring harmony and peace between the Israelis and the Palestinians, Jews and Arabs alike, we propose the following:

All present residents of the State of Israel shall have the right to be full-scale citizens of the State.

Second, that all Palestinians throughout the world shall have the right of return as full-scale citizens. The Palestinians' return

147

should be gradual and over a period of three to five years. Details to be worked out.

Third, that all Jews throughout the world wishing to immigrate to the State of Israel shall have the right to do so and to become full-scale citizens.

Human needs and the ability of the State to absorb immigrants shall be the only ground for immigration policy.

Jews and Palestinians alike will have the right to live in the State of Israel as full-scale and co-equal citizens.

All laws of the State shall apply equally and non-discriminately, without specifying any preferences in regard to religious sects or groups.

All citizens residing in the State shall have equal rights in voting and representation in the new government; every citizen shall be free to practice his religion and belong to associations of his choice.

The plan had been endorsed by several notable Palestinians, among them Dr. Mohammed Mehdi, the Secretary General of the Action Committee on Arab-American Relations, which was an Arab political-lobby group headquartered in New York. Its purpose was plain: To re-establish Israel not as a "Jewish State," not as a "Palestinian State," but as a sovereign nation composed of Jews and Arabs co-existing without official political and religious differences or disadvantages. It was, in a sense, a re-beginning of 1948—what should have happened in the first place.

I had no illusions that my proposal would gain much popular acceptance among Israelis or among Jews of the Diaspora. In theory, at least, it negated the whole concept of exclusive Jewish statehood— a concept that had been turned into a reality by the shedding of much Jewish blood.

Yet, it was precisely that reality that was at the heart of Israel's ongoing difficulties. It was as if the United States had evolved over its three centuries as an exclusively white and Protestant nation in which all non-white, non-Protestant inhabitants possessed fewer statutory rights than the white-Protestant founding establishment. As it happened, the U.S. developed in just the opposite fashion. As a result, despite its own history of internal social, cultural, and racial problems, in the 1970s, it was the model of a democratically pluralistic and ethnically co-existent nation.

I was convinced that by bringing the exiled Palestinian Arabs into a coequal political union, by integrating them into a Jewish-Arab social and cultural coalition, Israel would disarm the Palestinians into accepting peace. A separate Palestinian state on Israel's borders seemed pointless, since it would represent just another inimical force and produce a further intensification of hostilities.

Let the Palestinians have their state in Israel, I proposed. Let Israel in the future be a joint Jewish-Palestinian nation, with the religious and cultural traditions of each people preserved and protected by a common, non-secular, political law.

As expected, most Jews in America attacked my plan as either simplistically naïve or deliberately traitorous. Not a few Israelis did, too. What they all failed to realize was that as time went on, Israel was becoming more and more a Middle Eastern country—that is, a country surrounded and influenced by the values and traditions of the Arab world. So long as Israel clung to and maintained its Western outlook, so long as it refused to integrate itself into its surroundings, it would be resisted in the same way a human body rejects the implantation of foreign cells.

Many American and Israeli Jews argued, "Why should Israel abandon its Western outlook? Especially when it was a creation of the Western world."

My answer made almost too much sense for anyone to accept. "Because," I said, "the historical nation of Israel—the Biblical nation—was not a Western state." The entire rationale of Israel's right to exist as a sovereign Jewish State in the 1970s was based on the precedent of its existence in ancient times. Had modern Israel been established in the West, that would have been one thing. But the Zionist pioneers had insisted on reclaiming the land of the Biblical nation, the land they believed that God had given their ancestors. In Biblical times, the Jewish nation had been as much an integral part of its surroundings as the Arab ones. Indeed, the ancient Hebrew State had sprung from the pagan Arab culture of the region.

By re-establishing their state in Palestine, the founding fathers of the new Jewish nation, even though they were Europeans, should have realized that assimilation into the contemporary Arab world was the key to success. They did not do so. They sought instead to make

Israel a European and Western enclave in the midst of what was essentially an oriental landmass.

That had been Israel's Achilles' heel ever since. If modern Israel was to be truly and fully based on history, it should have started to integrate itself into its demographic surroundings early on—back in the first decades of Zionist settlement, back in the British Mandate period—rather than developing as a Middle Eastern outpost of Jewish Europe.

It was not too late to begin such a pattern of integration and assimilation. This was not only necessary, I argued, but inevitable if Israel ever expected to experience peace. By opening itself up to the displaced Palestinian Arabs, it would not lose its Jewish identity and unity. It would lose only its Jewish exclusivity, a trait that even in early Biblical times it did not insist upon. It was only later in the history of the first Jewish nation that exclusivity became an obsession. And it was largely because of that that the Biblical nation was destroyed.

In 1974, I felt that my proposal for resolving the Arab-Israeli impasse was an eminently rational one, especially in light of the fact that all other attempts at solutions had failed so abysmally. The eventual solution would have to come from within the two peoples, and I believed that my plan constituted a sensible starting point for the ultimate contacts, communications, interchanges, and negotiations that would be necessary before a successful modus operandi between the two was hammered out. Sure, the plan would undoubtedly have to go through countless alterations and refinements, but at least it represented the beginnings of a realistic transaction. Each side would be required to give up something historically important to get something else that was infinitely more important to them in the contemporary sense—to the Palestinians, de facto statehood; to the Israelis, de facto peace.

I had outlined my proposal secretly to many of my friends among the liberal and conservative political leadership in Israel following the 1973 war. I had received a number of interested responses, including one from Menachem Begin, the former Irgunist who was then the head of the small, right-wing Likud Party and who, a few years hence, would surprise the world by winning election as Prime Minister of Israel.

I had also circulated the plan, via various backdoor conduits, to several Arab and Palestinian leaders, most notably Anwar Sadat and a handful of moderate Palestinian activists. The feedback I received was also positive, for the most part.

For the first time, I began to sense that something conciliatory was stirring on both sides of the conflict.

Arafat's visit to the UN focused world attention on the Israeli-Palestinian wrangle. It was because of that that I decided to go public with my proposal and test it directly on Arafat himself. Mohammed Mehdi, who had endorsed the plan and knew Arafat well, arranged for me to meet with him during his brief stay in New York.

Arafat and I met in secret and discussed my ideas. Although non-committal, as I'd expected, he was politely open to what I had to say and foreclosed on nothing. Despite the threatening rhetoric of his UN speech, in person I found him earnest, intelligent, and likeable. Under other circumstances, I said, we might have been a Jew and an Arab sitting beneath a tree near Jaffa or Nablus discussing the state of that year's olive crop. We had a lot more in common than we had differences, I added, and I hoped aloud that we'd both live to see the day when we could embrace on a street corner in the Jewish-Arab state of Israel.

"Arab-Jewish state," he quippingly corrected me.

"Anything can be negotiated," I replied. "You give a little, we give a little."

He laughed easily and nodded. "We give a little, you give a lot."

"You never know until you try," I said, remotely hoping that he'd pick up my lead and say something like, "Who in Israel do I talk to?"

Although I sensed he was tempted to, he didn't. Instead, one of his aides whispered in his ear about another appointment. So, our "diplomatic banter" came to an end. Yet, for me it was a fruitful meeting, if only because I learned that Arafat was not some wild-eyed fanatic. He could be talked to. And as long as he wasn't talked down to, or patronized, he listened.

I now understand why, although they could easily have done so many times in the past, the Israeli secret service had never tracked Arafat down and killed him. As Golda Meir once told me, "Arafat is their Ben Gurion. We understand that, and we respect it in a curious way. We don't want to kill him. We just want to tame him."

Following my meeting with Arafat, Mehdi and I held a joint news conference at which I made the proposal public and Mehdi, speaking for the Arabs, enthusiastically seconded it. We began to make plans to promote the idea together in an attempt to insert it into the mainstream of international discussion about solutions to the Middle East dilemma. I was committed to an all-out financial effort over the next few years to bring Israel and the Palestinians to the negotiating table. My commitment was aborted, however, by the Israeli government.

Not long after the news conference, I received a call from the Israeli ambassador to the United States in which he asked me to cease and desist. With a national election approaching in Israel, the long-incumbent Labour government was confronted by possible defeat because of its handling of the 1973 war, its inability to control inflation, and recent financial scandals. The major threat to Labour dominance was being posed by the fiercely right-wing Likud Party headed by Menachem Begin. This was no time, the ambassador told me, for the Laborites to give the impression domestically that they would consider negotiating with the Palestinians over the establishment of a joint Jewish-Muslim state in Israel.

"Please," he said, "wait until after the next election before you begin pushing this proposal of yours. If you don't, it could contribute to the ouster of Labour. Once we've won the election, then we'll begin to publicly consider your ideas."

I could understand the government's nervousness, although I thought it shortsighted and, frankly, stupid. Yet, as a son of Israel, I could not ignore the plea. So, I put my commitment on the back burner for a while, at least publicly. Privately, I continued to lobby for the plan.

Oddly enough, I soon found a most enthusiastic supporter for it in a relatively obscure southern American Baptist politician who had the improbable dream of becoming President of the United States—a dream that in many ways was as unlikely as mine of becoming a senator. His name was Jimmy Carter.

CHAPTER EIGHTEEN: THE MAVERICK, PART II

The year 1975 found the United States in a political and economic mess. The aftermath of Watergate, including Gerald Ford's pardon of Nixon, had left the mainline Republican Party in tatters. It seemed inevitable that the 1976 presidential election would go to just about any Democrat who got on the ticket, even an unknown political innocent. Indeed, the presence of a political naif was almost mandated by public opinion, since the country was plainly disgusted with its familiar national politicians, Republican and Democrat alike.

Economically, the country was already in deep trouble, the Northeast considerably more so. New York City in particular was in the deepest difficulty. About to go officially bankrupt, it was saved only by an extraordinary takeover of its fiscal infrastructure by the State of New York, a takeover that was guided and administered by a committee of private-sector bankers and managers appointed by the governor. Uncertainty and instability ruled the day.

It was an amusing irony that despite the nation's, and the city's, fiscal miseries, my business was flourishing as never before. There is a rule of thumb in New York real estate that the rise and fall of property values runs in seven-year cycles. Boom and bust, the experts say, follow each other with predictable monotony.

Having been in the business in earnest since 1957, I'd found the rule to be true. At that time, I had started, although unknown to me, at the bottom of a down market. Roughly seven years later, in 1964, the market had risen to a peak by virtue of which the properties I'd acquired and developed were worth, on an average, three times what I'd paid for them. The early 1970s had proved to be another "bottom" period. During that time, I'd made another "killing," since I was able to pick up a number of valuable new properties cheaply. Then, in the mid-1970s, despite the encroachments of inflation and recession, values began to rise again. And rise, and rise.

It was here, though, that the rule did not follow its customary course.

Theoretically, the city's real estate market should have topped out again in 1978 or 1979. Instead, it paused for breath, then soared into the stratosphere—notwithstanding the steep and inexorable rise in mortgage interest rates. In the early '70s, the interest rate climbed from an average of 6 percent to one of 8 percent. By the late '70s, it was up to 10, and it proceeded from there to as high as 18 percent in 1984.

During that ten-year period, the demand for residential and commercial space in New York soared out of sight as well. Ordinarily, inflation and bloated mortgage interest killed demand. But in this case, the flight of capital from Europe and the Middle East, resulting from the political and economic turmoil there, plus the transformation of the American economy from manufacturing to service industries, put New York real estate—especially that of Manhattan—into a mass-hysteria of demand. With that demand went spiraling prices and spiraling values that hadn't been seen since the time Peter Minuit bought Manhattan from an Indian tribe for twenty-four dollars and change. If the 1960s had been the go-go era of the stock market, the late 1970s and early 1980s were the real estate equivalent. If one had the investment resources, it was almost impossible not to make tons of money in New York property.

I had the resources in the form of banks and investment partners. Thus, throughout the '70s, I engaged in the further buying, mortgaging, and maintaining or selling of commercial and residential properties. There was no end to opportunity. For example, Stanley Stahl and I acquired a pair of large apartment buildings, containing 600 units, just off fashionable Sutton Place in the East Fifties. The buildings cost $7.5 million cash, all of which Stahl put up, giving me 50 percent ownership in exchange for my promise to reap both of us a large cash profit through a re-mortgaging scheme. I re-mortgaged the buildings two years later for $10.8 million, for a gain to each of us of $1.6 million. Thereafter, we held on to the buildings and operated them as high-profit residential properties. Ever since, the profits have easily covered our mortgage, tax, and other expenses, and in addition, they have provided us with munificent annual incomes. What's more, today the buildings are worth easily $100 million.

My parking garage development continued apace. My biggest project in the area was the construction of a 1200-car garage adjoining Yankee Stadium, which was then undergoing a complete rebuilding under the auspices of the city. That experience was a perfect illustration of the differences between private and public construction projects. The stadium reconstruction, which was being run by city officials, went way over budget and failed by a year to meet its completion deadline. The construction of the parking garage, which was run by me, was completed nine months before deadline and at nearly $1 million under budget.

I continued to add profitable office buildings to my portfolio during the '70s, too. The most notable of these was 23 Park Row, a large, five-story structure opposite City Hall in lower Manhattan, and the Southern Pacific Building, a twenty-six-story property on busy East 43rd Street between Grand Central Station and the United Nations. In each case, I did as I had done with the Sutton Place apartments—took in a partner who put up the purchase money, then arranged for new mortgages at much greater amounts.

Throughout the period, I had to spend hardly any money myself. Investors were knocking down my door to get in on my purchase re-mortgage deals. Being in the real estate business was easier than ever, so much so that it was almost becoming boring. Which was another reason I entered the political arena. Making money was no longer the challenge it had been. I needed something new to invigorate my life, and public service seemed the most appropriate course.

My resolve to continue seeking public office was doubled by the greed, corruption, and incompetence I witnessed daily in New York politics. Many politicians were in the business of politics not to serve the people but to serve themselves, especially through the solicitation of private fees, payoffs, bribes, kickbacks, and other forms of legal and illegal income-padding. Since I had all the money I needed and more, no one could accuse me of pursuing public office in the hope of enriching myself financially. In fact, were I to gain office, I intended to donate my yearly salary to charitable causes.

Although I was thriving in the real estate business as never before in 1975, increasing numbers of ordinary citizens throughout New York State were encountering greater and greater financial difficulties as the cost of living continued to rise along with unemployment and credit costs. The government still had done nothing to try to control inflation except reapply tired, old economic formulas that had never been of much use in the first place, such as artificially manipulating the money supply and fiddling with taxation. It had done just as little to stem the alarming decline of America's industrial diversity during the previous ten years. In my view, things would only continue to get worse so long as some sort of stability failed to be achieved in the Middle East. The economies of all

Western nations were hostages to the political whims of the Arab oil nations.

Late in 1975, I was surprised to receive a phone call out of the blue from a man who, in a soft, Southern drawl, identified himself as Governor Jimmy Carter of Georgia. Carter told me he intended to run for the Democratic presidential nomination the following year. He'd heard that I was a knowledgeable figure in the New York Democratic Party, he said, and asked me for advice on how to go about approaching the state organization for support in the 1976 primary.

I must confess that at first I didn't take the call very seriously. But then he said something that rang a sympathetic bell. "A lot of people tell me I'm crazy to think of running. Except for here in Georgia, I have no great standing in the Democratic Party. I have no national recognition, no national organization, nothing. Already I'm being called a maverick candidate. But given the political climate today, I think a new face is just what the party needs to beat President Ford next year. I believe I'm as good as any other fresh candidate the party can come up with. And that's why I'm gonna make the effort."

"Pardon me, Governor," I said. "Did I hear you use the word 'maverick' to describe yourself?"

"Mr. Hirschfeld," he answered with a chuckle, "it's not my description. It's what other people say—the party leaders and the press."

"Well," I replied, "welcome to the club. That's what they're calling me here in New York ever since I ran for the senate last year. And I can tell you something. When you first said you wanted to go after the nomination, I didn't take you seriously. In fact, I didn't even know who you were. But if other people are calling you a maverick, then I say you have a chance. Therefore, though I don't know you, I'll do whatever I can to help you here in New York."

Out of that initial phone conversation, there quickly grew a close rapport between Jimmy Carter and myself. We met soon after, and he spent a long afternoon soliciting and listening to my political and economic ideas, particularly with regard to the Middle East. I told him about my Israeli-Palestinian reconciliation plan and meeting with Arafat, and about how I sensed that the time was ripe for the beginning of a realistic peace making process in the Middle East. Given his obvious reverence for the Bible, I thought that if he were to

156

succeed in gaining the Presidency, he might just be the man to get the process started.

My exchanges with Carter further fueled my determination to make another try for the senate. My gut feeling was that he possessed the freshness, charm, and novelty to win the Democratic presidential nod. And that if he did, the majority of American voters would value him over Gerald Ford if only because Ford continued to come across as little more than a bumbling and incompetent heir of the corrupt Nixon regime.

The senate seat that would be voted on in November of 1976 was occupied by James Buckley—a Republican, but one who was far to the right of the Republican Party's mainstream. Buckley represented a dilemma for me. In many ways, I was sympathetic to that part of his ultra-conservative philosophy, which preached a much-reduced role for government in private-sector business and industry, along with a sharp reduction in government spending.

On the other hand, Buckley had proved himself not terribly effective during his first term in the senate. He seemed little more than a single-issue legislator, and a point man for the Reagan movement that was then beginning to gather force across America. Reaganism did not particularly appeal to me, if only because it appealed so deeply to so many fringe-element groups in the United States that were, among other things, blatantly anti-Semitic.

I felt much about Buckley in 1976 as I had about Javits in 1974. As an incumbent senator, he was not objectionable in any specific way, but he was not as useful or effective as he should have been in tackling the major economic problems the country faced. Buckley did not suffer as much as other Republicans from the Watergate stigma, for he had been among the first to call for Nixon's resignation. Nonetheless, he was still in danger of being swept out of office if the Democrats, as I suspected they would, ran away with the first presidential election since Watergate.

At the start of 1976, then, I decided to run again for the Democratic senatorial nomination. The backstage resistance I encountered from the party leadership was even more pronounced than it had been two years before. I was still viewed as a maverick with little chance to win.

Again, I had no illusions that I could win. My principal goal at the start was to campaign against inflation and awaken the party, along with the voters of New York, to the economic dangers of the future if something practical wasn't done by the government to put a rein on rising costs and interest rates. Indeed, having had my say, I might have been prepared to step out of the race this time if I was rejected by the state party's June convention. But then something occurred at the convention that left me no choice but to press on.

After much testing-the-waters by various would-be candidates early in the year, by June, the race had settled into a contest between myself, Ramsey Clark, New York City Council President Paul O'Dwyer, and Congresswoman Bella Abzug, who was also from the city. As in 1974, Clark had little official support except in its most liberal sector. Abzug was objected to basically on the grounds that although she was a woman, she was not the "right kind of woman" to represent New York in the senate, an allusion to her loud, brassy personality. I, of course, had little official backing. That left Paul O'Dwyer, who was the favorite of the various Democratic county machines in New York City and its environs.

None of this sat too well with the upstate Democratic leaders, the most powerful of whom was Joseph Crangle, the former state chairman and still the head of the influential Buffalo-area outpost of the party. The fact that both of New York's senators had, for many years, come from New York City rankled the upstaters. Thus, as the June 15 convention in Syracuse neared, Crangle announced that he had persuaded the American Ambassador to the United Nations, Daniel Moynihan, to enter the race.

Presumably because Moynihan maintained a leisure "farm" in Delaware County, this made him an upstater, although he was basically a native and denizen of Manhattan. In addition, he was officially a resident of Cambridge, Massachusetts, where he was on the faculty of Harvard as a professor of economics. Crangle made it clear that his upstate organization intended to go all out for Moynihan's nomination to the September primary.

What bothered me about this stemmed from my past personal experience with Moynihan, plus my awareness that although a Democrat, he had spent time in the faithful service of Richard Nixon in the White House while formulating much of Nixon's domestic minority social policy.

Moynihan had been the American UN Ambassador at the time of my meeting with Arafat and the presentation of my plan to solve

158

the Israeli-Palestinian problem. He had made a number of unflattering remarks about the plan while at the same time pretending to be a vigorous supporter of Israel. I had pointed out in a debate that his support of Israel, though admirable on the surface, was really not very productive because it pandered to typical Western notions of what the Jewish state should be and ignored the reality of Israel as a Middle Eastern nation that needed to assimilate itself into its surrounding culture if it hoped to live in peace.

Moynihan had dismissed my ideas in the kind of supercilious fashion typical of Harvard professors who believe they know everything there is to know. It was exactly that sort of arrogant, knee-jerk, know-it-allism by its American defender that stood in the way of Israel making any real progress toward peace. When I pointed out to Moynihan that I had grown up in Israel and might know the Arab and Palestinian soul a little better than he did, he made a cheap joke out of it.

For all his outward concern for Israel, Moynihan, in my view, was no real friend of the Jewish State or Jewish people. He was a heavy drinker and poseur who was capable of no original thoughts about the Middle East. The only thing he seemed to think much about in 1976 was staying in the public limelight and exploiting his fake-Irish charm.

Clearly, I didn't like Moynihan. It could fairly be said that he liked me even less. I prefer to think that that was because he knew I could see through him.

But beyond personalities, there was the matter of Moynihan's identification with the Nixon administration. He was the author of the notorious "benign neglect" theory under which Nixon had proposed to deal with the social and economic problems of black minorities in America. The theory was consistent with the Moynihan I knew, a self-alleged liberal who in reality was always happy to tailor his beliefs to suit the needs of whomever in power was willing to give him a public platform. As far as I was concerned, it did not do for New York to have as a senator a man who was so calculatingly callous about the plight of Israel and of minorities in America. Moreover, a professional economist by training, Moynihan was totally blind to the parlous economic problems that were about to be visited on the United States. He was an economist who'd never met a payroll.

When the state Democratic convention gathered in mid-June of 1976, I tried to bring my concerns to its attention. I was completely throttled by the party leaders, who carried a grudge against me for having challenged their priggish authority in 1974. The O'Dwyer supporters from New York City did their best to try to stifle me so that I wouldn't rain on their parade of acclaim for their candidate. Stanley Steingut, a power in the State Assembly from Brooklyn and a longtime lieutenant of Brooklyn party boss Meade Esposito, threatened me with physical harm if I continued to make waves.

In the case of Steingut, this was more than the cold shoulder for an outsider. It was a personal betrayal that would lead me to unleash my anger in a way that some would define as my signature.

First, though, the betrayal. As Treasurer of the Democratic Party, I had known Steingut for many years, considered him a friend, and often defended him against charges that he was a hack of a politician who had no core values and could only make deals in Albany through threats.

Many around the state derided Steingut as an illiterate, clownish presence given to uttering pearls of wisdom such as, "This bill, if passed, will derail the ship of state" and "This session has been hit by an avalanche of creeping paralysis."

As someone who has uttered a non sequitur or two (hundred) in my time, I hardly considered this a stain on his virtue. I enjoyed his company and was pleased to help him. By example, Stanley had come to me a few years earlier wanting to join my country club, the Westbury Golf Club on Long Island, and I wasted no time in personally sponsoring his membership.

One day, we hooked up on the course to play a round. Stanley had another favor to ask of me. He desperately wanted his daughter to be accepted to Penbroke College, which was then the women's school at Brown University. He said he had met with the school's dean, tried to pull all the strings, but the school still kept on turning down his daughter. Knowing that Elie had graduated from Brown, Stanley came to me as a last resort, not knowing that Elie was, in fact, by now the head of the acceptance committee at Brown.

"Abe," he said, "I wouldn't impose on you for anything. But this is my daughter; she's my whole life, and this is her dream to go to Penbroke. Can you help out?"

I was touched by his love for his daughter, and I again moved to do him a favor.

"Stanley," I said, "tell her to reapply. She will be accepted tomorrow morning."

Still not aware of Elie's highly influential role at Brown, he was dumbfounded. "Really? Tomorrow? How?" he asked.

"None of your business. Just tell her to reapply."

"Abe," he said, practically in tears, "I'll do anything possible for you."

I did not call in that chit, as it is against my principles to acquire something I haven't earned or deserved. I never asked for any favor from Stanley Steingut. I didn't ask for his endorsement in my 1974 senate campaign, nor did I in '76. All I expected from him was fairness and respect for my right to earn the nomination. I got neither.

It was Steingut who pushed so hard for Lee Alexander in 1974, and at the time, I told him it was a shitty thing to do to me, but I let it pass. Now, however, he went further to end *my* dream of holding public office. During the convention in Albany, he sent me a very nasty letter all but ordering me out of the race. He tried to placate me with a condescending offer to give me my old job back as party treasurer, but I felt each word as if it were a knife going in my back. I was so enraged that when I heard that Steingut was having breakfast in his hotel with a bunch of his party clubhouse cronies, I briskly strode into the restaurant, went right up to his table, and glowered at him.

"You bastard. You liar," I screamed at him. Brandishing the letter, I said, "Is this how you'll do anything for me?"

I punctuated my screed with a well-aimed squirt of saliva that drenched his whole face.

Steingut, who prided himself on his pretensions of dignity and being in control of any situation, looked like a scared orphan boy caught in the rain. He merely sat in place, doing and saying nothing amid gasps, and a few giggles, from his coterie of flunkies who saw this Potemkin Boss for what he really was—a lying phony.

Steingut, after a few moments, got up, not to raise his hands to me—believe me, I was ready to mix it up—but to go to the bathroom to wash my spit off his red face. He never came back to the table, and he all but disappeared from sight the rest of the convention, no doubt embarrassed to show that face.

161

When word of the incident got out, the press ran with it and lay in wait for Steingut to pepper him with questions about what had prompted a long-shot candidate who should be genuflecting before him to expectorate at a party leader of his status. Instead, he avoided interviews like the plague, and the only time he surfaced was to hide behind Meade Esposito's skirt when that other Brooklyn phony, who was as corrupt a politician as has ever lived, made inane physical threats against me if I continued to run.

Behind the scenes, however, Steingut thirsted for retribution. Within months, the building in Albany that I had purchased from the Kennedy family mysteriously went from full to nearly empty, as almost all of the tenants were driven out with lies abut how the building was being managed. I lost millions by having to close up that beautiful and historic building, I firmly believe, because Stanley Steingut controlled the real estate circle of Albany, the city where he'd ruled for so long.

But I got the last laugh on Steingut by seeing his power erode, leaving him a broken, obscure man by the time he died in 1990, prematurely, at the age of fifty-six. And in case you're wondering if I regret having reduced his legacy from Speaker of the State Assembly to simply the man whose face Abe Hirschfeld spit in, the answer is a loud, ringing, "No." I would do it again, in a minute.

What's more, it was Steingut's betrayal that convinced me to avoid the party bigwigs and get on the September primary ballot on my own. I decided to stay in the race, if only to see if I could block Moynihan's election. He, O'Dwyer, Clark, and Abzug had all made it onto the ballot via the convention's selection system. Once more, I would be forced to go the nominating-petition route.

I spent the next few weeks rounding up the needed 20,000 petition names and campaigning hard against Moynihan, hammering home his record as an adviser to Nixon and pointing out that although he maintained a residence in the state, he had not voted in New York for at least twenty years. This led to a somewhat violent encounter between Moynihan and myself.

One day late in August, all the candidates gathered at *The New York Times* to debate the issues in front of that newspaper's editorial board. My staff by then had produced documentary evidence that Moynihan had never voted in New York in all the years he'd had a residence in the state. At the debate, I challenged the propriety of his presence in the race on that ground.

Moynihan, suppressing his rage, proceeded to lie as he attempted to fend off my challenge. "I most certainly have voted," he insisted, "many times. I always vote in New York City, not upstate where my farm is." Then, with great smugness, he added, "Mr. Hirschfeld's detectives have obviously been looking in the wrong place."

"If that's so," I answered, "perhaps you'd care to tell us just where in the city you were registered to vote. There seems to be no record of any registration address."

"Most recently," he said, after fumbling about for a reply, "I've been registered at 145 East 35th Street. Yes, I've done all my voting from that address for the past fifteen, twenty years."

"Really?" I said. "You mean that's where you've been living all that time?"

"If you must know," he answered, with great self-righteousness, "it's my residence in the city. I have an apartment there."

"Is that so?" I rejoined. "Well, Mr. Moynihan, now I know you're lying. You see, I happen to own that building. I've owned it for as long as you say you've lived there. And I know for a fact you don't have an apartment there."

Moynihan reddened and began to sputter in embarrassment. But before I could elaborate on my charge, which really was no more than a bluff, the chairman of the *Times* editorial board stepped in to save him. "Let's go on to something else," he said.

Notwithstanding my efforts, it became clear a week or so before the primary that the race had narrowed down to a choice between Moynihan and Bella Abzug. Abzug exploited the fact, that, if elected, she would be the first female senator the state had ever had, a prospect that seemed to stimulate a lot of otherwise indifferent women voters. Moynihan, backed heavily by the upstate Democrats and press, was able to play off his UN ambassadorship to attract the party's large, male, middle-of-the-road constituency. Despite his nominal support by the New York City party regulars, the phlegmatic O'Dwyer was never able to connect with the voters. As soon as the regulars saw his chances slipping away, they abandoned the O'Dwyer ship and swam to Moynihan shores.

The grim, self-righteous Clark was out of it early, which was surprising in the light of his strong challenge to Javits in 1974. In fact, he was never really in the race from the beginning. Nor, for that matter, was I.

Moynihan eked out a win over Abzug in the September primary, garnering an edge of less than 10,000 votes in one of the closest and most lightly attended elections in the state's history. To me, the result was depressing for two reasons. First, I still believed that Moynihan was not suited for the senate, philosophically or otherwise. Second, less than one-quarter of the state's enrolled Democrats had voted, a shockingly low turnout. That told me that citizen apathy and cynicism about politics were still strong in the wake of Watergate. The phenomenon was understandable, but it boded ill for the future. By its very apathy, the Democratic electorate was charting hard times for itself ahead. Hardly any Democratic candidate anywhere in the industrially sagging Northeast and Midwest was equipped to deal with the coming national fiscal crisis.

As soon as the primary was over, the party leadership did an about-face and began to plead for my support of Moynihan in November's general election, mainly because it knew of my value as a fundraiser. Even Jimmy Carter, who'd won the Democratic nomination to run for President against Ford, got on the phone and urged me to back Moynihan. I told Carter I would certainly work my tail off for his own election, but that I couldn't bring myself to do the same for Moynihan.

I rejected all demands that I endorse Moynihan. I declared instead, a few days after the New York primary, that I'd thrown my weight behind Buckley's re-election effort. Not because Buckley had a strong following among the state's radically right-wing elements but because he was the only candidate committed to dealing realistically with inflation and fiscal prudence in the operation of government—and because "it's my opinion that Daniel Moynihan is an opportunist who has always spoken out of both sides of his mouth, whereas Jim Buckley is at least consistent and the voters know what they're getting with him."

I became head of the Democrats for Buckley during the fall senatorial election campaign. At the same time, I worked vigorously for the election of Jimmy Carter as President. When questioned by journalists about my "divided loyalties," I had this answer.

"Gentlemen, I started out my life in this country a Republican. Then I became a Democrat. In body, I'm still a Democrat. In spirit, I'm still a Republican. In body and soul, I'm still Abe Hirschfeld. And Abe Hirschfeld is the prisoner of no party.

"So, it's not a matter of divided loyalties. It's a matter of a single loyalty—to the United States of America. And to the proposition that a man best serves the United States by supporting and voting for those he thinks are best suited to run it, regardless of their party affiliation."

As might have been predicted, I backed the losing side again. Well, half the losing side. Jimmy Carter, of course, roundly defeated Gerald Ford in the nationwide presidential election, doing especially well in New York State. But Carter's success, plus Jim Buckley's lackluster campaign, made it possible for Moynihan to win the senatorial race. Riding on Carter's coattails, he defeated Buckley by about 586,000 votes.

So much for my political hopes in 1976, I thought at the time. But as I was soon to discover, I was not quite finished with politics yet.

Abraham (Abe) Hirschfeld

CHAPTER NINETEEN: THE PERFECT PARTNER

When Elie was growing up, I always assumed that eventually he'd want to join Hirschfeld Realty and then, one day, take over the business from me. Accordingly, when he was in his early teens, I began to tutor him in real estate. Later, I brought him into the company to work at various apprentice learning jobs during his high school and college vacations. I believed that between the formal education he was receiving at Brown and the London School of Economics (where he spent his junior year), and the practical schooling he was getting from me, he would be well-groomed to move into a position of responsibility at Hirschfeld Realty upon his graduation from Brown in 1971.

Indeed, I was really looking forward to his joining me. I did not just look on Elie as a son whom I loved dearly. To me, he was a brilliant young man and a good friend whom I liked, admired, and respected enormously. As I've said, we were almost polar opposites in temperament and style. Whereas I was impulsive and feverish, he was deliberate and cool. Yet, we shared the same inner strength and determination. I believed that he'd be a tremendous complement to me in the future progress of Hirschfeld Realty. I believed we'd make a terrific team.

I was more than a little surprised and disappointed, then, when Elie told me, while still in college, that he didn't think he could work with me. "Dad," he said, "I've seen you in action all these years. You're just too strong a personality. I feel I'd always be in your shadow. I need to have my own life, my own career."

After I got over my disappointment, I realized what a courageous thing it was for him to tell me that. "All right, son," I said. "Go ahead and make your own career. But remember, if you ever change your mind..."

We never discussed the matter again. Elie went off to law school for three years. Then, in 1974, he was recruited into Milbank, Tweed, Hadley & McCloy, one of New York's most prestigious law firms and a bastion of the city's WASP establishment. The pride I felt in this was without bounds. The idea that such a firm would seek out the son of a Polish-Israeli Jewish immigrant with an accent as thick as a slab of corned beef amazed me.

167

But it was not a tribute to me, I soon realized. It was a tribute to Elie and his native brilliance and style. "Nonsense," he joked. "The only reason they wanted me was because they thought they'd get a rich client in you."

I became more or less resigned to the prospect of Elie making his career at Milbank Tweed. In five or six years, he would become a junior partner, and thereafter, he would rise into the lofty ranks of senior partnership. If there was any consolation for me, it was in the fact that he'd decided to specialize in real estate law. At least, I thought, I'd had some positive influence on his life.

Like any beginning associate in a larger firm such as Milbank Tweed, Elie found himself working long, hard hours—often as many as twelve or thirteen hours a day. Nevertheless, he found time to manage my senatorial campaign in 1974 and again in the spring and summer of 1976. Those experiences had a magnetizing effect on him. During the day, he would be cloistered in the somber, starch confines of the Milbank Tweed offices near Wall Street. At night, he'd find himself thrust into the exciting, hurly-burly, uptown world of politics and real estate. (Even while vying for political office, I continued to run my business.) The contrasts were sharp, and Elie began to acquire a taste for the uptown business and political scene.

Finally, at the end of the 1976 campaign, he came to me and said, "Dad, I've decided I don't want to be a Wall Street lawyer the rest of my life. It's too dull for me. If you still want me...."

I threw my arms around him and said, "Elie, you've made me the happiest man in the world."

And so he left Milbank Tweed and joined Hirschfeld Realty on a full-time basis. I'm pretty sure he's never regretted it. I know I haven't. He's been the best partner I could ever have hoped for, and today, he's an even more important factor in the Hirschfeld organization than I am.

It was a good thing Elie joined me when he did because I was about to enter what would prove to be the riskiest and most frenetic period of my business career and personal life. In the past, I'd usually limited myself to one or two major projects at a time, building the company in block-by-block fashion. Now, at the start of 1977, so many opportunities began to present themselves that I was hard put to keep up with them. Only Elie's presence enabled me to do so. With his orderly lawyer's approach to business details, he freed me to concentrate on several major future enterprises simultaneously. Had it not been for that, Hirschfeld Realty would likely not have grown the way it has since the late 1970s.

Economically, 1977 was a schizophrenic year in New York, and it was that madness that propelled me along the various paths I followed. On the one hand, the city was virtually in bankruptcy. It was being run by the state-created Municipal Assistance Corporation, a private-sector financial junta that supervised and managed the city's fiscal affairs. On the other hand, private investment money was pouring into New York—especially into Manhattan—as it never had before. Much of it came from abroad, the result of the general fear in Europe and elsewhere of the trend toward more militant socialist governments and toward further unrest in the Middle East.

Suddenly, the United States seemed a safe haven for countless private foreign fortunes. And since New York was the financial capital of the United States, many of those fortunes landed in Manhattan in the form of major real estate and banking investments. Thus, although the city was in dire straits as a public entity, in many of its private-sector aspects, it was in the process of exploding into an era of unparalleled prosperity.

There was an ominous downside to the cycle, though. With practically all the new investment money concentrated in central and downtown Manhattan—the city's "glamour" centers—the demand for property in those areas, both commercial and residential, shot up like a rocket. That, coupled with the inexorable rise in inflation and interest rates during the late '70s, began to drive property values out of sight. By 1980, a building market-valued at $100,000 five years earlier would be worth $2 million or more depending on how favorably it was located. Three or four years later, its value might soar to as high as $9 or $10 million.

I had seen this trend developing as early as 1973, when I began to speak out publicly about inflation and interest rates. At the start of 1977, although few people outside the real estate industry had yet perceived it, it was very apparent to me what was going to happen. The combination of high-demand and high-inflation was going to create a new two-tier property structure in Manhattan. One tier would be so expensive that only the wealthiest people would be able to afford to own or rent residential and commercial space. The other tier would remain the traditional low-income, government-subsidized housing and commercial properties. The middle-income, middle-class component of Manhattan's socioeconomic mix would be driven out.

The irony of it all was that I knew that I stood to profit enormously from the coming real estate boom, yet I was dismayed by the awareness that my profit would come, at least indirectly, at the expense of many who could no longer afford to live or maintain businesses in Manhattan. It was not an earthshaking dilemma, but a dilemma nevertheless. I decided to try to solve it by running again for political office, this time on the municipal level. With the city in the trouble it was, and with no one as yet paying any real heed to all the signs of deeper fiscal trouble ahead, I believed I could help. My program would be as before: the need to stem inflation by putting a government cap on interest rates and the desirability of transferring many financially wasteful and hopelessly bureaucratic municipal services to free-enterprise business management.

This latter theme was one I'd developed in large part as a result of my long, consistently vexing experience with the city's governmental bureaucracy—the Dorothy Green incident being a case in point. The corruption and inefficiency in the multifarious municipal agencies, departments, boards, and bureaus under civil service "management" not only represented an enormous squandering of the city's public resources but it also functioned as a stranglehold on private-sector development—the very development New York so desperately required to generate the revenues necessary to sustain its logistically complex services citywide. A complete reform of governmental administration was imperative. The only sensible alternative to ineffective public-sector management was to transform the service bureaucracies into organizations managed in the spirit of free-enterprise business standards and principles, under which such values as cost-control, productivity, efficiency, budgetary integrity, and job performances were paramount.

Nineteen seventy-seven was a major election year in New York City, with the office of mayor, city council president, and other key executive and legislative posts up for grabs. The reason they were up for grabs was because the incumbent administration of Abraham Beame, a colorless lackey of the Brooklyn Democratic machine who had succeeded John Lindsay as mayor, had been so tragically ineffective in staving off the city's fiscal crisis.

At first, I thought of entering the mayoral race. But then, as many other well-known local politicians decided to challenge Beame's re-election, I realized that I might become obscured by the traffic. So, I set my sights on the presidency of the city council. In many ways, its president played as vital a role in the city's management as did the mayor.

The incumbent City Council President was Paul O'Dwyer, one of the men who had unsuccessfully run, along with me, for the senate nomination the year before. A lot of O'Dwyer's political ambition had been sucked out of him as a result of his poor showing against Moynihan in 1976—he had, after all, been the candidate of the majority of the state party's bosses. In talking to him, I sensed that he was tired; that after expecting to get into the U.S. Senate, he felt that a return to city politics was a comedown. He intended to run again for the city council presidency, all right. But I could tell that he would not put much enthusiasm into it.

O'Dwyer could be beaten, I decided. Besides, in 1977, an intensifying spirit of reform filled the air of New York politics, generated mainly by the fiscal crisis and by the sharply reduced quality of life in the city that had evolved during the Beame-O'Dwyer reign. Like Beame, O'Dwyer's identification as a Democratic Party "regular" did not stand him in good stead with the younger generations of voters.

I knew that almost as many politicians would run against O'Dwyer as would run against Mayor Beame. The difference was that none of them would have the notoriety of those in the mayoral race. Thus, except for O'Dwyer, I would not be eclipsed by longtime political figures who were more famous. This raised my chances considerably. What I didn't know was that a reform movement of another kind was rapidly gathering force in the city, one that would center on the contest for the city council presidency. This was the women's movement.

I announced my candidacy at the end of May 1977, including in my opening statement the promise that if elected, I would turn my salary back to the city and would refuse to use the car and chauffeur that went with the office. I meant it. It was such wasteful amenities as cars and chauffeurs for all major city officials that had contributed to New York's financial quandary. If the city's officialdom had been unable to make New York work while enjoying the convenience of cars and drivers, what was the point of its having such conveniences?

O'Dwyer declared his intention to seek re-election soon after my announcement. Others who formally entered the race were Carter Burden, a wealthy young Manhattan councilman, Leonard Stavisky, a state assemblyman, and Carol Bellamy, a member of the state senate from Brooklyn.

After campaigning through the summer, my hunch about not being obscured by other contestants' notoriety was proving correct. In mid-August, a *New York Times*/CBS poll showed that O'Dwyer led at 30 percent, and I was second at 18 percent.

Burden, who was spending freely on television commercials, was third at 14 percent. Bellamy had only 5 percent, and Stavinsky was practically off the board at 2 percent. The primary election was three weeks away.

Herman Badillo, the highly respected Puerto-Rico born, liberal, New York congressmen was one of those who was in the thick of the mayoral race against Abe Beame—a race in which no one had a clear lead. Badillo was running on a program of sharp reforms in city government. Since I was, too, he came to me and proposed that we join our campaigns into a single effort in the final weeks. I agreed, and in the days immediately following our joint announcement, our respective ratings in the polls rose appreciably.

The purpose of the September 8 local primary election was to select the top two Democratic vote-getters for each office so that they could then compete against one another in a second "runoff" election to be held two weeks later. The winner of the runoff would then become the sole Democratic candidate for the given office in the November general election, running against a Republican candidate chosen in much the same fashion. It was a crazy and expensive system. But there it was, and I, along with every other candidate, had to put up with it.

I did not expect to out-vote Paul O'Dwyer in the September 8 election. I simply hoped to come in second, thereby getting onto the runoff ballot, and then I would use the next two weeks to mount an even more intensive campaign by which to beat him in the runoff. All the poll signs in the week leading up to the September 8 election indicated that I'd take the required second spot.

So much for the polls. None of the other candidates were aware of the quiet, almost subterranean impact Carol Bellamy, the only woman in the race, was having on Democratic voters—most of them, naturally, women. Nor of the negative impact Bella Abzug was having in her attempt to win a spot on the mayoral runoff ballot.

Abzug was her usual loud, abrasive, and often repulsive self during her mayoral campaign. Bellamy on the other hand, running for the city council presidency, came across as forceful and determined, but at the same time, feminine and polite.

There was another factor at work, too. The summer of 1977 was one of the most chaotic periods in the city's history. In July, a citywide power blackout had ignited several days of violent rioting and looting in the city's more deprived ethnic neighborhoods. In August, the notorious Son of Sam multiple-murder case reached its climax with the garishly publicized arrest of the crazed David Berkowitz, a Jew. By the time of the September 8 election, the city was in need of some soothing balm.

Carol Bellamy filled the bill perfectly. Those many women voters who were too embarrassed by Bella Abzug's personal and political style to vote for her in the mayoral race were all too pleased by the feminine contrast Bellamy posed in the contest for city council president. Male voters, too, were attracted to Bellamy at the last minute, if only because she possessed none of the garrulously militant and threatening feminist traits of Abzug. It seemed that everyone who could not bring him or herself to vote for Abzug automatically felt compelled to cast a ballot for Bellamy for city council president—as a form of compensation.

As a result, Bellamy was a surprise runner-up to O'Dwyer in the September 8 primary, thereby gaining the right to face O'Dwyer in the September 19 runoff election. He got 225,000 votes; she received 187,000; I received 124,000. She went on to defeat O'Dwyer in the September 19 runoff and to easily win the November election against her Republican opponent. Edward Koch, another somewhat unexpected runoff victor, captured the mayor's office.

My ally, Herman Badillo, returned to being a congressman. And I went back to being a "wealthy real estate mogul," as the press continued to label me. I decided that if the citizens of New York could not see the wisdom of my programs for fiscal and economic

173

reform, I had no choice but to use the system as it existed to do the best I could for myself, my family, and my company.

In retrospect, it was a good thing that I did, and that I failed to achieve the city council presidency. For just as Carol Bellamy was, I would have been submerged in the subsequent aura of self-congratulation and antagonism the publicity-hungry Ed Koch created for himself as mayor, an aura the New York media were all too eager, and all too foolish, to encourage and abet. Koch is a nice enough man. But in the nearly ten years of his mayoralty, he mismanaged the city to the brink of another disaster.

This has proved, in my opinion, that professional politicians do not belong, in this day and age, in positions of high political responsibility and leadership.

Koch ran in 1977 as a radical reformer. He reformed nothing. Rather, in his overweening eagerness to remain mayor of New York all these years, he only succeeded in creating a further desperate need for reform of the political system in New York. Carol Bellamy, in the meantime, faded into well-deserved, if lucrative, private-sector obscurity, her own "reformist" ambitions having transformed themselves into a hollow, laughable relic.

CHAPTER TWENTY: THE VERTICAL CLUB AND BEYOND

I was sure my political career, such as it was, was over. As I said in the last chapter, in 1977, the economic conditions in New York were creating a plethora of enticing, new real estate developmental opportunities in and around the city, and I could not ignore them. Once my attempt to win the city council presidency failed, I resolved to concentrate on business again, this time mainly to help get Elie established so that he would have a greater base to build upon.

I was nearing sixty, after all. Although my mother, still in Israel, was already well into her robust eighties, my father had died at a relatively young age. I couldn't be sure whose genes I'd inherited in greater preponderance, his or hers. Anyway, when a man gets towards sixty, he'd begins to think about his own mortality. All in all, I was lucky to be alive in the first place. If not for a few fortuitous accidents in my youth, I would have likely been one of the six million.

So, I was concerned with giving Elie a proper start. But other events were happening in my life, too. With the children grown and on their own, Zipora and I had moved back into the city from Great Neck, buying a roomy co-op-apartment several years before in one of the choicest building on Fifth Avenue—not one of my own.

As a result of our move, I looked for another golf club to join, one that was closer to the city than my club in Long Island. I found a desirable one and applied for membership. To my amazement, I was turned down, even though I was rich enough to have bought the entire club. Soon, I deduced why. It was because I was not "old money," and probably because I was not WASH—a white Anglo-Saxon Hebrew.

At about the same time, the modern-day fitness craze was beginning to establish itself in New York. I had purchased an old property on East 61st Street between First and Second Avenue. Because the property was located by the exit ramps of the huge Queensborough Bridge spanning Manhattan and Queens, it was in a neglected neighborhood of cheap, rent-regulated apartments and small commercial buildings. I had been thinking long and hard about what to do with it when inspiration struck. Rather than buy the country club that had rejected me, I would build my own club. But instead of it being in the suburbs, it would be in the city, a club with every

175

amenity except a golf course. An urban country club that would be oriented towards the fitness fad and would not—repeat, would not—reject anyone who could afford to join.

That was the "moral" basis of my idea. There remained the question of how to carry it out. There were already a few fitness-oriented commercial establishments in New York – YMCA or Jack LaLanne-type gyms and swimming pool facilities where people could go and work out. But they were fairly limited in what they had to offer, and they also lacked the kind of upbeat, club-like ambiance I had in mind—a place where people could not only workout but also socialize.

The question remained in the back of my mind, unanswered, throughout the mid-1970s. Then, the city did something that, by accident, provided the answer. I had originally acquired the property on East 61st Street with the idea of transforming it into another open-air garage. Given its location at the Manhattan end of the Queensborough Bridge, it was a perfect site. But in 1977, the city council passed an ordinance barring the construction of anymore parking garages in Manhattan on the misguided theory that such facilities were becoming too numerous and were attracting too many cars into Manhattan at the expense of public transit. Suddenly, I was left with a site that I couldn't use for the purpose I'd intended. It was then, as I mulled over alternative uses for it, that I began to think in terms of using it for my urban "country club." If nothing else, it was most conveniently located on the trendy East Side.

It so happened that I had been able to start building one final garage before the Manhattan ban went into effect. The site was next to the Empire State Building on 33rd Street, just off Fifth Avenue. It so just so happened that, as his first major job for Hirschfeld Realty, I put Elie fully in charge of the garage's construction.

Elie performed with great competence and ingenuity, proving himself worthy of the task. Indeed, he probably did it better than I could have. For instance, soon after the start of construction, the United States was hit by its second fuel crisis, again orchestrated by OPEC and the Arabs. Suddenly, gasoline was almost impossible to find without interminable waits at service stations.

The art of constructing any large building within a budget is really the art of managing and coordinating time, materials, and sub-contractors. At the beginning, every step in the construction process is scheduled to dovetail smoothly one into the other. When one step is about to be completed, the materials needed for the next step should just be arriving at the building site, and the sub-contractors dealing with that step should be getting ready to go to work. When a delay occurs in one step, though, all the subsequent steps are delayed exponentially. As a consequence, the construction budget begins to run into major cost overruns. The more delays, the greater the cumulative overruns.

I had pounded the principle into Elie's head when I gave him the task of overseeing the construction on the 33rd Street garage. No sooner was excavation almost finished than the new fuel shortage occurred. Many of the jackhammers, drills, and other machinery used in the excavation were run from compressed-air generators powered by gasoline engines.

On the final morning of excavation, with that part of the job almost done and the next step—the start of foundation work—waiting to begin, the excavation contractors went to Elie and said, "Sorry, we can't finish. We've run out of gas for our engines and won't be able to get any more for a couple of days."

What that means was that the foundation work would begin to back up and a domino effect to budget-breaking delays would be put into motion. An ordinary construction manager might have accepted the situation with a shrug, writing it off as part of the frustration of trying to get anything done on time in New York.

Not Elie. Without telling me about his problem, he immediately raced over to Twelfth Avenue, which was packed with cars waiting to get into the gas stations that lined the street. At one of the stations, he found a fuel truck making a delivery. He went up to the driver and explained his problem. "I'll make a deal with you," he said. "After you finish your delivery here, drive your truck over to my construction site and give me twenty-five gallons. That's all I need to finish the excavation job on time. I'll make it worth your while."

The driver agreed, and Elie got his twenty-five gallons half-an-hour later. He gave the driver $100 for his cooperation. With sufficient gas to finish the job that day, the excavators were able to do so. In exchange for $100, Elie saved the Hirschfeld organization tens of thousands of dollars of extra cost that would have resulted from chain-reaction delays down the road had the excavation not been completed on time.

It was only later, as I was contemplating what to do with the East 61st Street site, that I heard about Elie's "save." To me, it was proof that he was eminently cut out for this business, and from then on, I was happy to listen to any suggestion he made. Because of that, the now-celebrated Vertical Club had its genesis.

Elie knew that I was in a quandary about what to do with the East 61st Street property now that I could no longer turn it into another garage. He knew, too, of my desire to build an urban "country club" in Manhattan. Also, as I've said, he was a superb athlete who was religious about keeping himself physically fit. Tennis was one of his best sports, in winter, when he couldn't get out of town to ski; he liked to play tennis regularly. The only trouble, he said, was that playing tennis at the various indoor "bubbles" scattered around town wasn't much fun—the artificial lighting was bad and the indoor air was unnatural. If only someone could build some "indoor" courts that weren't really indoors!

And so, the concrete idea for the Vertical Club took shape. Instead of building a vertical, open-air parking lot for cars, I would construct a vertical, open-air, club-like facility for urban athletes who were turned off by the usual cramped, stale-aired, indoor facilities. It wouldn't have golf, but it would have everything else a fitness buff could want—especially a congenial atmosphere.

When I told him my idea, Elie enthusiastically seconded it. And once we were in harmony, everything else about it fell into place. The key concept was its open-air aspect.

Structurally, it could be built with the economy, efficiency, and speed of a parking garage. As we sketched out the design, the only difference was that it would have retractable walls that, like huge, sliding garage doors, could be open or closed, partially or wholly, depending on the weather or season.

The final design called for a building 180 feet tall, the equivalent of an eighteen-story office or apartment building. Inside, on various floors, would be eight tennis, six squash, and three racquetball courts, a swimming pool, the world's longest indoor running track, plus numerous other health, exercise, and state-of-the-art fitness facilities. Spectator seating, elegant locker-rooms, showers and saunas, an attractive restaurant, basement parking, top-bottom elevators, and a swank, street-level entrance lobby completed the plan. As I envisioned the club, there would be nothing else like it anywhere in the world. It would be a first.

As is evident from the above, the original emphasis was on racquet sports. For that reason, Elie and I started out calling the project a racquet club. But as the building was going up, we found that more and more people in New York, in addition to tennis, were getting involved in aerobic and weight-training regimens in their efforts to maintain fitness. So, we added a good deal of space in which those forms of exercise could be carried out, and we began to rethink our name for the club.

We felt that by calling it a racquet club, we might limit its membership appeal solely to tennis and squash players. We wanted it to be an exclusive club that attracted all sort of physical fitness buffs, since that was where the market was going in the mid-1970s, especially among the city's high-income groups. From the start, we had in mind for our membership people from those groups, since the club would be expensive to operate and membership fees would have to be much higher than at the ordinary New York fitness center. I sensed that if our plan succeeded, membership in the club would become somewhat of a symbol. The building itself would be a unique New York symbol. Thus, it had to have a very special name.

The eventual idea I had of calling it "The Vertical Club" came to me seemingly from out of nowhere, although on reflection I know that it had been stored in the back of my mind for years simply by virtue of the business I was in. The "vertical" parking lot had been one of my early phrases in describing my parking garages. Almost all of my other past real estate projects involved verticality. Indeed, New York itself was known as the "vertical city." What could be a more appropriate and distinctive name for the facility we were building than the Vertical Club. Everything about it said: New York.

As it happened, the name instantly became a very valuable tool in producing membership. I was right: the club did become a status symbol among the city's fitness hoi polloi. It grew so popular that waiting lists for membership became the rule rather than the exception.

I only wish the actual construction of the club had been as easy as coming up with the name. Seldom in my career had I been so personally enthusiastic and so intimately involve in the day-to-day

179

nuts-and-bolts of a development project. And never before had I been confronted by such obstacles. Indeed, the club almost didn't make it.

Having secured the necessary financing, having successfully negotiated the torturous path of zoning and building permits, having solved the myriad design and construction problems such a unique building posed, I was sure I was home free once the actual construction started. But then, midway through the project, all hell broke loose.

First, the city began to raise a stink about our rezoning application and threatened to close down construction. Although I couldn't prove it, I had no doubt that it was due to the fact that I had become a regular critic of the Beame administration and its pussy-footing in the face of the city's fiscal crisis. Based on the city's harassment, my bank, Manufacturers Hanover, decided to withdraw its financing and demanded the return of the monies it had already advanced. And based on that, the Club Corporation of America, a club management company we'd contracted to set up and operate the Vertical Club once it was completed, abruptly pulled out.

I don't mind saying that it took a Herculean effort on my part, with a great deal of help from Elie, to surmount those problems. But surmount them we did. In a way, it was a good thing they cropped up because they served as a valuable baptism of fire for Elie in the entrepreneurial real estate business. Needless to say, it was all worth it. When the Vertical Club opened in 1979, it was an instant success and remains a success to this day. We continue to own it, and we operate it under lease with a very competent club-management organization.

But it was not just the construction of the Vertical Club that preoccupied me in the years immediately following my unsuccessful bid for the city council presidency in 1977. If I thought that another failed race had put an end to my involvement in politics, I was wrong. This time, however, rather than the platform of state and city politics, I would find myself trotting the international stage. All thanks to Jimmy Carter.

Carter had kept in close touch with me since his inauguration in 1977. One of his major presidential foreign policy commitments was to try to engineer the beginnings of peace in the Middle East, and he still seemed interested in my ideas. Not infrequently, he would phone me from the White House to chew over possibilities, and on more than one occasion, he asked me to serve as one of his unofficial eyes when I traveled to Israel.

No sooner was Carter inaugurated than, due to financial scandal, Yitzhak Rabin was forced to resign as Prime Minister of Israel. That event threw the domestic politics atmosphere of Israel into turmoil, with the long-dominant Labour Party suddenly faced with defeat by a coalition militant conservative led by Menachem Begin, the ruthless Irgun operative of the Independence years.

By 1977, I knew the aging Begin well. What I knew best about him was that he was no longer the rabid reactionary portrayed in the Western media. Publicly, he was always ready to appeal to the hawkish, right wing, anti-Arab elements in Israeli society to strengthen his position as the main opposition leader and get votes. But privately, he was a realist and pragmatist, and he knew as well as anyone that the high-tension enmity between Israel and the Arab countries could not go on forever. He had conceded to me that one day it would have to be settled. He simply wanted to ensure that when the day of settlement came, Israel would be in as strong a bargaining position as possible. He was not turning soft, certainly. But he was open to new ideas.

He was particularly open to my ideas, if only because he knew that when I had first presented them at the UN in 1974, the Labour government of Golda Meir and Yitzhak Rabin had tried to muzzle me. He listened to what I had to say. Though he didn't agree with everything, he indicated an interest in exploring the matter further in private if he and his conservative coalition defeated the Labour government in the national election that was scheduled following Rabin's resignation.

Encouraged, I return from Israel in 1977 and began to raise funds for Begin's election campaign. I also reported to Jimmy Carter, to whom Begin was an unknown quantity, that in my opinion, a Begin victory might open a key door to the peace process.

"You must be kidding, Abe," the president said. "From everything I've heard about Begin, he's a warmonger."

"Don't trust what you hear," I replied. "The Labour establishment is on the defensive in Israel. It's compelled to take a hard line these days, just to offset the growing appeal of Begin and his coalition. If Begin's elected, he'll be starting afresh. Publicly, he'll keep up his image as an unbending right-winger. But I can promise you, privately, he'll be open to anything that makes good sense. He's been waiting almost thirty years to gain power. If he gets it, he wants to go down in history as the man who made a difference."

Sure enough, Begin won the Prime Ministership. As a result, because I had talked him up in the United States, I became somewhat of a Begin "expert" in the eyes of the Carter administration. And because Begin was aware of my friendship with Jimmy Carter, to him I became an expert on Carter. Soon, I was a conduit of secret communications between the two.

No one who was alive and politically aware late in 1977 is likely to forget the dramatic public peace overture made to Israel by Egyptian president Anwar Sadat, or Menachem Begin's acceptance of it, or the subsequent visit Sadat made to Israel to speak before the Knesset and confer with the Israeli leadership. There are many, though, who still believe that the entire chain of events was spontaneously initiated by Sadat.

Not so. The idea was planted in Sadat's mind by none other than Jimmy Carter, through intermediaries. Among others, I was secretly deputized by Carter to learn from Begin how he would react to such an overture; and, if his instinct was to react negatively, to persuade him otherwise. By the time Sadat made his overture, the diplomatic ground had been well prepared. Begin accepted Sadat's challenge to invite him to Israel. The rest is history.

The climax of that very important historical episode was the Camp David Agreement, which was so skillfully orchestrated by Jimmy Carter and his White House deputies in 1979 in the face of great difficulties. Camp David did not constitute peace between Israel and the Arab world. But at least it was a beginning. It demonstrated that mediation and reason—and plain, good-old horse sense bargaining—had effective, leading roles to play in tempering the agony of the Middle East I'm convinced that if Carter had been able to win a second term as President, the peace process would have continued—with Jordan, certainly, and perhaps one or two other Arabs nations, eventually coming round. But an entirely different Mid-east crisis sabotaged his chances, along with his mediatory, as opposed to bellicose, instincts. The crisis was the seizure in Iran of the American Embassy and the kidnapping of most of its personnel late in 1979. Carter's personal agony and perceived inaction in response to that event tragically doomed his hopes of being re-elected.

The bitter irony of it all was that while Carter's so-called inaction succeeded in saving most of the Iranian hostages' lives, the "action-oriented" policies of his successor, Ronald Regan, would result several years later in the slaughter of nearly 300 Americans in another Mid-east capital—Beirut.

In relating in outline my modest role in the events that led to Camp David, I in no way seek to take even a modicum of credit for the widely praised result. Yet, I don't think it's inappropriate for me to add that Jimmy Carter invited me to Washington to be present at the formal signing of the Camp David Agreement between Sadat and Begin. Or that, afterward, Carter singled me out and said that without me, Camp David would not have been possible, as did Begin and Sadat. All three wrote me notes of appreciation after the signing.

Abraham (Abe) Hirschfeld

CHAPTER TWENTY-ONE: ME, DICK NIXON, AND THE DONALD

Oddly, my extensive contacts with Jimmy Carter were not my only personal involvement with an American president in 1979. All of a sudden, in a different contest, I found myself dealing with Richard Nixon, too.

The sprawling Fifth Avenue apartment Zipora and I had occupied since moving back into the city from Great Neck was much larger than we needed now that Rachel and Elie were out on their own. What's more, inflation and demand were driving East Side apartment prices up at a steep and rapid pace.

One day, I said to Zipora, "Let's sell this place. The way prices are climbing, I'll bet we can get a million dollars for it. We'll make history, not to mention a huge profit. We'll use part of the proceeds to buy something smaller here and the rest to get something nice in Florida."

Zipora agreed. She'd been wanting for some time to have a place in Florida during the winter. I liked the idea, too, since it would enable me to get out of New York's frigid winters and play golf in the sun occasionally. We'd both settled on Palm Beach, where we'd often visited friends in the past. So, in the summer of 1979, I put the apartment on the market at $1 million firm. I'd bought it the year before for $200,000.

Not more than a week passed when I got a call from Zipora. "Abe, you'll never guess who's here looking at the apartment," she said.

"Who?"

"Richard Nixon's daughter. The blonde one. Tricia, her name is. She says her father and mother are planning to move to New York from that place in California."

The next day, I received a call from Nixon himself in San Clemente. He'd just spoken with his daughter, he said, and she'd told him the apartment was as he remembered it from his days as a lawyer in New York in the 1960s. He'd really like to buy it, but he couldn't afford a million. Would I come down?

We bargained and settled on $925,000. I figured that the distinction on selling the place to an ex-President outweighed that of selling the first million-dollar apartment in New York. Nixon told me that his daughter and son-in-law, a lawyer, would come around the next day with the standard ten percent down payment.

"Would you prefer cash or certified check?" Nixon asked. I had to chuckle at that, remembering all the stories about his secret cash funds during Watergate. "Mr. President," I said, "from you a personal check will be fine. I don't think it's going to bounce."

True to his word, the next day, Tricia Nixon Cox and her husband appeared at my office, signed the purchase contract on her father's behalf, and handed over a check for $92,500. The deal would never go through, however. As soon as the rest of the building heard about it, many of the other apartment owners launched a campaign to prevent Nixon from buying on the grounds that his presence in the building, with Secret Service agents and other security protection, plus a constant stream of reporters and photographers, would disrupt their peace and quite. The campaign culminated in a lawsuit, brought by the building's board of managers, that sought among other things to enjoin me from selling the apartment to Nixon.

Naturally the press had a field day with the news of Nixon's intention to move to New York, and even more so with the issue of the lawsuit in which I found myself—what else could I call it?—an innocent victim. I was prepared to fight the suit, but Nixon wasn't. A short while later, he phoned me again from San Clemente, apologized for causing me trouble, and said that he'd decided he wouldn't want to live in a building where he was so unwanted. If I would let him out of the contract, he said, he'd stipulate that I could keep the $92,500 he'd paid.

"But, Mr. President," I said, "it's not your fault the deal can't go through. I wouldn't feel right keeping the $92,000."

"No, Abe," he answered, "it's my fault. I should have tested the mood of the building first. When you took my money, you were obliged to remove the apartment from the market. It's been off the market for several weeks now. During that time, you might have made another deal, a better deal. I want you to keep the down payment as compensation for any losses you might have suffered."

Who said Nixon was a chiseler and a crook? You couldn't have proven it by me. Although technically I was entitled to keep the $92,500, he could easily have made a case that I wasn't given the circumstances. Rather than do so, he had acted magnanimously. He was a lousy businessman, I thought, but an honorable one.

"Besides," he went on to say, "I've just made another, better deal for our move to New York. I'm buying a nice, twelve-room townhouse with a garden on East 65th Street. A real bargain—only $750,000. So, you see, I'm still coming out ahead."

"Mr. President," I said, "you've managed to get a townhouse on East 65th Street for $750,000?"

"That's correct. Right next door to David Rockefeller. I made the deal last night."

"Mr. President, if you could make a deal like that, how would you like to come to work with me?"

If he saw the humor in my question, he didn't show it.

Instead, quite seriously, he answered, "Sorry, Abe, I'll be busy writing books."

So, the Nixon's moved into their townhouse on 65th Street, the lawsuit fizzled out, and I subsequently sold our apartment for more that $1 million. The publicity over the Nixon affair had turned it into the most desirable apartment in New York.

Zipora and I moved into a smaller place near Sutton Place before I got wind that an apartment had become available at 825 Fifth Avenue, at 64th Street, which offered spectacular dual views of Central Park to the west and Madison Avenue to the east, as well as a private, full-service restaurant that was the envy of the posh Fifth Avenue set.

Indeed, Zipora and I belonged to the Fifth Avenue Synagogue, on 62nd Street, and every member's dream was to wean an invitation to dine at 825 Fifth.

The owner of the apartment was Fred Donners, the former Chairman of the Board at General Motors, and we quickly entered into an agreement for me to purchase the place for a very reasonable $400,000. When I would tell people of the deal, the universal reaction was a hearty laugh. They all told me I didn't have a popsicle's chance in hell of winning board approval. And on the surface, they had a right to believe that since it was an unwritten rule—scandalous as it may have been, but accepted as a kind of divine right of the old-world crowd of ant-Semites who ruled New York's white-glove buildings—that Jews simply would not be allowed to own an apartment there.

Leave it to Abe Hirschfeld, a man with no pedigree and a fifth-grade education, to break through that barrier, not with demands and threats but with the gentle art of persuasion. I went to the board

187

meeting, eager to tell the hoary WASPs of my life and my accomplishments, and wound up regaling them with my jokes. I was, in short, Abe Hirschfeld, a proud Jew who had come a long way from Poland to stand with the biggest real estate giants in New York. The meeting began at 5 P.M., and within an hour, Zipora and I had been approved unanimously.

Don't underestimate what a landmark event that was. That night, we went to dinner with Mayor Ed Koch and his good friend Bess Myerson. When we told them of our acceptance, they were stunned. Koch listed the names of some very prominent Jews he'd known who had tried to buy an apartment at 825 Fifth, only to be rejected.

That led me to wonder myself why, in fact, I had broken through as I had. I found out the first night Zipora and I dined in the building's restaurant and a very distinguished looking gentleman came over and said, "Mr. Hirschfeld, my name is Lynton Harrison Baldwin, and I was at the board meeting." Talk about old-world WASP family dynasties. This Mr. Baldwin pointed out that he was the grandson of President Benjamin Harrison!

"Mr. Baldwin, can you answer for me one thing?" I asked. "Why was I accepted while those prominent 'WASH' were not?"

He knew what I was referring to—White Anglo-Saxon Hebrews. He laughed and picked up on the theme.

"Mr. Hirschfeld, those others came in and gave us some famous WASP names as references," he explained. "You, on the other hand, were proud of what you had done as a prominent Jew and gave us the names of your *Jewish* friends!"

Moral of the story: If you are not proud of who you are and those like you, even those unlike you will never accept you.

Ensconced in our dream apartment, Zipora and I spared no expense tuning it into a showplace. We hired Adam Tahini, who designed Le Cirque and many of the world's most elegant restaurants. He tore out the small windows on the Fifth Avenue side and created huge picture windows that brought the majestic, sweeping views above the treetops in Central Park right into our living room and bedroom. The living room and dining rooms we filled with oversized, original Frank Stella murals and the rarest of Chinese art and ceramic vases. But before you get the idea that I am some kind of dilettante imitating the dilettantes who are snooty Fifth Avenue art

188

connoisseurs, most of the wall space is dominated by the caricatures of Al Hirschfeld, including the classic image of me beaming broadly, my arms upraised in victory and pure joy, and that incredibly flattering, one-of-a-kind "33-Nina" tribute to Zipora and me, surrounded by all those celebrity friends we'd made through the years.

Finally, I had found a sanctuary, a place to think and dream and savor so much of the city I loved, just by looking out the windows. And with Elie fitting so well at Hirschfeld Realty, I felt that I could begin taking more time off for relaxation. In fact, Zipora insisted on it. I was about to turn sixty, she said, and I should stop working so hard.

I didn't know what sixty was supposed to feel like. What I did know was that I possessed as much energy and ambition as I ever had. To me, work had always been my relaxation. Yet, to please Zipora, I promised to let up a bit and spend more time in Florida. Events, however, immediately conspired to defeat my promise. I was about to enter the busiest and most pressure-filled period of my life.

It began with another one of those phone calls from out of the blue. The caller was an agent of the Penn-Central Corporation. Penn-Central was the product of a 1960s merger of the financially troubled New York Central and Pennsylvania Railroads. By the late 1970s, the corporation was for all practical purposes out of the railroad business, its operations having been integrated into the federally run Conrail and Amtrak systems. But because of the merger, it still owned vast tracks of old railroad real estate throughout the eastern half of the country. Among its most valuable properties were two large former railroad yards on mid-Manhattan's West Side, bordering the Hudson River. One spanned several blocks of tracks and warehouses in the West Thirties. The other stretched from West 59th to West 72nd Street, between the river and West End Avenue.

In the mid-1970s, Penn-Central, then in bankruptcy, put the two properties up for sale. An aggressive young developer, Donald Trump, acquired an option to buy them for $62 million. He then announced a grandiose plan for each site: the construction of a huge new convention center on the West Thirties property; and on the other larger property to the north, which was commonly called the "Penn Freight Yards," the building of a mammoth mixed residential and commercial development.

By 1979 Trump, who was fast becoming known as the "Boy Wonder" of New York real estate, found himself unable to follow through on his plans and was forced to give up his options. Thus the two properties were once again for sale, and Penn-Central was now doubly anxious to unload them.

I had maintained a casual relationship with Penn-Central since the time I negotiated the purchase of 277 Park Avenue from the old New York Central. What's more, in 1979 Elie was engage to Marcia Riklis, the daughter of Meshulam Riklis, "Rik," as he is known, was also an Israeli who had arrived in America in the 1950s to make a fortune. His specialty was buying up retail merchandising operations, and he had built his small business into what today is the huge and fabulously successful Rapid-American Corporation.

Although we'd not known each other in Israel, Rik and I became good friends in New York during the 1960s.

One of his major financial partners in the expansion of Rapid-American was the financier Carl Lindner, who also became the chairman and principal stockholder of the bankrupt Penn-Central in the 1970s. Through Rik, I had gotten to know Lindner, and I'd often talked to him about Penn-Central's valuable real estate holdings.

The out-of-the-blue phone call I received from the Penn-Central official in 1979 was to inform me that Donald Trump had just relinquished his option to buy the West Side properties and to inquire if I would be interested in the Penn Yards parcel, which consisted of almost 100 acres. His call was being made, he said, at the suggestion of Carl Lindner.

By then, I was thoroughly familiar with the problems Donald Trump had run into over his plans for the site. I was also suffering from an emotional letdown in the wake of my financial, legal, and other difficulties in getting the Vertical Club built. Plus, Zipora was urging me to cut back my activities. So, my temptation was to say—no, I wasn't interested.

But then there was the other side of the coin. In real estate, if you expect to prosper, you can never stand still; you must always be scouting for opportunities. Besides, I asked myself, did I really want to rest on my past laurels? Finally, the Boy Wonder of New York, Donald Trump, had all but admitted that the Penn Yards was beyond his developmental capabilities. He'd said, in effect, that if he couldn't do it, no one could. Wasn't that, I wondered to myself, challenge enough?

Donald Trump was the son of the wealthy Queens and Brooklyn real estate developer Fred Trump, a man whom I had known and loved for many years. Fred Trump, may he rest in peace, always loved and supported me.

When I ran for office, no matter which, he always collected signatures in his buildings for my petitions. We often played golf at the Breakers Golf Club, and he and his lovely wife Marie and Zipora and I were two of the first four couples at Governor Hugh Carey's first dinner at the governor's mansion in Albany.

I did not then know his precocious son Donald, whom Fred had taken into his organization when he was fresh out of college and provided the launching pad for his boy's subsequent success. The first time I encountered him, I sized up this cocky young man and thought, he is just like his old man. Smart. Personable. A bit of a hustler. At the time, I was running for Daniel Moynihan's vacated U.S. Senate seat, and one day during a campaign swing through Buffalo, a reporter asked me if I thought anyone would be a more attractive candidate than me. My answer came quickly.

"Yes, there is one," I said. "Donald Trump."

You must remember that few had ever heard that name back then, and my praise served as his introduction for many people. For his part, Donald was profusely grateful.

Soon after, he invited me to have breakfast with him. This became a habit. In fact, for around fifteen years, we would have breakfast at least one day a week until, as you will see, I committed the cardinal sin of puncturing his ego.

The irony, of course, is that without my guidance, he never would have been successful enough to have that ego. At the beginning, Donald was a kind of apprentice, learning the ropes of the real estate game, and his father was eager for me to teach him the lessons that can never be learned in a textbook. Indeed, the case of the Penn Yards led me to believe that Elie would be a far better realtor than Trump. Elie was three years younger than Donald, and with my help, maybe he could succeed where Donald had failed. Maybe he could be the new Boy Wonder of New York real estate.

I told the man from Penn-Central that I'd call him back. Then I grabbed Elie and said, "Come on, son. We're going over to look at the Penn Yards."

Upon inspecting the site, there could be no doubt about it. What we saw was the most valuable piece of developable real estate remaining in Manhattan—a potential gold mine. Just to the east, the huge Lincoln Center development of the 1960s was flourishing, and because of that, the upper West Side, north of it, was in the beginning stages of a residential and commercial rebirth.

Damn the consequences! I thought. I must have it, if only to give myself a chance to experiment with its development potential. Even if nothing came of it, with land values rising the way they were, it would be worth three, four, perhaps five times what I paid for it a few years later.

When we returned to the office, I called back the man from Penn-Central and asked the price. He said $40 million.

"Wait a minute," I said, "you had a deal with Trump at $62 million for the Penn Yards together with the West Thirties site. The West Thirties site is much more valuable than the Penn Yards, since it's on the edge of midtown and has fewer zoning problems. The way I figure it, of the $62 million Trump was willing to pay, $38 million was for the West Thirties parcel, and $24 million was for the Penn Yards. How do you get away asking $40 million now for the Penn Yards?"

He answered that the Trump deal had been made in 1975 and that now, four years later, each of the sites was worth much more.

"Maybe," I said, "but not that much more. And I happen to know you're desperate to get rid of it since Trump's dropped out."

"Would you consider $30 million?" he asked.

"Why don't I come see you?" I said, figuring that I was finally getting somewhere.

The following day, we met at the Penn-Central offices. I got the price down to $28 million, but payable only on the condition that I succeed in having the parcel re-zoned from industrial to residential use within a period of two-and-a-half years. My idea was to expand on Donald Trump's original plan but to develop the site as a mixed-use, park-like, riverfront residential enclave containing 5,000 luxury co-op apartments spread through ten hi-rise buildings. In other words, a city within a city.

On that basis, I signed a contract. With only $400,000 up front, I was now the owner of the nearly 100-acre Penn Yards, the choicest chunk of undeveloped property in the greatest city in the world. Any idea I'd had about slowing down was now out the window.

Even today, Elie, who was with me through the whole rapid-fire process, expresses amazement at the way I carried it off. Once I'd negotiated the price and other salient terms of the purchase, the Penn-Central people incorporated them overnight into a contract that was nearly an inch thick. The next day, I returned for the formal signing. Elie said to me, "Dad, you're about to sign the biggest contract of your life. You haven't even looked at it, and you haven't had a lawyer check it out. How can you do this?"

"Elie," I said, "you're a lawyer; you check it out." When we arrived at Penn-Central, he picked up the contract and began to pore through it.

I said, "Elie, you could take all day reading that. Just tell me two things. First, is my name on the contract?"

"Yes," he said.

"And is the price?"

"Yes."

"That's all I want to know. I'm ready to sign."

I was trying to teach him an elemental lesson of real estate. You can't let lawyers and other advisers make your decisions for you. If you have a vision, and are sure of it, follow it through without delay. If it's solid, then it doesn't need lawyers. If it's not, it will end up in the hands of lawyers anyway. You won't always bat a thousand. But if you're good, you'll win many more times than you'll lose. One of my favorite forms of recreation is playing cards—gin rummy, poker, pinochle, that sort of thing. I don't keep a lawyer at my side when I play. The real estate business is very much like a card game. When you can see you've been dealt a good hand, go for the big bet. When your cards aren't so good, bide your time and wait for the next deal.

I didn't have to be a genius to know that in the Penn Yards negotiation, I had been dealt one of the best hands of my life. They cost almost nothing to acquire, and I had two-and-a-half years before I had to pay off the very favorable purchase price. And to find a partner to underwrite the development plan I had in mind.

The partner appeared quickly. Francisco Macri was a former bricklayer from Argentina who had built a financial and real estate development empire in South America during the 1950s and 1960s. In the 1970s, he had moved his organization into the New York City market with a bid to develop a 24-acre piece of city-owned land, along the East River, into a luxury hi-rise housing project. The Macri Group, as it was called, had lost the bid, but not its enthusiasm for expanding into New York. Not long after I acquired Penn Yards, I received a call from a man named Carlos Varsavsky, the chairman of a Macri holding company known as B.A. Capital Corporation.

He said, "Congratulations on beating us to that Hudson River land you got from Penn-Central. We're told you're looking for a partner to develop it. We'd like to be that partner. Can we meet and talk about it?"

I said, "Why not?" I already knew the Macri organization was a giant in the field.

The deal I made with Macri and B.A. Capital was a gem of its kind. Essentially, I sold the site to them for a hefty profit and a 35 percent partnership in a new joint company to be formed by us for the purpose of developing the Penn Yards according to my original mixed residential-commercial master plan. The beauty of it was that Macri and B.A. Capital would put up all the money—close to $1 billion—needed to carry the development out. My job—Elie's and my job—would simply be to advise and assist Macri in the process of getting the site rezoned. We called the new company Lincoln West Associates, since "Lincoln West" was what we intended to name the huge development.

Elie and I did our part—we succeeded in getting the city to rezone the property in 1982, despite a loud chorus of opposition from local community groups who complained that the development would result in an overpopulation of the West Side. Unfortunately, though, the Macri organization did not possess the flexibility and imagination needed to engage in effective and profitable real estate development in New York. In South America, it was accustomed to getting its way whenever it wanted something. It had little tolerance for the endless bureaucratic obstacles that are constantly tossed in a developer's path in New York and was not inclined to negotiate its way around them.

I did my best to show them how. "When in Rome, do as the Romans do." But the Macri people couldn't adjust. Moreover, their designs for the project became increasingly grandiose, unrealistic, and expensive, requiring repeated renewals of permit applications, environmental impact studies, and zoning adjustments. By 1983, it began to be clear that they would never be able to carry the development off. Not a spade of earth had been turned. They had poured tens of millions into their efforts to get started and were still where they had been three years earlier. The only people who made any money were the lawyers and architects they hired to get them out of the messes other lawyers and architects got them into.

In the meantime, as a result of the war over the Falkland Island between Britain and Argentina, the Macri organization was suddenly faced with a cash crunch. It appeared that unless something was done, the "filet mignon" of New York real estate would turn into hamburger. Finally, early in 1984, the Macri people conceded to me that they could go no further with the project. For all practical purposes, they were broke. Would I care to buy them out, they asked?

No, I answered, but I might find someone who would bail them out. Please do, they said. So, I told them to contact Donald Trump.

Trump, of course, already knew the property well from the days in the mid-1970s when he'd had an option on it and envisioned his own development. During the five years since he'd relinquished his option, his fortunes and reputation had soared. He'd just finished two of the most expensive and prestigious new apartment buildings in Manhattan. He was about to open a gambling casino and hotel in Atlantic City. He'd recently bought a professional football team. He had dozens of other big-ticket irons in the fire. Perhaps most important of all, he'd learned to play the city's political machine like a virtuoso, and he had a deep-pockets financial partner for most of his projects in the Equitable Insurance Company. If anyone could save the Lincoln West venture, he could. That was assuming Macri could persuade him to take it on.

It turned out to be no trouble at all. Now that we had done all the donkey work in getting the Penn Yards cleared for development, Trump was happy to take over the project. He agreed to buy the property from us.

Well, not quite. Since Elie and I had been so instrumental in getting the project off the ground, we decided that to remain in the loop, whereby we became a 20 percent partner in the company he'd formed to buy out Macri and take over the ownership of the Penn Yards. We would play no further role in its development, but we would get 20 percent of the profits once Trump's development was in operation in the 1990s.

There remained one question to be answered: Would Trump be able to succeed where Macri had failed? To me the answer was a resounding "Yes." If I had any doubts about Trump's brilliance as a developer, they were erased when he announced his own plans for the site in 1985. They were eminently practical, as well as beautiful, and there's no question in my mind that he'd succeed with his splendid new addition to Manhattan's skyline.

Or so I thought.

Two decades later, I wonder why Trump wound up squandering so much of his potential and legacy. Actually, I know the answer. It has to do with me.

I marvel at the twists and turns of my complicated relationship with this self-promotional genius who, yes, thinks he knows it all. Of course, I have been described in those exact same terms. The only difference is, I actually do know it all.

And when Donald Trump followed what I told him, he would be regaled as someone who did as well. Case in point is a project that is one of my proudest dreams come true, one that would become one of New York City's most precious and romantic pieces of land: the Wollman Skating Rink in Central Park, to which thousands of people stream every winter to ice skate on snow-white ice framed in a picture postcard fresco of a twinkling skyline beyond the park's treetops.

This wasn't always the case, however. In the mid-1980s, the rink was an oversized pothole, constantly in disrepair, and more apt to be visited by junkies and hobos. From my apartment nine floors above the park, I watched as workers repaired the rink, then tore it up, rebuilt it, and tore it up again in a comedy of incompetence that to me was a grand tragedy. Finally, in anger, I called the Parks Commissioner, Henry Stern, and invited him to lunch in my building's private dining room, which excited him to no end.

Henry was a former city councilman; he knew how I had built the Yankee Stadium garage so splendidly and under cost. And so I told him I had a proposition: I would take over the sputtering Wollman rink project myself.

"Henry," I said, "I give you my guarantee. I'll get this project done in six months. I will give you a letter of credit and a guaranteed date of completion. You can take my word to the bank."

He was captivated by the idea. It also didn't hurt that I implied he could regularly eat in the dining room if I got the go-ahead. Right then and there, he said he would have an answer for me in two weeks. In the interim, we met maybe twenty more times and I was ready to send in the construction crews. But New York being New York, a tangled web of pork-barrel politics, a lot of people who do little but dole out favors to fat-cat cronies simply did not want to hand me this plum, knowing I would not grease anyone's palm in return. Neither did they care to reward me after I had stepped on so many toes—and spit in one particular face.

After Stern had hemmed and hawed enough for me to figure it out, I realized the rink would get nowhere unless my plan was put into effect—but with a front man with connections who would pay heed to me. That man was Donald Trump.

At our next breakfast meeting, I told him of my obsession to save the rink, and Donald loved the idea. Actually, the idea he loved the most was that he would be getting the publicity and the credit. This was fine by me because he had a PR machine I could not hope to match and the beneficiary would be the city. He agreed to take over most of the cost, which was minimal to him and to me, and in return, he would reap an avalanche of fawning headlines that were critical to his future projects.

I also did not mind that in his press campaign, he never mentioned me as the power behind the throne. He could not have without slowing down the project. However, at the opening of the rink, I'm sure many people in the political clubhouses were stunned when Donald arose and thanked me by name for my vision and plan. The encomium was nice and was appreciated. But my greater reward was seeing that wonderful gleaming ice and all those happy people skating on it whenever I looked out my window in the winter.

Another byproduct of the Wollman Rink episode was that Donald learned from me how to open up his rather stiff personality and make himself appear to have a sense of humor. I would provide him with a new joke at each of our breakfast conclaves, which he would then tell when he gave a speech. The one joke that was his favorite, however, he dared not tell. This was the one I told him when he came in one day and said he was having problems in bed with his fancy schmancy Czechoslovakian wife Ivana, whom of course, he had made nearly as famous as he is. I told him the story of the man who was having sexual problems with his beautiful wife and went to a doctor complaining he could not get aroused. The doctor bragged that he had a new injection that would make him perform for two hours. So, the man takes the injection and hurried home, but his wife wasn't there. After an hour, he desperately calls the doctor.

"Doctor, please help me," he pleads. "I have only an hour left before I lose my erection. What do I do?"

"Here's my advice," the doctor says. "Go have sex with your neighbor's wife or your girlfriend for an hour."

"Doctor, you don't understand," he says. "With my neighbor's wife or my girlfriend, I don't need an injection."

The only problem was, I think Donald took the punch line of that joke a bit too literally. He may have needed an injection with Ivana, but he had no trouble porking Marla Maples all that time (and everything else female that moved).

Along with jokes, I also gave Donald a new brother-in-law. When he was the guest speaker at some function or other at the Waldorf Astoria Hotel about ten years ago, he invited Zipora and I to sit at his family table with his parents, his brother, and his two sisters. After I had related to Marie Trump that Zipora and I had had an arranged marriage, and that my mother had been the world's greatest matchmaker, Marie confided to me that her unmarried daughter, Elizabeth, was miserable. She was forty-five years old, held a high position with Chase Manhattan Bank, but she could not meet the right man.

"Maybe you can find her a husband," Marie said, quite seriously, adding, "We don't even mind if he's Jewish. Most of our friends are Jewish."

"Marie," I assured her, "I will have her married off within six months."

I set Elizabeth up with Jim Groh, a film producer for CBS, who was a widower in his late forties. Almost immediately, they fell in love. Thrilled, Donald made me a promise.

"Abe," he said, "I'll give you a $5 million matchmaking fee if they get married."

I hate to have to say this about Donald, but he welshes on his promises. They did get married. And Donald still owes me that $5 million.

On the other hand, the real estate advice I have given him is worth ten times that.

If you don't believe it coming from me, then read Donald's first book, *The Art of the Deal*. He mentioned me and my influence on him so often that when I read that book, I thought it was about me, not him.

I'll also give you some examples. In the early '90s, Donald called me and invited me to his office on the ninth floor of the Trump Tower, where on a big table he had a large glass model of a building—which he wanted to build at Sixth Avenue and 59th Street, on Central Park South, after tearing down the famous Barbizon Hotel, a great New York landmark which he had bought.

I was aghast. I couldn't believe he was serious about such a thing.

"Donald, are you crazy?" I said. "Why would you destroy such a beautiful art deco building like the Barbizon?"

I pointed out that, after having seen the blueprint for his new proposed building, it wouldn't have nearly as great an F.A.R.—real estate jargon for floor area ratio—given that the Barbizon had 12-foot ceilings, not the modern eight-foot ceilings. "You don't replace a gem like the Barbizon. You'd be slitting your throat."

Donald circled the table, studying the model. Then he picked up the phone and screamed to his architect on the project, "Take back this monstrosity. I'm going to renovate the existing Barbizon, not tear it down."

About three years later, we were having our usual breakfast when Donald told me that the remodeling of the Barbizon, which he'd renamed Trump Parc, had made him a profit of more than $300 million.

"Abe," he said, "I just want you to know you saved me at least $70 million by not tearing it down. If I'd done that, within two years I wouldn't have been able to give away apartments in that new building."

Not by surprise, then, he again called me when he was about to acquire the fabled Plaza Hotel. He had just made an offer to buy the grand dame of all luxury hotels from its owners, Lufthansa Airlines, for $390 million—which was $60 million less than what Lufthansa had paid for it. "Abe, what do you think?" he asked. Well, any real estate man worth his salt would have known that such a devaluation meant the Plaza was not worth its reputation.

"Donald, listen to me," I said. "It may seem like a bargain to you, but to me it means you will wind up selling it for $60 million less than what *you* paid for it. You're paying double the value of what the place is worth. Trust me, you're going to lose the hotel."

Trump by now believed he knew better about the vagaries of real estate than me. He bought the Plaza at the inflated price, renovated it beautifully, and restored its classic, old-world décor. He brought the matrons and beautiful people back to the Palm Court restaurant for high tea and tourists back to the reservation desk. Donald himself married Marla Maples in the hotel ballroom, an affair I remember so well because my beautiful Zipora stole the show by wearing a one of a kind designer gown I had found while I was in Seoul, South Korea. What a knockout she was in it! I was never more proud of her in my life.

So, Donald was on top of the world, having passed his blood rival Leona Helmsley—another of my students, whom I had sent on to work for (and marry) Harry Helmsley—as New York's most renowned hotelier.

And within a few years, the banks foreclosed on the Plaza, and he had to sell it for $290 million. So, I was wrong to believe he would lose $60 million. He lost $100 million.

That set in motion a downward spiral that saw Donald make disastrous decisions and lose nearly his entire empire of hotels and casinos—and for all his publicity stunts, he will never again be among the elite of the real estate game. It also was the beginning of the end of our once warm relationship. The final act was when he once more came to me, not for advice but for capital.

That came about when he wanted to bring in a foreclosure on a two-tower, thirty-story building in Palm Beach, where of course, he has his famous Mar-a-Lago estate. Donald made a deal with the banks to buy the building for $24 million and asked me to be his partner. Only when I checked into it, I found that the cost was really $24 million for *each tower,* or $48 million. Clearly, this was an outrageous price, and I told him I was not interested. Instead, Donald talked Lee Iacocca into coming in on the deal—and they both lost their shirts.

It has now been around five years since Donald and I have spoken, and if I had to guess why Donald turned against me, I think it was that I was right about the Plaza, and that he was so disastrously wrong.

This is the way Donald Trump's ego works. It masks a very insecure and unforgiving man. On some neurotic level, he may blame me for being right, as if things would have turned out better had I only played yes man. On that level, I am the bad guy in the drama. If he does believe this, I suggest he get a grip on reality.

It also may have eaten away at him that I once called his Trump Tower a monstrosity. But then, if you can't be honest with someone you love, then they don't really love you. Worse, I think Donald knows the building he designed as his epitaph is a monstrosity.

To sum up the matter of Donald Trump, I will say in all honesty that he is a good administrator, a great manipulator, and a poor builder. And to bring this all full circle back to the Penn Yard project, shortly after he presented a scale model of his planned development to a press conference, Donald sent me a letter.

"Dear Abe," it read. "As you know, the plans call for a new street to be created through the finished project. I thought I'd let you know that I intend to call it, with your permission, Hirschfeld Boulevard."

Again, his promise was unkept—mainly because the Penn Yards project ended in failure, broken dreams that were never built and unceremoniously abandoned. My twenty percent of the profits turned out to be twenty percent of nothing.

And yet, I will say pretty much the same thing I said to that Buffalo reporter when I made him famous. For all his faults and short-sighted self-delusions, I freely admit that if I can't own the world myself, the next best choice would be Donald Trump.

When New York City renovated legendary Yankee Stadium in the early 1970s, I was called in to build one of my signature open-air garages next to the stadium. Three decades later, it still stands as an model of engineering perfection.

At a book-signing party with my old friend and student Donald Trump. The Donald never made a move without me and credited me for him making a fortune. Then he stopped taking my advice and nearly lost his shirt, and my friendship.

FOUNDED IN 1801 BY ALEXANDER HAMILTON

NEW YORK POST
Founded by Alexander Hamilton in 1801
ABE HIRSCHFELD
Publisher
PETE HAMILL   ROBERT McMANUS
Editor-in-Chief   Deputy Editorial Page Editor
STEVE CUOZZO   MARC KALECH
Executive Editor   Managing Editor
THOMAS T. KO
Deputy Managing Editor
MARALYN MATLICK   MARY PAPENFUSS
MURRAY WEISS
Associate Metropolitan Editors
America's oldest continuously published daily newspaper

A simple idea of mine became the front page that saved the *New York* Post from doom and inspired thousands of imitators, and is today a collector's item. Although many disparaged my brief ownership of the paper, and conspired to take it from me, the *Post* has since lost half its readership.

204

Back when there was no Israel and the British ruled Palestine, I (seated in the middle on the truck) proudly served my time in the Haganah, the Jewish defense militia that protected Jewish settlements from Arab terrorists. Sadly, some things haven't changed in six decades.

CRAZY AND IN CHARGE

Brilliant tycoons have had a tendency to get eccentric, or worse

By ALAN FARNHAM

Only 21 of us are still alive

HOWARD HUGHES WAS A GENIUS ENTREPRENEUR BEFORE BEING DEVOURED BY HIS ECCENTRICITIES

A t first glance, the business world of the 20th century would not seem a propitious breeding ground for eccentricity. Businessmen and -women, in the main, pride themselves on probity, predictability. "Sober" and "well-rounded" are considered compliments. Little wonder, then, that a hectare of executives contains fewer kooks than just about any other sampling of humanity. Compared with poets and philosophers, bankers and industrialists have been relatively late adopters of berets, ferrets and home brewing. Yet, even so, the century has hatched its share of "true originals"—some of whom won fame and fortune, others who left only a gaudy afterglow.

The fetishes of Howard Hughes (1905-76) have entered folklore, to the point that Hughes is remembered less for having been an industrialist-aviator-Hollywood-producer than for having been a saver of urine (his own), a recluse terrified of dust, a man who, with the right audience (Mormon bodyguards), couldn't see *Ice Station Zebra* often enough. Yet for every celebrity eccentric, a dozen more labored in obscurity. Who remembers Brian Hughes? This 1920s box-manufacturing tycoon liked nothing better than to patrol the sidewalk outside Tiffany in New York City, an envelope tucked beneath his arm. When the moment seemed right, and pedestrian traffic sufficient, Hughes would let loose its contents, sending a spray of jewels (all fake) clattering across the sidewalk. The melee that ensued never ceased to please him. On rainy days, he would exit a restaurant and deliberately leave behind an expensive umbrella. When opened by a misappropriater, the umbrella released a shower of leaflets saying THIS UMBRELLA STOLEN FROM BRIAN G. HUGHES.

For sheer reclusiveness, Hughes (Howard, not Brian G.) had a worthy rival in candymaker Forrest Mars Sr. Virtually every detail of Mars' life—including his birthday—is kept a closely guarded corporate secret within Mars Inc., a secretive company. He has reportedly given but one interview in his entire career and that to a candy-industry trade paper in 1966. Yet even Mars' and Hughes' penchant for anonymity pales before that of Basil Zaharoff (1849-1936), a munitions king aptly called the "Mystery Man of Europe." Zaharoff systematically stole or destroyed all records of his youth and early manhood, making snooping into his past impossible. He

J. PAUL GETTY AND FRIEND PARTY AT MAXIME'S IN PARIS, 1952. THEY PROBABLY SPLIT THE BILL

employed several doubles and never permitted himself to be photographed until late in life, after he had retired. Why such secrecy? Assassins from many nations hunted him. He had made his fortune by simultaneously selling arms to both sides in a conflict. He grew rich—and hated.

Certain industries have yielded gushers of eccentrics. Oil gave the world two famous penny-pinching billionaires: J. Paul Getty (1892-1976), legendary for forcing guests at his estate to use a pay phone, and H.L. Hunt (1889-74), who every day either brought his lunch to work in a paper sack or, when not feeling quite so flush, cadged his secretary's sandwich. Less well known was oil and cattle baron James ("Silver Dollar Jim") West (1903-57).

Wearing a diamond-encrusted Texas Ranger's badge and hunched behind the wheel of one of his 30 automobiles, West loved to race alongside Houston police in pursuit of evildoers, throwing handfuls of silver dollars to startled onlookers as he sped by.

Real estate has produced ABE HIRSCHFELD, who made his fortune building parking garages. With his millions, he has tried—and failed—to win a variety of elective offices, ranging from lieutenant governor of New York to U.S. Senator as a member of, variously, the Republican, Democratic and Independent parties. Recently, he interposed himself into the Clinton sex scandal, when, uninvited, he offered to pay Paula Jones $1 million if she would drop her sexual-harassment suit against the President. A few years ago, a headline in the New York *Post* asked WHO IS THIS NUT? At the time, Hirschfeld owned the newspaper. Asked if he was crazy, he replied, with great good grace, "I am. Any person that achieves things and accomplishes things is a little crazy." Which brings us now to publishing. If ever there was a happy hunting

CARROTS, SEX AND COLD WATER WERE KEYS TO BERNARR MACFADDEN'S HEALTH-AND HAPPINESS EMPIRE

I like to say being a little crazy can't hurt, and the proof is that Time *magazine named me one of the top hundred builders and titans of the 20ᵗʰ Century, joining other "crazy" geniuses like Howard Hughes and J. Paul Getty. I'm sure they would have enjoyed my company.*

Libby Pataki
Ienia, Route 9D
R1, Box 4A
Garrison, New York 10524

Dear Abe,

Thank you for the magnificent flowers. We were so honored to have you think of us.

Thank you for the brilliant ideas you shared with our campaign. Your tremendous fundraising job and efforts at getting out the truth were essential to our success.

On to January 1ˢᵗ,

Libby and George.

1W80

Received Nov 25, 1994

George Pataki coveted my support in his campaign to unseat the loathsome Mario Cuomo as New York Governor in 1994. Pataki and his wife Libby credit my "brilliant ideas" and "tremendous fundraising job" for his election. Then Pataki, as did Cuomo, knifed me in the back and became a dismal failure.

Abraham (Abe) Hirschfeld

> HYANNIS PORT
> MASSACHUSETTS 02647
>
> 2.
>
> Dear Abe — October 23rd, 1992
>
> Thank you so much for being a part of the Golf Tournament. You parsed the course, without even taking a swing.
>
> I remember that Bobby was captivated by you from the start, meeting you for the first time in the unlikely surroundings of a golf course.
>
> To him you epitomized the diversity, strength and
>
> vitality that is America.
>
> He loved that you were smart, funny and always there for him.
>
> He found you frank with your advice, giving of your time and thoughtful about the future of our nation.
>
> Like Bobby, you are devoted to your family, loyal to your friends and committed to your country.
>
> I will always remember what you meant to Bobby and appreciate what you've done for his Memorial and for me.
>
> With love,
> Ethel

I treasure this touching letter from Ethel Kennedy thanking me for participating in her charity golf tournament in 1992. "Bobby was captivated by you," she wrote. "To him you epitomized the diversity, strength and vitality that is America." These words bring tears to my eyes.

My pride and joy: The Vertical Club, fulfilling my vision to build the world's first (and still the best) upscale health and fitness club. And the critics said it could never be a success.

When I helped elect George Pataki Governor of New York, he
coveted my advice. Then, like Mario Cuomo before him, he
betrayed me – and all New Yorkers.

The beautiful tableau of the Wollman Skating Rink in Central Park would never have been created had it not been for my vision and commitment to build it.

I became the "Garage King" for my invention of the open-air garage, which revolutionized the American economy. Shown here is my garage on 49th Street, one of my first and still the hub of the Rockefeller Center area.

In 1973 I commissioned this moving montage of Bobby Kennedy's life for the Children's Recreation Foundation. Designed by artist Ivan Chermayeff, the mural covered an entire wall at the foundation's offices at 120 East 87th Street in Manhattan, keeping alive Bobby's eternal spirit.

I never have had to be talked into going for a ride with my beloved wife Zipora. Here, we take a spin in a tractor to get a first-hand look at the progress of my Yankee Stadium garage project.

No, I'm not doing my Godzilla imitation. I'm standing over a scale-model of my proposed 1993 Yankee Stadium renovation, which would have made the rundown South Bronx a glittering showplace had not the politicians killed the plan to spite me.

I often pop in at the Vertical Club (now called Sports Club/LA) to check out the state-of-the-at fitness equipment -- and the state-of-the-art women who work out there. My son Elie will confirm that, having met his wife at the club.

My great friend Al Hirschfeld honored me by drawing this wonderful caricature that perfectly embodies my joy and wonder at coming so far from such humble beginnings. It is among my most prized possessions. If only a few of my election nights had ended like this.

Not before or since have I ever had a hero like Bobby Kennedy. My fondest memories are of working for Bobby – and my worst memory is the heartbreaking conversation we had just before he was assassinated.

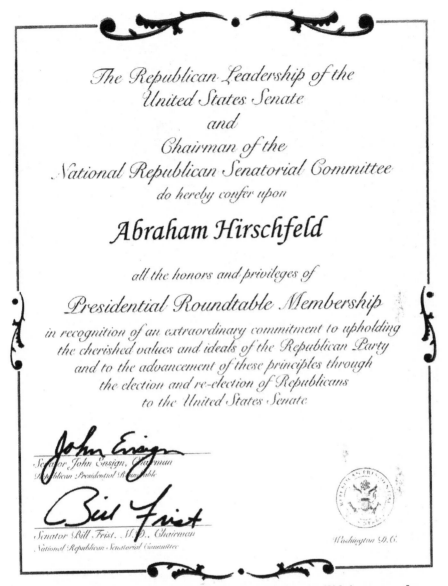

*The Republican Leadership of the
United States Senate
and
Chairman of the
National Republican Senatorial Committee
do hereby confer upon*

Abraham Hirschfeld

all the honors and privileges of

Presidential Roundtable Membership

*in recognition of an extraordinary commitment to upholding
the cherished values and ideals of the Republican Party
and to the advancement of these principles through
the election and re-election of Republicans
to the United States Senate.*

*Senator John Ensign, Chairman
Republican Presidential Roundtable*

*Senator Bill Frist, M.D., Chairman
National Republican Senatorial Committee*

Washington D.C.

**Despite George Pataki and Rudy Giuliani vilifying me, the
Republican Party's Senate Roundtable honored me with this
proclamation, signed by Senator Bill Frist, now the Majority
Leader. I also single-handedly elected George W. Bush president
– something I deeply regret now.**

Standing in front of one of my proudest achievements: the Clarion Castle Hotel, Miami Beach, 1990. I gave the city a beautiful luxury hotel and a dinner theater that revitalized all of south Florida – only to be closed down by corrupt politicians who couldn't buy me.

I came out early for Jimmy Carter and elected him president. A brilliant man who listened to my advice and gave me a key role at the Camp David summit, he never held a grudge that my endorsement of Ronald Reagan cost him the presidency. Today we remain good friends.

Politicians all over the world seek my advice, such as in 1997 when Tony Blair invited me to England when he was running for Prime Minister. I turned the election in his favor within days. But, as with George W. Bush, my support ended when the Iraq war began.

My life's mission has been to create peace in the Middle East, and my input was invaluable at the 1978 Camp David conference that produced peace between age-old enemies Israel and Egypt. Here, in my engaging way, I wheedle Israeli Prime Minister Menachem Begin to keep negotiating.

A picture of betrayal: Zipora and I pose at a charity function with Randy Daniels (top right), during the time I employed him when no one else would, and before I sent him on to work for George Pataki. Now, as New York's Secretary of State, Daniels won't lift a finger to help me.

At the podium during the first of my two campaigns for a U.S. Senate seat from New York, in 1974. As a politician, I have one fault – I tell the truth. This explains why the party bosses have never given me a fair chance to win any election I've been in.

Another picture of betrayal: New York's Lieutenant Governor
Carl McCall (standing, just behind Zipora) was eager to get in the
picture with the Hirschfelds and the Trumps, Donald and Marla
Maples (at right). But in 1997 McCall sabotaged my campaign for
Manhattan Borough President.

Blowing out the candles at my 75th birthday party, with the always-stunning Zipora at my side and my son and partner Elie and his wife beaming (far left). A decade later, I still have plenty of wind left in me for both future birthdays and battles.

Zipora and I, still hopelessly in love after 60 years of marriage. My wife is still one of the most beautiful and brilliant women in the world – and a victim of my ruthless enemies, whose obsession to ruin and imprison me have taken a toll on her health the last several years.

Dear Abe,
Thanks for your
friendship and
support.

Al D'Amato

Like many other famous New York politicians, Senator Al D'Amato beat a path to my door, only to turn his back on me when I needed powerful allies. But I got the last laugh. My election-day endorsement of Chuck Schumer in 1999 cost "Senator Pothole" his job.

With the great actor Anthony ("Zorba the Greek") Quinn and his wife. When famous people see me, they can't wait to talk to me. The same can't be said about the nagging woman next to Tony, *New York Post* gossip columnist Cindy Adams, who has written many vicious lies about me.

Media people have always wanted to hear what I have to say.
Here, I fill in David Brinkley on what was *really* going on in the
world back in the '60s when he was the biggest news anchorman
in America.

That's me, third from the left, at about 12 years old, standing
with a Jewish youth group in Tarnow, Poland in the late 1920s.
The dress code left no room for individuality, but even then I
went against the grain – rejecting the military-style cap for a
jaunty roadster's hat.

January 1992. President George Bush Sr. dedicates the new headquarters for the Drug Enforcement Administration's New York Field Division. The DEA bought the space from me after I turned an abandoned building into a palace – proving my real estate philosophy: look not for "location, location, location" but "garbage, garbage, garbage."

I've always been a big hit telling my stories on my campaign trails. Here, during my run for New York City Council President in 1977, I crack up then -Mayor Abe Beame and former Mayor Robert Wagner, seated to my left.

There are only a few people in the world as funny as I am, and
one is Alan King. Our friendship dates back to the Borscht Belt
days of the 1950s when the Catskill Mountains echoed with
laughter and love among the Jewish people.

"The Garage King" was among the invited guests when the future King of England, Prince Charles, visited New York in the early '90s. He even stole my script – speaking about "ending friction between religions" just days after I had used those words in a speech.

Don't be fooled by the smarmy smile on Mario Cuomo's face.
Never has there been a more vicious, cold-hearted politician.
When I ran for Lt. Governor against his hand-picked candidate
for Lt. Governor in 1986, my "old friend" smeared and had me
kicked off the ballot, which the *New York Times* called a "crime
against democracy."

Abe Hirschfeld

THE MOUTH THAT ROARED
PHOTO BY DAN FARRELL

If there is only lingering image of Abe Hirschfeld I would like to leave the world, it is this one. For all the pain and torture I've been put through, my life has been pure joy, laughter and wonder. And will be until my last breath.

239

When Donald Trump sought my advice his deals were successful.

My Je Accuse by Abraham Hirschfeld

I am back from prison where I was incarcerated for NO GOOD REASON. But now that I am a free man, I'd like to speak up on issues that are of major concern to us all.

First of all, the so called "Road Map" that President Bush proposed to achieve peace between Israel is NO ROAD MAP to peace, but rather a way to disaster.

President Bush intends to divide Israel into two parts. This is like dividing Manhattan into two parts between Blacks and Jews. Such a division will bring only further bloodshed and terrorism.

Secondly, President Bush had no right to go to war against Iraq. His excuse that Iraq is endangering Israel and the world because Saddam Hussein had chemical and biological weapons, has been proven false.

As reported in most newspapers the hunt for chemical, biological and nuclear weapons in Iraq has been fruitless. In view of some Democrats, President Bush has been lying about these and other matters, the way Lyndon B. Johnson lied about Vietnam, Richard M. Nixon about Watergate and Bill Clinton about his sex life.

For instance, Senator Bob Graham of Florida, the former chairman of the Intelligence Committee and a candidate for the Democratic presidential nomination, accused President Bush of "a pattern of deception and deceit" on Iraq.

In fact, a review of the president's statements found little that could lead to a conclusion that the president actually lied on either subject. But no more pertinent than whether the president told the literal truth is what factors he stressed and which ones he played down.

Certainly, a strong argument can be made that he exaggerated the danger posed by banned Iraqi weapons when he was trying to convince the country and Congress of the need for a pre-emptive strike on Iraq.

I therefore accuse President Bush in attacking Iraq for no good reason. The President is the mad ruler of America. I reproduce the front cover of my new magazine "ROYALTY" of December 20___ where I make these charges.

We cannot be silent, must condemn President Bush, he is the new Nero that we must deplore.

ROYALTY — DECEMBER 2003

THE DUKE
John Wayne rides again!

LADY BIRD JOHNSON
She showed LBJ the money

QUEEN LATIFAH
Sez who?

JFK JR. Truly,
he was America's Prince

THE DECAPPING
OF CARDINAL LAW

THE DETHRONING
OF THE WINDSORS
The butler did it!

THE CHIC SHEIK
OF ARABIA

HOLIDAY GIFTS FOR
A KING & QUEEN
From $1,000 to $1,000,000

KING GEORGE II
THE MAD RULER
OF AMERICA!
Shall we condemn him...
or commend him?

This specmagazine cover that Abe created was the foundation for his newest venture Royalty News.

This priceless Al Hirschfeld work showing Zipora and me surrounded by some of our many celebrity friends is one of a kind -- a "33-Nina," for the number of times his daughter's name is hidden in it. No other Hirchfeld had more than 11 "Ninas." Can you find all 33? And can you find Jackie Kennedy, Michael Jackson, Elvis Presley, Anthony Quinn, Jackie Mason, Jackie Gleason, Luciano Pavarotti, Carol Channing, Shirley MacLaine and Donald Trump?

DAILY ⊚ NEWS

NEW YORK'S HOMETOWN NEWSPAPER   Tuesday, December 7, 19

NEW PLAYER: Abe Hirschfeld yesterday unveils his vision for Yankee Stadium and surrounding area.

Builder pitches Stadium plan

By DAVID L. LEWIS

Developer Abe Hirschfeld said yesterday he needs a sales-tax break in the South Bronx so he can rebuild Yankee Stadium and attract shoppers to a retail mall in the surrounding neighborhood.

Unveiling a model of his proposal to put a clear dome on the stadium that would let the grass grow, Hirschfeld said shoppers could be attracted to the area if the city and state would make it an enterprise zone where they did not have to pay sales taxes.

"Everybody from Jersey and Connecticut will come shopping in the Bronx," he said.

In remarks prepared for delivery to the Bronx Chamber of Commerce last night, Hirschfeld compared the idea to the North American Free Trade Agreement among the U.S., Mexico and Canada.

"What we really need is a NAFTA between midtown Manhattan and the Bronx, between Wall Street and the River Ave., a NAFTA between blacks, whites and Latinos that will bring jobs, jobs, jobs to all sections of our city," he said.

Yankee owner George Steinbrenner, Mayor-elect Rudy Giuliani and Bronx Borough President Fernando Ferrer said they wanted to see details of the proposal and the financing before they would comment.

The developer said his proposal relies on turning the stadium into a year-round facility that would host pro football games and concerts in the five months when no baseball is played.

Hirschfeld said the project could be financed with revenue bonds or private investment. It would cost $210 million, not including the cost of moving the elevated train tracks underground.

"Can you imagine how this area will look when we remove the subway and we make River Ave. look like Park Ave., with a divider in between," he said. "That stadium will never have any future with the sub-

way sticking in there."

Hirschfeld, who made his name as a health-club and parking-lot guru before his failed foray into newspaper publishing this year, also said the stadium needs at least 18,000 parking spots — not the 6,000 planned by the city and state. He would build them on top of his retail and restaurant complex.

His proposal also calls for a luxury hotel over the stadium. He said the renovated Stadium, when complete, would be the first enclosed ballpark with natural grass.

He said he had the support of former Bronx Rep. Herman Badillo, who ran for controller on Giuliani's ticket this year.

"Basically, Steinbrenner has to like it, the city has to like it and maybe the governor has to like it," Hirschfeld said.

"When a project makes sense, you get all the approvals. When you talk pie in the sky, you get nothing."

Builder Pitches Stadium Plan

Abe with his beloved son Elie. Elie is an elected Brown University Trustee. All his life he would say "Dad why didn't you give me the tip of your nose, the smell of the deal." Now that he is working with me and following my advice he is achieving great success.

Abe Hirschfeld in Israel

Abraham (Abe) Hirschfeld

ראש העיר

August 11, 2003

Abraham Hirschfeld
KMH Realty, Inc.
328 East 61st St.
New York, NY 10021

Dear Mr. Hirschfeld:

I am still overwhelmed by your visit to Beitar and your vision for peace. I would like to thank you for allowing the City of Beitar to name our new park "Keter Avraham" in your honor. This park will act as a symbol for peace and will serve as a catalyst to bringing people together. Indeed, your efforts are historic in nature and will always be remembered and appreciated.

Your visit here in Israel left over a yearning and a desire for people to seek peace and to work on her behalf. Your accomplishments throughout your life have affected millions of people in a positive way and I am therefore convinced that this mammoth undertaking will achieve success in the very near future.

In conclusion, I would like to thank you for your generous contribution to our city, which will be appreciated by the 25,000 residents of Beitar including our 15,000 children. I eagerly look forward to hosting you in Beitar in the very near future.

Respectfully

Yitzchak Pindrus
Mayor

Office: 38 Rabbi Akiva st., beitar illit   בית העירייה: רח' רבי עקיבא 38, ביתר עילית

Letter from Mayor of Beitar , Israel

CHAPTER TWENTY-TWO: THE PENTA

In 1984, my beloved mother died. Her passing was a very emotional time for me, mainly because it brought back a rush of memories of my younger years and reminded me so strongly of what might have happened to us had it not been for a few curious twists of chance and fate when I was a boy. I recalled how reluctant she had been to join my father in Palestine in 1934, how in fact, she came close to refusing to make the trip or take my brothers and me there. I would have been perfectly happy with her decision had she not gone—only, no doubt, to end up in Hitler's ovens like so many other members of the Hirschfeld and Simon families. Zipora, Rachel, and Elie, my adventures and successes in New York, my political activities, my many friends, my golf, my houses and apartments—none of these things would have happened without my mother having made a right decision in 1934, which at the time she believed was dead-wrong.

Her death had another interesting effect on me. For most of my life, after leaving Poland, I had barely observed my religion. Out of a sense of obligation and gratitude toward her, however, after she died, I took time every morning for a year to visit a synagogue and engage in the Orthodox Jewish ritual of remembrance of the dead. I soon began to find a personal comfort in the experience. Ever since, I have become much more of an observant Jew. There wasn't any great intellectual transformation behind this. Nor was it a matter of my seeking the safety of religion in the light of my own advancing years—hedging my bets, as it were. It was simply a case of recognizing who and what I was and the things that made me that way. My mother's death made me think and feel deeply about those things, and I decided that the time had come for me to begin honoring them. Jewish social and cultural history is so ineluctably interwoven with its religious history that it is impossible to honor the former without paying homage to the latter.

One final effect of my mother's death was its impact on any thought I'd had about "slowing down" on account of my own age. She had not only lived to be ninety-four, but had remained vigorous and productive almost to the very end. I was sixty-four when she died. For years, people had been asking me about how it felt "to be getting old." Although I never "felt" old, I began to wonder from the constant stream of questions if I should start experiencing such feelings and acting old. I tried, but couldn't.

Then I realized that I must have indeed inherited my mother's aging genes, not my father's. If so, I had twenty-five more years to go before I'd begin to feel my age, for that's how it had been with her. So, what was all this talk about slowing down? At sixty-four, I was just reaching the peak of my powers. I was just entering the full bloom of middle age, not the start of old age, as the American insurance actuaries and the country's mandatory-retirement rules would like people to believe.

The realization sent me back to work with renewed vigor. Besides, I had no choice, for Hirschfeld Realty was busier than ever. In addition to the Penn Yards development, since 1980, we had spread our wings in several other profitable directions.

This was due to three factors. The first was Elie's maturing presence in the firm. He and Marcia Riklis had gotten married on Valentine's Day, 1980. Later that year, on Thanksgiving Day, Marcia gave birth to their first child, an exquisite daughter named Daniella, and Zipora's and my fourth grandchild. (I should add that American national holidays seem to coincide with the most blessed events in the Hirschfeld family. Our wedding anniversary falls on July 4 each year, and Elie's birthday is the same day as Christmas.) Marriage and fatherhood not only agreed with Elie, they seemed to strengthen his commitment to his partnership with me. That commitment gave me the freedom to concentrate more on future acquisition and development deals and to leave the everyday management of our existing properties to him.

The second factor was the volatile nature of the New York real estate market. As I've mentioned before, inflation and demand, much of which came about through tax-shelter syndications, had sent values skyrocketing in Manhattan. Although some were profiting, many residential property owners, unable to meet their sharply rising fixed-costs under rent controls, were obliged to co-op their buildings or to sell out to others who then co-oped them.

The same forces were at work in the arena of commercial real estate—office buildings and merchandising space. The great influx of people, corporations, and investment money from Europe and elsewhere, starting in the 1970s, had sent demand spiraling upward. Whole neighborhoods in Manhattan, many of them rundown, were being rebuilt and gentrified to accommodate the demand for new, higher-priced, uncontrolled housing and commercial space. Adding to the frenzy were the special tax-abatements awarded to developers and rehabilitators by the city to encourage such improvements.

The third factor was the city's ban on the construction of further parking garages. The garage on West 33rd Street, whose construction Elie had supervised, was the last one we were able to put up. We could expand the garage side of our business no further in New York and were thus practically forced by the city to invest our profits in other property expansion.

One of my primary real estate principles was, when looking for opportunities, to find what was needed and where, and then to invest in the "where" so as to profitably fulfill the demand for the "what." It became apparent early in the late-1970s explosion of the Manhattan market that a lot of middle-income citizens, who until then could afford to live there, would no longer be able to. As a result, there was destined to be a large-scale migration out of Manhattan in search of lower-cost housing to the areas immediately surrounding the island—the outlying boroughs and the New Jersey side of the Hudson.

Predicting that trend, and the consequent rise in demand for quality apartments there, we began to acquire and rehabilitate buildings in Queens and New Jersey. That was one component of our post-1980 expansion. We also continued to buy and co-op apartment buildings in Manhattan, most of them on the burgeoning upper West Side.

The opposite trend was occurring with respect to commercial and office space. Instead of an exodus, there was an influx of new businesses into Manhattan as it became the financial and commercial capital of the world in the late '70s. So, we expanded further into office and commercial buildings, too.

A pet project of mine was the acquisition of 35 West 33rd Street, adjacent to the Empire State Building. I planned to put up a twenty-five-story apartment and hotel building on the site and call it Empire State Tower. The area around the Empire State Building had long been an intensely commercial district—nearby were Penn Station, Madison Square Garden, the General Post Office, the garment center, and a dozen major department stores. With the construction of the huge new New York Convention Center underway just to the west, I felt that the area, which had grown slightly seedy, was due for a major upgrading once the Convention Center was finished.

It was the feeling that soon got me into my biggest project yet, not counting Lincoln West. The Zeckendorf organization owned a celebrated old hotel on Seventh Avenue, opposite Penn Station and Madison Square Garden, called the Statler-Hilton. Between the 1920s and 1950s, the New York Statler, as it was then known, was one of the city's top deluxe commercial hotels, on a par with the Waldorf-Astoria and Astor in its worldwide fame. Since the 1960s, however, it had gone downhill, even though it had been under the management of the Hilton chain. Finally, in 1983, Hilton decided to pull out, and Zeckendorf put it up for sale. I called William Zeckendorf, Jr. and said that I might be interested in buying the hotel. I knew nothing about owning hotels, of course, but since I'd stayed in so many over the years, I couldn't resist the idea.

"How much?" I asked.

"Sixty million," Bill Zeckendorf replied.

"Give me a tour," I said.

What I saw on my tour was a magnificent skyscraper building containing one-and-a-half million square feet, nearly 2,000 hotel rooms and suites, acres of ballrooms, conference rooms, and an imposing, football field-size main lobby. It remained the only hotel of any size within easy walking distance of the new Convention Center. I said to Zeckendorf, "Are you crazy? Fix it up a little, and you've got a gold mine here when the Convention Center opens."

"That's three years away," he said. "I can't wait. I need the money. I'll tell you what, Abe; I'll let you have it for $55 million. You and I both know it would cost five times that to build today."

I told him I'd think about it. Then I went back to the office and talked to Elie. "How'd you like to go into the hotel business?"

The idea caught his fancy. "But how?" he wondered. "We don't know anything about operating hotels. We'd have to get someone to run it for us."

"So, let's talk to some hotel operators."

Which we did, all to no avail. The most interested was the Holiday Inn organization. But they could only see turning the Statler into the equivalent of a high-rise motel—something that might be profitable, perhaps, but not what I had in mind.

I was now thinking in terms of sharply upgrading the hotel. Where before I had expected the mid-thirties district between the Empire State Building and the new convention center to undergo a kind of spontaneous renaissance, it occurred to me that with the Statler, I could pioneer and force such a rebirth. In the decade ahead, millions of people a year would be attending weekly conventions at the sprawling convention center. If the Statler was returned to a semblance of its former glory under an effective modernization regimen, it would become the main hotel for out-of-town convention goers. And since it actually contained more hotel rooms than it knew what to do with, the lower floors could be profitably turned into commercial office space—the latest trend in new apartment and hotel developments.

During the time I was mulling all this over, I had to take a trip to Israel. While in Tel Aviv, I stayed for the first time at the Carlton Penta Hotel on the city's beachfront. The hotel was not only doing a booming business but unlike most Israeli luxury hotels, it was superbly run.

Since I had grown curious about the hotel business, I arranged to meet the manager of the Carlton. After congratulating him on the smoothness of his operation, I asked him how he accounted for it when so many other top-rated hotels in Tel Aviv were sloppily run.

"There is only one answer," he said, with the kind of fussy superiority only a Swiss hotelier could exude. "It is because we are a Penta hotel."

"Penta, shmenta—what is that?" I inquired.

He explained that Penta was a consortium of three major European airlines that owned and operated hotels throughout Europe and the Mediterranean, which was why the hotel he managed was called the Carlton Penta. Penta managed and had a financial stake in it. "I like to think we're the best at what we do," he said. "Better than Hilton, better than Sheraton, better than Intercontinental—you name it."

"That's funny," I said. "I've never heard of Penta in the United States."

"No doubt because we don't operate there," replied my Swiss friend, as if Penta was his personal company.

"Why not?"

"Simply because we've not found the right opportunity. But I happen to know we're eager to get involved in America."

"In New York?"

"Especially in New York—if we found the right property."

"Well," I said, explaining further who I was, "I may have the right property. Who would I talk to about it?"

"Our managing director," was the answer. "Mr. Dillman. He's located in London. It's the headquarters of the Penta organization."

Talk about coincidence. At that very moment, Elie was in London on a brief holiday with Marcia.

"Would you phone Mr. Dillman?" I said. "Ask him if he will see my son tomorrow? My son will explain everything to him."

"Of course." The manager called London and arranged a meeting the next day between Elie and Fred Dillman. Then I got on the phone and tracked down Elie. I told him the story and said he was expected the following afternoon at the Penta executive offices.

"Tell the Penta people all about the Statler-Hilton," I said. "If you can sell them on coming in with us, we'll buy it and they can run it."

Elie not only made the presentation but he sold Penta on becoming our partner and, over a period of two days, on his own, negotiated a very favorable deal. Upon my return to New York, I called Zeckendorf and offered him $40 million. We settled at $46 million and the Statler was ours.

The key to the deal, as it so often is in such transactions, was that I was able to get an immediate $60 million mortgage on the building. We had acquired the magnificent old hotel without having to spend a penny in cash. Instead of pocketing the $14 million profit, however, Penta and Hirschfeld Realty invested it in a total renovation and modernization. We also changed the hotel's name to the New York Penta. With the convention center recently opened, the New York Penta was on its way to a completely new and profitable life as a landmark first-class city hotel.

CHAPTER TWENTY-THREE: HOW MARIO CUOMO STABBED
ME IN THE BACK

My attempt at electoral politics in the 1970s had been
motivated by my desire to right some of the wrongs and defects I saw
in the system. After failing three times to achieve office, I had more-
or-less put my ambitions aside, figuring that there were not enough
people in New York interested in genuine reform to make any further
efforts on my part worth the time and trouble. I was a Don Quixote
all right, tilting at windmills, but no one seemed to want to join my
crusade.

But then in 1985, after my experience with Sportsplex, and
having gained a greater insight into the corruption and ineptitude that
remained endemic in the governance of New York City and State, the
old political juices began to boil in me again. Perhaps, I thought, I
should make one last try. With Elie thoroughly on top of things at
Hirschfeld Realty, with Zipora recovered from an illness that had
struck her down the year before, and with Rachel thriving, I felt that I
had the time to devote to another political campaign. Added to that
was the fact that a political situation had developed in the state which
almost cried out that I do so.

When Mario Cuomo narrowly won the gubernatorial election
in 1982, Alfred Del Bello, also a Democrat and the former
Westchester County Executive, was voted in as lieutenant governor.
The lieutenant governor's office in New York is largely a ceremonial
one; its only real purpose is to provide an automatic successor to the
governor should something occur to remove him from office during
his term. Del Bello quickly grew bored as lieutenant governor, and in
1984, he resigned to take a high-paying position in private industry.
Under New York law, once a lieutenant governor leaves, the office
cannot be filled again until the next gubernatorial election. Since
1984, then, the state had been without a lieutenant governor. The next
election would not be until the fall of 1986.

In 1985, it was clear that Cuomo would seek re-election in
1986. But it was also becoming evident that he was priming himself
to go after the Democratic Presidential nomination in 1998. If he
succeeded, he would have to resign as governor not long after the start
of his second term, handing over his office to whomever the
lieutenant governor was. The more I thought about it, the more I

thought that man should be me. If events went according to the scenario, I would have a chance to be governor of New York for at least two years, and would be able to use that time to effect some meaningful reforms in the management of the state.

In the fall of 1985, I tested my idea on various political friends around the state. The response was overwhelmingly in favor of my making a run for the lieutenant governorship. Just about the only people who weren't enthusiastic were Cuomo's. "The governor would prefer to pick his own running mate in 1986," they said, making it clear that he would not pick me.

That was no surprise. Yet, there was no rule that said the candidate for lieutenant governor had to be the choice of the governor. The governor could select his own candidate at the 1986 state Democratic convention and automatically put him on the ticket. But through the petition process, others could also get on the ballot in the September primary election. As I'd done when I ran for the senate, that's the course I resolved to follow. In the early spring of 1986, I announced my candidacy.

I made my announcement at a press conference in a New York subway station, a move that was designed to symbolize one of the chief themes of my campaign—the dire need to bring effective management to the city's atrociously decrepit subway system, in many ways its lifeblood. Another of my principal targets was New York State's sales tax system, under which every clothing purchase is subject to sales tax.

This was an abomination. Clothing is as much an essential in most people's lives as food. The sales tax on clothing was particularly punitive to the middle-and lower-income classes, and doubly so to those income earners who had large families to clothe as well as feed. New York's neighboring states had no taxes on clothing, which tended to send many New Yorkers out of state to make their clothing purchases, much to the detriment of New York merchandisers. What's more, the New York sales tax created a much higher propensity for shoplifting in New York stores than would otherwise exist; shoplifting statistics in New Jersey and Connecticut were significantly lower than in New York State.

Finally, a case could be made for the fact that the clothing tax was directly responsible for recently driving out of business such major New York department stores as Gimbel's, Alexander's, and

Ohrbach's. The full, economic effects of those and other likely future closings had yet to be felt. One effect could be the collapse of at least two of the city's major daily newspapers, which until then had relied heavily on the millions in advertising revenues provided by the defunct stores.

These were but two of the programs I developed as I mounted my campaign to win the nomination for lieutenant governor during the spring and summer of 1986. The September primary was three months away.

For a heady but all-too-brief time, I was in fact, Mario Cuomo's running mate. Because Cuomo hadn't announced his choice for the position, I was technically the only candidate for lieutenant governor. A *Daily News* article that ran in April 1986 read,

"Hirschfeld is incumbent Mario Cuomo's running mate in the November election. They are unopposed so far."

That would have sounded delightful in November, but alas, within a few days, Cuomo made his pick, naming a relatively obscure upstate politician with nothing to say, Stan Lundine, a congressman and former mayor of Jamestown. And of course, Cuomo, and everyone else expected me to simply go away so that there would be no primary on September 9. But as many people have learned, I don't go away so easily.

I was in the race to stay, not only because I was the right man for the job but to write a merciful end to the Byzantine "tradition" of snubbing democracy for the sake of a governor's massive ego, and in this case, his presidential aspirations. On April 13, I had a $1,000-a-plate fundraising luncheon at Donald Trump's Mar-a-Lago estate in Palm Beach, which admittedly was a long way to go to raise money for a race in New York. However, in politics, as in real estate, you go where the money is. Unfortunate, but true. And Donald held sway among the money set in ritzy Palm Beach.

I, of course, could be called one of that set. Zipora and I had been winter "snowbird" residents of Palm Beach for many years, and by now we had purchased a condominium at the Palm Beach Towers and a penthouse at the Palm Beach Hamptons. We were also members of the distinguished Poinciana Club. And our friends sent us back to New York well-fortified for the campaign.

So, we began in high gear and high spirits. By April, I had no problem obtaining over 70,000 signatures to be legally on the ballot—50,000 more than was required—and had spent some $460,000 of my own money. This was probably $460,000 more than everyone who had ever run for lieutenant governor had spent combined, but it was just the start for me. All told, I would spend around $2 million, opening the door to the now-habitual practice of wealthy people financing political campaigns out of their own pockets. My message was radiating: creativity in government and economic development. When I made my announcement in the subway, I had suggested building underground shopping malls in subway concourses. Now, people were starting to say what a wonderful idea that was.

Mario Cuomo, however, was aghast at my rise and decided he had to get me off the ballot, by hook and by crook. At first, he was hoping his cronies at the state Board of Elections would simply remove me. But on July 31, the Board legitimately ruled that I was indeed a qualified candidate. That's when Cuomo got mean and nasty. Even before then, Cuomo's people had been leaking anonymous quotes aimed at Democratic voters that if I won, I would "embarrass" Cuomo and damage his widely-presumed run for President in 1988.

The implication was that Cuomo would not run if it meant New York would be left in the hands of Abe Hirschfeld—who was merely a visionary and fundraising genius—rather than in the hands of a party hack like Lundine. I guess that explanation didn't fly because, now, Cuomo himself got in the act. He came out and said I was "unfit" and "unqualified" to be governor and, reaching for any straw, made a big deal that I had been the Chairman of Democrats for Ronald Reagan in 1980 and 1984, as if I had been the only one of those in two elections when Reagan swept New York State. Actually, the message there helped me: I would be nobody's rubber stamp, not even Mario Cuomo's.

Then Cuomo's campaign coordinator, Drew Zambelli, said Cuomo would go to State Supreme Court to disqualify me based on "fraud" and "forgery." The only fraud and forgery, it turned out, was in Cuomo's head—and in his dirty hands. Because that day, Lundine's lawyers—I suppose Cuomo wanted to make it look like he wasn't behind it, although everyone knew he was—subpoenaed all of the petitions from the election board. Once these documents were in

Cuomo's hands, I believe his people changed them to make it look like I hadn't followed proper procedures.

While that happened, Lundine himself ran and hid. We had both agreed to debate in the office of the *Long Island Jewish World* newspaper in Great Neck, Long Island. I showed up and debated an empty chair, which probably knew a lot more than Lundine did.

Lundine—Cuomo, really—carried through his lawsuit with amazing fervor. He called dozens of people who'd signed my petitions to testify when the case was heard in Albany in early August before Judge Vincent Bradley. Indeed, *The New York Times* described my battle with Lundine "the most heated issue" of the campaign.

How determined was Cuomo to do me in? Lundine subpoenaed my payroll records, computer tapes, and most disgustingly of all—even my naturalization papers. I guess if all else failed, he wanted to say I wasn't an American citizen. Of course, they couldn't have said any such thing, and when word of this got out, they revoked the order for the naturalization papers, with egg all over their faces.

I fought like a banshee against these Gestapo moves. But what I couldn't fight was Cuomo's control of the whole election process. When Lundine sued, I had asked the head of the Board of Elections, Daniel DeFrancisco, to recommend a lawyer I could use who specialized in election law. DeFrancisco put me together with Robert Muir, who within weeks I fired because I suspected Cuomo had planted him to undermine my campaign.

I didn't need a lawyer to find various discrepancies in the records, including one volume of signatures that had 150 pages written up as having only 126. Cover sheets—which summarized which congressional districts each volume had come from—were doctored. When I found these errors, I fired Muir—but it was too late to rectify all the little technical mistakes by the time Judge Bradley looked at them.

Bradley, too, was a curious problem. The original judge on the case had mysteriously gone on an extended vacation, so they brought in Bradley, a judge from Kingston, and made him a Supreme Court justice for my case. And Bradley ruled me *off* the ballot—not because of fraud but because of the very technical violations I noticed had cropped up in my petitions. Bradley cited signatures that weren't grouped properly and couldn't be traced to any district. In other words, picayune stuff—which perfectly symbolized the petty thief level of Mario Cuomo's crusade against me.

I stood on the courthouse steps that day and tearfully spoke with the press, shattered that my dream of elective office had been taken from me. I decried Cuomo's "dictatorial" ways and said, "I don't know if they're trying to annex New York State to Russia." The best reaction, though, came from Andy O'Rourke, the Republican candidate for governor and the Westchester County Executive. He said, "Abe Hirschfeld has had everything happen to him but getting his legs broken."

What's more, *The New York Times* agreed with me whole-heartedly that Cuomo had sullied the state. In an editorial, they called the Supreme Court ruling "a defeat for democracy" and a "national embarrassment that leaves the governor looking more like a clubhouse pol than potential President."

To this day, I don't know why Cuomo took such a low road, or why he trashed democracy to beat me. I believe we would have made the perfect team. He's a talker; I'm a doer. I would have gotten things done for him that he never did get done, which was just about everything except high taxes. Because I'm an implementer. I turn word and ideas into action.

But because I'm also a realist, I knew that, because of Cuomo, my days in the Democratic party were numbered. All the people I had supported with my pocket book always made promises to stand by me. And now, when I came to them for support, they deserted me. The party of Bobby Kennedy had become the party of fear and corrupt values and practices. I wasn't the only one the party was running out. Within a decade, it would become unable to even compete for the governor's seat. For that, it can blame Mario Cuomo, who of course had claimed *I* would be the ruination of the party.

I vowed to press on and appeal the Supreme Court ruling to the Appellate Court. But I ran into the same brick wall. Cuomo had the judges in his pocket—the Appellate Division upheld the ruling without a hearing, as did the Court of Appeals. That only crystallized why I had run and why Cuomo had opposed me so virulently. As treasurer of the state Democratic Party, I had seen a corrupt system burgeon in which judgeships were bought and sold at a price. There was a list price for judges as if they were menu items in a restaurant. There was—and still is—a price for a Supreme Court judge, for a civil court judge, for every office there was a price to be paid, as if by the pound. A judge was expected to earn that price to move up.

Judge Bradley, I might add, later became an Appellate Court judge. Was that his payoff for the ruling against me? Was the ruling *his* price?

What it came down to was that Cuomo and the party didn't want me because I was going to make an issue of stopping the selling of judgeships. That was the most dangerous thing any candidate could have promised—which is why no candidate ever does. The next one who does will be found with cement shoes at the bottom of the Hudson River.

They did that to me, too, figuratively. I paid my own price. I must have been the only candidate in history to have spent $100,000 on lawyer's fees to battle my own party while running for office. I was also so humiliated that I was immediately receptive to Andy O'Rourke wooing me to support him. Tall and regal-looking, O'Rourke was a very nice man. He even offered to get rid of his running mate and put me on the Republican ballot in the same lieutenant governor spot.

"Keep your running mate," I told him. "I'll be more valuable to you just by endorsing you."

And so, we came to an agreement that I would hold a press conference to announce my support a few days later, on September 16. When word got out, Cuomo became deathly afraid and sprang into action. Suddenly, he was my best friend. He called me himself and he and his son Andrew, who was also his campaign manager, came to my apartment and for hours they seduced me like I was the head cheerleader. Cuomo talked about the good of the party, about the legacy of Bobby Kennedy, and promised he'd consult me often. I believed he was implicitly assuring me that my real estate business would be the beneficiary of state business, which he would route my way.

He also invited Zipora and I to Albany, where he wined and dined us. As it happened, I had revitalized the capital city. I had turned the downtown area around by building a thriving series of apartment and office complexes, and the city became so energized and exciting that Joseph P. Kennedy chose to live there during his last years, in a house I put him in. And Cuomo, mindful of all that, praised me lavishly for it.

After all that seducing, I knew why Cuomo was such a successful politician. He could talk. He couldn't do, but he could talk. He knew a good pickup line. If I had been a woman, I would have become pregnant just talking to him. He was also smart enough to know he needed me, or more accurately, that he needed to keep me away from O'Rourke. And so, I swallowed my pride and agreed to endorse him.

There is no doubt that I saved Mario Cuomo's behind. I also saved Andy Cuomo's behind. Late in the campaign, it came to light that even while Andrew was orchestrating the plot to get me out of the race, he was actually on my payroll. He's a very fine lawyer, and at the time, he was working with the Blutrich, Falcone & Miller law firm in Manhattan. I'd hired him the year before to represent my real estate company in a disputed closing, and the firm was still representing me. This meant there was a definite conflict of interest for Andy, who was still collecting fees from me.

When news of this broke, the state Appellate Division's disciplinary committee investigated the matter and things could have gotten sticky for him, especially had I decided to press the conflict of interest charge. Instead, I bit the bullet and decided to say nothing. I even let Andy get away with the outright lie that he had had nothing to do with his father's effort to get me removed from the ballot. In the end, they let Andy slide. So, should he decide to run for office again—after pulling out of the 2002 governor's race during the primary campaign—he will bless his stars that I was so accommodating.

And gullible. I bought into Cuomo's promises and lies. And I still feel very bad about what I did to Andy O'Rourke. On September 16, two hours before the scheduled press conference we'd called for me to endorse him, I instead endorsed Cuomo at a hastily-called press conference in Albany. That left O'Rourke speechless. And petulant. The polls had begun to close up and O'Rourke was only a few points behind. He had hoped my endorsement would create a bandwagon that would carry through to election day. Now he had no chance.

"I believe Mr. Hirschfeld's actions speak for themselves," he said acridly in a prepared statement. "I feel strongly about keeping commitments."

He was right, of course, if also a bit disingenuous—this was politics, after all, where the Marquis de Queensbury rules don't apply.

Moreover, at that point, I wanted very much to stay a Democrat, and I really believed I would be a valuable ally and adviser for Cuomo.

"With me," I had told him, "I guarantee you will win and that you will be President."

After he trounced O'Rourke, however, I never once heard from him. He never so much as sent me a Chanukah card or bought me a pastrami sandwich at the Carnegie Deli. All he did was use me and walk out the door. Not once over the rest of his time in office did he deign to consult me or consent to speak with me on the phone. Often I had found office buildings that I could have turned into space for any number of state agencies I knew were seeking new homes in New York City. Cuomo had told me not to hesitate to submit these blueprints to his housing administration, yet now I was told not to bother. I grew absolutely infuriated by Cuomo's cold shoulder, and by the sad truth that I had been had.

Still, I believe that what you reap you shall sow. And Cuomo reaped a lot of trouble. In the end, he reaped his own political suicide, because I got rid of Mario Cuomo. For all of the chattering about his presidential ambitions, Cuomo chickened out of running for the White House in '88 and that memorable plane waiting to take him to the New Hampshire primary never made the trip. Cuomo absurdly claimed he had no time to run because of the crush of state affairs in Albany.

By 1992, after he had won another term as governor, Cuomo's time had passed for national stardom, totally eclipsed by the star of Arkansas Governor Bill Clinton. By then, he was merely an old-time pol who had overstayed his welcome and had accomplished little. The irony was that a man with so much anger in him, and so capable of playing dirty tricks on me, had so little fire in his belly and so little conviction that he couldn't bear the thought of actually running for President. He let down scores of his political sycophants, and many people nationwide who saw so much in him, yet he thought nothing of that. He thought only of himself and his insecurities.

Cuomo, more out of habit than conviction, wanted one more term as governor in 1994, intending it as a coronation. I had taken a leave from New York when he ran for re-election in 1990, as you'll see in the next chapter, but by 1994, I was back and absolutely committed to depriving Cuomo of that honor. I quickly supported the then-obscure Republican candidate, George Pataki, the mayor of

Poughkeepsie, whom no one in the state had heard of but in whom I saw a man with solid ideas and values.

I gave a good deal of time and money to his campaign and was candid about saying Mario Cuomo was not an honest man. And people listened, because I speak to the common person. And the common people are the ones who elect politicians, not the intellectuals. Intellectuals most of the time don't even vote. They are much like Mario Cuomo. They're too high and mighty for such drudgery.

The moral of the story is that Pataki defeated Cuomo and exorcised Cuomo's demonic influence on the state. For my support, Pataki pulled strings and made me the Republican Party's Man of the Year in 1995—though, as you will see, Pataki's gratitude was very short-lived, and when he tasted power his values became anything but admirable.

Just as gratifying as being named Man of the Year was the sheer bliss of being able to put Mario Cuomo in his place, face to face. After Cuomo was out of office, I ran into him at some affair or other. I approached him, shook his hand with a flourish, and acted like we were still best friends. Then, with delicious timing, I lowered the boom.

Remember that I told you that you would be President?" I told him.

"Abe, I sure do," he said with a laugh. "And I appreciate it."

"Well, I still believe you will be President."

"You do?"

"Yes—but only of your co-op board."

Seeing the look on Mario Cuomo's suddenly drop-jawed face was as good as winning any election could have been.

CHAPTER TWENTY-FOUR: MAROONED IN MIAMI

Needless to say, the backstabbing, two-faced manipulations of Mario Cuomo left a bitter taste that lingers to this day. As soon as 1986 faded into a bad memory, I experienced a period of depression that my political ambitions and all the positive change I could have made had been sacrificed to the altar of a man who had thought nothing of snooping through my naturalization papers eagerly seeking to brand me as some sort of illegal alien.

I still think about this whenever I see Cuomo on television or read his name in a newspaper. What a colossal waste of talent he was. What a colossal failure. And what a colossal ingrate. Almost immediately after I had endorsed him in '86, the more my mind drifted back to the '86 campaign, the more my mood soured. This was compounded by the realization that Cuomo had no intention of consulting me or responding to my plans that would have benefited the state.

Sitting in my apartment as the decade of the '80s was ending, watching the dreary winter turn Central Park brown and barren, I decided that the only way out of my doldrums was to literally get out of New York.

I am known for my quick, decisive decisions, but the truth is, I make those decisions because I know that if I give myself time to think, I'll talk myself out of what my gut tells me. And so, through the first months of '87, I talked over with Zipora the idea of moving to the *second* land of my people—Miami Beach—and making the same positive changes there. Not surprisingly, she had been reading my mind and agreed readily that it was a good idea.

I made arrangements to leave Hirstan in the hands of others— who would, unfortunately, break my heart by betraying my trust—and Zipora and I flew to Miami Beach with the boundless optimism of a young turk and the instincts of a wily old genius. Miami represented renewal for me, and for the city itself was heaven-sent because the place had been progressively unlivable in the past decade.

I had frequently visited there during that time and was horrified at how grungy the downtown area had become. Crime was sky-high; there were terrible racial tensions between the aging, white, Jewish populations and the emerging population of Cubans. There was also an unchecked problem of police brutality, a topic I will return to shortly.

It was clear to me that the city's fathers were handling these problems all wrong. They merely wanted to gauze over, or bludgeon over, the rifts and strains. I knew where the solutions to recovery were—in its greatest natural resource, as a worldwide tourist attraction.

Most alarmingly to me was that the chain-link of hotels along Collins Avenue going southward to the Fontainbleu and further on to South Beach were dying on the vine. Many of these once-proud hotels were in a shambles; many were either now cheap fleabag motels or boarded up.

You know already of my biggest credo in real estate development: it's not "location, location, location" but "garbage, garbage, garbage." Thus, the dilapidations of Miami Beach in 1987 offered the perfect opportunity for me to do my thing. I had no dearth of renovation possibilities, but the best situation to kick off the renewal process was the Konover Hotel, another stately art-deco palace on Collins Avenue that had been built in the late 1960s and had its heyday when Hugh Hefner owned it for a while as the Playboy Hotel, but it was, even now, teetering on the verge of bankruptcy.

The Konover's management probably thought I was delirious when I offered, and they eagerly took, $14.5 million for the place, but I figured they were the real pigeons because of what I had planned for the hotel: to make it no less than the entertainment capital of South Florida.

The Konover was an enormous place, but most of its five acres were unused. Immediately, I set forth plans to not only refurbish the 800 rooms and grand ballrooms but to construct a much better dinner theater and a Vertical Club-style health spa. I wanted the whole world to beat a path to my doors here, and I wasted no time in beginning the project in May 1987.

While the work proceeded, I turned my sights to the attractions I could bring into the theater, which, again, was a dump when I bought the hotel. I wanted to create no less than a Broadway of the South.

For me, this was a logical extension. I have been a member of the Tony Award voting committee since the 1970s, and the Friar's Club since before time, and I longed to become a theater impresario.

That I would have to go to Miami Beach to become one was the result of a hard lesson—failing miserably in my first try at conquering the "big league" of theater, on Broadway.

I must admit, I always saw myself as another Sol Hurok, a guy who could not only spot a good show and a good actor a mile away but who could also drum up business through the force of his larger-than-life personality. I suppose my mistake was shooting for the stars right off the bat. Blinded by the bright lights of Broadway, I leaped right into the thicket of the New York theater scene, assuming it would be no problem to find people who would follow my directions. This, however, was sheer naïveté, given the entrenched culture of Broadway, its sleazy financial angels, its corrupt unions, and its pampered, self-indulgent, and self-important theater critics.

Not experienced in dealing with any of these folks, I merely concerned myself with finding the right property to produce. I chose a wonderful musical treatment by the brilliant composer, arranger, and orchestrator, Don Sebesky, whose sole credit up until then was the musical *Peg,* a one-woman show by singer Peggy Lee that opened on Broadway in 1983—and closed after five performances. This was an expression of my philosophy, which is not to rely on the hoary establishment but to give life to the most ingenious ideas, no matter anyone's track record.

Don put together a magnificent score, with lyrics by Gloria Nissenson, based on an original novel by Evan Rhodes that told the story of a twelve-year-old boy, J.J., who runs away from a Staten Island tenement after his mother dies and lives in a cave in Central Park. As the story goes, thugs try to steal his prized possession, a keyboard, but he's befriended by a mysterious park dweller, who protects J.J. in exchange for his songs. Eventually, he finds happiness with a mother and a father who lost their own son—a remarkable parable of life as told through the eyes and fantasies of a troubled child living on the outer edge of reality. The role of J.J. was handled to perfection by a young actor named Richard H. Blake, who had appeared in the Broadway revival of *MacBeth,* though the show's headliners were JoAnne Worley—whose antics on the old *Laugh-In* TV show overshadowed the acting and singing skills she displayed in the original stage production of *Hello Dolly*—and the wondrous singer-dancer Adrian Bailey, the star of *Your Arm's Too Short to Box With God* and *Sophisticated Ladies.*

My director/choreographer, Tony Tanner, was a proven Broadway veteran, having performed in *Half a Sixpence* in the '60s and directed and choreographed *Something's Afoot* in the '70s and *Joseph and the Amazing Technicolor Dreamcoat* in the '80s.

Prince of Central Park was first staged at the Jan McArt Cabaret Theater in Key West, Florida, and I made Jan co-producer, fulfilling her own Broadway dream. I also brought in as executive producer, Karen Poindexter, who ran Burt Reynolds's dinner theater in Jupiter, Florida. I can only imagine the resentment among the old-line Broadway hacks when they saw these out-of-town theater people come to town. And yet, I would be misstating the case if I laid all the blame for what befell the show on the paranoia of the Broadway cognoscenti. In truth, I take the blame myself.

Although I had intended to be a hands-on producer, other pressing business matters took my attention away from the daily grind of the show when it went into three weeks of previews at the Belasco Theater on October 24, 1989. Instead, I delegated much of the decision-making authority to Jan McArt. Big mistake. Without my guiding hand, everyone involved began to deviate from my vision for the show. I had given strict instructions and warned that if they were not followed one hundred percent, they would destroy the show.

And damned if they did just that. One week before Opening Night, I came to the theater and was aghast. What I saw was a completely different show. They had put in new parts, new scenes, including a totally extraneous shopping scene set in Bloomingdale's. After the audience had filed out, I called a cast and crew meeting and did not mince words.

"Ladies and gentlemen," I began, "the show you have made is so horrible that I am going to announce on Opening Night that it will only play one night. Whatever reviews we get, good or bad, I don't care."

Whether they believed me or not, I do not know. But on Opening Night, November 9, on what should have been one of the proudest moments of my life, I stiffly went through the motions, doing acting on my own, playing the part of Sol Hurok but knowing full well I was going to pull the plug on a play I loved but which had been ruined.

As it happened, the reviews weren't universally terrible. Even so, I had no argument to pick with the reviews that panned the show.

In my mind, it was as big a bomb as the one dropped on Hiroshima, and I was honest enough to admit it, certainly a rare quality for a Broadway producer. But then, I have an intractable philosophy that defines whether a show is a hit or a stinker. Unless I hear the audience giving the cast a half-hour standing ovation, that show is not complete. That night, there was barely a sound when the curtain dropped. That was all she wrote, although I allowed the show to play four performances out of respect to the actors before I sent everyone home.

I did not, however, discard *Prince of Central Park*, which I believed in and would re-enter my life, as you will see. I also did not hold any of the actors to blame and was pleased that my show was a springboard for many of them. Richard Blake, for instance, went on to star in the original Broadway runs of *Rent, Saturday Night Fever,* and *Aida*; Adrian Bailey would appear in *Jelly's Last Jam, Smoky Joe's Café,* and *The Wild Party.*

The *Prince of Central Park* debacle was a learning experience. And one of the things I learned was that I neither desired to wade into the murky waters of Broadway again any time soon, nor did I believe I needed to. I was far more turned on by the notion that I could create from scratch a burgeoning theater culture in Miami Beach. To most show people, the notion was rather idiotic. After all, how could there be a thriving night life in a place where people eat dinner at four o'clock in the afternoon and are ready for bed by eight in the evening? As one of my favorite jokes goes, Jesus Christ couldn't have been Jewish. If he had been he wouldn't have come to the Last Supper – he would have come to the Early Bird Special.

Clearly, the *Prince of Central Park* fiasco did nothing to change my mind about leaving New York. But if truth be told, I was committed to going regardless of how the show fared. My mind was in South Florida. I saw a different Miami, a changing city with a burgeoning cosmopolitan atmosphere. I saw terrific potential here— potential that would surely grow once I put my energies into renovating the entire south Florida area. I had in mind something far more vital and important than dinner theater. I saw fertile territory to stage productions that weren't pale versions of New York or London theater but *better*. I wanted big stars, big audiences. And so, I again called on Karen Poindexter, and I did not mince my words.

"Karen," I told her, "you are the person who can make my theater into the best in the country."

Karen had a little trepidation.

"Come again?" she said.

Her reaction was justified. Because of her work, Burt Reynolds's theater was thriving. Mine was an unopened shambles. But, as I explained to her, I would spare no expense in giving her a free hand to make the theater radiate with magic. Within a few minutes, she had given Burt notice and was on her way from Jupiter to Miami Beach to be the executive director of the Hirschfeld Theater—named not for Abe Hirschfeld but for my wonderful friend Al Hirschfeld, whom I loved like a brother and wanted to honor for bringing so much magic to Broadway with his drawings. A man who lived as long as Al Hirschfeld and loved the theater like he did deserved his name over the doors of a theater.

Next, all the details had to be nailed down. To make the financing of the hotel feasible, I did something I do better than anyone else: I convinced a much bigger money angel than myself to enter into a partnership, whereby they could front the cash and I would pay it back when the profits streamed in. That partner turned out to be one of the largest hotel chains in the world, Clarion, which put the hotel into its upscale line of Choice Hotels International. By agreement, we called the place the Clarion Castle Hotel and Resort. We were really on the way now. During the construction phase, the publicity alone sold out the entire hotel months in advance of its opening, which was scheduled for fall 1989.

The politicians in Miami Beach were less excited—I seem to breed contempt among the professional politicians for one reason: my strict aversion to allowing myself to be bought and bribed and manipulated by the very people politicians are supposed to keep in line. Miami Beach was no different in that sense from New York, with its bought judges and media liars. In fact, the only honest politician in Miami was the man who made it possible for me to renovate the city without having to grease the palms of shady crooks.

That was Mayor Alex Daoud, who would pay both for his support for me and for his honesty later. Alex, a big, jolly teddy bear of a fellow, did everything he could to make certain I didn't have to pay protection money to organized crime when dealing with the unions. It was Alex, too, who made me a wonderful suggestion—that

I should, myself, become a city father of Miami Beach, the better to work with the inner sanctum that was the Miami Beach City Commission.

City commissioners, elected to two-year terms, met just once a week, yet, they heavily influenced commerce, industry, and building in Miami Beach. Moreover, each of the commissioners is installed as deputy mayor for two months every year. As locked as the commissioners were into their roles as grease-my-palm politicians, I believed I could talk sense into them for the city's common good. And, as deputy mayor, I would be able to work closely with Mayor Daoud to get things done quickly and economically.

I kept that suggestion in the back of my mind as I pressed forward with my plans. Zipora and I moved into a room in the hotel even as it was being renovated. And Mayor Daoud made sure I would be welcomed like a king. On May 19, 1989, he held an "Abe Hirschfeld Day" in Miami Beach and presented me with a beautiful proclamation. It read:

City of Miami Beach Proclamation. Whereas: Miami Beach's Konover Hotel, built in the late 1960s, will be renamed the Miami Beach Castle, Premier Beach and Resort; and whereas New York Real Estate magnate Abraham J. Hirschfeld, the new owner of the property, will renovate the hotel, including the update of the rooms, ballrooms and theater, and the construction of the Vertical Health Spas; and whereas the new Miami Beach Castle, Premier Beach and Resort promises to become one of the finest hotels in the City of Miami Beach, not only helping to promote our tourism industry but also increasing the city's economy and beauty.

The hotel renovation was completed on schedule, and though I had not yet made up my mind about running for City Commissioner, so exhilarating was my arrival in Miami Beach in October 1989, that within one hour of stepping off the plane, I impetuously announced my candidacy.

This time, there was no Mario Cuomo skulking behind me with a dagger.

People have at times accused me of not knowing every facet of every issue, and they have been right. My focus is on several critically important issues, seen from a broad perspective. My genius is to see the big picture and what needs to be done—and then make it materialize, very quickly and simply. What's more, in this case, I didn't even know the name of the commissioner whose seat I was trying to take away. I still don't. To me, that person, just like Stan Lundine, was magnificently unimportant when compared with a visionary like me.

The people of my district must have agreed with me. Or should I say, enough did. Although many people in the district knew nothing of me, I was able to make the case for an exciting new crown jewel of South Florida and on November 8, election day, I won by all of 227 votes out of several thousand cast.

I knew what George W. Bush and Al Gore felt like years later, because my squeaker of an election also had to be verified by a recount, which in Florida can be, well, let's say touch and go. When the recount was done, though, I had again prevailed—by a whopping 120 votes.

For those who like to claim that I am obsessed with money, may I point out that the job paid all of $6,000 a year, yet I never would be happier than I was living out my dream of holding public office. Indeed, I waded right into the business of government. And needless to say, I immediately began to ruffle feathers on the corruption-ridden City Commission.Only a month later, in December 1989, I acted on my biggest pet peeve about politicians—their pompous verbosity, or is it their verbose pomposity. Either way, people simply did not want to listen to politicians prattle on. And so, I convinced the loudmouths to limit speeches during commission debates to three minutes. I put a light on the speaker's podium that turned green when it was time to talk and red when it was time to shut up.

The reaction was predictable. "Personally, I resent this light," said one of the more pompous commissioners. One time I was forced to turn the light red when a commissioner named Hal Hertz, a very good friend of mine who had helped me win my election, spoke too long. "I was humiliated and felt my presence violated," Hal moaned, just slightly exaggerating the effect of a little light. Later, I went over to him and put a big kiss on his cheek, to show him I still loved him. It was, I imagine, the first time anyone had ever kissed a politician during a spirited debate. Unless, of course, you count clandestine meetings in hotel rooms or brothels in a "red light" district.

Hal may not have liked the red light (the commission cravenly repealed the rule only three weeks after it had been approved), but he loved me. Later that day, he told the press, "Abe's got his finger on the pulse of the city's business beyond what I expected a freshman commissioner to have after only three weeks in office."

He wasn't the only one to notice. My good friend, Mayor Alex Daoud, was shocked at what I was getting done. In my first week on the job, I noticed that the city was losing thousands of dollars every week because city administrators did not require the Jackie Gleason Theater of the Performing Arts to pay all the rent called for in their contract with the city. I went to Alex with this startling information, and he launched an investigation. Result: the money was collected.

It was also my leadership that fostered positive changes in the city's police force. The first thing I did was to call for a rule requiring the police commissioner to live in the city, not some cloistered suburb where blacks and Cubans weren't allowed to live; clearly, such a homogenous environment could create a mindset hostile to Miami Beach's non-Caucasian majority. The commission approved the rule, and though they backed away from my proposal to require every police officer to live within the city as well, they enacted another of my proposals that would turn into one of the most important and far-reaching solutions in the area of police/community relations.

In Miami Beach, police brutality was rampant in the late 1980s. My take on it was typically simple and effective. I proposed that every police car on duty have one white and one African-American or Hispanic cop. It was just that simple. Police teams should always reflect the racial composition of their communities. And within days of this law being passed, complaints of police brutality all but vanished in Miami Beach.

Rather than to just "go with the flow" and buckle under to corruption and a don't-rock-the-boat attitude, I was working to get rid of that attitude. When I arrived in Miami Beach, I saw first-hand the undue influence of the City Manager, a scoundrel named Rob Parkins, who had cost the city around $12 million hiring contractors who charged off a mass of cost overruns. Parkins's waste and mismanagement also cost the city a new sports stadium that was built instead in suburban Homestead.

271

I made it my business to get Parkins fired, along with his minion, a bumbling city attorney, Arnold Weiner, who himself had cost the city $30 million by failing to properly defend a lawsuit that wound up in a judgment against the city. When this "dumb and dumber" were gone, I had the judgment reversed.

Similarly, I saw that the city's new downtown Convention Center project had been so badly managed that it was close to being abandoned, not unlike the Wollman Rink had been. One problem was crippling cost overruns. So, I had my personal construction manager check the books, and he found that the city actually owed $65 million *less* than what the books claimed. There was a clear case of fraud somewhere in those books, but I persuaded the city to settle with the contractors at the lower cost to keep the project on track. Next, I got the seven top builders in Miami Beach to serve without pay on a commission to oversee the project, and as a result, I saved the city $6 million more. This was a manifestation of another of "The Hirschfeld Rules"—that only builders could be on the commissions, not politicians or lawyers. Put those crooks on any commission and it degenerates into the usual corrupt cesspool. I steered the Convention Center past them, and it became a showplace, a magnificent building.

One more example. When the Miami Beach Arts Festival was slated to close because traffic was always snarled getting there on the I-95 highway, I had another typical Abe Hirschfeld remedy: simply by changing the highway from four lanes going north and one going south to a two-and-two scheme, traffic would be eased. Of course, it worked perfectly, and the Festival was saved.

The *Miami Herald,* which was itself filled with reporters who were bought and sold by corrupt forces, and was poised to attack me from the get-go, nonetheless had no choice but to praise my contributions. On March 11, 1989, they wrote: "His rough-and-tumble, shoot-from-the-hip manner rubs some people the wrong way, but supporters say his business acumen is just what the Beach commission needs."

One of my fellow commissioners, Stanley Arkin, said this: "He offers a different approach to our agenda and method of operation. He doesn't care if you have ordinances, committees, rules, or a Sunshine Law. He's a nuts and bolts person who wants to go directly to the problem, but we weren't able to do that in a governmental setting [before]."

272

I was, then, a big hit. And there was no doubt that my Castle would be, too. With my ability to juggle so many different balls, even as I threw myself into my commissioner's role, I was immersed in the business of opening my hotel and theater. I had already lined up the first production that Karen Poindexter imported, a revival of *Anything Goes,* starring Marilyn McCoo and Bebe Neuwirth from the "Cheers" TV show. On the glorious night we opened the doors of the theater, Al Hirschfeld—who had lived in New York seemingly since the Indians paid twenty-four dollars for Manhattan—did something he had never done before. He came to Miami Beach just to see a show. Weeks before, knowing I had named the theater for him, he had called and begged for a ticket, which of course he need not have done.

"You have a permanent ticket here," I said. "But Al, you don't fly. You're afraid of airplanes."

"So, I'll drive," he quickly assured me. "Just have my ticket waiting."

And that is when Al Hirschfeld, who then was around eighty-seven years old, drove from New York to Miami Beach to see my show. At *his* theater.

Within weeks of the opening of the Castle, we were doing a goldmine business. Rooms were completely booked, and as I had predicted, the entire corridor of the Gold Coast was vibrant and kicking. Taking a break from the mundane political grind, I went on a theatrical scouting mission to London and was invited to co-produce a new version of *Hair.* That '60s standard, ironically, was a lesson in new-age theater economics, as it cost only $2.5 million to stage—the scenery was a mere $50,000. (Of course, having actors prance around naked did save on wardrobe costs.) I took the lesson back to America, proving that any show I touched would become a smash—provided, unlike with *Prince of Central Park,* everyone involved understood that there would be no deviation from my instructions.

That golden rule guided thirteen productions to tremendous success at the Hirschfeld Theater. These included *Evita, Broadway on Ice, 42nd Street, Romance, Romance, Nunsense, Ain't Misbehavin', They're Playing Our Song, Peter Pan* (starring Cathy Rigby), *Hair* (Danielle Brisbois), *Oliver* (Davy Jones), *The Prince of Central Park,* and finally, the biggest smash of all, my biggest pride and joy outside of Zipora and my children: *Phantom II of the Opera.*

But trouble was brewing, the kind that seems to breed around me wherever I go.

The trouble was that, as usual, I was just too good at doing what I did. And thus a big threat to people who wanted it done differently—for their own good, not the community's.

Karen Poindexter tried to warn me, telling me, "Abe, no one *needs* to pay you off. They know they can't control you."

The consequence of that became more than just conjecture only three months after my election. By then, the hotel and theater were bustling. And one fine morning, with not a minute of advance warning, I was blindsided by the lowlife building director of Miami, Paul Gioia—another slug who I had not yet gotten around to firing—who cited me for five violations of the building code.

I was outraged by what was obviously a hit-job. I strongly suspected that Gioia had been put up to it by Rob Parkins, out of revenge, and I was told it only came after Gioia had tried to solicit a bribe from one of my hotel's suppliers. Although Gioia denied this, the evidence compelled Florida's then attorney general, Janet Reno, to investigate before, in an inevitable whitewash, deciding against taking any action on the matter. There was no way she could have—as it would have halted the obvious goal of closing down my hotel and theater and driving me back to New York.

How phony were these building "violations?" Consider how they came about. It was not because of any complaints, any incidents, or any of the dozens of inspections that accompanied every phase of the hotel's renovation. It only came to be an issue after I made the mistake of cooperating with one of those devious *Miami Herald* reporters, who asked me how much I had spent on the renovation. I told him around $9 million, which included converting the top-floor solarium into a penthouse. This guy then ran to Paul Gioia, who sent an inspection crew to "find" fire violations in the penthouse and to insist—incorrectly—that I had not obtained building permits.

I could only point to the obvious. I was living with my wife and daughter in a hotel Gioia insisted I knew was a firetrap. Furthermore, there had not been a single fire in the entire history of the hotel, going back to the '60s—and not a single violation found in all that time! It was only after I had taken over the hotel that all these "violations" magically arose.

"The only violations this building has," I told the media, "are political violations."

At first, I sued the city, which in turn countersued me. But in April 1990, I agreed to call Gioia's bluff and make the necessary repairs to fix those "phantom" violations. I spent at least $10 million on this, but nothing I did would suffice. Always there were more inspections and more violations. My enemies were bribing my construction crews to foment strikes so that hotel guests would have to run the gantlet of picketers to get in and out. I even gave in to their demands for more money. But after a time, I just could not go on with this game of deceit.

Nor could I counter the daily cacophony of slanted stories in the *Herald,* mainly by a horrible liar named Bonnie Weston, who is as much a reporter as I am an Arab sheik. On June 12, for example, the *Herald*'s headline was "Beach hotel a 'disaster waiting to happen.'" The source for this accusation was a court-appointed referee who never asked me to provide evidence to the contrary.

But what ripped it for me was the ultimate disgrace—the rape of the Hirschfeld Theater. In June, we had opened the run of *Phantom II of the Opera.* This was my most ambitious production of all and a sure loser according to the "experts." Many longtime theater observers believed a second *Phantom* was extraneous given that the Andrew Lloyd Webber original had won so many raves during its London run. Now the Broadway version was about to begin its own long and successful run. However, I had sought out a production that more closely adhered to the 1911 Gaston Leroux novel on which at least four *Phantoms* have been based. I wanted the relationship between the Phantom and his victim Christine to be better developed, acted with more passion. I wanted a more varied music score. I wanted some comedy. I wanted, as the old-time Borscht Belt performers used to say, more *schmaltz.*

I hired two veteran Broadway composers, Paul Schierhorn and Lawrence Rosen, and to write the script, I hired Bruce Falstein. The best thing I can say about this triumvirate is that they listened to me. And I listened to my daughter Rachel. I had stewed for weeks that the ending of the show wasn't quite right, that it needed something unique. Rachel provided the answer.

"Daddy," she said, "why don't you end the show like it begins; have the Phantom give the spirit of music to another girl."

Once I ordered this ending to be put in, everything jelled. Audiences passed my half-hour ovation test. They would not leave. And so, I would come out on stage and tell them, "If you want to see it again, you'll have to buy more tickets." And they did. Over and over. My *Phantom,* starring Elizabeth Walsh and David Staller, took off. The critics were captivated. The *Sun-Sentinel*'s Jack Zink wrote of the score, "It has a sweep and style, from soaring ballads to ragtime and pop in a cohesive whole."

Variety used some of the most glowing terms ever in a review:

The Hirschfeld Theater on Miami Beach has created a new seriocomic musical . . . that is nothing like the hit Andrew Lloyd Webber pop opera....[It] sports a romantically enticing book that follows closely the original novel, plus a bright musical score that ranges from pop to traditional theatrical musical comedy stylings....[The other "Phantoms"] are turgid by comparison....The treatment was commissioned by theater owner Abraham Hirschfeld...and as assembled from scratch in just under six months....In some ways, Rosen and Schierhorn's music is more challenging and complex than the celebrated Webber version.

Originally, Karen booked the show for a two-month run, but ticket demand became an avalanche, and it was in its eighth month, breaking box office records and creating a tremendous word of mouth excitement. Indeed, demand was so great that we decided to record the show on videotape, and it played all across Florida on public television, garnering ratings that beat out the regular networks' programming. Then the videotape ran in New York, at the 57th Street Playhouse—a direct challenge to the Weber musical that was ensconced on Broadway. Even the acrid New York critics who carried no truck for me loved it. The *Times'* review read: "Surprise: It is not half bad....Mr. Falstein's concise libretto makes the allegory much clearer than Mr. Lloyd Webber [has]...[The] music is as unabashedly romantic as Mr. Lloyd Webber's, although the melodic edges of their songs are softer and the orchestrations more diaphanous."

All of the raves were so gratifying to Karen and me. But then, just like that, the music stopped and the lights went out.

276

I wasn't in the audience that night, but I received a phone call from Karen, who was frantic.

"Abe," she exclaimed on the other end of the telephone, "the police have come into the theater and are demanding the show be stopped in mid-performance. They say the theater is in violation of some zoning laws or other. We don't know what to do."

Neither did I. As stunned as I was, I could only think of the audience. All I wanted to do was to get the show completed. Then I would confront these zoning allegations.

"Karen, tell the cops to please wait until after the performance before closing the theater!" I pleaded.

"We told them that," she said. "But they say no. They're saying, 'Either stop the show or we'll arrest all of you.'"

"Just keep the show going," I said. "Forget about the intermission. Try to get it done as fast as possible." Karen passed along the word to the cast and production crew. Then I heard loud voices arguing. Then she came back on the phone.

"Abe, we tried to go on, but they said they're going to interrupt the show—right now."

Before I could say anything, I heard a commotion in the background as the curtain was being dropped, the lights were turned on, and the audience was being told the performance was over. Those nice people in the audience must have been absolutely bewildered and as livid as I was. I had an announcement made that refunds would be issued at the box office, which at that moment, I could imagine being a surreal scene from out of a Fellini movie, with people milling about in a state of shock and confusion.

Once my mind had a chance to focus on what was going on, it became clear to me that this criminal act committed in the name of justice had not a thing to do with "zoning violations" of the building code. It had to do with my success as an interloper, an outsider who was beating the stranglehold of corruption in Miami Beach and making a real difference in people's lives.

In many ways, this despicable intrusion was a worse rape of my civil liberties than when New York cops would enter my apartment a decade later. The indecency of it cannot be overstated. I cannot imagine why any American authority figure would ever treat another American the way Hitler treated his own people. These newest alleged zoning violations could easily have waited until the next morning. Were they so callous to the fact that hundreds of people had paid their hard-earned money to see a quality show? Do human beings mean nothing to political hacks such as those who so resented me in Miami Beach? You know the answer.

Worse for Karen and I, on that night, the audience included Tom Mallow, a big producer who had national dinner-theater connections and wanted very much to take our production of *Phantom* out on the road. We were to meet with Tom the next morning. As well, we had just contracted to bring into the theater as our next production *A Chorus Line*. That would be the next casualty of the Miami Gestapo.

The next morning, I raised holy hell in the media about the city commission, from where I believe the order emanated to close the theater. All of the commissioners were bastards. Not one had the courage and dignity to stop the order. As to the charges themselves, they were remarkably bogus and highly selective.

The only thing I understood was that the theater was an inviting target. This was the very symbol of my renewal plan for the city. Sending in storm troopers sent a chilling message to the largely Jewish population of Miami Beach—to stay away.

And so, with no other option, in late October I announced that I was closing the hotel and the theater, meaning that the City Commission of Miami Beach and the *Miami Herald* were responsible for 1,200 people of meager means losing their jobs. One woman named Josephine, a seamstress, was sixty-five years old. She had come to America twenty-five years ago and had worked at the hotel for the last twenty-three years. "Abe, this is my whole life," she told me through tears that sad day. Now her life was gone.

The city's humiliation of me was not over. They barred me from holding a press conference or even being inside of my own hotel. Then they got their hand-picked judge to dock me $23,000 to pay for the city's legal tab.

I put the Castle up for auction for $20 million—a real bargain considering that it was now worth around $35 million. In late October, two dozen or so businessmen came for the auction held in the hotel's ballroom—yet, not one put in a bid. They had no doubt been warned not to enrich me. The game plan was clear: to strip me of my hotel and theater and not allow me to walk away with a cent in my pocket.

There was someone else in the ballroom that day, Bonnie Weston, the lying *Herald* reporter whom I had specifically ordered to stay away from the hotel. When I saw her, I asked her what she was doing there. Assuming a Queen of the Nile pose, she arrogantly said, "I go where I please."

Now I welled up with anger and rumbled over to where she was standing.

"You bitch. Get out of here!" I thundered.

When she refused to budge, I was as outraged as I had been when Stanley Steingut had backstabbed me in 1976. And my reaction was exactly the same.

As TV cameras began moving in to capture the scene, I expectorated in her smarmy face.

Still she sat, motionless, humbled, humiliated, shocked, and wearing a look of total befuddlement that perfectly matched her clueless existence.

I wasn't through yet. I took another swallow and let her have it again, my saliva stream landing on the back of her head as she turned it at the last moment.

"You bitch, get out!" I screamed at her again, but before the words were out, she had made tracks for the door, dripping wet, before I could load up again.

I will tell you right here that I do not regret either spitting incident; both Steingut and Weston amply deserved what they got. I might say, too, that I happen to believe that spitting is the perfect weapon of retribution. It hurts no one, yet it humiliated them beyond words. You can dry off saliva in two seconds but the stigma of being spat upon in public lingers with you an entire lifetime. When Stanley Steingut died, the first thing anyone wrote in his obituaries was that he was the guy Abe Hirschfeld spit on. Bonnie Weston will carry her own scarlet letter to the grave.

Though the human barnacles on the city commission censured me by a 6–0 vote for the incident, and many demanded an apology from me, I never wavered in my belief that spitting in Bonnie Weston's face was perfectly justifiable. I even called it an act of "self-defense" given how she had vilified me every day in the paper, with assumed impunity. Now, hopefully those in the media who believed they could tear apart someone's reputation and hide under the cloak of journalistic immunity would know there was no sanctuary, unless of course they planned to take an umbrella with them wherever they went.

Indeed, as many people told me in the succeeding days, "I would like to spit at the *Miami Herald,* too!" I was also gratified that during the knee-jerk condemnation of me in the media, in which I was called nuts, sick, evil, disgusting, abhorrent, foolish, and even "filthy," I came across a number of letters to the editor in the *Herald* that took my side. One of these pointed out that "the Miami Beach Commission has been symbolically spitting on the people for years by maintaining an arrogant, what's-in-it-for-me attitude." Another, from a man named Herbert Davis, offered a brilliant analysis of the situation:

The *Herald* has long been on a crusade of total destruction against Mr. Hirschfeld. The *Herald* thinks, or wants its readers to think, that it has the right to try and destroy a man and his business. Your justification is "in the public interest." Well, that's a good blanket to hide under. You have labeled him boorish and a disgrace to the people of Dade County, but is it because Mr. Hirschfeld is an aggressive, overbearing businessman, who is wealthy to boot and who does not answer to your beat as the drummer? Since when did the *Herald* become the Emily Post on proper behavior?

I am sick and tired of the *Herald* trying to tell us what to vote for and the characters of [those you dislike]. As if the *Herald* knows what's good for us.

Abe Hirschfeld is not your patsy or a dog that can be kicked around. I think that he is refreshing in light of what has been going on in Miami Beach for too many years. This man is above reproach. How do you control somebody who has everything? He can't be bribed, and that is a lot more than can be said for some other people on the Beach. If you had half of his guts and brains, you might be very well off and not sitting behind that desk trying to save the world.

Indeed, when the high-and-mighty commissioners censured me and worked to remove me from office, I hit them with the truth: any one of them had committed far worse crimes, including more than a few who had been nabbed driving drunk and others who spent more time in brothels than at City Hall. The very same man who had called an emergency meeting of the commission to demand my resignation, a fool named William Shockett, put in the motion that I had committed "repeated deliberate acts inconsistent with the standards of conduct expected and required" of a commissioner.

Yet, this man was hardly a saint. When I was interviewed on Channel 4 on December 26, I candidly told the host that "Many times [Shockett] comes to the commission drunk."

In response, Shockett sued me for slander, asking for $10,000 in damages. Though he never got a penny, it highlighted how phony and cowardly these crooked people were. Nearly all were the vilest creatures I've ever seen, corrupt and immoral and evil. But the first time anyone would call them on their behavior, they attacked. With me, they never stopped attacking. Before one commission meeting on December 19, I tried to calm everybody's frayed nerves by telling a good-natured ethnic joke. Shockett was not amused. He stood up and demanded that I be censured *again* and even called a special session over the Christmas holiday to pass it, though by then it was deemed so absurd that the motion was withdrawn by unanimous vote, even Shockett's. (They probably realized not laughing was for me far more hurtful than a censure.)

As an aside, I am still amazed that anyone could ever take offense at the joke I told, a wonderful and charming old saw that actually skewers racism and anti-Semitism and could have come right from the gentle story-telling mouth of Sam Levenson. I have told it many times, to great gusts of laughter from rabbis and civil rights leaders, and I'll tell it again now so that you can decide for yourself. It goes like this:

There was a kosher restaurant in Miami Beach where the Orthodox Jews went everyday. One day, two black men came in for dinner, and the waiter Johnny didn't know what to do. He went over to Sammy the owner and told him these black men wanted dinner.

"Johhny," said Sammy, "we don't discriminate against blacks here. Dinner is nine dollars—but charge them one hundred dollars, and they won't come back."

So, the men ate a nice dinner and left a big tip. Next day, Johnny says, "Sammy, we have a bigger problem. There are ten blacks here. What do we do?"

"Tell them it's two hundred dollars for dinner, and they won't come back."

The ten black men ate and left a thousand-dollar tip.

Next day, a whole busload of blacks come in. Johnny says, "What do we do?"

And Sammy says, "Johnny, I told you, we don't discriminate against blacks. Chase out all the Jews."

You tell me: Is this joke cause for wanting to draw and quarter me? I hope not, because it's one of my better ones.

Far more damaging to me than a bunch of thin-skinned commissioners was the *Miami Herald*. This paper was out to destroy me, pure and simple. Drunk with their own power, it violated every rule of journalism. They played up the labor strikes at my hotel and never mentioned that I'd settled them. When a judge threatened to hold me in criminal contempt, it was on page one; when he said he would not do it, it got not a single word. The same thing happened when Shockett wanted to censure me for the joke, never bothering to report that the censure motion was also withdrawn.

Following the *Herald*'s lead, other smaller papers and magazines did the same. One, *New Times,* took a favorable story written about me in which the author called me "funny and charming," edited out all the nice things, and headlined it, "Nobody likes Abe." When the writer, Joshua Weinsten, saw how they'd butchered and twisted his article, he quit. But the *Herald*'s reporters didn't have that kind of integrity. They did what their cowardly publisher David Lawrence and his stooge of an editor Jim Hampton ordered them to do, which was to get me.

Why? Don't ask me. Ask them. In fact, when people would call the Hirschfeld Theater confused about why it had been shuttered, I instructed the operator to tell them to call Jim Batten, chairman of Knight-Ridder, which owns the *Herald,* just as I instructed her to tell folks who wanted to make reservations at the Castle Hotel to call Paul Gioia. Both of those horrible men received hundreds of phone calls and I hope much discomfort.

The funny thing, tragic really, is that Bonnie Weston would apologize to *me*. This astonishing event took the form of a letter dated January 24, 1991, which had to do with the joke censure distortions. The letter read:

Dear Commissioner Hirschfeld:

Please accept my apologies for an item in today's paper incorrectly reporting your censure by the Miami Beach Commission. As you know, the item was in fact withdrawn by the unanimous vote of your fellow commissioners. I regret the misunderstanding and any distress it may have caused you.

Sincerely,

Bonnie Weston

You may be surprised to know, as well, that Bonnie Weston and I have become friendly since those turbulent days. I do not hold grudges against anyone and am quite willing to forgive and forget, as long as the person who wronged me is big enough to apologize for it. In fact, in the spirit of healing old wounds, I apologized to Rob Parkins for running him out of town on a handrail. In the months since, the former city manager had gone to Palm Springs, California to take a similar position and had continued to advise the Miami Beach Commission, with some very helpful advice. I stood up during a commission hearing and effusively praised Parkins and called for a motion to pay him for his good advice.

As the healing continued, I found that more and more people who had criticized me in the past were now agreeing that I had been treated unfairly by the city, though it was too late to save my beautiful hotel and theater. Given the good vibes I was getting, I seriously considered running for mayor of Miami Beach after Alex Daoud was convicted on phony charges of taking graft and removed from office. That conviction reeked of reverse anti-Semitism. Alex is a Catholic, a rare commodity in Miami Beach, and he wouldn't cooperate with the "Jewish Mafia" of crooked politicians and bureaucrats that run the place. I wanted to continue his policies while, of course, introducing my own agenda of progress and productivity.

I named a campaign manager in mid-1991, and my ruminations about running for mayor were revealed in a very nice story in the *Herald* by none other than Bonnie Weston. Her lead paragraph read: "Unfazed by his first rough and tumble term as Miami Beach Commissioner, Abe Hirschfeld—politician, hotelier, amateur comic—may raise his political sights and run for Mayor of Miami Beach."

However, by then I could read the tea leaves; my time in Miami Beach had run its course and I could hear New York City calling me back home. Zipora was more than ready, having urged me for months to stop banging my head against the wall of injustice and opposition in Miami Beach.

On July 28, 1991, I closed the Castle for good and sold it to Russel Galbut of the Alexander Hotel chain—at a $30 million loss. Unsurprisingly, the hotel was allowed to re-open quickly, but only briefly, as it turned out. Within a few years, it was sold again and converted into luxury condominiums, the Camelot that it had represented to the city when I'd turned it into the entertainment capital of south Florida now long gone. My legacy, however, would remain intact. Within a few years, the prosperity I fomented in Miami Beach would spread to South Beach—which had been a virtual Skid Row when I developed several dilapidated hotels and converted them into luxury, art-deco co-ops. As a result, South Beach became the "in" place for people to go to be seen. Again, a case of "garbage, garbage, garbage" becoming "diamonds, diamonds, diamonds."

The saddest thing of all was not the money I'd lost making Miami Beach profitable or the slurs to my dignity I'd had to put up with. It was that I could have done so much more. As it is, I made Miami Beach the hottest spot in the country. For doing this, I was the most popular person in the state, among the people, if not the politicians. More people recognized me than the state's governor. The spitting incident drew worldwide attention and made me into some kind of populist folk hero (did anyone say Don Quixote?). People from all walks of life knew my name. When I was invited to a fundraiser for Governor Bob Martinez, the cameras didn't move from my table. The governor had no cameras!

But now, it was time to leave. When my term as city commissioner was done, I jumped on a plane and came back home to New York—blissfully unaware that, at age seventy-two, I was just now embarking on the most rewarding and controversial years of my life.

CHAPTER TWENTY-FIVE: CLOUDS OF WAR

My Miami Beach adventure was costly in many ways. Not only had I lost around $32 million in the Castle Hotel fiasco, when I returned to New York in 1991. I found I needed to sort out some loose ends in my real estate business that had unraveled in my absence. For one thing, Elie had become quite an important real estate lawyer and was ready to move into his own business in real estate.

Up until then, Elie had been proof perfect of my theory for raising perfect children. When he was eight years old, and I was thirty-four, I sat him down and shared my theory. As usual, it's a very simple theory, so simple that it's simply beautiful.

"Elie," I told him, "we should work as partners. We will discuss everything. That way, nothing can go wrong between us."

He looked at me, puzzled.

"Dad," he said, "what happens if we disagree?"

"If we disagree," I replied quickly, "you will do it my way."

Elie practiced the rule all throughout his brilliant academic career. And he practiced it during his biggest period of success when he worked with me, well into his twenties. There was only one time we ever disagreed about something. That was when he was eighteen, and he decided he wanted to buy a little European sports car.

"Listen to me," I told him. "Forget that sports car. I'll buy you a big Cadillac, a safe car."

"Dad, you remember our agreement?" he said. "Well, I take my veto now."

I never had any reason to believe we would ever clash on anything more serious than that. And while he adhered to my rules, he prospered and excelled, such as by his work helping to get the Vertical Club built. Another glittering example was our joint venture that culminated in one of my most lucrative deals ever. It began as it always does for me—with garbage, garbage, garbage.

In the mid-1980s, I saw that the old American Refrigeration Building was sitting vacant, and it was the kind of beautiful eyesore that can be turned into gold. This twelve-story building was huge, taking up the entire block of 17th Street between 10th and 11th Avenues on the West Side. It had once been used to store much of the frozen foods that were distributed to stores and markets all around the city. Now, though, there was no need for a central storage facility

285

because installing freezers had become cost-efficient, so the building was a tomb. Nobody wanted to touch it.

When I spoke with the building's lawyers, they were thrilled to no end, as they had not been able to find a buyer anywhere.

"How much do you want?" I asked.

"Seven million," the lawyer said, a bit unsurely. "But you can make me an offer."

"No," I said, "if I like something, I pay full price for it."

"Okay, then, seven million."

"You have a deal."

I'm sure that man believed he had suckered me so badly that he wanted to laugh out loud. Of course, he didn't know that when I make a deal like that, I always laugh loudest, and last.

The first thing I did was convert the building into a luxury condominium. And as so often happens when I convert a building, people say to themselves: *"What does he know? He must know something."* Immediately, all kinds of wealthy people began lining up to buy condos in the building. I sold one floor, the twelfth, for $7 million alone, meaning that just with that sale, I had effectively bought the building for exactly nothing.

It got better still. I had taken Elie in on the project, forming a holding company called Able Empire Group. Most companies need years to get off the ground. We needed no more than a few weeks. This was because we found out that the federal government was looking for a large building because they needed to move the Drug Enforcement Administration to a new location in the city, to house the New York Field Division. And through Elie's efforts doing what he does best—shmoozing with the intellectuals who run government agencies—we were able to make a deal to lease the building to the DEA under a lease negotiated by the U.S. General Services Administration.

This was precisely the kind of inspired and useful building process I had envisioned when I gave Mario Cuomo my endorsement in 1986, and which I have excelled at carrying through my whole life as a builder. Remember, I'm not an architect. I don't design exteriors, even though my buildings are invariably beautiful and aesthetically perfect. I design *functional space.* Cuomo, by callously rejecting my plans, not only shafted the governmental agencies that needed splendid new office space, he also shafted me personally.

The Federal government, on the other hand, had no desire to screw itself by screwing me. They saw what I could do for them – provide a home for the largest task force of Federal and local law enforcement agents and the largest joint center for drug intelligence in the country. Here, the agents would be in the same venue as the labs, making for a better and tighter chain of command. Little wonder that soon after its its opening, the drug trade and drug crime began to plummet in New York, which of course is the gateway to the entire country.

Not incidentally, it also produced an enormous profit for Elie and me.

One of the most gratifying moments of my life was when President George Bush came to New York in January 1992 to dedicate the opening of the new DEA office. Which meant I had now witnessed two U.S. Presidents dedicating my buildings—Jimmy Carter had done the same at the Vertical Club.

With his share of that investment, Elie went out on his own, with an open invitation to return to me at any time. Of course, not all had been wine and roses between us. We have had our disagreements about business matters—as I have with my daughter Rachel—yet, I think of this as a healthy thing. I did not raise my children to be mannequins but flesh and blood people who can stand on their feet. My love for my children could never be impinged upon, even though both Elie and Rachel have become occasional adversaries of mine in courtrooms over strictly business matters—though I must emphasize that I have never sued Elie or Rachel, and I never would.

The pity of it is that my *real* adversaries, as you will learn, have thought nothing about using these painful, private family matters to damage me. That they have so willfully and blithely tried to exacerbate my relationships with my children may be the single most venal and unscrupulous thing they have done, and that takes in a lot of ground. Because everything he did, he did because I told him what to do. The bottom line on my relationship with Elie is that he has helped me enormously, and without his input, I would have been lost.

I have rewarded Elie well for his ideas, his energy, and his encouragement. As soon as he reached manhood, I gave him a 16⅔ percent interest in Stahl Associates, one of the two holding companies I co-owned with Stanley Stahl, and the one I managed, in which I held a 32⅔ percent interest. (My brother Menasha I gave 1 percent.) This was a similar structure to Hirstan Associates, the company managed by Stahl, in which Stanley and his sister Sonia Schlossberg had the same stock arrangement. In Hirstan, I owned 48 percent, and I gave my daughter Rachel 1 percent and Menasha 1 percent.

Remember these figures because, later on, the issue of family blood and how it pertained to both Stahl Associates and Hirstan Associates would become extremely important.

This is my introduction to my war with Stanley Stahl, a man with whom I had never had a cross word or as much as a two-word argument with in twenty-five years.

Let me clarify that by adding that we rarely, if ever, had more than a two-word *conversation* in all those years, either. People were always curious about the relationship between Stanley and me. We were such different people that few could figure out how we would ever tolerate each other. I suppose the answer—other than our mutual instinct for making money—is that our peccadilloes actually fit in a polar-opposites-attract sort of way.

Stanley was as quiet, even sullen, as I am gregarious. As long as I knew him, Stanley was a lone wolf, zealously fanatic about his privacy and obsessively focused only on his business. If I saw him smile once, it was once in forty years. Although we had a very good business relationship, I never saw the inside of his apartment, nor he of mine, though I invited him many times. We would have lunch together and regular meetings, but other than that, we maintained separate orbits. He generally made the business decisions, with my consent, and we normally had the same ideas for our properties.

And yet, Stanley was no saint, as neither am I. *New York* magazine once quoted anonymous executives who had done business with Stanley. It seemed to matter much more to Stanley than to me that he got most of the credit for our burgeoning business empire. The truth was that I had brought almost all of the buildings we owned to Stanley. But it's true as well that he ran them as a single-minded compulsion, while I branched out to involve myself in politics, government, and the arts.

In that symbiotic way, we had the perfect mixture, and I would get offended when Stanley would claim that I was no more than a cipher to the business. In truth, Stanley made a lot of money for me, and I made a lot of money for Stanley. Unfortunately, he could never quite bring himself to admit the latter. As time wore on, he seemed to become more and more annoyed that I was even around.

That was fine with me as long as the partnership was strong. I had no problem with Stanley socializing with his elitist snob billionaire developers—those hoary fossils whose names seem to be moaned when a good wind blows through the canyons of Park and Madison Avenues. I was never much for humoring or hobnobbing with the snobs. Their lives are too miserable for me to want to bring their depressing ways into my life.

That was the big difference between us. We were both from humble stock—Stanley was the son of a Brooklyn butcher—but I never lost touch with the common man. Indeed, that is the very key to my rough-hewn genius. I formulate and build my dreams out of what I know the common person wants, because all through history the institutions that have endured the longest have been those not actualized by intellectuals. An intellectual knows nothing about the real world because his head is always in the clouds. Look back through the tunnel of time. Who has made a difference in our lives? Was it the Platos or Aristotles or has it been the Rockefellers, the Fords, the Wright Brothers? All of the latter began with nothing. The Rockefellers began as paperboys. And I, of course, began as a sixth-grade dropout in Tarnow, a place that is still inside me.

Stanley, on the other hand, didn't ever want to look back at where he had come from. He had no affinity or loyalty for our mutual success. I actually pitied him for that.

When I returned to New York in the early 1990s, I felt a distinct chill in the air when Stanley came into the same room with me. It became progressively clearer that he regarded me as an obstacle and that he wanted to push me out at a time when property values in New York City were skyrocketing. For many years, Stanley had looked down his nose at me—to him, I was a kind of peon, a tagalong little brother even though I was older than he was. It was as if he had been merely tolerating me.

To anyone who knew of Stanley's business dealings, such a situation would be cause for great concern. Though I did not know him that well personally, I knew that in Stanley's methodology, if he had no use for you, you had little chance of fighting him. Unlike me, Stanley would never have been an ideal candidate for the Nobel Peace Prize. His methods were more Vito Corleone than Mahatma Ghandi.

Never has there been a more ruthless man in any endeavor. Stanley Stahl, quite simply, had no intention of ever losing a round in any business deal or any court of law.

In 1977, for example, Stanley was convicted of bribing an IRS agent in order to lower the value of his father's estate. But he didn't stay convicted for long because he had the most powerful lawyer in the city, Milton Gould of the giant Shea Gould law firm—whose partner was William Shea, the man who was powerful enough to bring the New York Mets into baseball, after the Dodgers had left Brooklyn, and for the Mets' stadium to be named after him. Milton Gould was able to get the man who made the bribery charge against Stahl to change his story, and the conviction was reversed on appeal. It was the best magic trick since Houdini.

However, not even Milton Gould's power could rival Stanley Stahl's, nor could he save his own law firm a few years later when Stanley fell out with him. In the end, Shea Gould was completely bankrupted and destroyed, and he was put out of business for good. Within just a few years, in fact, Stahl had effectively put out of business dozens of former associates in a purge of anyone whom he felt might have stood in his way. This happened in earnest when, in 1990, Stahl had acquired the Apple Bank in a hostile takeover, fueling his megalomania. The first test of his power and thirst for conquest was a lawsuit brought against Stahl in 1993 by another of his real estate partners, Joseph Comras, who claimed Stahl had willfully withheld $2.5 million.

I wish I had paid more attention to that particular lawsuit, because it was a primer on what would later happen with me. From the start, Stahl launched a blizzard of countersuits against Comras, which Stahl was able to "consolidate" under the aegis of a judge favorable to him. And despite massive evidence of breach of contract on Stahl's part, in the end it was Stahl who prevailed, and it was Comras who was put out of business in total bankruptcy.

He wasn't alone. During that three-year period when Stahl's purges were at their most brutal, virtually anyone who had a grievance against Stahl was figuratively liquidated. Even Stahl's only child, his son Gregory, was committed to an insane asylum.

All this bloodletting had been carried out by Stahl's new lawyer, David Rosenberg of the Marcus Borg Rosenberg and

Diamond law firm. From 1992 on, I would become very familiar indeed with David Rosenberg.

I am sure that to Stahl and Rosenberg, I was supposed to be the next on that long list of victims standing in Stanley's path. I'm sure that I was also supposed to be properly frightened—and to give in to his lust for power or else. Only I was too naïve, or too rooted in an old-fashioned sense of righteous outrage, to be frightened. Surely I was too naïve to know how far Stahl would go to crush me. What's more, at the time I actually believed our long relationship still meant something.

Indeed, given the $30 million bath I had taken in Miami Beach, I asked Stanley for a $500,000 loan, and he readily agreed. Within a year, I had paid him back with interest. In turn, I had guaranteed for Stanley a $3 million loan. Why would I have had any reason to believe that we did not still share a special bond?

But, by 1992, Stanley Stahl was rather drunk with power. I began to see little deceits that disturbed me because of my sense of honesty and fair play in business.

The hints began when I returned to New York and surveyed our holdings. Most strikingly, I found that our three most profitable luxury apartment-office buildings had no fewer than thirty apartments and four commercial spaces sitting vacant. The breakdown looked like this: 360 East 55th Street, 11 vacancies; 404 East 55th Street and 405 East 54th Street, 19 vacancies and four commercial spaces. When I confronted Stanley about this situation, which of course was costing us many thousands of dollars a month, he became very indignant, as if I had no right to ask why so many profitable apartments and offices were being kept off the market.

I could only deduce that it was his aim to force, by attrition, all the tenants out of the buildings so that he could then exert the leverage to convert the buildings into condominiums or co-ops. But the more important point was that Stahl was operating under the radar screen, without my advice and consent, to keep rent-controlled and rent-stabilized apartments away from prospective tenants, which was against the housing laws.

A further inspection of the tenant list led to another revelation—racial discrimination. The fact was, Stahl was not renting apartments specifically to any black people. (He was even trying to drive out of one building one very distinguished resident who happened to be black, the great singer Harry Belafonte.) Just to prove what Stahl was doing, I sent three very fine, upscale African-Americans with impeccable references to these buildings' rental offices, and all of them were rejected out of hand by Stahl's hand-picked rental agents. They all then filed complaints with the New York State Civil Rights Bureau, which I encouraged.

And, reluctantly, on December 2, 1992, I decided I had no recourse but to file papers in New York Supreme Court to bring about the dissolution of our partnership, by reason of Stahl's mismanagement, waste, and breach of fiduciary duties. On that day, I moved for the appointment of a Temporary Receiver to manage the buildings while the case was being heard. On February 18, 1993, Judge Harold Tompkins granted my application, and on March 12, an order to that effect was granted.

Predictably, Stahl reacted to the charges and my lawsuit not by mending his ways but by attacking me with his customary legal overkill. First, he filed an appeal on March 15, and rammed through a stipulation that "pending termination of this present action, the authority to solicit, approve and rent apartments to prospective tenants shall rest with the managing agent of the buildings, Charles H. Greenthal & Co." I read this stipulation literally—that Greenthal, whose employees were hand-picked by Stahl, had "authority" to rent apartments but that nothing in the language prohibited me from fulfilling my obligation to rent these apartments. Thus, in August, I felt nothing prevented me legally from placing ads in the Real Estate section of *The New York Times*.

On this fine point, Stahl went absolutely ballistic, accusing me of breaching the stipulation and abrogating Greenthal's "exclusive" authority to rent these apartments, an authority that did not exist. Stahl, through David Rosenberg, asked that I be held in contempt.

Stahl, moreover, openly insulted the forty or so people who had responded to my ads, many of whom were minorities, in the most sickening ways, which seemed more appropriate for a member of the Ku Klux Klan. These people, he said in court papers, were "a parade of horribles" who could foment "great disturbances" and pose a "threat to the security" of the existing tenants. He also trashed them en masse, saying they "might not qualify because of their credit history."

Stahl's way of attracting tenants, he insisted, was through "reputation" and "word of mouth"—simple euphemisms for what he was actually doing, engaging in racially discriminating practices.

Only after seeing how out of control Stahl had become did I ask to dissolve our partnership in 1992. My final attempt to keep it out of the courts was when I came to Stanley and offered to buy him out of the partnership for $9 million so that I could maintain the integrity of those beautiful and stately buildings. That was when he responded with the remark that defined his nefarious plans against me:

"Abe, I will buy *you* out for $3 million -- or I will put you in jail."

Still, while this would be no idle threat, I believed the courts would protect me and come down on the side of equal opportunity housing. I even believed it might be possible for a judge with Solomon-like wisdom to save the partnership through prudent intervention.

In fact, Judge Harold Tompkins was an honest, well-intentioned judge who was sympathetic to me. However, I learned quickly that David Rosenberg knew the ins and outs of manipulating the legal system. He began launching caseloads of tenuously-related lawsuits—including, most disgustingly, personal business lawsuits filed against me by Rachel designed solely to muddle the main issues and allow Stahl to pick and choose the judges he wanted to preside over the case.

For example, Stahl accused me of failing to distribute profits from the buildings to our two companies. This was absolutely ludicrous, as not only have I always distributed every penny, but I saved our companies over $1 million simply by making it unnecessary to call in accountants. But it gave them the excuse to open a second legal front against me.

Then they hit me with yet another charge, something about overcharging for asbestos removal at a restaurant and garage we owned—when in fact I had done the job for $260,000 and not the $1.5 million that Stanley had agreed to.

Both of these bogus adjunct cases—and many more to follow that were stranger than fiction—were intended merely to make it possible for Rosenberg to argue that another judge should come in to consolidate all the cases. And that's what happened. First, a brilliant

Supreme Court judge named Sheila Abdus-Salaam took over the case, and she, too, was sympathetic to me. Thus, as you will see, that would set the stage for an acting judge with no judicial standing to send his clerks to take away the papers from Judge Salaam. His name was Ira Gammerman. Remember the name, because you will not believe what this man did and said in his tenure as presiding judge in this case.

Even before this, I had begun to feel the sting of Rosenberg's onslaught. I was found guilty of contempt on the issue of the newspaper ads, and I lost the asbestos removal case. It all had begun to fit into a pattern. Over the next ten years, I would not be given a single hearing to state my case; my time in court was spent answering bogus "contempt" charges. From 1992 on, Stahl and Rosenberg stopped me from receiving monies owed to me, which amounted to around $7 million a year from Hirstan and $6 million a year from Stahl Associates. They would close my bank accounts and have my mail re-routed to their own private mailboxes.

Clearly, it was still early in a never-ending legal war between Stanley Stahl and me. But even in 1993, the stakes were high. I was already in a fight for my life, with Stahl's sharp daggers lurking around every corner.

CHAPTER TWENTY-SIX: "WHO IS THIS NUT?"

My problems with Stanley Stahl notwithstanding, I did not lose touch with what was going on in the world. The early 1990s saw war in the Gulf, which from my perspective was wholly justifiable once Saddam Hussein invaded Kuwait. Unlike my feelings twelve years later, when another Gulf War arose, I did not see a serious threat to Israel, though the thirty or so SCUD missiles that Saddam launched against Israel—an innocent bystander during the war—was an outrage that should have, in itself, led George Bush Sr. to go in and forcibly remove him, put him on trial in the Hague, and then execute him as a war criminal.

Still, war or not, I knew Bush could never win re-election after his gross mismanagement of the economy. Part of this was not his fault; it was Ronald Reagan, whom I had supported twice, who let the budget deficit get out of hand. By the early 1990s, poor Bush had to deal with the mess of an economic policy he himself had once described perfectly as "voodoo economics."

So, now, the chickens had come home to roost. Unemployment was at 7 percent, the cities were crumbling, and nobody was spending any money. The pins were all sticking in the voodoo doll of George Bush, whose 90 percent poll ratings after the Gulf War melted away like snow in July. My problem was that I had no candidate I could support. Bill Clinton, pretty much an unknown governor from Arkansas, said some very enticing things, and he was an engaging man, but I could see he had a problem keeping his fly zipped even before the election, when he had finessed (read: lied) his way around the Gennifer Flowers affair.

Little did I know at the time that I myself would have a sort of "affair" with another of Clinton's playthings a few years down the road.

Another negative factor against Clinton was that he was a lawyer, as was his very brilliant wife, Hillary. The two of them were billing themselves with the slogan, "Two for the price of one," but with what I was beginning to see with my own lawyers, I didn't even want to pay for one. Two was more than I could stand. Lawyers, I can now say without fear of contradiction, are nothing but crooks, thieves, and liars. I would even venture that lawyers are the single biggest problem this country has.

Only lawyers and could have screwed things up as badly as they have in areas of lobbying and campaign finance corruption, and in protecting the status quo of crooked and bribed judges and district attorneys, because lawyers protect each other with fanatic determination. Nearly every issue you can think of has been put into a grab-bag of special interest favors; instead of dealing with these issues, they are merely pretexts for lawyers to wring money out of fat-cats to preserve the status quo. Just look at Clinton, Al Gore, and the Chinese money they took—and at George W. Bush and his slavish subservience to Enron. Their lawyers made sure the money spigot would always remain open.

Bill Clinton, I could tell even then, would face the consequences of having two heads. You're asking, two heads? Yes, because that is what he had. He would become the hardest-working President in all of history. He would work twenty-four hours a day because he had those two heads—his upper head and the lower head.

There is no doubt Clinton did become a magnificent President in terms of policy and management, but his instincts as a lawyer almost destroyed him. He looked for every loophole to enrich himself. And, of course, he left that famous legacy of a lawyer—"It depends on what *is* is." In fact, his habit for getting caught in the red tape of legalese—and the fact that his lower head worked as hard as his upper head—would be what brought me in to save his hide. But we're getting ahead.

The candidate I finally chose to endorse was a rebel like me, a maverick who pulled no punches and also like me, a very successful businessman. It was Ross Perot, in fact, who sounded the alarm about Bush's rising deficits, and though Perot was—also, like me—a little *meshuga,* I saw a lot of potential in this little man with the big ears.

And Perot saw a lot in me. Not my money, which was a refreshing change. No, Perot had all the money he needed, and more. What he saw in me was the man who had led the way in the now-commonplace practice of wealthy businessmen financing their political campaigns with their own money, which was unheard of when I did it first back in the 1970s. A wise man, Perot wanted to tap my store of knowledge about running such a campaign.

And so Perot invited me to his enormous home in Dallas, Texas—in fact, I was the first Jew that ever played on his golf course. Perot sent his private plane for me and pumped me for information, but what I remember most about our meeting was that when I was there, Perot's daughter came to the house with her fiancée, who happened to be Jewish—an Orthodox Jew, no less—something I'm sure Perot wasn't completely prepared for. I don't know if this sat well with Ross because he began grilling the young man.

"So," he said to the kid, "you want to marry my daughter. How will you support her? First of all, what do you do for a living?"

"I study the Bible, sir."

"That's very impressive, son, but how will you provide for my daughter?"

"Well, sir," the very intimidated boy said, "God will help."

"And how will you provide for your future children?"

"God will help."

Finally, the kids left, and as I was sitting with Ross and his wife, Ross said, "Abe, I like that boy very much."

"Why is that?" I asked.

"Because he thinks I'm God."

Having been in the same position with my own children's marriages—and there have been more than a few of those—and the help I have given them, I understood exactly what he was talking about.

Perot wasn't the only would-be leader who would covet my special advice. In 1997, when Tony Blair was the head of the Labor Party in Great Britain and was running for Prime Minister against incumbent John Major, very few observers gave him any chance. He was young, only forty-four, and there were doubts that he had any real depth. To most, he was a mannequin with a pretty face.

That was where I came in. Blair, whom I had not met, called me and invited me to his home, which is on the border of Scotland and England.

"Abe," he told me, "you've never missed an election. Whoever you support wins. My chances right now are slim. What do you think I need to do?"

At the time, I was completely unfamiliar with the issues of British politics. I needed to stick my educated nose into the soup bowl.

I said, "Tony, I need a week or two to analyze the country. Then I'll tell you." I needed the time because I am a people-reader. I don't just make guesses. I go out and talk to people on the street.

Well, that's what I did, all over England. And after two weeks, I came back and told him, "Tony, tomorrow morning you will be Prime Minister."

He looked puzzled. "But Abe," he said, "the election is still two months away."

"It may be two months away, but I'll make you Prime Minister tomorrow."

"How?"

"Very simple. The VAT"—which is the Value-Added Tax, a tariff paid on all sorts of goods by the British people—"is very, very high, especially on power and gas prices. Tomorrow morning, you will announce to the nation that you would end the VAT on power and gas."

"Then why shouldn't I say I want to eliminate all VATs?"

"Do that and everyone will laugh at you, call you an opportunist who will wreck the economy. You must understand, this is a symbol. It will have little real effect on the economy, but by taking this cautious position, it will show that you are a creative thinker. And tomorrow morning, when people are waiting in line at the gas station, they will be saying, 'This wouldn't happen if Blair was in power. He'll eliminate these lines.'"

The next day, he came out against the VAT on power and gas, and from then on, he zoomed past Major in the polls and had an easy victory. Unfortunately, Blair is not a man of deeply-held values, which would be amply demonstrated by his blind support for the Iraq war. If he had called me before he took that blind leap, he would not be in the trouble he is in now.

As for Perot, I consider it something of a miracle that, as a third-party candidate with an erratic, volatile nature, the man got 20 percent of the vote, some 20 million votes in all, though he probably spent $100 million to get them. At $5 a vote, I can think of more efficient transactions. Still, had he not bounced like a pinball in and out of the race and just stayed in from the start, I believe he would have won.

For me, politics and advice-giving was merely a sidelight. More important was making a positive difference to the economy of New York. This didn't necessarily apply to buildings, though I would make just such a difference with my renovations in Soho and a remarkable project on Wall Street that I'll tell you about shortly.

In 1993, however, I had my sights on a building at 210 South Street on the lower East Side, for it was here that an important New York institution was in need of salvation—the *New York Post*.

The oldest newspaper in the history of the United States, the *Post* was founded by Alexander Hamilton in 1801 and had gone through a long, winding road of many changes and limited financial success. Until the mid-1970s, the paper represented New York's liberal, staunchly, anti-Communist tradition. Under publisher Dorothy Schiff, the *Post* featured some of the most respected liberal columnists in journalism, including Arthur Schlesinger Jr., James Wechsler, and Max Frankel. It was very intellectual, very sedate, and dull as sawdust.

A seismic change came when Australian media baron Rupert Murdoch bought the paper in 1976, gaining a foothold in America after conquering the scurrilous and lurid tabloid market in England. Murdoch's papers were famous for their sex-drenched stories, punch-in-the-face headlines, and loony, right-wing agenda, which the editors carried from the editorial page to the news pages with slanted stories. The concept seemed new and daring, though it was a throwback to the yellow journalism of the early 1900s.

The novelty of the *Post,* with its unforgettably tacky headlines—such as the classic, "Headless Body in Topless Bar" and "Granny Executed in Her Pink Pajamas"—and Murdoch's raids on the hapless *Daily News,* resulted in huge sales. By the early 1980s, the *Post* had tripled its circulation to around 900,000, a close second behind the staid *New York Times* and ahead of the once-mighty but now pathetic *News,* which at the same time was junking its legendary Red-baiting editorial policies and becoming more mainstream.

But Murdoch was doomed to failure because, unlike the *News,* the *Post* had little connection to the real tabloid audience, the low and middle-class population of Italians and minorities who lived in the Bronx, Brooklyn, and Queens and who read their papers while riding the subways and buses every morning. Murdoch's minions liked to chide "limousine liberals," but his paper, while courting "Reagan Democrats," was as elitist and Manhattan-oriented as any liberal snob. Practically no blacks or Latinos bought the *Post,* and Murdoch seemed not to care at a time when the city had become primarily black and Puerto Rican.

Inevitably, the paper's circulation slid to around 400,000 and began coughing up red ink—losing over $7 million by 1992, when its advertising market share was an embarrassing 5 percent, behind in New York City even to the Long Island-based *Newsday*.

Murdoch, whose News Corporation empire made $385 million in profits on over $7.6 *billion* in revenue worldwide that year, lost $150 million on the *Post* from 1976 to 1988. Clearly, Murdoch had not bought the *Post* for its money-making potential. Rather, he wanted to own New York as the multi-media cornerstone of his global empire. That became evident when Murdoch, in the mid-1980s, bought a local TV station, Channel 5. He did this despite an FCC rule that prohibited cross-ownership of a TV station and a newspaper in the same market.

Murdoch expected a waiver from the rule from the powerful allies he had made in politics, but Senator Edward Kennedy, whom Murdoch constantly ridiculed in his other newspaper, the *Boston Herald,* denied him the waiver, and in the early 1990s, Murdoch had to make a choice. Seeing the future of TV over print, and his own cable news channel to push his conservative agenda, he chose Channel 5 over the *Post,* which went up for sale.

For the next several months, the oldest newspaper in America was put on a sordid merry-go-round. The ride began when Murdoch sold the paper to businessman Peter Kalikow, who neglected to tell the bankruptcy court that he had dozens of creditors after him. When the court found out, Kalikow had to declare bankruptcy as well (he has rebounded well; today he is the chairman of the Metropolitan Transportation Authority, which runs New York's bridges and tunnels), and in short order, *he* sold the paper, in early February 1993, to another businessman, Steven Hoffenberg, who spent $6 million to own it.

That's where I came in. I had known Hoffenberg for years, and he called me and told me he needed other investors to keep the *Post* alive. It seems that the $6 million he put up was merely to guarantee a line of credit for the paper, and he was restricted from using funds from his company, Towers Financial Corporation— fittingly, the city's largest debt-collection agency. Hoffenberg accepted all the *Post*'s liabilities, but he was strapped for cash.

Hearing this, I didn't delay one second in helping out. It was a longtime dream of mine to be part of owning an important newspaper, and here the opportunity was dropped in my lap. That day, I pledged to give Steve $3 million to help him meet the payroll, and in turn, he named me chairman of the *New York Post.*

The *Post*'s unions, except for the Newspaper Guild, supported Hoffman and me, although other potential owners were now popping up, including a Texas oilman named Lester Euell. But Bankruptcy Judge Burton Lifland granted Hoffenberg control of the paper on February 19.

That was the good news. The bad news was that Hoffenberg neglected to tell the judge a little detail, too—that Towers was in the midst of a Securities and Exchange Commission probe for fraud for using false financial statements to sell more than $400 million in securities.

When this came out—making it seem as though Murdoch had left a curse on the *Post*—the court did an about-face. On Friday March 12, Judge Lifland looked around the courtroom, which was full of people who had said they wanted to buy the paper, and asked, "Is there anyone here with a check and a pen?" And the whole room fell silent. Then I spoke up.

"Judge," I said, "I told you, if nobody will buy the *Post,* I will. I will write a check for $3 million right now."

Judge Lifland then asked Rupert Murdoch, who also was there, "Mr. Murdoch, you have the first right to purchase the *Post.* Will you let the paper go, or do you want to keep it?"

"I don't want it," he said. "Let Mr. Hirschfeld have it."

In the dizzying swirl of that day, I was the toast of the town—and the scourge of the *Post* newsroom. Looking over the ruinous financial conditions left to me, I saw a bloated staff choking the payroll. So, in all, I issued pink slips to seventy-two employees—including some very big names, such as columnist Jack Newfield and the gossip columnist Cindy Adams, both of whom I considered worthless. But the biggest pink slip went to the most bloated worthless employee of all, Pete Hamill.

New Yorkers were very familiar with Hamill, who had been a columnist for the *Post* during its liberal days and since then had written novels in a faux Hemingway style. He made sure to be seen nightly at Elaine's Restaurant on the Upper East Side with other self-important writers and actors and briefly dated Jacqueline Kennedy. Not a particularly handsome man, Hamill's entire *shtick* was to pose as a rugged, macho *mensch,* a man's man who with all his wealth was supposed to have a love for working people. The truth was that Hamill was a rather soft, pampered elitist whom I don't think had ever been in a fight and might have wet his pants if a real man came at him in anger.

With Hamill, reputation was everything. He had, again, become a very rich man because of it. Indeed, Steve Hoffenberg had been seduced by Hamill's aura and had given him the job of editor of the *Post* at a salary of $500,000 a year, which I considered absurdly excessive. No editor has ever sold one newspaper, and I could not justify keeping Hamill at that price, so I gave him his walking papers on that morning of March 12. I expected him to take it like a man's man. Instead, he took it like a spoiled brat, refusing to leave the building.

By lunch, because of his example, all hell had broken loose on South Street, and I was in the center of the maelstrom.

First, the fired employees, egged on by Hamill, refused to leave as well. And I was prevented from being on any floor of the building except the sixth, where the management offices were. Of course, I could have legally brought in the police and the marshals and had them all forcibly evicted for trespassing, even had them thrown in jail. But I sympathized with them. These people were about to lose their jobs. And while the egomaniacal Hamill was the ringleader of this illegal insurrection, I even felt for him. After all, losing that half-million dollars would have severely crimped his social life.

I suppose I could have sat them all down and given them a simple lesson in economics: that Murdoch's mismanagement in hiring too many people was what had brought the paper to bankruptcy. And that Hamill's salary was an affront to all of those who were about to lose $20,000-a-year jobs. Instead, I talked to them in small groups, pledging to hire back as many of them as I could once the money situation had stabilized—and provided Hamill would voluntarily cut his fat salary, which of course, he wouldn't, even if it meant jobs would be saved.

And so, instead of a smooth transition, Hamill stoked an ugly and needless confrontation in which Hamill became obsessed to deflect the issue of his salary and blame me as the enemy instead of the only person who could save the paper. At the time, I was negotiating with the unions to hire back nearly all of those who had been fired. Yet, because Hamill was so obnoxious and so obstructive, all of those working people Hamill claimed to love were in limbo and afraid of being arrested if they remained in the building. But their plight didn't disturb a whisker on his expensively-trimmed beard.

Neither did it disturb Hamill to defame me, a sixth-grade dropout who had lost most of his family in the Holocaust yet who became an American success story. Perhaps it never occurred to Hamill that Abe Hirschfeld and Alexander Hamilton himself share the honor of being in the Immigrant Hall of Fame. Worse, this self-proclaimed champion of minorities turned his venom on a black man whom I had hired to be the *Post*'s editor, a *real* editor, Wilbert Tatum, who had turned the small African-American newspaper *The Amsterdam News* into a force in the city's media landscape.

Hamill's ham-fisted Huns blithely threw around the words "racist" and "anti-Semitic" about Wilbert and me—and, amazingly, they even called *me* anti-Semitic. But I felt worse for Wilbert, a very good and honest man who, ironically, happened to be a Jew himself! Bill had converted to Judaism some years before, and his wife is also Jewish, as is their daughter. Because *The Amsterdam News* had taken a strong point of view on social issues that departed from Hamill's views, and that of the city's white ruling class, it hardly meant that Tatum was a back racist. It only meant he was opinionated. That should be treasured because it produces an effective dialogue. I wonder if Pete Hamill would like it if someone called him "anti-Irish" because of an opinion he had.

What's more, with the benefit of 20-20 hindsight, it turns out Bill was right about many things. For example, he had publicly supported the young black men who were arrested and then convicted in the infamous "wilding" gang rape of a woman who was jogging in Central Park. Tatum, of course, was blasted as a racial arsonist blindly supporting certain criminals merely because they were black. But only last year, long after these boys had done time in prison, DNA evidence came to light that cleared them of the crime, and their convictions were expunged from the record. But I don't expect Hamill or anyone else who raised holy hell will admit they were wrong. Contrition isn't a word in their dictionary.

The bottom line was that Bill Tatum was a great editor with a proven record, not an overpriced dilettante like Pete Hamill, who would also drive the *Daily News* into the ground and be fired there as well after he was made that paper's editor in the mid-1990s.

Still, I never evicted Hamill's ass from the building. Until a judge would have the final say about his firing, I even tried to forge an alliance with him during the first few days of my ownership, to end the bitterness and the squatters' occupation of the building, which was making it difficult to get out a paper. On the second day, I defied the ban on me being in the third-floor newsroom, strode to Hamill's office, and pushed open the door.

"What the fuck are you doing here? You're not supposed to be on this floor," he said, exhibiting his normal glittering personality.

I met his tough-guy act with some attitude of my own.

"Who the fuck are you to tell me I don't belong here? I own this paper. You don't. And I can get your ass out of here in two minutes. But, Pete, this is getting us nowhere. I came here to make this paper work, and it's not. So, let's try to be human beings and make it work."

Then I laid it out for him.

"Pete, listen. This paper is dying. Murdoch couldn't save it. Schiff couldn't, Kalikow and Hoffenberg couldn't. I can do it."

"Oh yeah? How?"

"Pete, have you ever gone fishing?"

"What the fuck does that have to do with anything?"

"Well, how is a fish caught?"

"I don't know. With bait."

"No, I'll tell you how. A fish is caught only one way—when it opens up its mouth."

By that, I meant that the public would buy the *Post* only if, like a fish, it would open its mouth to feed on what we could give it. "And, Pete, right now, the fish are opening their mouths. I'm the bait—*we're* the bait."

It was true. From day one of my ownership, even with the bitterness and the logjam in the building, the paper's sales went through the roof. Because of the soap opera of all the new owners— but mostly because the owner now was Abe Hirschfeld—we were hot. In fact, among newspapers, we were the only game in town. Hamill couldn't deny that. Still, he was hostile to me.

"Just remember one thing," I told him, concluding our tête-à-tête. "I am a very good writer. I write something that will keep you alive."

"And what's that?"

"I write the checks."

As detentes go, it wasn't exactly the nuclear non-proliferation treaty. But I believed we had reached a non-aggression pact. I was wrong. Hamill could not get over the fact that while I would take back many of those I'd fired, I held firm on five editorial people I did not respect—Newfield, Adams, editorial page editor Eric Breindel, City Hall bureau chief David Seifman, and Albany editor Fred Dicker.

"I'll tell you the only people I want writing for the *Post*," I had told Hamill. "Those who never graduated college. I don't want the intellectual snobs. Intellectuals don't buy the *Post*. Common people buy it. I want this paper to talk their language."

I also had plans to merge the *Post* with *The Amsterdam News* and the Hispanic *El Diario*. That would have put our circulation over one million, more than the *Times*.

"My intent," I told one interviewer, "is to unite, not divide the people. Jews and blacks must kiss! Protestants and Catholics must kiss! Everybody must begin to kiss. We only have one planet, so we must all kiss!"

Already, my personality and my plans were working. I had been wearing a tie since I took over the *Post,* which was designed in the form of a newspaper crossword puzzle. To my amazement, people were talking about the tie all over the city. That led me to put together a promotion whereby anyone who subscribed to the paper would get a free crossword puzzle tie. Anything I did, it seemed, was attracting attention, to the benefit of the paper. Suddenly, even the intellectual magazines were sending reporters to interview me.

One such hoity-toity magazine, *The New Republic,* ran a story about my takeover of the *Post* and gave us the kind of favorable publicity money couldn't buy. Of me, they wrote, "His style is that of an overgrown urchin with the boundless, effervescent chutzpah and childlike naïveté of the successful entrepreneur who makes money but not friends. [His life] is so colorfully surreal that it belongs in a miniseries written by Philip Roth, acted by Jackie Mason, with music by Jerry Bock.

"Never in the history of media barons have a rambunctious tabloid and its proprietor been better suited....The man is so singular that 'Hirschfeldism' will undoubtedly go into the language defined as what happens when deluded grandiosity, originality and a lack of inhibition combine to create farcical charm."

I was so delighted with such attention that I didn't even mind the part about delusions. How deluded could I be if I came to own the paper everyone now wanted to read? Another high-falutin' literary magazine, *The Nation,* went so far as to blow the whistle on the phony Hamill revolt. It called the alleged "working class" uprising an "Intifada" and went on:

The city is enthralled; the national media are dishing it all over the country. [But] the lines aren't so clear as the doughty rebel reporters would have it. Slime time at the *Post* started 17 years ago when Rupert Murdoch bought the paper. Since then it has been consistently poisonous to every decent effort to improve the city's uncivil society....

The righteous anger of the staff at the disorderly takeover by the vulgar and erratic "terrible two" loses force in the mouths and word processors of hypocrites. New York is a radically diverse city, but the new non-European, unhomogenized majority is excluded from the media mainstream. The Hirschfeld-Tatum idea of a multicultural paper is pretty good....The *Post* has a chance to make it in New York, but as a paper that digs—not bashes—the new city.

But leave it to Pete Hamill to flush this great opportunity down the drain. His mindlessly slanderous rants rose up like a geyser on Tuesday, March 16—one day after a mysterious computer glitch stopped the paper from being published on a Monday for the first time in its history. On Tuesday, Hamill filled the *Post* with a stream of twenty-four pages of invective directed at me and Bill Tatum. Rather than inform New Yorkers of the events of the world, Hamill printed every public incident in my life such as the Dorothy Green "hostage" farce to my spitting episodes with Stanley Steingut and Bonnie Weston.

Adorning these negatively-twisted stories—in which the rules of journalism were damned—were headlines such as, "Honest, Abe Doesn't Know About Journalism" (clearly a case of the pot calling the kettle black) and "Who Is This Nut?" Over the Weston incident, it read, "Part Of Her Job Was Taking a Gob From an Angry Slob." Insidiously, they labeled me "anti-Semitic" and Bill Tatum – who had been in real civil rights fights while Hamill was sipping daiquiris at Elaine's -- "a force for evil."

That March 16, 1993 "mutiny" edition of the *Post,* of course, is probably the single most famous newspaper edition in all history. The front page is the reason. On the cover was an illustration of Alexander Hamilton, a tear running down his cheek. There were no headlines, no words at all, just the image. People all over the world bought the *Post* just to keep that edition for posterity. Today, an original copy of that front page is a collector's item, worth hundreds of dollars, and more if it has my signature on it. Along with the 1948 *Chicago Tribune* front page incorrectly declaring "Dewey Defeats Truman", the March 16, 1993 *New York Post* is the most famous single item of journalism history in the history of mankind.

While the message of that cover was intended as a slap at me—though I would bet Alexander Hamilton would have cried over what Hamill had done to pervert his paper rather than over what I was doing to save it—I found it to be a wonder. It was great; it was ingenuous.

And it was because of me.

That's not idle braggadocio. The fact was, that cover was my idea. I had told Hamill that there was no reason why a front page had to blind you with big letters, that a single, compelling image was the greatest subliminal inducement to get that fish's mouth open. Today, the concept is used again and again, always with the effect of selling a ton of papers.

The anti-Hirschfeld crusade, meanwhile, continued after a judge ordered me on Wednesday morning to keep Hamill as editor, though his illiberal prejudices kept the great talents of Bill Tatum submerged, and soon Bill bowed out. Still, keeping Hamill was fine with me, as long as he did his job and stopped the jeremiad against me. In fact, I waited in front of 210 South Street that morning and when Hamill arrived, I planted a big kiss on his cheek to highlight my "everybody must kiss" campaign.

I guess my kissing needs work because, blessed by Hamill, the next day, the "rebels" who still hadn't been taken back staged a rally outside the building where they listened to speeches against me by the likes of has-been, publicity-starved celebrities like author Norman Mailer and actor Danny Aiello. This was another absurd distraction, but on Friday it got serious when the Hamill brigade asked Bankruptcy Judge Francis Conrad—in a petition reprinted on Page One—to take away the paper from "The Madman," meaning yours truly.

Judge Conrad's reply was succinct.

"It's a done deal," he said, upholding my ownership and not so subtly telling these people to get over it and get on with their lives.

That seemed to defuse the situation, and for the next two weeks, things settled into an uneasy but workable calm. However, by then, it wasn't a lightweight like Pete Hamill who was posing the biggest threat to me. He, and the other insurrectionists, receded before the specter of political corruption.

Rupert Murdoch, seeing the circulation figures zoom as they never had under his rule, now suddenly decided he wanted the paper back, despite what he had told Judge Lifland. And who did he turn to in order to get it back? None other than Mario Cuomo, a man experienced at stabbing me in the back.

One would think that Cuomo, with his liberal pretensions, would have welcomed a better, more multi-cultural *Post*. Instead, one year before his well-deserved political oblivion, he again showed what a magnificent phony he is. Behind the scenes, this unethical man—who had been regularly attacked by Murdoch in the *Post*—worked to get the bankruptcy court to strip me of the paper I was making so successful.

I was scheduled to be guaranteed full control of the paper on April 2. But the *coup-de-etat* was underway in late March. Murdoch had gone to Albany to make God knows what kind of promises and *quid pro quo* deals with Cuomo, who also lobbied Senator Al D'Amato—a man who had often praised me, only to stab me in the back when I needed him—and Teddy Kennedy to backtrack and give Murdoch his FCC waiver from cross-ownership rules.

Talk about spineless hypocrites! Teddy Kennedy went from staunch defender of the law to a weak-kneed toady within sixteen days. Having known and revered his brother the way I had, I was almost glad that Bobby Kennedy was not around to witness such a capitulation to selfish, privileged interests.

Then, they trotted in Senator my old nemesis Daniel Patrick Moynihan, the lying crook that he is, to cement the waiver. When in doubt, send in the clowns.

As these moves were being made, the *Post*'s creditors and employees made a pilgrimage to court, falsely claiming that I was refusing to pay the bills. If Judge Lifland had been there, he surely would have thrown them out on their ears. But, as it happened, he had suddenly taken a "vacation" *to Australia* and a different judge was brought in from upstate New York.

Does this sound familiar to you from the last chapter? It should, because I am convinced that all these moves were in fact orchestrated not by Murdoch or Cuomo but by Stanley Stahl. You might dismiss this contention right now as paranoid ravings, but you won't feel that way after reading on. You will understand why the last thing Stahl wanted was for me to have the prestige and the forum of the *Post*. He needed to make me seem like an outcast, a leper. As I was finding out, Stahl's tentacles—and the reach of his bribery—were everywhere I tried to go. And so on Friday, March 26, the bogus judge did his part in the sordid scenario, ordering me to sell the paper to the man who had buried it.

The deal was that Murdoch would pay me the $3 million I had invested. The next day, Saturday, Murdoch and his son came to my lawyer's office to finalize the deal. But they came without a check. I turned to my lawyer and said, "I'm here to sign an agreement. Where's the check?"

A typical crooked lawyer, he was as limp as oatmeal, stammering, "You know Mr. Murdoch is good for the money. You don't have to worry. He can't get you a certified check on a weekend. He'll give it to you on Monday."

When Monday came around, the judge called me at 7 o'clock in the morning. I must sign over the *Post* to Murdoch at once, he said. "If you don't," he warned me, "I'll give it to him for nothing."

I was outraged and deeply offended. And I didn't give a damn that I was talking to a judge.

"Fuck you, Judge. Drop dead," I said, and I hung up the phone.

An hour later, my lawyer called. "Abe," he said, "I got the judge to split the difference. Murdoch will give you a million and a half."

"I agreed to $3 million," I reminded him.

"Abe, sign the papers. Don't fight."

So that's how my tenure at the *New York Post* ended—with a crooked lawyer acting in concert with a crooked judge forcing me to sell at a $ 1½ million loss to a crooked publisher with crooked friends in high places, and the string pulled by a crooked man trying to destroy me.

I've had better days.

But I would have worse days to come.

Still, I left the *Post* with my head held high. It was an exhilarating ride, and one that proved my genius. Never has the *Post* been as successful as it was during those wild sixteen days, not before and certainly not since. In fact, in the decade since, Murdoch has taken the paper into the grave for the second time. Its circulation currently is back down to 400,000—with thousands of copies given away daily to pad the figures.

Post employees, it has been reported, "come and go like the weather"—including, of course, that bastion of stability Pete Hamill, who was fired by Murdoch yet unlike with me said not a peep in protest. (If what I heard was true, the reason had to do with the fact that Murdoch quietly bought out Hamill's contract for several million dollars, something I never would have considered. So much for Hamill's "working class" affiliation.)

The editor of the Sunday edition of the paper, Marilyn Matlick, was fired in the spring of 2002 and filed a complaint with the Equal Opportunity Commission, claiming the *Post*'s coterie of all-male executives shun women in favor of Brits and Australian men. Business reporter Dan Cox was fired in 2002 after he said he was forced to report unconfirmed stock tips from Murdoch's fat-cat, insider-trading cronies.

Journalism shouldn't be a nasty, ugly business, but Murdoch has made it so. He has tainted and corrupted this most fundamental instrument of democracy, discriminating against those with no voice in decision-making and buying off supposedly principled journalists who suddenly have nothing to say about these desecrations of their beloved profession. And for all that, what hath Rupert wrought? Still no one in the outer boroughs or anyone with black or brown skin reads his paper. Just think of the simple beauty of my plan to make the paper a reflection of New York's wonderful diversity, championing the little people who need a break yet have no voice to the Murdochs of the world. That would have been the greatest newspaper ever. For 16 days, it was.

Now, it's a cheap, money-losing rag serving one evil man's media megalomania.

And for that we can credit those two famous liberals and friends of the common man, Pete Hamill and Mario Cuomo.

Some would call this irony. I call it tragedy.

Abraham (Abe) Hirschfeld

CHAPTER TWENTY-SEVEN: DIRTY POOL, A DIRTY DA, AND JACKIE MASON

The seeds of Stahl's ultimate plot to obliterate me were planted in the mid-1990s. Remember, I had sued Stahl—the case number 32380/92 is burned into my mind—on the very narrow issue that our partnership should be dissolved in a manner fair and equitable to both of us. I merely wanted a judge to act as Solomon and bring the matter to a quick and mutually acceptable conclusion so we could get on with our lives.

However, Stahl was not a man who would settle anything halfway: it had to be on his terms and anyone impudent enough to challenge him had to be destroyed—no matter who it was and no matter how many people he had to bribe and judges to bribe or buy.

Thus, while I expected things to move apace in New York Supreme Court, what happened instead was that I had to step over piles of judicial junk and legal land mines laid down by Stahl and his unscrupulous lawyer David Rosenberg.

The first big hurdle for me in Stahl's diversionary, muddy-up-the-water strategy was when he filed a motion to force me to pay $4 million toward a mortgage Stahl Associates had on two of our beautiful, luxury apartment buildings, 260 East 55th Street and 405 East 54th Street. As you'll recall, I had found these buildings and Stanley had bought them for $7.5 million, all of which he'd put up. He then gave me a 50 percent ownership if I could reap for him a nice profit by re-mortgaging them.

I did just that for $10.8 million—with the mortgage, ironically, from Apple Bank, before Stahl took Apple over in a hostile takeover. That meant I had earned a $1.6 million profit for each of us. Stanley was always saying he did all the work in our partnership, and in a sense, he did. Stanley made a lot of money for me for which I did nothing, But by the same token, I was very good for him. I didn't see him turn down that $1.6 million, either. And I did that sort of thing with other buildings as well.

Now, by the mid-1990s, Stahl had re-mortgaged the buildings again, with the Morgan Guarantee Trust Company, for $16 million. He did this without my knowledge—and, of course, without my signature—under the aegis of Stahl Associates, the profits of which we split 50-50 but the affairs of which he managed and controlled all the books to. (I do the same for out other company, Hirstan Associates, which owns far fewer properties, mainly a garage and two restaurants.) Stahl also unilaterally increased the buildings' expense fund by $2 million to $7 million.

Keep in mind, too, that ever since I'd filed my lawsuit in 1992, Stahl had withheld from me my share of our profits from Stahl Associates, or some $8 million a year. He said he was holding that money in escrow pending the settlement of the suit—which, of course, he wanted never to end because he could go on keeping my money for himself. Not by coincidence, he kept all that money in his private Apple Bank account. He claimed he did this to pay real estate taxes, some $1.25 million a year. Remember that detail, too, because it becomes very important.

Let me also point out that I frequently gave Stahl money from my own pocket when he screwed up the books with his little tax dodges. For example, Stanley would refuse to take his share of Hirstan Associates because he didn't want to pay taxes on it, and would put it in an escrow account to hide it. From the beginning, tax sheltering was on Stanley's mind. That is why the partnership agreement for Stahl Associates was written as it was in 1975. Although he would control 50 percent of the profits, Stahl officially took a 1 percent share, putting the other 49 percent in his sister Sonia Schlossberg's name so he wouldn't have to pay taxes.

Anyone could see through Stahl's shenanigans. Clearly, he was trying to steal the buildings we co-owned for himself. I can recall now that, a few years after we began our partnership, I happened to discover a document Stahl had written listing the share-holders of Stahl Associates. In it, he listed with me the names of my wife Zipora and my son Elie—even though at that time he had no reason to even know their names. Even then, he was attempting to play divide and conquer with my family, a strategy that would soon come into play again, as I will tell you about shortly.

You can imagine the gall Stahl had when he claimed that I should have to pay $4 million for a mortgage I had nothing to do with. Yet, through legal red tape and subterfuge, this ridiculous claim gummed up the case for two years.

"[E]ven after Abe Hirschfeld [pays] $4 million," Rosenberg told the court snidely, "he will have over $8 million in his pocket [from Stahl Associates], which is not a bad return since Abe Hirschfeld never paid a penny for his interest in the partnership."

Happily, Judge Sheila Abdus-Salaam would dismiss the motion and tell Stahl to pay his own loans. But this was just one battle in a coming war in which my own motions were dismissed out of hand, with no hearings. One was for the appointment of a receiver to oversee the Stahl Associates bank accounts, which Stanley was preventing me from seeing. Making the ordeal even more torturous, every lawyer I hired to present my case eventually worked against me. To this day, no less than twenty-four have come and gone, some of the biggest names in the legal profession, including Gus Newman, Barry Slotnick of Bernhard Goetz ("The Subway Shooter") fame, and Alan Dershowitz, whose treason against me in another case I will relate a bit later on. Others were Robert Chira, Kelly Drye, Ross Andrews, Al Aidaly, Edward Dudley, and Chris Lynn.

All of them bled me dry. Over a two-year period alone, my lawyers' fees in this case amounted to over $5 million. I wonder how much they pocketed in all when their bribe money was figured in. Increasingly, I was coming to the conclusion that there was only one honest man I could hire to represent me. That man was me.

For all of Stahl and Rosenberg's roadblocks, they were really after bigger kill. By 1994, that became easier to do when they drew another partner in crime into their web of lies—Manhattan District Attorney Robert Morgenthau.

This tall, gaunt man had a tremendous pedigree. He was the son of Franklin D. Roosevelt's Secretary of the Treasury and grandson of Woodrow Wilson's Ambassador to Turkey. Morgenthau, who was born the same year as me, 1919, had a reputation for straight-arrow honesty ever since John F. Kennedy appointed him State's Attorney for the Southern District of New York in 1961. In 1974, he won the first of his eight elections as Manhattan DA.

Over the years, he won fame for prosecuting organized crime, tax fraud, and corruption. The mind-numbing irony was that, by the mid-1990s, Morgenthau had become a servant of those very vices. I have no compunction calling Morgenthau exactly what he is—a crook and a liar. Because, as you will see, he was actually proven to be just that for what he did to me starting in December 1994. That was when he empanelled a grand jury to get me indicted—at Stanley Stahl's behest—for tax evasion, all too often a crime concocted to "get" people when all else fails.

The man who preceded Morgenthau as Manhattan DA, the unimpeachable Frank Hogan, once spoke the immortal words, "A DA can indict a ham sandwich if he wanted to." And over the next eleven months, Morgenthau had his grand jury subpoena my banking records, combing through every decimal point looking for something amiss. Now you know the real reason why Stahl kept my money from Stahl Associates while insisting he did it to pay my real estate taxes. Stahl, with "Morgy" as his puppet, held all the cards to jigger around the numbers and make it look like I was the criminal.

Those were the records a real DA should have subpoenaed, because it could have led to an open and shut case of fraud by Stahl. Instead, they gave this DA a way to railroad me on income I never saw.

Morgenthau didn't stop there. He bullied and badgered and threatened everyone who worked for me who might rat me out for something, anything. The biggest pigeon he found whom they could manipulate and try to make into a stool pigeon was my longtime secretary, a woman named Rosemary Singer, a hard-working lady and a devout Catholic—her daughter is a nun—who had a strong sense of values. Or so it seemed.

I had hired Rosemary Singer in 1965, and in time, she became my closest confidante, my right arm. She knew the ins and outs of my business. I thought I was blessed to have her, and in appreciation I bought her a house, I got her son a good job at Cross and Broom, a big real estate firm, and paid for his wedding. I prided myself on developing long and loyal bonds with my employees, and when Rosemary wanted to be paid off the books, I thought nothing of it. I did it to accommodate her, though it would be her responsibility to declare these earnings and pay the taxes on them.

The first inkling I had that perhaps Rosemary wasn't Mother Teresa arose in the mid-1990s when I went through the books—something I almost never did, but my famous, educated nose tip smelled that something wasn't right. That happened when my driver, Victor Ocampo, had gotten his paycheck, and it was twice the normal amount. Victor came to me and said, "There's a mistake; it's too much."

So, I checked the books, and I found that the salaries of Rosemary and the bookkeeper, who was Victor's wife, had been doubled. In Rosemary's case, she had been collecting double salary for many years. When I confronted her, she admitted she had done it, leaving me no choice but to fire her on the spot.

Maybe it's my bleeding heart, or my naïveté, but I felt bad about losing Rosemary so suddenly after all those years, so I brought her back at half her usual salary, but only until I could find a replacement. Then I let her go again. As it happened, I fired her too late, because in that interim Morgenthau's goons pored over my books. They, too, found Rosemary's double-salary scam, and discovered that Rosemary hadn't paid tax on the phantom income, amounting to many thousands of dollars.

Bingo! Morgenthau now had his opening.

He trampled this poor lady, threatening her with jail if she did not give him some kind of evidence against me. Of course, there was no such evidence—I take great pride in the fact that the only illegality I have ever committed was to get a parking ticket—so the goons put in the wringer: she would either wear a hidden microphone and trap me into saying something Morgenthau could use to crucify me or face the prosecutor herself.

Naturally, I knew none of this was happening at the time. In fact, I didn't know Morgenthau was so obsessed with me or that he was in Stanley Stahl's pocket. I was still just trying to be heard in my court case against Stahl, to no avail. Still, I won a round when Judge Abdus-Salaam ruled against Stahl on the Morgan Guarantee matter. Clearly, this must have frightened Stahl and his mouthpiece David Rosenberg to no end because, one night after court business was over, a clerk came into Judge Salaam's office and removed all of the documents relating to the case. The next day, with no explanation, Salaam, a respected Supreme Court judge, had been removed from the case and replaced by an obscure Acting Judge named Ira Gammerman. In the coming years, Gammerman would earn every bit of Stahl's favoritism. But in so doing, he would turn himself into a judicial jackass and a prosecutorial prostitute.

Even then, again unbeknownst to me, Morgenthau had violated the canon of judicial ethics, nakedly breaking the law when he wrote in his subpoenas for my bank records that "a criminal action was pending" against me. This was in 1994 and 1995, two years before any such action was taken, making what he said a dirty and prejudicial lie.

Morgenthau didn't care. He was following Stahl's blueprint to the letter—right down to the moment he chose to finally indict me for a bogus crime. In typical fashion for these crooks, they did it by stepping on a big moment in my life.

This was in the spring of 1997, after I had gone ahead with my plan to run for Manhattan Borough President. The office had been a stepping stone for David Dinkins to become mayor, and his successor, a non-entity named Ruth Messinger, was trying to emulate him by challenging Rudy Giuliani that year, though she would be deservedly crushed at the polls.

I chose to run as a Republican, despite the insulting treatment I had received from Giuliani and George Pataki. For me and the Party, it was a golden opportunity to win an office held by Democrats seemingly since the days of Peter Minuet. Because my platform was geared to real people, it was radically different from those of the bland, corrupt politicians.

First, I would complete the long-promised Second Avenue Subway, which was begun in the 1980s, then abandoned and left as a hole in the ground to this day. I also had a plan for the overall renovation of Harlem based on my model on 102nd Street, which would make Harlem part of Manhattan, economically. I would rebuild the city's schools the way I had rebuilt Miami—by naming commissions that would have no politicians and no lawyers, only builders. And I would put trees on every street and avenue, every twenty-five feet. Crazy? Hardly. They do that in Paris and London, and not just for aesthetic reasons; trees keep the air clean of automobile pollution. The pundits said the borough presidents had no influence. That's because I wasn't a borough president.

In my naïveté, I believed the always-dormant Manhattan Republican Party would wake up and jump at the chance to finally win this office, but I had no intention of running the usual Republican way, by ignoring minorities. In fact, I ran as well on the Independent Party line. This is a party brought to influence by black people like Lenora Fulani, a very bright and dedicated black woman who had run for office many times and who was blithely and unfairly branded by liberal snobs like Pete Hamill as a "black racist." I proudly named her

318

as my campaign chairman in Harlem. But I did run like a Republican in one sense: I spent a lot of money.

I set the announcement to declare my candidacy for May 10. I reserved the VIP Room at Le Cirque that day for a 10 A.M. press conference. But Robert Morgenthau beat me by five hours. At 5 A.M., I was awakened when—for the first time but not the last—Morgenthau's uniformed goons came to my door and hauled me off to a jail cell in the district attorney's office. At 9 A.M., I found out why: Morgenthau, beating my press conference by an hour, brought me before a judge and had me indicted for—of all things—state income tax fraud. He then went out onto the courthouse steps and told the media what a rat and a cheat Abe Hirschfeld was.

That of course meant there would be no press conference for me. I spent all that day relating my shock about being charged out of the blue with this crime and insisting on my innocence. It was exactly what Stanley Stahl wanted.

I will not even bother to give any credence to the charge by getting deeply into it. In fact, there were precious few details to it. Morgenthau offered some kind of mush that I had illegally shifted profits and losses from my businesses and from my Broadway production of *The Prince of Central Park* in 1989 to different companies to keep from paying tax. Ironically, while I never did this kind of "shifting" of the books, Stanley Stahl did it with yawning regularity. But then, he was calling the shots.

Amazingly, Morgenthau indicted me on 123 counts and yet *118* counts had no dollar figure at all, they were left blank and clearly just thrown in to pile on. Only five counts had a figure, and their total of $3.3 million was the sum total on the indictment. A first-year law student would have seen through Morgenthau's phony indictment like cheesecloth. But I was in for three years of exhausting court time and legal fees on this pathetic sham of a case.

I resolved to run my race for the borough presidency despite the indictment, because I am a fighter, and I didn't want to let the crooks stop me. But the indictment gave Giuliani and Pataki cover to ignore me—a case of the Republican Party cutting off its nose to spite its face. Rather than put forward a candidate to run against me, they preferred to let me drown so they could be rid of me. This of course was right out of the Stanley Stahl playbook, but I suspect it went deeper. Pataki and Giuliani knew I would never be another of their puppets who say nothing, do nothing, and take bribes to be yes-men. I had felt the same thing when I ran for office in Florida, which only proves that no matter the geography, there is one constant in politics—corruption.

The pity is that the Democratic primary produced a very beatable candidate, Harlem councilwoman Virginia Field, a nobody whom *The Village Voice* called "a complete embarrassment and the poster child for Democratic Party mediocrity." I would have wiped out Field had I been able to secure the line of the Liberal Party, a party which is liberal in name only and far more inspired by power than agenda—witness their habitual support for Rudy Giuliani. With that line, thousands of Democrats could have voted for me without a problem. But, under orders from Giuliani and Cuomo, Liberal Party boss Ray Harding put forward as his candidate in the primary, the African-American New York State Comptroller Carl McCall.

In truth, McCall had no intention of running in the fall. The object was to keep the line away from me, which they did. That McCall went along with this con showed what a spineless coward he too is, and I enjoyed greatly his comically inept and pathetic run for governor against Pataki in 2001. No one ever deserved being crushed as much as McCall did. Better still, no one will ever take him seriously should he re-enter politics. Some stories just have a happy ending.

The unhappy problem for me was that, without the Liberal line, I knew I had little chance of winning in heavily Democratic Manhattan. I did hire two respected Republican consultants, Ed Rollins and Kieran Mahoney, who took a lot of money for doing very little. I should have listened to the best political consultant in the world—me. But I knew the race was rigged when Virginia Field refused to debate me and no one made a stink.

Besides, all during the campaign, my opponent wasn't Field as much as Robert Morgenthau, who kept me so busy that I virtually stopped campaigning. In the end, I did get my message out in TV commercials I spent around $3 million to run, ten times what Field spent in total. And given the circumstances of running as an indicted criminal—which a cynic might say immediately qualified me to run for any political office—I did pretty well. I garnered 12,444 votes, or 23 percent, behind Field's 37,777.

Those were 12,444 of the smartest people in the world, and I love them all.

Maybe it's good that I'm a little *meshuga* because all my travails in 1997 would have driven any sane person crazy. Yet, despite the best efforts of Morgenthau, Stahl, and Gammerman—which contributed to me getting high blood pressure in addition to the skin cancer that grew on my face and hands—my mind was sharper than ever.

In this same time frame, my activities were remarkably eclectic. In 1996, for instance, I tried to get back into the newspaper game by founding a new evening tabloid called *Open Air PM.* My inspiration was not the lurid, money-losing *Post* but Tel Aviv's *Maariv* daily, which thrives on one ingenious concept—death—by selling pages and pages of obituaries. This isn't as crazy as it sounds. Do you know any of the people whose obituaries are printed in *The New York Times*? Every person has a right to an obituary, not just a famous person. In New York, over 1,000 people die every day, and their family and friends have a story to tell about each one.

I hired some fine people to get the paper off the ground, including Avi Alkalay, who had worked in the New York bureau of *Maariv;* Richard Gooding from the *Post;* and Laura Durkin of the *Daily News.* However, once again I ran afoul of the egos of the New York literati. Running the operation from the office I still kept in the Hotel Pennsylvania, I wanted to bring out the paper in April 1996. But instead of following the blueprint for success, Gooding and Durkin wanted to imitate the *Post* and do more news and feature stories.

"You want to write stories," I told them, "go work for Doctor Seuss. Just do what I say, and we will all get rich."

Not only did they not listen, they also wanted to increase the size of the staff, which was only six people. That is all you need to run a paper like this. So, I had to fire and replace them, meaning the target date was pushed back to June. However, a bigger problem was outside the office.

The dirty secret of New York newspaper publishing is that you must make secret kickback deals with the unions for the pressers and the delivery people. These unions themselves are fronts for organized crime, and unless you cooperate by paying "protection" money, your paper will sit in the pressing plant, or in garbage cans on the street, and never be delivered. Since I had 800 newsstands ready to sell *Open Air PM,* and a circulation goal of 100,000, the unions had me over a barrel.

At first I played ball with them, but because I was going to spend $10 to $15 million on the paper, I simply could not survive financially by forking over millions to the Mob. The paper waddled on for six months before I was forced to close it. It was a noble try at cracking a corrupt monopoly and another learning experience.

A far more glorious experience, however, occurred that same year. This was my return to show business. I did it by making it possible for a man to return from the dead.

The man was Jackie Mason.

Jackie, whose acerbic Yiddish-tinged jokes and monologues made him the second-greatest Jewish comedian in the world after me, had been tremendously popular when he made his first comeback in the 1980s—a comeback he owed to me. At the time, I suggested to Jackie that he consider taking his deflated career to Broadway, with a one-man show composed of his monologues about life seen through the eyes of a Jewish *schlub.* The problem was, there was probably no one on Broadway who believed he could pull it off.

Strictly as a friend, with no financial interest, I laid the foundation for my idea. Looking around, I saw only one possible means to that end, Mayor Ed Koch, who was one of my closest friends. Koch consulted me regularly about building issues during his three terms and trusted my judgment. And when his brother was married on the lawn outside Gracie Mansion and the mayor invited Zipora and me to attend, I took the opportunity to bring my own guest, Jackie Mason, whom Koch had never met. I introduced the two, they hit it off, and thereafter, we went everywhere together and were photographed so often we could have been dubbed The Three Jewish Amigos.

Koch and I worked to get Jackie his Broadway gig. I exerted my influence with the Tony Award committee and the theater people, and we convinced the Shubert Organization that operates the theaters that Jackie would be a good investment. We found producers who would be willing to work with him despite his reputation as a hard-ass with people. Result: Jackie Mason became the biggest star in America. He starred in three one-man shows, received a Tony nomination, won two Outer Critics Club Awards, and made millions.

However, because of his natural tendency for self-destruction, which springs from his terrible insecurities and low self-image, he threw it all away.

I won't mince words. I can tell you without fear or reservation that Jackie Mason is likely the world's worst human being. This is a man with absolutely no gratitude for anyone, who will not listen to anyone's advice but his own, and who will give credit to no one but himself. How do I know? Because Jackie could never bring himself to thank me for what I'd done for him. He became so touchy when my role in his comeback was revealed that he became apoplectic, spewing invective about me all over the newspapers. In one such tirade he called me "a sick bastard," "a pig," and "a common deranged maniac," and wished that I "should drop dead by Thursday."

During my tenure at the *New York Post,* the editors had smugly printed these remarks as though Jackie Mason was some kind of sage instead of a bitter, unappreciative yutz. And yet, I was hardly alone. He offended producers, stagehands, critics, even audience members, and thought nothing of it. Thus, it seemed a given that he had dug for himself his own grave, with a headstone reading: "Here lies Jackie Mason. Who gives a damn?" I was frankly shocked when I saw how down and out he was now. His act was tired and his public utterances embarrassingly witless, such as when he called Mayor David Dinkins "a fancy *schvartze* with a *yarmulke.*" There was no sadder sight in my mind than this little, aging comic with dyed henna-colored hair trying to be funny.

I could never have envisioned hooking up with him again. On the heels of his irrational bitterness toward me, Jackie filed an even more irrational defamation of character suit against me, again, for saying I had saved his career. (Wisely, he let the doomed suit drop.) But I'll give Jackie credit for one thing: he knew where his *challah* was buttered. As he slid further into oblivion, he obviously did some thinking and concluded, correctly, that I was the only man who could resuscitate his career—again. Poverty no doubt made Jackie see the light. A notorious spendthrift, he was broke and suicidally depressed when he rang me up in 1996, begging me to let bygones be bygones.

It was, of course, an act of unspeakable *chutzpah,* and I was somewhat wary, not knowing if he was going to screw me again after getting him back on his feet. To be honest, many show people warned me not to get involved. Logically, they were right. It would take a superhuman effort to convince the Shuberts again. And while Ed Koch was still tight with Jackie, he was out of office, though Jackie's lawyer was close friends with the current mayor, Rudy Giuliani.

Still unpersuaded, I agreed to have dinner with Jackie and his girlfriend and manager Jyll Rosenfeld, and the lawyer. I knew how difficult the task would be when the lawyer told me that Giuliani wanted Jackie to get another show but that even he couldn't get the show people to listen.

"They won't give him a theater," he said dejectedly. "They won't let him on Broadway."

I must admit I was pricked by the challenge. I also must admit, as all my friends know, that I am a sucker for a sob story and far too forgiving for my own good. I've not let a grudge stand in my entire life. And so, yet again, I was out there pimping for Jackie Mason. I use that word in the literal sense, because this time I did not do it out of the goodness of my heart. This time, I would do it for the money.

I made it clear at the dinner with Jackie that I would take on the challenge, for a title—producer—and that I would personally bankroll the show in return for a 50 percent cut of the profits. I expected Jackie to put up a fuss about that, but the fact that I would commit to bringing Jackie back from the dead thrilled his lawyer.

"Abe," he said, "If you can swing this, we'll give you *52 percent.*"

I wanted more than that, however. Not more money, but my usual complete, one-hundred-percent control of everything involved in any show I produce. Including the material Jackie would perform on stage. The last thing I wanted to feed theater audiences was Jackie's timeworn *shtick* about being picked on by Jew-haters. I wanted a softer, more human, even cuddly Jack Mason.

"Jackie," I said, "you are going to talk about family, about friends, about neighbors. I even have the perfect title for the show."

"What is it?"

"Love Thy Neighbor."

"Okay, but forget about the title for now. Let's talk about the money. I don't have a cent."

"Jackie, I will put up all the money. How much do you need?"

"Two-hundred-thousand."

I was about to stun him.

"Jackie, when I do something, it has to be perfect or it won't be done at all. I don't want you to get out there on stage and be a *schmuck.* You need full scenery. You need material. I will give you $350,000, and I will give you your jokes."

For once, Jackie was speechless. After taking a few spoonfuls of his chicken soup, he said one word that set his new comeback in motion.

"Fine."

Within days, we had signed contracts—and if I could do one thing over again, it would be looking over every word and semi-colon in that contract, for reasons that will become clear momentarily. But I was by then immersed in finding a theater for *Love Thy Neighbor.* After a number of meetings with the Shuberts, Abe Hirschfeld was back on Broadway. And Jackie Mason was reborn, again.

Love Thy Neighbor turned out to be Jackie's biggest hit. It opened at The Booth Theater on March 24, 1996 and instantly became Broadway's hottest ticket. The critics loved it—and loved it for two years of sellout shows in New York and Miami Beach that elevated Jackie to stratospheric heights. HBO recorded the show to show on pay-per-view, and he won an Emmy for it. He also received Grammy nominations for the album of the show and parlayed his new fame into hosting a talk show on PBS.

This was another new Jackie Mason, one who could brilliantly poke fun at life's conventions and its absurd ethnic divisions, yet with humble, moving wit—with a feather duster instead of a slashing machete. His transformation was hailed by the critics. In the *Post,* Clive Barnes noted that he was at "his superlative best" and "roaringly funny." The *Times* wrote that he "ranks among the all-stars." I received little notice, but after the debacle of *Prince of Central Park,* I was ecstatic simply to have stitched together a smash hit.

The only problem was that you cannot change Jackie Mason for the better. You cannot make a potato into a banana, and you cannot change a bastard into a nice guy. Though my nagging doubts about working with Jackie were never far from my thoughts, it was not until *Love Thy Neighbor* ended its Broadway run, after 234 performances, on January 5, 1997, that my doubts were borne out. Jackie and I took the show to Miami Beach to play at the Jackie Gleason Theater. There, we again sold out every show. I remained in

New York, unable to get away due to pressing business. That, too, turned out to be a mistake—one that Jackie took advantage of. That became evident when one day, a call came from the theater informing me that the regular performance of the show had been postponed, and refunds were being given to the 3,000 people who'd come to see the show.

When I asked why, I was stunned.

"Jackie Mason ordered it closed," I was told.

"Why? Is he sick?"

"No, Jackie's here. He rented the theater out for a bar-mitzvah."

I didn't know if this was some sort of practical joke, if I was being ribbed, or if it was Jackie's idea of humor. As it turned out, it was his idea of conniving.

Here is where the contract I had not read comes in. According to a seemingly innocuous clause Jackie and his lawyer had put in, he was given the right to perform at private functions such as parties, weddings, and bar-mitzvahs. Only a devious mind would have believed that gave him the right to close down the theater and use it for those private functions. Now you know what kind of mind Jackie Mason has. Imagine what kind of empty, pathetic soul would stiff a whole house of people who had paid good money to see him, just so he could pocket a hefty fee to do a private show. And he had arranged to close the theater for a whole *week,* so he could do more of these private gigs.

Refunding the audience's money was hardly enough for me. I wanted to use Jackie's next paycheck to refund them double their money. It was my most humiliating moment since Paul Gioia closed down The Hirschfeld Theater fifteen years earlier. When I called and confronted Jackie about what he had done, his attitude turned ugly—his true colors. Instead of being contrite, he became typically arrogant and demanded that I close the show.

"I'm going to re-open it with myself as the producer," he said, which struck me as having been his plan all along.

"Jackie," I said, "you can either be the star or the producer. Which would you rather be? I'll make it easier for you: I don't want to be the star."

He repeated his intention and hung up. That was the last time I spoke with Jackie, the man I had saved. I sued him for breach of contract and recovered what I was properly owed, which I'm sure Jackie considered a reasonable price to pay to live out his fantasy of being a showbiz genius.

But Jackie Mason could not save himself. He re-opened the show on Broadway, listing Jyll Rosenfeld as producer (he scrubbed my name off all literature about the show), but he had to charge half of what I'd been able to charge. This in itself proves how little he knows about show business; he doesn't understand the reverse psychology that if you cut ticket prices drastically, people will think the show is a dog. And people did. His production of *Love Thy Neighbor* was a total failure.

Neither did he learn from his failure. In 2002, looking half-dead and embalmed, Jackie came back to Broadway with yet another one-man show, having suckered some poor dupe into financing him. Out of curiosity, and to prove to myself that this man could never thrive without me, I bought a ticket for opening night. Fifteen minutes into the show, I was out like a light, having been put to sleep faster than if I had inhaled Valium. Nor was I alone. I heard more snoring in that theater than you would find in an army barracks at 3 A.M. The good news was that the show closed after one performance.

I am sure Jackie Mason will call me again, begging for forgiveness and for my help in getting him another gig. I can assure him I'm not that much of a sucker for a sob story. I will tell him that his career is over and that if he wants to tell jokes, the only place he should do it is at Bingo Night at his Florida condo.

The only lingering regret I do have about Jackie Mason is that, as a result of our falling out, I lost my friendship with Ed Koch. In retrospect, I wish I had never introduced him to Jackie. I would gladly exchange the money I made on *Love Thy Neighbor* to have kept Koch as a friend. What saddens me is that for years, Jackie told lies about me to Koch, and Koch believed him. Someday he will learn what it feels like to be used and betrayed by this malignant munchkin. When he does, I will welcome his call, and we will go share a plate of pickled herring at the Stage Deli.

The ups and downs of my Jackie Mason saga may have been an exhausting roller coaster ride, but it hardly consumed all of my time and energies in the mid-1990s. Just as rewarding to me was brainstorming the third major invention of my lifetime—after the magnetic seal on refrigerators and the open-air parking garages.

The idea, as it often does with me, came out of the blue, as I was riding in my car in Florida on the road from Palm Beach to Miami. The road ran parallel with the railroad tracks on which a train was running in the same direction. I noticed that while we had to stop for traffic lights while the train kept going, we still beat it to Miami.

I thought: "Why was that train so slow?" And it came to me. It was all because of its steel wheels. It dawned on me that every vehicle in the world, whether a car or a baby carriage, has rubber wheels. Only the train doesn't. Why? Because when the train was invented, rubber tires didn't exist. That's not a good enough reason to keep it in the 19th Century.

Rubber wheels took over because they provided a smooth, fast ride. Steel wheels on steel rails are loud, slow, and inefficient. They also require constant track replacement. A train also needs enormous weight to get any traction, yet you can walk on that track wearing sneakers and have plenty of traction.

Rubber on steel—that was the answer. And from that simple premise, I worked out a brilliant plan for rubber wheels for high-speed trains that can go up to 150 miles per hour—or from Penn Station to Boston not in five hours but in an hour and a half. Thus was my idea born—the Bullet Train.

Imagine how wonderful the Bullet Train would be for our archaic rail transit system. It would not require new trains or tracks. The rubber wheels will absorb vibration and be quiet as a mouse. The Bullet Train would vastly improve our quality of life because as train travel increases, traffic decreases, and with it, the pollution and congestion it creates.

The railroad companies are today going broke. My invention will create a new demand in rail transportation, just as similar rubber-wheel trains have done in Paris and Tokyo. The difference with my rubber wheels is that those trains rely on magnetic elevation, a very expensive technology that requires new trains and tracks. With my Bullet Train, only the wheels are new.

My detailed plans covered two designs. One is L-shaped with the steel rim fitting over the inside of the rail; the other is U-shaped, the two rims fitting over the rail. While I knew nothing of the mechanics, the experts added the technological things, such as microprocessors that constantly measure and adjust the trains' speed according to track curvature and send "signals" to the hydraulic system to tilt each car and keep them on the track.

With it all, it still boiled down to a simple plan. When I received a patent in June 1997, the national media regaled me for it in stories that ran in publications from *The New York Times* to *Rubber and Plastics News*, which wrote:

Real estate tycoon Abe Hirschfeld made millions in parking garages, produced Broadway shows, once bought the *New York Post* and has run for [office]....Now, at 78, he's ready to start a rubber revolution.

I fully expect the revolution to happen. In Florida, the House immediately began exploring how to implement the Bullet Train to connect Miami, Orlando, and Tampa. Once the railroads' habitual resistance to new ideas recedes, as it must for them to survive, it will be a reality. Maybe I won't be around to see it, so I will take my bow now.

So, while my courtroom wars would intensify and get even uglier, my instincts were still very much "steeled."

And they would lead me to my most famous episode: that of saving the hide of the President of the United States.

Abraham (Abe) Hirschfeld

CHAPTER TWENTY-EIGHT: ME AND MRS. JONES

As outrageous as Morgenthau's indictment was, it was only the overture of his plot with Stahl to destroy me. As it was, by the fall of 1997, the fallout from the bogus indictment had begun to eat into me like battery acid. You will recall my wonderful plans for 25 Broad Street and how I foresaw that it would be bought by the New York Stock Exchange, and how I had lined up three other Wall Street buildings to buy for $30 million (and which today are worth $1 billion).

All those plans unraveled after the indictment. First, Morgenthau had all of my credit accounts closed, which came on top of Stahl getting Ira Gammerman to approve the closing of all my bank accounts while my lawsuit was pending—which of course, Stahl intended to drag on forever. So, unable to get credit or even know how much was available to me, I had no choice but to put 25 Broad Street up for sale. I came away with $1.5 million on a building today worth close to $200 million.

But all that was nothing compared to the hit Morgenthau landed on my good name—though even before the trial could begin, he landed an even harder and more outrageous blow.

This, of course, was the fantasy scenario he cooked up that I had tried to hire a hit man to murder Stanley Stahl.

Typical of a crook like Morgenthau, he had someone else do the dirty work of defaming me. Before he had the decency to even interview me or call me to a grand jury, he leaked his bullshit murder-for-hire scenario to one of the lackeys in the press who was in his pocket, Mark Kriegel of the *Daily News*. On November 8, Kriegel wrote a front-page column "revealing" this laughable plot in which I had supposedly paid $75,000 to a man to hire a hit man to kill Stahl; when the deed was done, the bizarre tale went on, I was to have paid this middleman $75,000 more.

This nonsensical story, like that of my "tax fraud," was as full of holes as Swiss cheese. Most absurdly, trying to explain away the inconvenient detail that Stanley Stahl happed to be very much alive, Morgenthau said that the middleman was discovered, beaten up, and called off the "hit," at which point he just kept the $75,000, and I just forgot the whole thing!

I've seen more realistic plots on *The Gong Show*.

One element of the fable did ring true, though it broke my heart and further disgusted me about Morgenthau. Only now did I learn that the DA had bullied Rosemary Singer into wearing a wire and trying to manipulate me into implicating myself.

Now I knew why Rosemary had badgered me with disjointed talk about Stahl, why she had led me to talk about Stanley out of the blue, saying things like, "If only someone would murder Stahl," or "Wouldn't you just like to kill him?" I, of course, passed such talk off as nonsensical chatter and, like anyone else in that situation, went along with the charade. Usually, I wasn't even listening to what she said. Still, I wasn't angry at Rosemary as much as I was at Morgenthau for bullying her into becoming my Judas.

The same went for the alleged "middleman," a construction and demolition sub-contractor I had known for many years. Veltri had done work for me on the Yankee Stadium garage project and at 21 Hudson Street in Tribeca. He was an expert in his field; he did excellent work for me. And so, when I began my renovation at 21 Hudson Street, I hired him to subcontract the project. Again, he did a wonderful job, and in appreciation, I had given him a $75,000 bonus as a gift. At first, I was going to pay him $50,000, but Joe was going through a very painful divorce and asked for more. Me, being me, I gladly gave it to him.

This was not out of the ordinary for me, to reward good work with a token of appreciation. In fact, for that same project, I had also given Randy Daniels $50,000. But in Joe Veltri, Morgenthau found another pigeon to coerce. Joe was around sixty years old, and with his financial problems stemming from his divorce, he was an easy target. I can only imagine Morgenthau threatening to sic the IRS on Veltri, throw him in jail for tax evasion on the $75,000, whatever it took to break the man. (An interesting aside to the story is that Randy Daniels escaped similar scrutiny and pressure by putting the money I gave him in his daughter's name.)

In retrospect, both of these fair-weather friends had forced me to talk about the nutty notion of having Stahl killed. Remember that when I take you through the entire ludicrous litany of bogus conclusions Morgenthau would ask the jury to believe. But I will, at this point, give you the only fact you need to know. Knowing of my problems with Stahl, Veltri called me one day and proposed that I pay a half a million dollars to have Stahl killed. I didn't know whether this was some kind of a joke—tough-guy macho posturing—but my response was unequivocal.

"I won't pay you five cents."

Later, Rosemary ran in all hot and bothered and said that Veltri was going to blow the whistle on me. "He's gonna say you wanted Stahl murdered!" she bellowed. "You're gonna go to jail!"

That is when I realized it was no macho posturing and certainly no joke. It was, I strongly suspected, a clumsy extortion plot against me by Rosemary and Veltri. I also suspect that when Morgenthau's snoops found out about it, he took the usual Morgenthau slimy approach. Instead of prosecuting them, he told them he'd let them walk if they would twist the details and lie that I was behind it all.

So, in Morgenthau's dirty hands, the $75,000 I gave Veltri became the "smoking gun," though in truth it wasn't even a smoking cap pistol. It was just steaming manure. Now all this "respected" DA needed was a motive. That would take a little longer, and when he came up with one, it would be the biggest lie of all. But we're getting ahead.

As soon as I laid my eyes on the *Daily News* story, my life was shattered. Here I was being called an attempted murderer in black and white. This rat Kriegel never even called me for a response. I was completely blind-sided. It was, in every way, a "hit" on my reputation.

I immediately called my lawyer, Ted Kupferman, and he felt that I should sue the moribund *News* for every cent it had (granted, that wouldn't be much). Instead, I was not interested in money; I wanted the paper to be forced to be an instrument of the truth, not lies. And so, I sued the *News* in Manhattan Supreme Court—for exactly two cents in libel damages, a public apology on page one, and to have a receiver operate the paper until a new owner could be found who would not tolerate this kind of character assassination.

I did not want that new owner, I might add, to be me. I had little interest in this near-irrelevant paper, though I do have a personal loathing for its publisher, Mort Zuckerman. This classic limousine liberal Canadian, who also publishes *U.S. News and World Report,* knows nothing of New York beyond the circuit of high-society cocktail parties he lives to be seen at. But his real failing is that, as a

Jew who has appointed himself spokesman for Israel and its Zionist leaders, Zuckerman has been one of the people most responsible for the failure of peace in the Middle East. How? For years, he has refused to report anything about my peace treaty, the only vehicle that can possibly bring a lasting peace to that war-ravaged region. War and pain, then, is Zuckerman's legacy.

It came as no surprise, given the above, that when Zuckerman *did* put me in his newspaper, it was a repugnant, unethical, trip-job designed to ruin me personally. And he came close to doing just that. After I filed my suit, when I walked out onto the courthouse steps to meet the press, I was in tears.

"They destroyed my mentality," I told them. "I can't go to synagogue. I can't go to the store. I walk in the streets, and my friends don't want to look at me."

You must keep in mind that, at this point, there was no indictment on this "crime," and there would not be for over a *year*. The tax fraud case wouldn't go to trial for *two years*. Yet, I had to live with these Swords of Damocles hanging over my head every single day.

Worse, Morgenthau hand-picked another compliant judge named Herman Cahn, whose jurisdiction was Queens, to replace the judge slated to hear my suit against the *News*, Stuart Cohen. Cahn dutifully scheduled the case extraordinarily fast, within a week, leaving me no time to prepare a detailed case for a receiver, although Kupferman made an eloquent case when he explained to the court, "If the paper were bankrupt, the court could appoint a receiver. Well, the *News* is morally and journalistically bankrupt."

But on November 21, Cahn blithely dismissed the case. I considered amending my complaint and suing for $50 million, but I knew the deck was stacked. Besides, I could only spend so much on legal fees with so many other court dates pending. The remarkable thing was, as the new year 1998 dawned, not only was I still standing, but I finally got the pleasure of seeing Morgenthau exposed as a crook.

When the arrogant DA had indicted me, he tried hard to cover up his slimy practices, but I could put two and two together. But when it came to light that his subpoenas for my banking records in December 1994 and October 1995 contained that false statement that a criminal action was pending against me, I immediately petitioned the State Supreme Court to let me sue Morgenthau for abuse of authority, an offense that could get him removed from office.

My lawyers told me I would never win the motion, that such a thing was unprecedented. That's why I hate lawyers. I went ahead, and on February 11, 1998, Justice Phyllis Gangel-Jacob ruled in my favor. This was a monumental victory, and now that Morgenthau's true colors were revealed, I believed his cases against me were mortally compromised. That was enough of a reward for me, so I did not file the suit against him. I don't like to sue people, anyway. So, I let him keep his job.

Once again, I was stupid. As much as I expected the media to plaster Morgenthau's lying all over the papers and airwaves, I neglected to take into account Stanley Stahl's bribe-facilitated hold on the media. While AP did break the story the next day, almost no one else touched it. The *Times* was the only paper that did—in a three-paragraph story not on page one but in the Metro section, blandly headlined, "Judge Lets Developer Sue Over Inquiry." Anyone reading that would think it's about a couple of guys named Moe and Murray.

So, even when I won in court, I still lost. And Morgenthau went right on with his sleazy tactics, aided and abetted by his bought judges. Another example came two months later, in April, when I petitioned Judge Gammerman to approve a Special Referee in my case against Stahl, to get a full and honest accounting of the finances of Stahl Associates—which I could not do because Stahl was keeping all the records from me.

Gammerman named as Referee a man named Julius Birnbaum, a one-hundred-percent honest man who directed that Stahl and I cooperate with each other's requests for documents. However, Stahl never even responded to my requests and *two years* later, told Birnbaum he would give me nothing unless so ordered by Gammerman—who of course, never would have gone against Stahl. Exasperated, Birnbaum suggested to Gammerman that he name an independent accountant to examine all the records. I agreed. Stahl refused. Birnbaum then told the judge such an appointment did not require the consent of both sides, that Gammerman could do it anyway. Gammerman ignored him. He just kept the case stuck in the mud.

This, then, was the predicament I was in in the fall of 1998, caught in the revolving door of a corrupt system, going nowhere. And yet, I wasn't the only powerful man in that predicament.

In Washington, D.C., the most powerful man in the world was being jerked around by *his* enemies, seemingly with no way out.

Until I gave him the way out.

Bill Clinton's problems with Paula Jones had begun in 1991 when, as Arkansas governor, he made his famous "sexual advance," dropping his pants and asking her to "kiss it" in a Little Rock hotel room, though I never quite understood why else she was in his room. Three years later, with Clinton in the White House, she suddenly decided she would sue Clinton for sexual harassment.

When the Supreme Court, ludicrously, ruled that she could sue a sitting President on a petty thing like this without taking him away from his duties, it became the seed from which an unimaginable scandal grew, beyond all logic, around another of Clinton's habitual sex acts—the most infamous blow job in history. This was revealed only because yet another imbecile judge allowed Jones's lawyers to question Clinton about his affair with Monica Lewinsky, which was hardly harassment.

As I have mentioned, I believed Clinton was the hardest-working President we've ever had, a man who worked for us twenty-four hours a day with his two heads. He was also manna from heaven for comedy writers. And the Paula Jones and Monica Lewinsky episodes were wonderful comedy fodder for a brilliant jokesmith like me. One example I would tell at the time went like this:

When Barbara Walters interviewed Clinton, she said, "Mr. President, Monica Lewinsky says that you have a very, very small penis."

And Clinton said, "Oh, no, that's only because she has a very, very big mouth."

More seriously, and ominously, the Lewinsky affair gave Clinton's version of Jean Valjean, the scurrilous Ken Starr, the opening to—in Morgenthau-esque fashion—engineer a ploy to catch Clinton in a perjury trap he fell into by denying it under oath. For two years, the scandal was all the country heard about, and Clinton's lie that he did "not have sexual relations with that woman" plunged his administration and the country into complete paralysis.

By the summer of '98, the economy was going south, the stock market eroding, crazy terrorists running around. And, as usual, only I saw the solution that would lift this albatross from around Clinton's neck and let him handle these issues. All it would take was a million dollars.

For four years, Clinton and Jones had gone around and around on money. She originally asked for only $175,000 to drop her case but like any other hooker kept raising her price. Now she wanted $700,000. Clinton refused and a circus trial loomed that would have been the ruination of the country and the presidency.

As it was, a witch hunt in the form of impeachment hearings were set to begin in the congress in November on the silliest of pretenses about "crimes and misdemeanors"—the same crimes and misdemeanors every single congressman practiced on their lunch hour. And while the Jones case was dismissed by a district court judge in Little Rock on April 1, Jones's lawyers were appealing to a Republican-stacked, three-judge federal panel, so it behooved Clinton to get rid of the case for good.

That's where I came in. On October 2, I publicly promised to pay Jones $1 million to settle her lawsuit. Of course, few took me seriously, putting me down as usual as a publicity hound. However, Paula Jones did. Or rather, her leech-like mob of lawyers did. She had so many lawyers who had glommed onto her case, looking to bleed and torture Clinton, that I wonder if Paula Jones, who is not among the deep thinkers of our time, knew how many had taken advantage of her and how much in legal fees she owned them all.

In fact, Jones was now on her second or third set of lawyers, two guys named Wes Holmes and Donovan Campbell, from a law firm in Dallas called Rader, Campbell, Fisher & Pyke. She also had a lawyer named John Whitehead from some right-wing front group called the Rutherford Institute, who seemed to be in it just to get Clinton. But she also had two previous lawyers, Joseph Cammarata and Gil Davis, who had placed an $800,000 lien on any settlement of the case. Between all the lawyers, Jones would have been lucky to come away with enough money to buy a pack of gum. But that wasn't my business. I would give the money; they would have to divvy it up among themselves.

That plan seemed to work for the Jones camp. That October 2, I got a call from Wes Holmes, who said Paula would take the offer. I was willing, I said, to send a bank check for the million dollars, to be kept in an escrow account until they settled the suit with Clinton. My deadline would be October 16. Holmes said fine and that he'd send me a contract with all these terms.

Three weeks later, after the deadline had passed, I still had not received a contract, nor heard another word from Holmes. By now, the press was breathing hot and heavy on the story. And of course, when nothing happened, it was cause for another round of blasting "Abe the publicity hound." I maintained, however, that I was still amenable to doing the deal.

"I have the money, and I'd like to spend it," I told the AP on October 28, "but I think it's a wasteful wish."

Trying to keep the offer alive, I called Holmes and suggested that if Paula was really interested, she had one last chance, but she had to physically take the check in a public forum, in front of all the nation's media. That seemed to excite Jones's people. I was put in touch with her spokesperson Susan Carpenter MacMillan, that shrill blonde lady who was on TV all the time vilifying Clinton, and whose husband Bill was *another* lawyer lurking around on the case. Susan and I made the event for Saturday, October 31, before the National Press Club, at the Mayflower Hotel in Washington, D.C.

The Jones entourage was all very nice at that point, as well they should have been given that I paid for all their plane flights and hotel accommodations. Before going to Washington, I spoke again with Holmes, and he and my lawyer, Harvard Hollenberg, hammered out the deal: I would draw a teller's check for $1 million from my personal account at the Israeli Discount Bank on Friday and take it to Washington with me, hand it to Paula Jones, and she would give it to Holmes to deposit in escrow in his firm's account at the Nation's Bank in Dallas. The check would be negotiable until November 30, by which time the Clinton lawsuit must be settled.

I also insisted that the check be made out not just to Paula Jones but also to all of her lawyers, past and present. As the agreement read:

Mr. Abraham J. ("Abe") Hirschfeld, a public spirited citizen of the United States, who resides in the State of New York, has determined that it would be in the national interest for the [Jones vs. Clinton] Lawsuit to be settled as expeditiously as possible…and has heretofore indicated a willingness to underwrite a final settlement of the Lawsuit in the amount of ONE MILLION DOLLARS ($1,000,000.00)....

It has been brought to Mr. Hirschfeld's attention that several parties in addition to Mrs. Jones, namely her attorneys at several stages of said litigation, have expressed or may express a claim to all or part of any settlement of the Lawsuit....Mr. Hirschfeld's intention is to make no individual party of attorney whole, but only to facilitate said settlement....

Whereas, the individuals and or parties who may foreseeably attempt to enforce a claim against a settlement in the Lawsuit are the following:

Paula Corbin Jones
Joseph Cammarata, Esq.
Gilbert K. Davis, Esq.
Rader, Campbell, Fisher & Pyke
The Rutherford Institute (John W. Whitehead, President)
William McMillan, Esq.

The first time I laid eyes on Paula Jones was that Saturday morning at the Mayflower Hotel. My first reaction was that she was a nice lady but, frankly, I didn't know what Clinton had seen in her—I knew one thing: I wouldn't go to bed with Paula Jones if she paid *me* a million dollars. For the TV cameras, I led her by the arm into the conference room. I handed her the check, which has become a great artifact in American history, and kissed her on the cheek. She then called me "a wonderful person," and I told the media why only I could have made all of this happen.

"I have a clear head in dealing with the nation's problems," I said, something everyone would know if they only listened to all of my solutions.

Indeed, just since my offer was made, there had been a discernible effect on the country. "Already," I pointed out, "everybody is happy. The stock market has been up every day. That's not a coincidence."

Alas, leave it to the lawyers to mess up such a good thing.

The first sign of trouble came when I handed the check to Paula Jones and, within minutes, she was told to give it back to me. Remember that, the fact that the check was Paula's to keep, yet she didn't. If you're not counting, that made *two* times that the check had not been taken. Instead, Holmes insisted that we rework the agreement that day and that I would wire the million dollars on Monday to the Nation's Bank account. So, to answer a question many have asked, the check I gave to Paula Jones was perfectly negotiable, until November 30, 1998.

Maybe Holmes had a good reason for the change; that's why they pay lawyers. But remember what I said about my educated nose tip? I sensed something was rotten in D.C. that day. It struck me that these people were hiding another agenda, and having gotten their free trip and their million dollars' worth of publicity, they were looking for ways to place roadblocks in the way of the deal. I had the sneaking suspicion that they were using me as leverage to get Clinton to settle for the $700,000 he was offering in a package deal that, with my million dollars, would bring the whole payment to $1.7 million, and that they wouldn't legally take my money until they knew what Clinton would do.

They had read Clinton correctly. Because after I went back to New York that night, I got a phone call from Clinton's big-shot lawyer, Bob Bennett. Apparently, the scene at the Mayflower had convinced Clinton that this was the time to settle with Jones. Bennett said he appreciated my help in moving Jones to the edge of a settlement, and I was appreciative they recognized that fact. However, in the next breath, Bennett took a different path.

"Abe, the President likes and respects you," he said, "but he wants you to know he cannot enter into an agreement with Paula Jones if you are involved in a settlement. It has nothing to do with Jones getting more money than she deserves. It's that you happen to be under indictment for tax evasion. We simply can't partner up with you under those circumstances. The President hopes you understand."

I did understand. I understood that Bill Clinton was a coward and a hypocrite. This man who used the Oval Office as a hot sheets motel was worried about being associated with *me!* Bennett was polite, so I politely told him to go fuck himself. Then I called Harvard Hollenberg and told him I don't like being used, and I wanted to call off the deal with Jones right then and there.

Harvard cooled me off. "Abe, forget about Clinton," he said. "Whatever he does with her, if you back out you'll be in breach of contract, and you'll make everyone who hates you look good."

He was right, of course. As it was, most of the media coverage of the Mayflower event ridiculed me as a huckster. Everyone wanted to inspect the bank check to see if it was real. So, I made sure to say the deal was still on. I'm not sure Jones's lawyers wanted it to be.

Indeed, more ominous was that on that same weekend, Jones's old lawyers, Cammarata and Davis, were raising a ruckus. When I got into my office Monday morning, a certified letter was waiting from them informing me—threatening me—that they had a claim to the first $800,000 of any settlement. Meaning that, since they had not signed off on the deal with Jones, they would not abide by the indemnification clause in it, and there was no way Jones's current lawyers could enforce the clause. Conceivably, if Cammarata and Davis took $800,000, Holmes and the others would still insist on their million.

Given this complication, I could not possibly go ahead with the wire transfer that Monday. And of course, the media took the easy way out and blasted me for "reneging." Some even said with supreme ignorance that my check had "bounced"—even though a bank check cannot bounce. Many also assumed that the deal was off. That, too, was a lie. The fact was, my deadline for giving Paula Jones a million dollars was November 30. If she settled with Clinton by then, she had a right to the check, provided her lawyers would get Cammarata and Davis to indemnify me from their claim.

However, it became all too clear that the Jones camp had no desire to do that. According to my educated nose tip, what was rotten was that the Jones people knew they were going to get their money elsewhere. I smelled a rat. A rat named Stanley Stahl.

The last thing Stanley Stahl wanted during our court warfare was for me to be regaled as a national hero. And I wouldn't because a chain of events that took me out of the Jones picture. First, Bob Bennett kept sliming me in the media, saying the President would give Paula Jones $850,000 if there were "no strings attached"— meaning Abe Hirschfeld. Then, appropriately, on Friday the 13th, Bennett said that Bill MacMillan had sent him a letter stating that my million-dollar offer was "off the table" and that I would be no part of any settlement Jones made with Clinton. A *New York Times* story included the nugget that "(N)o one in the Jones camp regarded Hirschfeld as reliable in anything but his ardor for publicity."

That was the day the announcement was made of a settlement between Jones and Clinton.

"It's over . . . I'm glad," Jones cried on cue before the cameras. But, as you'll see in a minute, it wasn't over yet with me.

Let me say this without equivocation: I do not believe for a second that Bill Clinton paid a penny to Paula Jones, and by that I also mean his insurance company or his defense fund didn't pay, either. Again, I believe Stanley Stahl, a man with a $5 billion empire and every politician in his pocket, funneled a hell of a lot more than $850,000 for Clinton to give to Paula Jones, and whatever it took to take care of Cammarata and Davis.

By now, you should understand that this isn't idle blustering. You should understand that, like the parody song about Elvis Presley, Stanley Stahl was everywhere. Stanley Stahl was everything.

I would say that everyone made out like a bandit, but all these people were already bandits.

Meanwhile, the only honest person in the bunch had been slandered, used, insulted, and pushed aside. Still, the country had been spared a convulsion, and Clinton kept his presidency, only because that honest man had had the foresight to get involved. I even got to keep my million dollars. Overall, not a bad deal for an old wheeler-dealer like me.

Not that Paula Jones hasn't tried to get her grubby hands on that million dollars ever since. Having apparently grown accustomed to the high life, spending thousands of dollars on a nose job and various other luxuries, in February 2000, she filed suit against me in District Court in Dallas, claiming with unmitigated gall that I breached the original agreement. This despite her rejecting two million-dollar checks and her lawyers' letter to Bennett saying my offer was "off the table." Keep this in mind, too. After her settlement with Clinton, Jones and her lawyers had seventeen days to ask for the million dollars. They did not. Because they could not.

How did Jones try to get around these painful truths? With weasel language, such as this particularly embarrassing bit of nonsense, when instead of saying, "I expected and had a right to be paid," she hemmed and hawed:

"I never expressed or indicated in any manner that I no longer wanted the payment owed to me by the defendant."

Is it any wonder that her suit was thrown out on September 19, 2000, simply because it had no business being filed in Dallas. Undeterred, she then filed this doomed suit in New York on August 15, 2001. As of this writing, it is still pending, but I fully expect it to meet the same fate.

Not that I have any sympathy for this woman who had her fifteen minutes of fame, but Paula Jones has allowed herself to be conned and cheated by so many people, and apparently the only way she will learn that lesson is by winding up penniless and back in the trailer park again. Some people never learn the lesson. If Paula Jones does, she will understand that I was the only one who ever tried to help her without trying to hurt her.

I learned a lesson myself. No matter my good intentions, someone will do Stahl's bidding and try to make me look like the bad guy. And now it would be Bob Morgenthau's turn—four different times—to pull out all the stops to turn me into a convicted criminal.

Abraham (Abe) Hirschfeld

CHAPTER TWENTY-NINE: "A POLITICAL VENDETTA"

How petty and obsessed was Morgenthau when it came to ruining me? The answer to that question could always be seen whenever anything that happened elevated me in the public mind. By late 1998, not only had I monopolized the headlines for weeks during the Clinton-Paula Jones matter, but the December 7 issue of *Time* magazine gave me priceless publicity by naming me one of the 20th Century's greatest business geniuses.

I, of course, had known this all along, but I must admit that it felt good that a powerful media giant had finally recognized me for my achievements. Even during the Paula Jones saga, when I was the biggest name in the country, no one wanted to interview me. The only one who did was CNN's Larry King. Someone from his show called me when I was in Washington on that Friday, October 31 and said King would have me on his show the following Wednesday, but only if I would be "exclusive" to King, that is, promise not to go on any other show. I figured Larry King would have the largest audience, so I agreed. Then, when Wednesday came around, the same guy called and said, "We're sorry, Mr. Hirschfeld, we've canceled your appearance."

I can only surmise that this whole thing was a ruse to keep me off television, and it worked.

After that, the people from other networks who had begged me to come on their shows stopped calling. Not to sound overly redundant or paranoid about this, but I could sense Stanley Stahl's hands all over this crude plot.

Time made up for all that. This was the magazine's third Top 100 list—the first was of the century's greatest leaders, the second its greatest artists—and one can barely put into words the feeling of accomplishment and honor of being included in the company of "Builder and Titans" such as Howard Hughes, H.L. Hunt, and J. Paul Getty.

That we all were grouped in a section called "Crazy and In Charge" only proved to me that my ideas, like theirs, were, and are, far ahead of their time. Anyone whose mind works in ways that most people cannot fathom will always be labeled as "crazy." In truth, of course, we are light years ahead of the intellectuals, who consider themselves the smartest people on earth, for one simple reason: We come from humble beginnings and never lose touch with the people whose lives we can improve. We don't build ivory towers, as the intellectuals do. We think "outside the box." To the Philistines who can't, the easiest way to dismiss us is to call us "crazy." I say, the crazier we are, the more we will change the world for the better—and the more we will have an unquenchable thirst to improve the world until the day we die.

I was also greatly flattered that *Time* chose to print in the issue the caricature of me drawn by my "brother" Al Hirschfeld, my two arms upraised in a victory gesture, my grin ear-to-ear. I could not have been any higher atop the world when the issue came out.

And then, only days later, with timing hardly coincidental, Morgenthau spitefully brought me crashing down to the gutter he lives in.

After a year in legal limbo, Morgenthau just couldn't wait to have his goons arrest me in the middle of the night and drag me half-naked downtown and thrown onto a cold jail floor so he could stand on the courthouse steps the next morning and breathlessly tell the world he had indicted me for "criminal solicitation," which in the fable he had concocted meant I had tried to hire a hit man to kill Stanley Stahl.

This story, of course, with its melodramatic Cain and Abel script of betrayal and murder, albeit one that never happened, was all over the place that day, and for Morgenthau, I'm sure it seemed like a *coup de grace,* after having already indicted me on the bogus tax fraud charge. And, as I had done before, I had to defend myself against another Morgenthau litany of half-truths, no-truths, and concocted "evidence." As I suspected, all of it came from the undercover tape recording the traitorous Rosemary Singer had been forced to make without my knowledge.

As Morgenthau spewed out his misinformation, the whole house of mud rested on two things I had said on the tainted tapes—most of which actually proved I was innocent!

The tapes mainly centered on what happened during and following a phone call Joe Veltri made to me. Veltri, you recall, was my construction manager at 21 Hudson Street, and through our conversations, he knew well of my legal tussle with Stanley Stahl. I had not the slightest inkling, however, that Veltri would call and out of nowhere tell me he was going to kill Stahl. But that is what he said when he made that call. I literally could not believe my ears when he told me he had paid a hit man $75,000 and that I would have to pay $500,000 to complete the "hit."

From reading these pages, you already know something is fishy here. Why? Because you know that I had paid Veltri $75,000 as a gift upon the completion of 21 Hudson Street. And now here he was using the same exact figure in this loony "plot." Having been squeezed by that allegedly ethical Morgenthau, Veltri had clearly told him of the $75,000. And Morgenthau just as clearly knitted it into his hokey scenario. The implication was clear: I had paid Veltri the money expressly so that Veltri would hire a hit man to kill Stahl.

When Veltri made the demand, I was so stunned that I didn't fully connect the dots to Morgenthau. I merely figured that Veltri, who was in deep money straits, was trying to hit me up for more money in an extortion plan. And I was having none of it.

Outraged, I vented my anger in no uncertain terms. "Go to hell!" I raged at him. "I won't pay you five nickels! I don't want Stahl murdered."

Veltri then muttered something about "going to the cops" to tell them I wanted to kill Stahl.

"I'm going to put you in jail," he threatened.

"I don't care what you do. I'm going to put *you* in jail for extortion!"

A few days later, Rosemary Singer, her wire well concealed in her underwear, came into my office and told me Veltri was trying to call, and he was demanding I pay him more money.

"This guy's a thief," I said. "He fooled me all along. And if he talks much more, I will put him in jail. I'll sue him for a refund of the money I gave him."

When I did connect the dots, I would realize that Rosemary had apparently cooked up an extortion plot with Veltri and that both of them, in order to save their own behinds, had "flipped," meaning that in exchange for not being prosecuted they would do, and say, whatever Morgenthau wanted them to.

Indeed, you can see how Rosemary was trying to lead me by how she proceeded with her comments, which I recount here verbatim, exactly as it appeared on the transcripts of Morgenthau's tapes.

"Money for what?" she asked.

"I gave him money. He told me he could do things, and I gave him a lot of money. But he stole the money and did nothing."

"He's going to say you wanted Mr. Stahl murdered. You're going to go to jail."

"I never wanted him to go through with the murder."

Now, you will notice that never once did I say I gave Veltri any money for murdering anyone. In fact, I expressly said I *didn't* want him to murder Stahl. And yet, believe it or not, that last remark of mine—proving my innocence—became Morgenthau's prime evidence *against* me! I can only imagine how difficult it is to make lemons out of lemonade, but Morgenthau was going to try his damnedest.

Another example was his other big "bombshell" from the tapes, which was me telling Rosemary, "Yeah, I wanted him murdered. So what?" Of course, this hardly constituted proof of anything. If everyone who ever used those words about someone else were prosecuted, no one would be left on the streets.

Yet, Morgenthau plunged ahead with his pitifully weak case, having squeezed Veltri into making up an absurd fable about being a middleman between he and a shadowy hit man—whom Morgenthau could never produce—who reneged when I didn't pay more money, leading Veltri to "rat me out" to the intended "victim," Stanley Stahl. In reality, this ludicrous story had it exactly backwards. The truth was that Stahl, with Morgenthau as his stooge, planned to frame the real victim, me.

Perhaps even Laura Dryer, the judge at my arraignment, knew how flimsy and clumsy the case was when she smiled at my offer to give her the Paula Jones check to cover my million-dollar bail, and then let me go after taking my word that I would post bail the next day—which, combined with the bail on the tax fraud case, made this the second million dollars I had paid to the crooked Morgenthau.

So now, I had two trials to prepare for, facing up to fifteen years in prison on the first if convicted and seven years on the solicitation charge. As Morgenthau planned it, the tax fraud trial would begin in July; if things went badly for him, he would rush me right into the other trial, turning me into a human pinball bouncing from courtroom to courtroom, hoping my head would be in a haze.

Here again, the timing was not coincidental. Because early in 1999, I was openly talking about running the next year for the U.S.

Senate seat being vacated by my old foil, Daniel Patrick Moynihan. My bumpy run for Manhattan Borough President, sabotaged as it was by Rudy Giuliani and Carl McCall, had a positive effect in that it solidified my allegiance with the Independence Party, which as an outgrowth of Ross Perot's Reform Party was by now established in every state in the country.

The party would have its convention in June 2000, and while another man from upstate New York was running as well, I knew the nomination would be mine for the asking. After all, a man prepared to spend $10 million of his own money is going to be very popular in any party. I intended to make my announcement late in the fall. Morgenthau wanted to finish me off by then.

So, you can guess what happened. By the time summer arrived, Morgenthau had me practically living in the courtroom. First came the tax fraud trial, on that fallacious 123-count, $3.3 million indictment of which only five counts and $114,000 were accounted for. (Again, most of the charges centered around my Broadway production of *The Prince of Central Park,* and to demonstrate how bogus the indictment was, Morgenthau never mentioned that I had actually *lost* $3.5 million on that production. It's rather difficult to hide income when you lost $3.5 million of it.)

If Morgenthau expected me to roll over instead of fighting him, he learned I would be more than a thorn in his side; I'd be a thorn bush.

The first thing Morgenthau tried to do was to bully me by preventing me from having decent legal representation. I hired one lawyer after another, including Gus Newman and many other top lawyers—and each of the eleven was notified by Morgenthau that they should not represent me. Some of them clearly acted against my best interests, forcing me to fire them. Before the trial even began, I had thrown away at least $150,000 on crooked lawyers.

So now I put into reality my theory about who could best represent me. I filed a motion with the court to allow me to act as my own attorney.

The judge in trial was Supreme Court Justice Bruce Allen, who was considered a laid-back, non-dictatorial judge. At first, he came off as a fair man, though I felt somewhat insulted when he wouldn't let me represent myself until I underwent a court-ordered psychiatric examination. Believe me, I may be a little crazy, but I am still far more sane than any judge or lawyer on the planet. But if that's what he needed to prove it, so be it.

"What you decide," I told him, "I accept."

And so, for three hours, I sat with three psychiatrists whom I captivated with my thoughts on life and my jokes. Then they gave Judge Allen their evaluation—rating me in the 75-percentile rank in rationality among all human beings. You should know that most people are in the 40-percentile rank. In light of this ringing endorsement, Allen did what I'm sure Morgenthau dreaded—he allowed me to represent myself.

Morgenthau was right in his dread. When the trial began on July 12, I ran rings around his assistant DA, a nervous young woman named Gilda Mariani, keeping her constantly on the defensive by exposing her false evidence. And I didn't even get to do what I wanted. For example, given the power to summon any witness I wanted, I intended to call former Presidents Jimmy Carter and George Bush as character witnesses. I also wanted to call Rudy Giuliani, for one simple reason—to ask him why he'd had me evicted from the Lincoln Day Dinner. I figured that if he were under oath, I'd finally get the answer.

I had one more witness in mind as well, the controversial and outspoken Reverend Al Sharpton, because of a recent incident that I suspected Morgenthau was behind. I had met with Sharpton, another man many of my Jewish friends despise but whom I always respected for his intelligence and commitment to black causes. Or so I thought. I was all set to announce my plan to end police brutality, which had worked so well in Miami Beach—by integrating all police cars with at least one black cop in all minority areas of the city. Sharpton was very excited by the plan, and he agreed to appear with me at a press conference in front of the Police Academy. I was thrilled, knowing his support would galvanize both the black community and the media.

Then, as I was driving to the conference, my cell phone rang. I recognized the voice on the other end as Sharpton's.

"Abe," he said, sounding oddly subdued, "something urgent came up. I can't go to the press conference."

I was completely taken aback, and right then and there, I lost all respect for him. This is a man, after all, who once betrayed his own people as an FBI informant and who was captured by a television surveillance camera allegedly trying to make a drug deal with undercover cops.

"Now I know who you really are!" I yelled into the phone. "You don't care about the black community, only yourself. You don't know how to create opportunity. All you do is create talk."

Predictably, while the press conference drew reporters, not one story was written about it because Sharpton wasn't there. I had every suspicion that Morgenthau—by order of Stanley Stahl—had gotten Sharpton to ruin another moment of glory for me.

Indeed, the Stahl-Morgenthau axis became much clearer when I discovered a direct link, a "smoking gun" that tied them together. This was a man named Stephen Kaufman, who was Morgenthau's personal tax lawyer, not to mention the best man at Morgenthau's second or third wedding. Kaufman also happened to have been Stanley Stahl's personal tax lawyer. You can bet that if I could have called Morgenthau himself to the witness stand, I would have, to expose what a perfect phony this man is. Not that it had any bearing on the case, but it offended me a great deal as a Jew that Morgenthau goes to synagogue every Yom Kippur in my Upper East Side neighborhood, duplicitously pretending that he is a Jew even though he converted to Protestantism some years ago and is married to a gentile woman. That is the kind of dishonesty that drives him.

Unfortunately, Judge Allen forbid me from calling any of these high-visibility men. Instead, I decided I would simply address the jury not as a lawyer but as a man whose life had been torn to pieces by the DA's lies. Rather than wearing a suit and tie, I dressed in a short-sleeved shirt and slacks—you don't want to be in an un-air-conditioned New York City courtroom in July—and began my opening remarks by getting these nice people to know who I was, who I *really* was, not who Morgenthau wanted them to believe I was.

I told them my life story. I also told them jokes. When I got to the one about Jesus Christ not being a Jew because if he was he would have gone for the Early Bird Special, even the judge laughed.

As the *Times* described it, my presentation was "part memoir, resume, and Catskills comedy routine." It was more. It was a perfect defense. I did not, however, arrogantly dispute those five specific counts and the $114,000.

"If there were mistakes, they were made by accountants, not by me," I told the jury. "If I go to a doctor and he gives me a prescription, I take it. I am ready right now to give the court a check for $114,000. But all the other counts are pure garbage. They were simply made up, and the $3.3 million figure pulled out of thin air. The indictment was written on toilet paper."

I boiled my defense down to very simple terms. Because there were no monetary figures on those counts, I asked, "If you get a bill from Macy's without a price, how much money do you owe Macy's?" I concluded: "I promise you, Miss Mariani won't deliver you one honest witness."

And that was the case. Most of those witnesses were "witlesses," former employees of mine who, despite being squeezed and threatened by Morgenthau, had zero credibility. Not one could come up with any motive for me cheating on my taxes. It is well-known that I have no great lust for money, that money has been a byproduct of my business acumen. I have given away millions to charity and spent countless thousands on travel to meet with world leaders about my Middle East peace treaty. If I were as obsessed about money as Stanley Stahl, I would today be one of the world's wealthiest men. In fact, as you will learn later, I once tried, in vain, to send back to the government my Social Security checks, which I and many other well-heeled Americans do not need.

I am many things, but I am not a greedy man. I'm the kind of man who could lose $3.5 million on *Prince of Central Park* and work for ten years on making it into a movie, as you'll also see, only because it's such a good story, with no hope of making money from it.

After four weeks of testimony, I sensed I had gotten this point across and that things were going my way. Evidently, so did Judge Allen because suddenly he became less jovial. In fact, he was downright surly after the jury got the case on August 12 and they still had not reached a verdict three days later. The prosecutors and the judge were now grumbling about, well, just about everything.

One thing was that some friends of mine organized a rally on the courthouse steps, proclaiming and carrying signs that read, "Hirschfeld Is Innocent!" Another was that I had discreetly left a few copies of a *New York Times* article favorable to me on a bench outside the jury room. Although there was no law that precluded me from doing these things—which was simply my exercise of free speech— Mariani, a nervous woman to begin with, was nearly hyperventilating when she demanded that Allen hold me in contempt for tampering with the jury. I held her in contempt for incompetence.

Fortunately, as anxious as Allen was, he saw through Mariani's bull and did not hold me in contempt because by then, he could read the handwriting on the jury room wall. On August 14, the jury came back with convictions on the five counts I did not contest, but they were deadlocked on the other 118 charges.

Allen would not accept this. He told them to go back and keep trying to reach a verdict. Eight days later, they were still hopelessly deadlocked, thanks to a lone holdout juror who had to be the smartest person on earth. When they came back in and told the judge, Allen, according to the *Times,* looked "visibly disappointed." Again, he berated them to go in and come to a verdict—which really meant, "Go find him guilty." That set *me* off. Livid, I rose to my feet and berated *him.*

"Listen, Judge," I told him, "you must be a crook or a liar. The jury doesn't have to find a verdict. All they have to do is vote their conscience. And I *order* you to tell them to vote their conscience!"

With that, I turned and began walking out of the courtroom.

"Mr. Hirschfeld, please come back," Judge Allen pleaded. "We're not through yet."

"I don't give a damn," I told him. "I don't like these manipulations. Goodbye."

Though I was acting out of anger, I have since discovered that it is no sin to speak to judges in this gruff manner—especially the crooked ones—since they have such little self-respect and seemingly need to be abused. Such talk acts as a slap in the face and frequently prods them into doing the right thing for a change.

That's exactly what happened with Bruce Allen that day. He did as I said and ordered the jury to vote their conscience. And as soon as he did, I knew I was home free. As the jury deliberated, I took my wife and some friends to lunch and bought them champagne. After a while somebody said, "We better get back for the verdict."

"We don't have to go back," I said. "We won the case."

When we did go back, the jury came in still deadlocked. And I walked out of the court with at least one of Morgenthau's knives out of my back, though I knew this vengeful man would not accept his defeat gracefully and would try the case again, and again, and again if he had to.

But for now, I had cause to celebrate. And to reward those hard-working jurors for their diligence, I told the press I would pay each of them $2,500. For those skeptics who expected another Paula Jones "stunt," I showed how sincere I was. I arranged a big party at a nice restaurant downtown on Friday, September 3 and invited all the jurors to come and pick up their checks. All but one did.

My largesse to the jurors is one of the most misconstrued acts in judicial history. From the moment I announced my intention, every lawyer and judge in captivity mewled about it, as if I had committed a heinous crime. The hysteria was typified by Norman Goodman, the New York County Clerk, who oversees Manhattan jurors. "I found [the payments] mostly reprehensible," he said. "I thought it kind of diabolical." The *Times'* Clyde Haberman, taking the obligatory pot shots at me, defined the alleged problems with the payments in a September 9 column that read:

This might be shrugged off as merely another wacky moment in the life of a millionaire developer and perennial political candidate who, over his nearly 80 years, has led newspapers to exhaust their supplies of synonyms for "bizarre." But with another Hirschfeld trial coming up, it seems fair to conclude that potential jurors now know that a pot of gold may await them if only they produce the right verdict, or even no verdict.

Bluntly put, did last week's handout, however legal, amount to tampering with future juries?

Well, if Norman and Clyde had calmed down, and come down from their high horses, they would have known that what I did wasn't only completely legal, as Haberman said, but was reasonable compensation for vastly underpaid jurors—people whom the legal system doesn't give a damn about. That is one of the great failings of the system and has been forever. What's more, Judge Allen had no objection. In fact, it was he who told me what to pay!

That happened after everyone came back from lunch and as we were awaiting the final verdict, I approached Allen to broach the idea of paying the jurors.

"Judge," I said, "these jurors have been here three months. They're all crying about losing their wages. They're making $40 a week. I want to give each of them $5,000."

Allen's only quibble was the amount. "Five-thousand is too much," he said. "Give them twenty-five hundred." I have at least fifty witnesses to him saying that—even though Allen later would try to cover his behind by saying what I did was "inappropriate."

Obviously, I could not have been tampering since my offer was made *before* the verdict and because I was going to give the jurors the money regardless of whether they found me guilty or not guilty.

But never have facts gotten in the way of judges, lawyers, or reporters. Not when Abe Hirschfeld is involved. Indeed, this same crowd made no stink when the notorious boxing promoter Don King, after he was acquitted of insurance fraud charges a few years ago, took his jury on a vacation trip to the Bahamas! When I did what I did, they all began screaming for a change in the law that, in 2001, culminated in the New York State Legislature enacting a statute that prohibits any "benefit" upon any juror as a reward for his service. To do so now is a Class-A misdemeanor.

The statute is Penal Law 215.22, but it is far better known as "Hirschfeld's Law." Besides the "Son of Sam Law" prohibiting a criminal from profiting financially from a crime, it is the only law I know of specifically named for a person in the U.S., and for that I am extremely proud.

Yes, you read that right. I am absolutely in favor of the law. Though I did what was proper and legal at the time, if it highlighted a need for a change in the law to bring integrity to the system, I was all for it. And, indisputably, I was an agent of change toward that end. Again, it took Abe Hirschfeld to change the world for the better.

I have only one "objection" to Hirschfeld's Law, and that is it should also apply to judges. Judges should not be permitted to be paid or even to be friends with a lawyer in a case he hears. Even if they had lunch once, he should not be on the case. I have more credibility than anyone in calling for this measure, since nearly all of the judges who have sat in judgment of me have had a hidden conflict of interest with the other lawyers. The legal system had simply become far too chummy a club for judges and lawyers. This club must be closed.

Of course, these judges' corruption went way further—all the way up to Robert Morgenthau and Stanley Stahl. I could not have possibly corrupted the system. How can you corrupt something that is already a sewer of corruption from top to bottom?

Before I leave the tax fraud trial behind, I would like to clear up once and for all the nonsense that I somehow tampered with the jury. After the trial, the lone holdout juror, a man named Morgan Godwin, wrote me a three-page letter telling me of his anger at being subjected to Morgenthau's twisted attempt to railroad an innocent, seventy-nine-year-old man into prison. It is one of the most brilliant, heartfelt letters I have ever read, and I would like to share it with you so that you can better appreciate how the judicial system serves not you or me but those who manipulate it within the club I have spoken about.

The typed letter bore the title, "A Juror's Trials" and came with a hand-written note reading: "I have come to believe that what you...said during the trial is true—that the charges and the circumstances surrounding the trial were politically motivated."

The letter reads:

My first experience as a juror will, I hope, be my last. Recently called for possible jury duty, I found myself selected to serve as a juror in a criminal fraud case held in the New York State Supreme Court. Being a newcomer to the role of juror, I found each step in the process interesting and often fascinating....What I brought to the role of juror was a belief in the tradition of blind justice. I had no prior awareness of the trial or the circumstances leading to it. I do not read the local newspapers or watch local television....

The prosecution charged the defendant, Abraham Hirschfeld and several of his business enterprises, with 123 counts of criminal fraud...I believed that the defendants were presumed to be not guilty unless the prosecution proved otherwise beyond reasonable doubt. Therefore, the burden of proof was on the prosecution. Imagine my surprise when the prosecution's two principal witnesses proved to have signed cooperation agreements with the district attorney's office to avoid prosecution for crimes they might have committed.

If that wasn't sufficient to raise reasonable doubt as to the veracity of their testimony, their manner on the stand, underlined by countless "I don't know," "I'm not sure," "I don't recall," and other examples of seeming lapses of memory or perhaps selective recall, cast their testimony into the gravest doubt in my mind...their body language further undermined their credibility.

As the case progressed, I began to feel that the district attorney's raid on the defendant's offices had been more a fishing expedition than a search for specific evidence...The jury did find one of the defendants guilty on five counts relating to the 1989 Broadway production *The Prince of Central Park.* In that instance, the evidence appeared to indicate that there had been irregularities, and I was persuaded to vote guilty with the eleven other jurors on those five counts.

During deliberations, I was accused of setting a different, excessively high level of reasonable doubt in relation to the remaining 118 counts. It was clear that there was one [juror] who was determined to move the jury toward a vote of guilty on all counts. That juror acquired several supporters who focused their efforts on shifting those who wished to vote not guilty to guilty. Several did change their votes as a result of the small group of "find them guilty" activists. When it became clear that...they were just not going to get everyone to vote guilty on all counts, the group shifted their efforts to getting various jurors to trade votes so that even if the defendants were found not guilty on some counts, at least there would be unanimous votes on all counts.

To me there is something fundamentally wicked to trading votes that could result in a defendant's fate being decided just for the sake of consensus and unanimity. When I was asked to vote guilty on certain counts in return for unanimous not guilty votes on others without regard to the defendant's guilt or innocence, I refused. At that point, I became the object of increasing verbal assault. My intelligence was questioned, as was my objectivity...I sent a note to the judge asking if it was legal and just to trade votes...

The judge's response reinforced my belief that to trade votes could not be fair and just for the defendants, and I again refused to change my vote. The result was the declaration of a mistrial—a result that was a profound disappointment to me since it left the prosecution with the option of retrying the defendants.

I feel more than ever that the prosecution simply failed to make its case. In my view, their case had holes in it that you could have sailed the Queen Elizabeth II through.

While a mistrial may have left the question of guilt or innocence unanswered, it was, in my view, a price worth paying to ensure that injustice did not occur for the sake of consensus.

If it comes to a choice of consensus or justice, consensus be damned!

Most of the jurors, I found, believed I was a skillful lawyer. Not only that, when the mistrial was declared, many in the media who had ridiculed me in the courtroom began to praise me as a kind of Jewish Perry Mason. The *Times,* for example, wrote:

All of the jurors agreed that Mr. Hirschfeld's decision to represent himself gave him a legal advantage. He was able to present himself to the jury and rebut testimony in the cross-examinations without ever having to testify under oath and undergo cross-examination.

"He was very shrewd," said Ray Brooks, [a] juror who favored conviction.

Far be it from me to disabuse anyone of the notion of me as a legal genius. But, in truth, I just followed my instincts, not the law, secure in the knowledge that I was innocent. In fact, I actually *wanted* to testify. Judge Allen said it would be unnecessary.

Still, I was a victorious "lawyer," and the experience prepared and steeled me for round two versus Morgenthau, who would make sure his next hand-picked judge wouldn't allow me to represent myself as the State began its biggest vendetta—and Morgenthau presented his biggest lie.

CHAPTER THIRTY: MAKING MINCEMEAT OF MR. MORGENTHAU

You may have noticed that I have not said much about Zipora in recent chapters. This should not be taken that she meant any less to me than she did for half a century before when her toughness and innate sense of seeing complicated things down to the nub had propelled me to achieve my own potential. Zipora had been a kind of extension of my mother, whose earthy wisdom and practicality took me out of the idealistic rut my father had instilled.

She could still bring me down to earth when I needed to, or pump me up when my spirits were flagging. Given the horrendous persecutions I have faced, I am not stretching matters when I say I literally do not know if I would have lived through all of it without Zipora. Or when I say our romance is today as strong as it was on that glorious July 4, 1943 day when we were married. It simply amazed me that she seemed not to age. At seventy, she was as youthfully beautiful and energetic as she was at thirty. Often, when we would be invited to parties, the host would joke, "Abe, don't take this personally, but we really wanted to see Zipora, and she wouldn't come if we didn't invite you." How could I be offended when it was so true?

I always believed Zipora would make a wonderful diplomat. In fact, I have told my good friend Henry Kissinger, "Henry, you're good. But if you really want to know about statesmanship and making everybody feel good, talk to Zipora." You will recall how Mario Cuomo wooed me to endorse him in 1986 after working to kick me off the ballot. It was only because of Zipora that I did. Zipora did something else, too. Just before Cuomo and I went out to give our press conference, Zipora told Cuomo, "And you'll be coming with your wife Matilda."

Cuomo said, "No, she'll stay home. There's no need for her to be there."

Zipora wouldn't budge. "Are you forgetting that women vote, too?" she lectured him in her always gentle and persuasive way. "If Matilda isn't going, Abe and I aren't going, either." Needless to say, Matilda went.

Being a product of an old-world family, and being of a generation where few even talked about such things, I am very much a prude about sexual matters, so there is not much to kiss and tell about in my life. But I can honestly say I have never given much thought to adultery, not only because I am guided by the Bible but because no woman has ever seemed as alluring as Zipora, and I have known many of the sexiest actresses in the world. The closest I came to adultery is a story that centers on one of those great actresses, Shirley MacLaine.

Back in the 1960s, both Shirley and I worked extremely hard for Bobby Kennedy, and we were drawn together by the shattering tragedy of his death. We began seeing a lot of each other as mutual comfort and quite naturally, our emotions and feelings became more romantic in nature.

I am very attracted to brilliant people, and I have met few people in any walk of life as brilliant and caring as Shirley. I would have loved to produce a movie in which she could star, but we never could find the right vehicle. Shirley, though, was more into a different kind of collaboration. One day she got right to the point. She told me she was in love with me, and she wanted me to go with her to Japan while she made a movie. This was preparatory, she said, to me getting a divorce and marrying her.

Well, if there has ever been a more flattering moment in my life, I can't recall what it is. Imagine a man of my humble origins and, to put it mildly, non-movie star looks, being proposed to by one of the most glamorous and famous movie stars in the world! Of course, I had to let Shirley down, and I truly believe she knew I was hopelessly in love with Zipora—people have always told me I look at Zipora as if I'd just laid eyes on her and been hit by a thunderbolt. Still, my imagination has done a few flips when I think about what life as "Shirley MacLaine's rich businessman husband what's-his-name" would have been like. I'll leave those ruminations to me and my imagination.

Not for a minute, however, have I been let down as Zipora Teicher's husband. I have watched in endless fascination as she gave of herself to the cause of Israel and peace. One of the great joys of my life was when, rewarding her energies in service to so many charities and foundations in the country, in 1976, the Israel Education Fund of the UJA named the first kindergarten-nursery school in Safed, at Zipora's request, after her father Elimelech Teicher. We traveled to Safed for the dedication ceremony on October 29 of that year, and tears came to my eyes as Zipora gave a speech so full of metaphors of hope, faith, and love for her father.

"He was my teacher. I was his pupil," she said. "From my father, I received the courage to understand the purpose of being here and the meaning of life. He paved the road and poured the foundation for me to continue…The only way I can compare the life of my father is like a needle and thread. He threaded those little needles, one by one, day by day, and formed the fine fibers of life, and it became a beautiful tapestry, colorful with depth and meaning."

She concluded with these wonderful words:

"It is an appropriate time to remember the young men who gave their lives for their country and that the wars were not in vain and not in vain will it be. I hope that those little children who will enter this school, and have a better and more secure future, will achieve peace here in Israel and all over the world. I would like to thank my husband and my family who helped me achieve my dream, and now that we are one nation and one heart, there is no more wandering Jew, no more yellow star on our back; we have a home and we are proud, and I promise to continue in my father's footsteps."

That was Zipora, an uncommon woman who could make you believe anything good was within the realm of possibility.

I say "was" in sadness and anger because I watched her health deteriorate rapidly as the inquisitions against me intensified in the late 1990s. This vibrant and stunning woman seemed to age twenty years overnight as her stress about losing her husband to long jail terms weakened her immune system to the point where Alzheimer's and Parkinson's Diseases ravaged her body and mind.

I don't think Zipora ever recovered from the shock and trauma of that terrible night when the police stormed into our apartment, treated me like a common criminal, and dragged me into the street in my underwear. Even as her health failed, Zipora would insist on going to court every day of my trials, for even the most minor of motions—even if the session lasted only a few minutes. By the end of the decade, though, I had to find her an assisted living home to live in, as she was unable to do even menial tasks and had a tenuous grip on reality. Though her eyes were still sharp and knowing, my beautiful bride had wasted away.

For that, I hold one man directly responsible. That man is Robert Morgenthau.

What's more, the harshest indictment against Morgenthau is that he didn't care how much damage he did to my family. Anyone familiar with my life may well know that both of my children have contested me in court over matters that had not a thing to do with my lawsuit against Stanley Stahl. These were petty, intra-family squabbles over the interests in my business I'd given them, and over Rachel's attempt to become Zipora's legal guardian instead of me.

And yet, while Morgenthau was not the cause of these personal matters, I believe he sought to use them to muddy the waters of my courtroom wars with Stahl. Indeed, I have no reason not to believe that Morgenthau encouraged these cases being brought to trial (where they all were adjudicated in my favor). I fervently believe others were put up to suing me—again, never have I filed suit against my children, and I brought Elie back to work with me in the mid-1990s. but Rachel was suing me. Doing Stahl's bidding, Morgenthau clearly encouraged these intra-family battles, the better to further damage my reputation and to allow his hand-picked judges to consolidate unrelated lawsuits into the Stahl docket. Doing just that, my original suit against Stahl was all but unrecognizable by the mid-1980s.

All the while, Morgenthau was serving not the interests of justice but of Stanley Stahl. The Stahl mob is a nest of vipers. They look for a chink in the armor, an opening to do dirty business, and then they strike. And they exploited my children. With Rachel, it was my anger that she had turned her back on Judaism, which I have fought so hard to preserve, and converted to Christianity. Using this wedge, they inveigled her to sue me for a greater percentage share of my business, even though through no work of her own she has profited handsomely; as an officer strictly on paper, she has been enriched by millions of dollars. Later still, Morgenthau would use Rachel as a pawn even more insidiously.

Morgenthau's role was to work hand in hand with Stahl's lawyer, David Rosenberg, to find the right judge to continually rule against me. This was how Gammerman took over the case and why he sat on the case for a decade without holding a single hearing. This was also why he would automatically issue motions requested by Rosenberg without notifying me to appear in court—and then threaten to find me in contempt for not being there! My objections were routinely slapped down without comment, often without my lawyers being notified.

Not by coincidence, many of these rulings occurred while I was preoccupied and under the shroud of the two criminal cases Morgenthau was orchestrating. I had scant time to breathe after the mistrial in the tax fraud case before I was right back in the courtroom, on trial on the ludicrous charge of trying to have Stahl murdered.

Only one thing was missing when the trial got underway in October 1999, and that was Stanley Stahl himself. After years of ill health, he had died on August 5 at age seventy-five, apparently of a stroke.

Even though I was battling him so bitterly in court, I think I was the only person in the world who was genuinely saddened by Stanley's death. As I've said, I had no personal grudge against him, and I still valued our long relationship. For all his faults, and mine, we had one of the most successful businesses in the world and oversaw the best buildings in New York, buildings Donald Trump could only have dreamed about owning. Not only was I saddened when he died but I was outraged by the fact that even before his body was cold, his own associates were manipulating his estate for their own greedy purposes.

For example, in their obituary of Stahl, *The New York Times* took note that Stahl's real estate holdings totaled around four million square feet of office space and residential buildings with more than 3,000 apartments and "numerous" retail buildings, and then placed his net worth at $430 million. In truth, Stahl's net worth from these holdings and his ownership of the Apple Bank was somewhere in the neighborhood of five to ten *billion* dollars, but the Probate Court was "persuaded" to set the estate at $500,000, saving Stahl's successors millions of dollars in taxes.

This was the handiwork of two men who were the trustees of Stahl's empire, a couple of lawyers named Richard Czaja and Gregg Wolpert, whom Stahl had hand-picked and groomed to take over his business, Stahl Real Estate Company, of which Czaja now became executive vice-president. (In his will, Stahl left Czaja no less than $1 million and Wolpert $750,000 *per year*.) Obviously, a good part of their grooming was how to continue Stahl's war of personal destruction against me. Because the moment Stahl's heart stopped,

Czaja and Wolpert, with no legal authority, elevated themselves into Partners in Stahl Associates.

Again, you may call me *meshuga* or paranoid, but something about Stahl's death did not smell right to my famously educated nose. I have known many people in the world of cut-throat business who would do literally anything to get their hands on a $5 billion pot of gold. Could Czaja and Wolpert be among this crowd? Could they have actually had Stahl killed, doing what Morgenthau had accused me of wanting to do? I wondered because I was told that, rather than being sick at the time of his demise, Stanley had been in rather good health. The night before, he had gone for a brisk swim at a health club where I have many friends.

If Czaja and Wolpert, or anyone else, had gotten rid of Stahl—and I have no proof this—then the remaining piece of the puzzle was to get rid of the surviving Managing Partner of Stahl Associates: Abe Hirschfeld.

Their strategy to do just that, in fact, would become crystal clear during Morgenthau's second attempt to put me in jail.

When the criminal solicitation trial began, Morgenthau's stooge, Assistant DA Gilda Mariani, laid out the case against me. I had had a preview of their bogus arguments when I testified before the grand jury that Morgenthau had called to rubber-stamp his indictment. I did this, by the way, against the advice of my lawyer, who didn't want me saying anything that could be used against me at the trial. But I had nothing to protect, nothing to hide; all I ever can do in these persecutions is to tell the truth to real people—working people—who understand me.

Mariani's line of questioning, which would be repeated almost word for word during the trial, went like this:

Q. Mr. Hirschfeld, did you ever tell anyone that you wanted Stanley Stahl murdered?

A. No.

Q. Did you tell anyone anything that could be interpreted that you wanted Stanley Stahl murdered?

A. I don't know such a thing....

Q. Did you pay anyone money to find someone to kill Mr. Stahl?

A. No.

Q. Did you—did anyone ask you or tell you that they could find somebody to kill Mr. Stahl?

A. No.

Q. Did anyone suggest to you that a way to deal with the dispute you were having is to have Mr. Stahl murdered?

A. I never had this discussion.

Q. With anybody?

A. With anybody.

Q. Did you ever say to anybody that you wanted Mr. Stahl taken care of?

A. The best thing that I can do is say that Mr. Stahl should live forever. I make millions and millions with him without investing a penny. He really made me what I am...

Q. Did you ever give Mr. Veltri any money to find somebody to murder Mr. Stahl?

A. No.....

Q. Did you ever tell Mr. Veltri that you wanted Mr. Stahl hurt?

A. No.

Q. That you wanted him scared?

A. No.

Q. That you wanted him shaken up?

A. No.

Q. Did you ever discuss with Rosemary Singer whether or not you paid money to anybody to murder Mr. Stahl?

A. No.

Then she badgered me about those tape-recorded remarks I'd made to Rosemary about Joe Veltri's extortion demands, which as I pointed out, exonerated me:

Q. Mr. Hirschfeld, do you remember that conversation?

A. Yes . . . I remember this conversation with Singer....[S]he tried to tell me [Veltri] is going to the newspaper [or] maybe to [the DA]. I said, let [him] go to all of them....

[Veltri] tried to threaten me to go to the paper, to write to you people. I said go wherever the hell you want....The conversation [struck] me, why the hell would such a conversation be. I couldn't figure it out….It was very strange….I just thought it was some kind of a crank or whatever…..[S]omething was suspicious going on.

I also knew, and told Mariani, that Veltri had been put up to it by Rosemary Singer—Morgenthau's big pawn:

Q. On the tape you called Joe Veltri a thief. What did you mean he's a thief?

A. It was a complete misunderstanding. Rosemary was the thief; she was pushing me into it…into pushing me for money. You have to give him money. You have to do this. You have to do that. And I thought it came from Joe Veltri, but it came from Rosemary. [It was all] based on Rosemary's conversation with me. Before I knew what Rosemary was [doing] I told you, he's an honest man. He worked well with me. We worked for twenty years. We never had a problem, but it was all Rosemary's manipulations….I [now]understand Rosemary's a crook….She probably influenced him into it.

Q. What kind of conversation did she have with you or did Mr. Veltri have with you about money?

A. I told her each time she told me about money. I told Rosemary he should go to hell. Rosemary should have gone to hell….

Q. But on this tape, you admit you gave him money….When did you give him money?

A. I was always giving Joe Veltri money. I gave him bonuses. I give my employees good money.

Q. Mr. Hirschfeld, on the transcript you said he wants to push me for more money. That means you gave him money with respect to something. What did you give him money for?

A. When he finished 21 Hudson Street . . . I gave him seventy-five thousand. I gave Randy Daniels fifty thousand, [he's] the number-three man in the state….

Q. Mr. Hirschfeld, this conversation you're having with Rosemary Singer is a conversation about murdering Stanley Stahl, about him going to the newspaper about a story that you wanted to kill Stanley Stahl. So, what money did you give him in connection with that?

A. I didn't give any money in connection with it.

Q. Do you remember giving Mr. Veltri seventy-five thousand dollars in cash?

A. Yes.

Q. Do you remember anybody else in the room with you?

A. I don't know.

Q. Do you remember what time of day it was?

A. People can go in and out of my room all the time....

Q. What did Mr. Veltri do with the money when you gave it to him? Did he put it in his pocket, in a briefcase?

A. I didn't pay attention.

Q. You didn't pay attention.

A. It's none of my business.

Q. Well, he's in the middle of New York City walking out with seventy-five thousand dollars in cash. Weren't you interested to know where he's going to put this money?

A. It's not my business. It's his money.

Q. How thick is seventy-five thousand dollars in cash?

A. I don't know.

Q. Was it thick? Could you put it in a wallet?

A. I don't know.

Q. Were they hundred dollar bills?

A. I don't know. I could have told you I gave him ten thousand, but I tell you what I give.

Mariani questioned me for six hours on nonsense like this, continually trying to twist the words Rosemary had put in my mouth. I had a simple, unwavering defense.

"I did not want to pay, and I didn't pay anybody to kill nobody," I said, and no Morgenthau pawn was going to prove otherwise.

I even turned the tables on Mariani. Whenever she had me listen to the tapes, I picked out nuggets from the transcript that showed I was innocent. This was one such moment:

Q. Mr. Hirschfeld, did you hear that?

A. No, but I want to read it out loud.... "I never wanted him to go through with the murder."

[That] means I didn't [and that] he goes to jail for soliciting money for such a purpose....

He's the one who is guilty.

Perhaps knowing how flimsy the case was, she finally got to Morgenthau's "ace in the hole," which was nothing more than his Big Lie.

Q. [I]f Stanley Stahl were murdered you would be sole managing partner. You could sell the building[s], isn't that right?

A. No, it's wrong. Why don't I read you the agreement? I cannot do nothing. There's a special clause...number twelve, about death, which shows exactly that nobody gets nothing by death. Here it is. Signed by all the partners....Page twelve will tell you that nobody has benefit in my death or [Stahl's].

This was the trial balloon, so to speak, for Morgenthau's desperate attempt to find a motive for me wanting to murder Stahl—that there was a "survivor takes all" clause in the partnership agreement Stanley and I had signed in 1975. In truth, there was no such clause; in fact, as I told the grand jury, it says so specifically on page twelve of the agreement. Here is how the clause reads:

Upon the death of any partner, unless the interest in the Partnership of the decedent passes to a member of his immediate family, the surviving partners shall purchase the decedent's interest in the Partnership from his legal representative, pro rata according to their respective interests in the Partnership at the date of death of said partner. The purchase price shall be equal to the "fair market value."

In other words, I had not a penny to gain from Stahl's death, and in fact, this was put to the test when he did die and I did *not* get his interest in the partnership—nor did I claim it. Yet, how shameless and disingenuous was Morgenthau to use this canard at the very same time that Czaja and Wolpert were *breaking* the agreement illegally, since the agreement also clearly states:

No interest of any Partner may be sold, assigned or transferred [other than to] a spouse, son(s), daughters(s), sister(s), brother(s), mother or father...Any purported assignment which does not comply with [this] provision shall be null and void and of no legal effect whatsoever unless approved of in writing by all the Partners.

Stahl's death, then, meant that I was indeed the only Managing Partner left, and while I had no right to claim Stahl's 50 percent interest in Stahl Associates, I did retain the right to *buy* his share at "fair market value" from his surviving *blood relatives*, who would inherit his interest. Yet, not only had Czaja and Wolpert—who shared not a drop of blood with Stanley Stahl—made themselves full-fledged partners, they named another man I'd never heard of, James Matera, *co-Managing Partner,* not of Stahl Associates but of *Hirstan* Associates, which I operated with Stanley but managed by myself.

At first, I thought perhaps Matera could have been a blood relative of Stahl, until I read in the *Times'* Stahl obituary that he had a stepdaughter named Simi Matera; James Matera was her husband, meaning that he was Stanley's son *in-law.* And so here were three no-blood relatives illegally hoarding all of Stahl Associates' money, including that which was due me, and refusing me my right to buy Stahl's interest at *any* price. Their whole thing stank like rancid lox.

Of course, when all this became clear, I filed an immediate motion with Judge Gammerman to void these "promotions." Knowing exactly how Gammerman would rule—against me—Czaja and Wolpert did not even wait for the ruling before they made other illegal moves. They pressured and threatened Citibank to close all of my accounts, not just those related to Stahl and Hirstan Associates, but *all* of my accounts. They also diverted Stahl and Hirstan Associates mail addressed to me from my office to *their* office, advising the U.S. Postal Service with magnificent arrogance that because Stahl had been the *de facto* Managing Partner of Stahl and Hirstan Associates, the mail had to be kept from me, claiming with no supporting evidence that I was no longer Managing Partner!

Czaja and Wolpert were right to be smugly confident of Gammerman's eventual ruling. Amazingly, but hardly unpredictably, this crook of a judge quietly and automatically ruled that these two smarmy bandits could do all of the things they had done!

I could feel the walls closing in on me. I was trapped in an Alice in Wonderland of nefarious DAs and judges patently ignoring illegalities and established procedures. It was getting harder to keep my resolve. Like Zipora, my own health was failing—during the trial, I was diagnosed with skin cancer, and I was always a step from fainting in exhaustion.

But I am a fighter. And whenever Gilda Mariani took the floor, my resolve stiffened. If she wasn't stumbling and bumbling, she was threatening me with contempt of court motions. Always, she was mocking and rude to me, leading me to tell her, "Ms. Mariani, let us be human beings," in vain, as it turned out. Once, before the grand jury, when a nice man on the jury asked a very good question, she shushed him, saying the question was "irrelevant."

"Excuse me," I said. "This man is entitled to ask a question. He's a gentleman. He makes an honest living, and you don't."

Though the grand jury was ordered to indict me, I knew they were on my side. As was the jury in the trial. Never did Mariani get anywhere, and she blew it big time when on October 5 she put her "star witness," Joe Veltri, on the stand.

It would have been great fun for me to have torn apart Veltri's story—which was, of course, Morgenthau's story—on the stand, but unfortunately, Morgenthau had learned he had to keep me from representing myself. That became clear when State Supreme Court Justice Harold Beeler, who presided at the trial, began his reign of terror. I came before Beeler in good faith to request a hearing on what is called the Huntley Law. This statute explicitly says that one cannot be the subject of a wiretap unless he or she is notified in advance. Had Beeler given me an honest hearing, he would have automatically invalidated Rosemary Singer's tape recordings. Instead, he refused to rule *at all,* a cowardly way of avoiding the issue altogether so that the tapes would be heard in the retrial.

What is more, Beeler would not let me come to any session without a lawyer—a blatant violation of the Fifth, Sixth, and Fourteenth Amendments to the U.S. Constitution. Every American, of course, has the right to represent himself in a court of law. But, with Morgenthau and his judges, I learned, no law is sacred or enforceable. They don't live in the same America that you and I do.

So, I watched from my seat in horror and pity as a good man who had been ensnared by Rosemary Singer and bullied by Robert Morgenthau make a fool of himself.

Morgenthau and Mariani had hauled Veltri into their office twenty times to drill him on what to say on the stand. They stripped him of his immunity from prosecution when they'd brought him before the grand jury and forbid him to have his own lawyer, which is unheard of. Any slip-up, any deviation from their bullshit story, they said, and they'd put him in jail.

All that bullying backfired. On the stand, even during direct examination being guided and spoon-fed by Mariani, Veltri was a jumble of nerves—sweating, stammering, and hardly able to speak without knowing if he was digging his own grave. It no doubt enraged

Morgenthau and Mariani that he was so unconvincing, despite their best efforts to coach him.

Veltri tried to stick to the farcical cock and bull scenario scripted for him: that I had given him that $75,000 not as a bonus for his work but for him to meet up with a shadowy, unidentified "hit man" waiting on the corner of 26th Street and Seventh Avenue South in a black Lincoln Continental with, of course, black-tinted windows.

According to this stranger-than-truth tale—which would have been rejected in two seconds by *NYPD Blue* as too silly—Veltri, saying, "This is from Mr. Hirschfeld," slips the envelope through a two-inch opening of the window, whereupon a mysterious man looks in the envelope, counts the money, and, in "a rough voice," (no doubt like Edward G. Robinson in *Little Caesar*) tells Veltri, "It's less than half" of the $75,000 and "There are no pictures," and orders him to go back to me for the rest. So now, two weeks later, I give Veltri *another* envelope—this time with another $75,000, two photographs of Stahl, his address, phone number, and license plate number (which I never knew), and Veltri goes back for another clandestine meeting on 26th Street and hands it to the now presumably contented hit man.

But wait, it gets better. Now it seems Veltri is getting very nervous about what he has done and begins calling me day after day, threatening that he will go to the press and the DA, and tells me, "You put yourself in the middle of an ocean." And I tell him, "You put yourself in the middle of the ocean," and to go to hell. (Not by surprise, Veltri's story includes nothing about his extortion demands.) So, now he decides to ring up not the authorities or the press but Stanley Stahl to tell him about the "hit" that never happened. Stahl, in turn, calls his buddy Morgenthau, who erects his *grand bouffe* of a bad story using as "evidence" Rosemary Singer's tainted tapes.

One can almost palpably feel the pressure Morgenthau must have been under from Stanley Stahl to come up with *something* he could get a jury to believe. In the real world, however, the reason I had given Veltri a photograph of Stahl and his address was a much less harrowing story. What happened was that I had designs on buying the building where Stahl lived, 923 Park Avenue. Because I would have again used Joe Veltri as my construction manager in refurbishing the building, Joe wanted a picture of Stahl so he would know who he was and be able to talk to him about the building's condition, such as its asbestos situation given the building's old age.

Mundane, but true. And compared to this simple, credible explanation—denied by Veltri under oath, which was a clear case of perjury—Morgenthau's story was rendered ridiculous from the get-go.

Indeed, even while being steered by Mariani to give answers they had rehearsed for weeks, Veltri cracked open like a three-minute egg. How sure was Veltri that I'd wanted to have Stahl killed? Not very, it turned out. Read the transcript of these parts of the *direct* examination, which came before my lawyer even began his cross-examination, and ask yourself that question.

Q. Did the defendant, Mr. Hirschfeld, ever ask you to do anything that was unusual?

A. Yes....He asked me if I knew anybody that wanted to take care of one of his partners that was giving him a lot of trouble. I answered him; I said are you crazy?...I walk away. I walked out.

Q. You were in his office at the time?

A. Yes.

Q. Was anybody else around you when he said that?

A. At that time, no. We were walking through to the corridor.

Q. Did he say it in a loud voice?

A. No, not loud. Just when you talked to somebody, very low.

Q. Did he tell you who the partner was?

A. No.

Q. Did he say some kind of problem or trouble?

A. He was giving him a lot of trouble.

Q. Did he explain what that was, what trouble?

A. No....

Q. Mr. Veltri, he said what to you?

A. He says can you do me a favor. Can you take care of—I have a lot of problems....I answered him. I said, you think I am Italian and every Italian is in the Mafia?...I says you are crazy.

Q. When you said this, taken care of. What did you understand that to mean?

A. *My understanding* is he wanted to kill somebody. To take care of somebody. [Emphasis added]

On cross-examination, my lawyer, Arthur Aidala, plucked Veltri like a prize turkey.

Q. By carrying an envelope that you didn't know what was inside of it, you [felt you] did something wrong? [For example] Did you know if that envelope you were carrying was being handed over to an agent for one of the top models in New York City?

A. At that time, no.

Q. Correct. So that envelope and that conversation could pertain to anything, right?

A. No.

Q. Could "taking care" of Stahl have possibly meant bribing him?

A. That's not my *interpretation.* [Emphasis added]

Q. Is that your common sense or is it all your assumptions, which one is it?

A. I don't know how you want to put it. *Common sense is it looks like a hit to me.*

[Emphasis added]...

Q. But you didn't think it was important enough to consult an attorney?

A. First of all, I couldn't afford an attorney. Second of all, I was telling the truth.

Then came Veltri's lie about when he first knew of the $75,000, and the $300,000 "plot."

Q. You spoke with the Prosecutor about $75,000 being in that envelope that you delivered, correct?...

A. That's what I told her.

Q. And you [said] you knew it was $75,000 because the guy in the car told you it was $75,000, right?

A. Yes....

Q. Do you remember [during grand jury testimony] being asked this question and giving this answer:

"QUESTION: The first time you knew there was money in there was when?

"ANSWER: When the guy tell me this is not even half."

Do you remember being asked that question and giving that answer?

A. Yes.

Q. Do you remember being asked this question:

373

"QUESTION: Did you know how much money—did you ever learn how much money was in the envelope?

"ANSWER: It was $75,000."

Do you remember being asked that question and giving that answer?

A. Yes, sir.

Q. Do you remember being asked this question:

"QUESTION: Who did you learn that from?

"ANSWER: I think from Mr. Hirschfeld."

Do you remember being asked that question and giving that answer?

A. It could have been but....

Q. Do you remember being asked this question:

"QUESTION: Did [the man in the car] tell you how much was not even half?

"ANSWER: No, he didn't tell me how much exactly."

And that was approximately one year ago when you testified in the Grand Jury after this took place, yes?

A. Yes, sir.

Q. So it is fair to say that your memory was more clear than it is now?

A. No....

Q. So two years ago when you testified in the Grand Jury you [said] the person in the car did not tell you how much money was in the envelope, correct?

A. The first time, yes.

This refers to the fact that Veltri was rushed back by Morgenthau and Mariani for a second stint before the grand jury—at which point he changed his story.

Q. After you testified in the Grand Jury the first time...did you meet with Ms. Mariani after that?

A. I think I met her once. I'm not sure....

Q. On that morning you spoke with the Prosecutor?

A. Yes.

Q. And then you went in and testified again, right?

A. Yes.

Q. When you went in and you testified that you changed your story, right?

374

A. Well, I told her that I forgot to mention that because I just—the first time I ever went to the Grand Jury, I was a little nervous.

Q. So on the two different times when the Prosecutor asked you in the Grand Jury where the money was, how much money there was in the envelope, you gave the wrong answer because you were nervous?

A. Not really. I have never been in front of the Grand Jury before in my life....

Q. How long after you testified the first time in the Grand Jury...did you realize that you lied to the Grand Jury?

MS. MARIANI: Objection, your honor.

THE COURT: The objection is sustained.

Q. How long after you testified did you realize you mischaracterized the truth to the Grand Jury?

MS. MARIANI: Objection.

THE COURT: Sustained.

Q. How long after that time did you realize you made a tremendously big mistake as to when—

MS. MARIANI: Objection.

THE COURT: Sustained.

Q. When did you find out you were wrong when you said I found out from Mr. Hirschfeld it was $75,000 and instead it was from the guy, the voice from the car?

MS. MARIANI: Objection.

THE COURT: Overruled.

A. Right after.

Q. As soon as you walked out of the room?

A. When I went home. I said I made a mistake....

Q. Where did you hear that there was a $300,000 contract on Mr. Stahl's life?

A. I was *just assuming that* . . . I didn't jump to any conclusions. I went right to the facts. *It's my opinion.* [Emphasis added]

The rest was easy. Indeed, Gilda Mariani, in her closing statement, made a rather odd request to the jury.

"You don't have to believe Mr. Veltri alone," she said, effectively blowing off her star witness.

It was apparent that Judge Beeler was deeply concerned the jury would go my way, and he was determined to put me in jail himself, one way or another. Two days before the case went to the jury on October 20, this pompous ass—who had placed me under a gag order so I could not talk to the media—called in the same media and recycled Judge Bruce Allen's insipid moaning about my "jury tampering."

What sparked this tantrum was that, as in the previous trial, ads had appeared attesting to my innocence in the *Daily News, Post,* and two Manhattan weeklies, *The Resident* and *The Spirit.* Though I did not pay for these ads—they were placed by a close friend of mine from Israel, Abraham Alcalay—I was nonetheless happy to see them because the gag order was patently unfair and an intrusion of my right to free speech. If I couldn't talk, these print ads could speak for me. They didn't even need to use my own words; instead, what ran was merely a reprint of an October 7 *Daily News* article headlined, "I assumed Hirschfeld wanted hit, sez witness"—referring to Joe Veltri's admissions that he had no knowledge of the alleged "hit" against Stahl, that he'd only "assumed" it existed, in his "opinion."

Beeler, feigning outrage, vowed to "get to the bottom" of the ads and to put me in jail for criminal contempt if he found out I was responsible for them.

But, first, Beeler had to suffer, as Bruce Allen had, when after four days of deliberations the jury was still out. Two days later, October 26, Beeler became infuriated when I came to court wearing a yarmulke and prayer shawl, reading the Bible. I did not do this for attention or sympathy. I pray every morning, and I had been summoned to court very early that day because the jury was expected to give its decision. Even so, Beeler, in his lowest form of indignity, ordered me to remove the shawl and to *stop reading the Bible* when the jury was in the room.

Yes, this is a man who believes reading a Bible is tampering with a jury!

Later in the day, the jury filed back in and announced that they were hopelessly deadlocked. Another trial, another hung jury, another mistrial. I was now two-for-two against the assembled forces of Stanley Stahl and Robert Morgenthau. And though, again, I knew Morgenthau would try to find a fixed jury to retry the case for, I hoped against all hope that he would now end this sick crusade.

After all, Morgenthau wasn't fooling anyone anymore. The *Times'* story the next day read,"(J)urors who favored acquittal said there were many holes in the prosecution's case and that Mr. Hirschfeld was a victim of a prosecutorial vendetta." Does that sound familiar? Those were the very words used by Morgan Godwin in blasting Morgenthau's case in the tax fraud trial. One of the jurors in this case, a middle-school teacher named Thelma Hines, told the *Times,* "It was a railroad. The defense did a great job."

I was so gratified and relieved by the verdict that I could not keep myself from crying the moment it was announced. All those terrible long hours of stress and worry were over, at least for now. I walked down the courthouse steps a free man, weeping uncontrollably, leaving it to Artie Aidala to sum up my summer and autumn of torture and humiliation succinctly.

"When you look at the two cases, the tax case and this case, and the contempt charge," he said, "it's very obvious that the New York County District Attorney's office is focused on one thing: putting Abe Hirschfeld in jail."

Those words, sadly, would prove prophetic.

Abraham (Abe) Hirschfeld

CHAPTER THIRTY-ONE: BLIND, DEAF, AND DUMB JUSTICE

After my two victories in Morgenthau's war of lies, I had no intention of shriveling up and waiting idly for the double-dealing DA to come after me again. Having spent a solid year under his dirty thumb, I was ready to live my life once more and make up for lost time. The first order of business wasn't business at all; it was my unrequited yen for public service. The prize: the U.S. Senate seat I'd had my eye on since my old foil Daniel Patrick Moynihan announced he was retiring.

While Morgenthau and his partners in crime—including my new, illegal "business partners"—no doubt expected I would not be able to present my priceless solutions for world peace and to remedy the problems facing New York State, by late August 1999, I was running for the seat and building great momentum. I was truly gratified by the number of people who were eager for new ideas and amazed at the outpouring of sympathy for me because of how I'd been hounded by Morgenthau.

Suddenly, Abe Hirschfeld was a "hot commodity." Television stations that had avoided me like the plague were sticking microphones in my face wanting my take on current affairs. As always, I had much to say and did. I even had a startling prediction that few thought possible, given the booming state of the economy at the time.

"There will be a recession in two years and a depression in five," I said, adding that these things need not happen. "I have a plan that will make America recession-proof. I have single-handedly taken the country out of two recessions, and I can put my plan into effect within six months." Of course, the first part of that equation would sadly come to pass, as will the second unless those plans are heeded.

If you want to know if I have political clout, ask Al D'Amato, because he's still feeling its sting.

The man they called "Senator Pothole" for his alleged ability to get federal money for New York to fix the notorious craters on the city's streets, ran for his third term in 1999. As election day neared in November, I believed D'Amato had betrayed New York State by spending so much time in his role as Senate Judiciary Committee chairman investigating Bill Clinton's land deals and sex escapades. I also resented him for backstabbing me. I had helped elect him twice,

379

yet when I was on trial and needed powerful supporters, he shunned me.

I used to. believe Al D'Amato was an independent man, a maverick like me. But he became far too comfortable in the seat of power, and obsessed by political self-preservation, he was now just another tired old bolt in the corrupt Pataki-Giuliani-Morgenthau machine. It was high time to put him out to pasture, even if it meant the sure election of a Democrat, Charles Schumer, whom I considered no more than a vacuous publicity-seeking lightweight with no *sechel*—a Yiddish term for "sense." Yet, right up until election day, D'Amato was well ahead in the polls.

On election eve, I was interviewed by Channel 5, and I'm sure D'Amato expected a ringing vote of confidence from me. Instead, he got a ringing non-endorsement. I said that for the good of the state and the nation, he should be defeated. Within hours, the polls completely turned around and Chuck Schumer was elected convincingly. Again, I can take my bow.

A few days later, on November 9, I announced my own candidacy with a speech at LeCirque. It was a speech I had been itching to make for what seemed like forever. I began:

"My reason for running is I believe that I am the best qualified person...in terms of what is needed for New York in the 21st century. I have the track record to prove it, and I am not part of the dominant ruling class of America today—lawyers. By contrast with my prospective opponents Hillary Clinton and Rudy Giuliani, both lawyers, I am a builder, a job creator, and an inventor. The new millennium will call for new, innovative solutions to the major concerns of our time, such as universal healthcare, high quality education, housing for all Americans, and good jobs for everyone who wants and needs employment . . . . I think—in fact, I know—it is time to have people from all walks of life involved in the running of this country. It is time to break up the dominating monopoly in city, state, and federal government, namely lawyers....

"Prior to the last forty years, people from every profession were involved in government. Farmers, craftsmen, and journalists—everybody could be found. At that time, we had a government for the people and of the people. Today, we have a government of the lawyers, by the lawyers, and for the lawyers.

What makes lawyers' participation in government any better than anyone else's? Nothing!

"Today, we have the greatest building technology the world has ever known. Yet, they cannot build the Second Avenue Subway in eighty years. Ninety years ago, the subway system was built by people working for the most part with picks and shovels. And they built the best subway system in the world in four to six years. I can do the job I propose in one or two years. Today, we have powerful earth-moving equipment that can literally replace thousands of people working with primitive tools. So, why can't the Second Avenue Subway be built? I will tell you why: because of special interest groups and their lawyers. And lawyers seek only to create chaos, not order."

Among my platform ideas were:

* Full employment at a living wage.
* Full medical and pension benefits for all Americans.
* My practical method for raising perfect children.
* Utilization of my high-speed Bullet Train to create fast and efficient urban rail networks.
* A national urban redevelopment dedicated to eliminating slums by creating low-cost, livable housing.
* Converting the decrepit New York Coliseum of 59th Street into an elegant, Off-Track Betting gambling casino, lowering taxes and creating hundreds of well-paid jobs for minority workers.
* Construction of a new, elevated Robert Moses Westside Highway in two years that would relieve the congestion of the mess created by George Pataki when he tore down Moses' brilliant design and left the western edge of Manhattan in ruins. Today one cannot walk to the edge of the Hudson River because Pataki removed Moses' elevated highway and ran it along the edge of the river. As a builder and planner, who do you trust, Moses or Pataki? We must revive the Moses plan.
* Proven solutions to the drug and crime problem.

One thing you can never say about Abe Hirschfeld is that he is a conventional politician. And if anyone needed any confirmation of that, there was my line about Hillary Clinton.

"If she can't please one man," I said impishly at every stop, "how can she please a whole state?"

I had no jokes about George Pataki, but much bitterness, as was displayed in my speeches. I had every intention of running for the Republican nomination, and had I done so I would have had much ammunition against Rudy Giuliani. Of course, Rudy pulled out of the race when he was diagnosed with prostate cancer, leaving the nomination wide open. That logically should have been Pataki's cue, as the nominal leader of the GOP in the state, to come to me and pledge his support. But logic is not the mother's milk of politics, and of politicians like Pataki.

As with Mario Cuomo, Pataki – whose election would not have happened but for my endorsement in 1994 – never followed through on his promises to consult me. And if Cuomo had been unresponsive to my plans for selling the state office space in New York City, Pataki was absolutely barbaric in his opposition to my ideas. One such idea, in particular, sent him into a psychotic rage. This happened when I was close to acquiring the old Altman's Department Store premises on 34th Street. This was a landmark building, a huge space running the entire block from Fifth Avenue to Sixth Avenue. It would have made a splendid state office building, in a high-visibility area. Given the depressed economy, the price tag, I found, was quite affordable, less than $10 million. However, as I closed in on the building, suddenly Pataki became obsessed with the building himself, yet had no intention of dealing with me for it. Instead, he wanted to shunt the building to one of his cronies (I'll say more about this later, because it is a very ugly tale of political corruption), and made it bluntly clear to me that I would have no part in any deal.

His injunction came in a phone call that I will always remember as the moment that George Pataki's Doctor Jekyll became Mr. Hyde. As soon as I heard his voice, I was stunned. His anger and lack of respect made him seem like a completely different man from the kind-hearted, soft-spoken Poughkeepsie mayor I had elected. Without even a perfunctory greeting, he launched right into a tirade.

"Abe, I want you to listen to me," he said, as if with the hissing of a rattlesnake. "Stay away from Altman's. You're making it difficult for us, and if you persist in trying to buy the building there's going to be trouble. Again, stay away."

With that, he hung up, leaving me speechless for one of the very few times in my life. I didn't quite know what to make of this bizarre threat from no less than the Governor himself. But I knew that without the state's partnership I would have little viable use for the Altman's property. I dropped my plans to acquire it and moved on.

Perhaps I should have purchased the place out of spite; after all, one does not threaten me and get away with it. It is my nature to fight, no matter the opponent.

However, in this case I was more saddened than emboldened. If there had been a man whom I believed could break the mold of corruption and sleaze that bathes the world of politics, it had been George Pataki. And now he had revealed *his* true colors. He was no less vile and bankrupt in his soul than Mario Cuomo. I am constantly saddened when I think of the gross waste of potential that is George Pataki, whose capitulation to the forces of greed and sell-interest suggests the fall of Caesar. For me, my relationship with him can be summed up in three words:

"Eh tu, Pataki?"

The fallout with Pataki meant there was zero chance I could get the GOP nomination. And so, as the certain Independence Party candidate, I set out on my latest quixotic campaign of ideas—not in a private plane but in a red, white, and blue motor home. My first stop was in Buffalo, which typified all of upstate New York and its problems. This grand old city was dying from the neglect of George Pataki and the state's congressional delegation. Standing in downtown Buffalo amid vacant office buildings, I shook my head in disgust.

"This is the most beautiful downtown I've ever seen," I told a large media turnout. "They have astonishing assets, but what good is gold if you don't mine it?"

Having revitalized so many blighted neighborhoods, I felt right at home. A renaissance in Buffalo, and in all of upstate New York, could happen, if I could find builders like me willing to invest in garbage, garbage, garbage. As senator, I would persuade the state government to move some of its offices into the city, which would boost property values, as had been the case when I'd sold office space to the DEA. In Buffalo, office space was renting for $10 a square foot. What a bargain that would be to the government, and that investment would spread as it had in Tribeca, with new stores, restaurants, and businesses. Everyone would benefit from a better economy.

My message was getting through, and as I looked down the road, I saw clear sailing to victory in November.

And so, of course, as was the case whenever things looked promising for me, my enemies conspired to throw a monkey wrench into the works, no matter who would suffer for it.

In July, after I had officially secured the Independence Party nomination, Judge Harold Beeler finally decided the time was right to find me responsible for the heinous "crime" of having left a newspaper on a bench during the first criminal solicitation trial. Rigging a fixed "non-jury trial," he found me guilty of criminal contempt of court. He would hold a fixed hearing on March 8 to decide if he would send me to jail, though my only question was "how long?"

Not that I had any intention, again, of putting my full and varied life on hold until then. My campaign went ahead, as did my renewed show business plans. As I began my eighth decade on earth, I was just beginning to do the things I'd wanted to do for so many years. Foremost among them was to produce a movie. The *Phantom of the Opera* video had broken the ice, and now as I looked toward a full-length feature film. I traced a similar path by adapting another of my properties, *The Prince of Central Park,* into a screenplay.

As I've mentioned, the failure of the Broadway production of the play may have broken my heart but it did not prevent me from wanting the world to see this wonderful New York tale of a young man's coming of age amid family crises and unknown dangers. I was intent on getting it filmed and in the late 1990s, I began looking for a star to take top billing. Finally, I chose Steven Seagal, who had made all those violence-soaked "action" movies. Even though I am not a fan of those pulp movies, I saw in Seagal something more subtle and inscrutable, a guy who had inner vulnerabilities, which made him perfect for the part of the mysterious "Guardian," the park-dweller who befriends the young runaway, J.J. Somerled.

Seagal liked the script and the idea of playing a role with more depth, and I was willing to go along with anything he wanted, including teaming up with producer Jules Nasso, with whom he had made some of his big action pictures. I knew little of Nasso, but I was impressed with how he used his influence to get the movie into production. By late 1999, we had hired the rest of the cast: Kathleen

Turner, Cathy Moriarity, and Danny Aiello, as well as Nasso's teenage son, Frankie, a fine young actor, in the J.J. role.

As the project was structured, I was executive producer, and I made Karen Poindexter, who had of course produced the show at the Hirschfeld Theater in 1990, co-producer. Pre-production began with our director John Leekley, who wrote the screenplay, ready and eager to oversee his first feature film. Everything was on schedule—everything, that is, except Steven Seagal.

For weeks, the production was bogged down because Seagal kept saying he had other business to attend to. "Tomorrow," he would tell me, "tomorrow for sure." But tomorrow always turned into another tomorrow. Then one day he told me his mother was sick, and he was dropping out of the picture. Of course, everyone was enraged, and it killed Steven's relationship with Nasso.

It also ruined my picture. We did get it made, replacing Seagal with one of my favorite bad-guy-with-a-good-heart actors, Harvey Keitel. Harvey did a creditable job on very short notice, but the chemistry we'd had with Seagal was lost. When the movie came out in 2000, it was received as a noble effort to depict gritty family drama—told from the viewpoint of a troubled teenager—but it was not the same movie I had envisioned. Of incidental concern, at least to me, it didn't make much money at the box office, although it has done well in the video market.

That made it two times I had struck out with *Prince of Central Park*. But it did teach me a valuable lesson about Hollywood and betrayal by actors with oversized egos. I have steered clear of the pitfalls as I have embarked upon my next movie project—which will be a hip-hop version of my *Phantom of the Opera*. The concept has brought me a flood of calls from many movie big shots, and with reason since I expect that when it is made, hopefully within the next year or two, it will break all box office records. However, I am consciously steering clear of known actors in favor of young, unknown talent. The lucky ones whom I choose will become instant stars from this breakout vehicle. And that will give me greater satisfaction than trading on any actor's name.

The saga of *Prince of Central Park* didn't end there. In fact, its epilogue is that Steven Seagal's rift with Jules Nasso has mushroomed into a drama worthy of any movie, especially if it's a gangster movie. In 2003, Seagal accused Nasso of being involved with the Columbo crime family—whom he said had been trying to muscle in on the movie industry. Seagal claimed the "wiseguys" threatened him into making more movies for Nasso and paying out $3 million in protection money, I assume to keep his legs from being broken or his handsome face in one piece—and sued Nasso for damages.

However, Steven may have a vivid imagination or a serious problem with reality. When he testified in court, even his own friends called him delusional. But then, I've been called the same thing, so I will reserve judgment. All I know is, this alleged tough guy was less than a man in screwing me over, and as a result, his career is finished. That is some form of justice.

As for me, I moved on from that less than satisfying experience back to my first love: the theater. I thought a lot about the glory days and the Hirschfeld Theater, and now I felt I owed something to the good people of Florida who had been screwed by their own crooked politicians when the Clarion was shut down, and then by Jackie Mason's arrogance that killed *Love Thy Neighbor*.

I had, in fact, been waiting for ten years to revive my greatest production, *Phantom II of the Opera*. By early 2000, the time was right. The videotape made of the Florida Public TV presentation had by now become a cult classic. And, propitiously, Karen Poindexter had recently become executive producer at the Clematis Street Theater in West Palm Beach, and she was looking high and low for a good production to bring to the theater. Even so, after several weeks of auditioning singers in West Palm Beach, I could not go ahead with a *Phantom* revival until I found a leading lady who moved me with her voice and presence.

And then, as so often is the case in my life, God came to my aid. One Saturday morning I went to services at Temple Emanuel, the synagogue near my longtime beachfront condominium, and I happened to hear the voice of an angel. I looked up from my prayer book and saw a beautiful young woman singing the *kaddish* in the pulpit. I asked who she was and was told that she was the wife of the rabbi, Leonid Feldman, and she had never performed in a major stage production. Yet, right then and there, I was ready to reopen my pride and joy with a new leading lady named Melissa Feldman.

My agreement with Karen was that I would co-rent the theater with her for a two-month run of the show, from February 16 to April

16. And when we opened, within a week, nearly every performance of the run was sold out. The nice people of Palm Beach discovered what critic Jan Sjostrom of the *Palm Beach Daily News* had in her review: "Even if you think you've had enough of *Phantom of the Opera*," he wrote, "make room for more."

It occurred to me that the same thing could have been said about Abe Hirschfeld.

While the New York literati had pronounced me dead, a non-entity, and of course a hopelessly deluded *meshuga,* the people who streamed into the Clematis Street Theater literally could not get enough of me. The result of that adoration was good news for the show—and, indirectly, for George W. Bush.

Indeed, I do not exaggerate a smidgen by saying that I single-handedly elected him President of the United States.

No, I did not give him any money—nor did he need any from me, having raised stratospheric amounts of it from some of the country's biggest, and as it turned out, most corrupt corporate CEOs. My contribution was on the only level I work on: talking to people. I had decided by the spring of 2000 that Bush, a non-lawyer, was preferable to Al Gore, a lawyer. I believed Bush may not have been all that bright a man, but the truth is that no intellectual has ever been a strong leader of any nation in the world. The truly powerful leaders in history, good and bad, were not gifted with high intelligence. And I believed America needed a strong leader, one without artifices or a wall of lies to hide behind.

Then, too, while I could not abide the Republican Party in New York, given Pataki and Giuliani's constant attempts to defame me, I was held in high esteem by the national Republican Party. In 1999, in fact, after working for a number of GOP candidates nationwide, I was presented with a certificate of honor from the senate's top-ranking Republican leaders, John Ensign, Chairman of the Republican Roundtable, and Bill Frist, Chairman of the National Republican Senatorial Committee (soon to be Majority Leader).

So, I felt quite comfortable coming out for Bush, whose father I had known and liked, and who was kind enough to dedicate the DEA Building I had built in 1991. And just how did I elect his son? Again, by going to the people, 500 of whom came to see *Phantom II of the Opera.* These people were so overjoyed with the production, so personally affected, that when the curtain came down, they would stand and cheer for fifteen minutes. They would not sit down or leave unless the cast came back out and sang an encore.

That was my cue. Instead of the cast, out I came to thank them and to make them a deal: if they would promise to vote for George W. Bush in November, I would send the cast back out. They all said they would—and I'm sure you remember what happened on election day. Bush did unexpectedly well among the elderly Jewish residents in Palm Beach, and in the squeaker that election became, that made the difference for Bush in Florida and in the election. Some pundits attributed the Palm Beach anomaly to confusion stemming from the "butterfly ballot" that caused many to mistakenly vote for the anti-Semite Pat Buchanan. That may have been, but the *Phantom of the Opera* vote was what made the difference.

Unfortunately, in the months that followed, I would come to regret putting this man in the White House, for I saw very troubling signs that Bush and his bunch of arch-conservative, religious-right fundamentalists were going to destroy Israel with their insane mix of religion and world colonialism. But I will get to that.

Unfortunately, as well, my smash revival of *Phantom* marked my last triumph and was a temporary oasis of calm before the final nails were hammered into my legal coffin by the unscrupulous Robert Morgenthau, Richard Czaja, Gregg Wolpert, David Rosenberg, and their dutiful lackeys in the New York media, craven men like Mortimer Zuckerman, Rupert Murdoch, and Gary Rosenblatt, publisher of the *New York Jewish Weekly*, who refuse to publicize my Middle East peace treaty.

I can only imagine how irked Morgenthau and his overlords in the Stahl mob were by my glowing aura in Palm Beach. On February 27, the *Palm Beach Post* ran an article about me entitled, "All his world's a stage." And with me about to extend *Phantom's* run, Morgenthau—through his crony, Judge Harold Beeler—made sure I wouldn't have the chance. The March 6 sentencing hearing for Beeler's trumped-up contempt of court charge was nearing, and I requested a two-day delay—which Beeler accepted. But he could not resist pricking me by issuing an arrest warrant, as if I was some sort of serial killer on the loose.

When I arrived back at LaGuardia Airport on the seventh, as soon as I stepped off the plane, Morgenthau's goons were there to slap the handcuffs on me and once again hold me in jail until the hearing the next morning.

Beeler had only just begun to humiliate me. At the hearing, he perfunctorily sentenced me—not to 30 days and a $1,000 fine, as prescribed by law; instead, he gave me *90* days and an *$8,000* fine. Beeler's attitude about how he could get away with this seemed to be, "Because I can."

It was the arrogance of a legal system gone haywire, a system not of blind justice but of bribed injustice. It is the shame of our nation, stripping law-abiding citizens of their rights every day of the year.

And so off I went, my legs shackled, my hands manacled behind my back, to the Tombs, the filthy, rat-infested mausoleum of a jail in Lower Manhattan where hard-bitten murderers and rapists are held until they can be routed to more permanent prisons.

This was my first sour taste of the Tombs, but it wouldn't be my last. I would come to know again the stench of urine and feces in the corridors, the feeling of wearing an orange jumpsuit with no pockets, the steep staircases one must descend to meet visitors, the cramped cells, the one-inch plastic mattresses on cold steel cots, the backed-up toilets and clogged sinks, the two hours of sunlight and fresh air a day.

Oddly enough, though, I also felt something of an epiphany. The old saw that every man must spend at least one night in jail for his own good has a lot of truth in it. Deprived of freedom, forced into contemplation. Living with those poor souls trapped on a treadmill of crime and spit out by a racist society, I learned that the spirit of survival is man's strongest quality. I found myself bonding with people I had always been conditioned to believe were worthless chaff, to be feared rather than respected. And, in turn, seeing my sincere receptiveness to them, they instantly bonded with me, craving to hear my wit and wisdom. My own resolve became stronger, my thoughts clearer, my mission to fight my enemies more urgent.

This, of course, was exactly what Morgenthau and the Stahl mob did not want to happen. Clearly, they expected me to have a taste of my future, of more days and nights behind bars. To them, the 90 days was supposed to drum into me that the next time I would be on these premises, I would not come out alive.

It was they who would learn how counterproductive their bloodthirsty aims were.

When I was let out after 45 days, I was friskier than ever. And I had some business to settle. For months, I had been steaming about how the *Post, Daily News,* and *Times* had printed as fact Morgenthau's big lie that my motive for wanting Stanley Stahl to be murdered was the "survivor takes all" clause that did not exist. I had written letters to all of the papers explaining the true story, but not one of them had the decency and journalistic integrity to print them or to correct the lie.

My recourse was to go to court, not to sue these irresponsible newspapers – one of whom was Cindy Adams, whom of course I had fired from the *Post*, before Murdoch had hired her back. My intention was not to sue for millions in civil court but instead to sue the individual reporters who had written the stories for $3,000 in Small Claims Court. Money was not my objective; it was only to tell the truth unencumbered by crooked judges and lawyers and to have it on record that these reporters had lied.

To do this, I was willing to go through the Hades of Small Claims Court. I sat for five hours with a hundred people in an airless courtroom, spending the time having some very nice conversations with these mostly lower-class New Yorkers whom I so identify with. In fact, I respect them far more for standing up for their dignity over even a few dollars than I do any millionaire with a battery of high-priced lawyers.

Based on my understanding of state law, I believed that Small Claims Court prohibits such lawyers from representing the contestants, not that they would want to anyway given that they wouldn't make enough money for their three-martini lunches off these petty cases. However, I learned yet again that mere laws do not apply to me. When my case was called and I approached the bench, I expected to state my case to the referee—judges usually don't preside in Small Claims Court—only to see the man arise from his seat and leave the court. He was replaced by Judge Herman Cahn, who had come from no less than the Supreme Court just to hear this case!

You knew Cahn from a previous lawsuit I was involved in, when he had rendered a patently unfair judgment against me. That pretty much told me that even in this court, I would not be dealt with fairly. What's more, none of the reporters I had specifically sued had shown up in court. Normally that would mean I would have received a default judgment in my favor. Only this time, the rules were changed and new law made on the spot right before my eyes. It happened when a man came before Cahn and identified himself as the lawyer for all three reporters.

"Wait a minute," I protested. "This is against all procedures. The law says that lawyers cannot represent a person in Small Claims Court."

Cahn looked at me hatefully with his cold eyes.

"That's my decision," he sneered haughtily. He then ruled instantly that the lawyers could in fact represent the reporters.

At that point, my eyes turned just as cold and hateful as I stared at yet another venal judge, one who had been dispatched to a court he probably never frequented in order to slap me in the face.

"If that's how you rule," I said with frozen loathing, "against the law and against all sense of fair play, then fuck you."

With that, I turned on my heel and left the room, to the sound of many of the people in the gallery applauding me.

If only that could have been my parting shot to the court system, and that I would never have to see the inside of one of these kangaroo courts again. Unfortunately, it would not be long before I'd be walking back into another courtroom. And when I did, for the retrial of the farcical criminal solicitation case, it was clear to me that if Morgenthau would go to the trouble of importing a Supreme Court judge to screw me in Small Claims Court, he would do anything to prevent me from ever getting a fair trial.

For the redo of his silly story about me hiring a hit man to murder Stanley Stahl, he lined up Supreme Court Judge Ira Beal – bringing him in from Staten Island, his normal jurisdiction, just to hear this case. In the pretrial hearing, I was going to formally file a motion to represent myself *pro se*. But before I could even speak, Beal was prepared to short-circuit me.

"Mr. Hirschfeld," he said, "where is your lawyer?"

"Judge, I would like to represent myself, as I have done in the past and quite well, I might add."

His response left no room for further debate.

"Not in my courtroom, you won't," he hissed.

As with that other judicial giant, Harold Beeler, Beal acted with total disregard for the law and my constitutional rights. I tried to appeal to any sense of decency he might have had by suggesting a compromise: I would represent myself, but I would retain a lawyer to sit beside me at the defense table.

Not only did Beal reject it—he deceitfully ruled that the mere mention of this suggestion meant I had *forfeited* my right to self-representation! That way, he would not have to specifically rule against my *pro se* motion, which would be illegal and provide a certain cause to overturn a conviction. Instead, he sat on my motion without ever ruling, and my Sixth Amendment right went right into the toilet of justice.

Beal then went further in trampling my rights—I would not necessarily be permitted a lawyer of my choosing. Any lawyer I chose would have to be approved by Beal himself! This was the predicate for Beal to set up other legal red herrings. For example, because so many lawyers were rejected, and others fired by me for working directly against me, I had to file continuances delaying the trial. Beal would then be able to rule that these "delaying" tactics abrogated my right to request a hearing on the matter of suppressing Morgenthau's tainted tapes.

These were the lengths to which Morgenthau had gone—all the way to Stalinist Russia. His pet judge would, over the next nine weeks, head me off at every turn and dictate to the jury what they were to believe and not believe. Rosemary Singer and Joe Veltri, brought back to reprise their pathetic lies, were treated like royalty, immune to any surgical cross-examination. The same questions that had exposed their fabrications in the previous trial were now, by rote, ruled out of order. The many problems with the prosecution's case simply melted away as if by magic. This is how it is done in a police state.

In every possible way, Beal all but ordered the jury to convict me. After the case had been presented, Beal could divine that the jurors were sympathetic to me, despite his ham-handed rulings. He then unctuously told them he would not sentence me to more than one year should I be convicted, because of my age. I knew full well he had no intention of keeping that promise, but the jury would fall for it. On June 16, they returned after two days of deliberation with the verdict Beal had ordered them to arrive at—guilty.

My head sank into my hands and Zipora began to cry uncontrollably behind me in the first row of the gallery. I immediately filed an appeal, but I was allowed freedom only until August 1, when Beal would hold the sentencing hearing.

Having gotten their pound of flesh, Morgenthau and his stooge Gilda Marian now wanted to cut out my heart. And they were, as usual, very willing to skirt the law to do it. During the first criminal solicitation trial, Morgenthau had illegally fed false and damaging information about me to *New York* magazine for a negative article about me entitled, "Crazy As He Wants To Be." He then had sadistically scheduled the retrial of the tax fraud case to begin on July 31—one day before the sentencing hearing. This assured that I would look like a hardcore criminal.

Morgenthau played his last ace card at the hearing, when Beal opened the court to the "victim's" family. Up stepped a woman who identified herself as *"Genese* Stahl, Stanley Stahl's widow."

Were my eyes deceiving me? I knew Stahl's wife. Her name was *Cherise,* and she was a small woman, unlike this "Mrs. Stahl," who was a very large and obese woman. Was this damned court so twisted and perverted that it was now acceptable procedure to send in an impostor posing as someone else? And to do so even while clumsily getting her name wrong!

I wondered if this woman had been hired for her acting abilities. Handkerchief in hand, fake tears rolling down her cheek, "Mrs. Stahl" gave a virtuoso performance, begging Beal to send me up the river. The script was straight from Morgenthau's typewriter:

"While it is true that Mr. Hirschfeld's hired assassin never pulled the trigger of his gun," she caterwauled, "Mr. Hirschfeld is responsible for Stanley's death just as surely as if he had taken a gun and shot him himself."

Bringing it all full circle back to Morgenthau, the impostor absurdly claimed that Stahl had read the aforementioned *New York* magazine article and was so upset he'd had a stroke, became gravely ill, and died ten days later. (Never mind that he had been in good health when he'd suddenly died.)

The faker went on. "I was angry that his life was over, that Mr. Hirschfeld's crime had robbed us of happiness during our last two years together."

With that performance over, Beal took his cue. First, with magnificent insincerity, he oozed, "This was a mean-spirited crime by a very wealthy man—out of greed. The community has a right to see some form of punishment."

In truth, of course, what the community deserved was a top-level investigation of the crimes of Morgenthau and all of his courtroom stooges. But then again, that would mean the criminal and the scumbags would be investigating themselves. What happened to me should never happen again to anyone, yet it will, again and again.

Next in the scripted proceedings came Beal's announcement of my sentence—a minimum of one year and a maximum of *three years*.

The jury had been hoodwinked, and I had been railroaded to what my enemies surely assumed would be a death sentence.

Given a chance to make a statement, I decided I would not dignify the crime perpetrated against me by addressing the court.

"All I would like to do," I said, "is to kiss my wife goodbye."

Zipora was destroyed by the entire crusade that began on that horrible night when Morgenthau's storm troopers burst into our home. By now she had gone over the edge of mental illness, and I could only wonder if that had been a sort of defense mechanism to insulate her from any further pain inflicted by these monsters. She was all I thought about as I contemplated spending the foreseeable future in prison. I worried far more about what it would do to her than what it would do to me.

And all Ira Beal could say in answer to my simple request was a haughty, "No." He then gave the sign to two court officers to handcuff and shackle me, to take me away.

Ask yourself a simple question: What kind of a heartless, bankrupt soul could have denied a husband a last kiss to his wife of fifty-six years? When Ira Beal comes face-to-face with his maker, he will beg for forgiveness.

And his simple request will bring a simple response: "No."

As I was being shackled, I did my best to throw appropriate manure on Beal's court. I yelled every expletive I could think of. Those who rule like pigs should be covered in pig shit. I hope all my words are still ringing in Beal's ears.

Like yesterday's trash, I was shoved into a police van—something I had become quite accustomed to—and transported to a familiar destination: the Tombs, to begin a journey that was supposed to end my life but which would become the greatest experience of my life.

Abraham (Abe) Hirschfeld

CHAPTER THIRTY-TWO: MOSES IN A JUMPSUIT

The appeals process began, against my instincts and wishes, with the hiring of yet another world-renowned lawyer. This was Alan Dershowitz, the scruffy Harvard professor with the oversized ego who has made his fame overturning verdicts on appeal for high-profile clients, most notably Claus Von Bulow's conviction for trying to murder his heiress wife—though Dershowitz was less successful trying to overturn the tax evasion conviction of my old friend Leona Helmsley, the hotel baroness dubbed "The Queen of Mean" by the same New York media that had labeled me "Crazy Abe."

(Just to digress for a minute, I would like to say that Leona Helmsley is a very fine and dedicated lady who, like me, has been the target of a vendetta by Robert Morgenthau and, like me, convicted on the flimsiest of evidence. But then I admit I'm a bit prejudiced, having given Leona her start in real estate, taking her into my business as a complete novice and teaching her all that she knows of our trade before sending her to work for Harry Helmsley. Harry Helmsley was another grand old friend of mine, who if he was alive would tell you how much he'd benefited from my advice as he went about gobbling up great big chunks of New York real estate such as the Empire State Building.)

It was my brother Menasha's idea to hire Dershowitz.

"Abe, you need a lawyer who can articulate better than you all the abuses and improprieties of the judge," he told me after the conviction. "So you may as well go out and get the best."

For all my reservations about lawyers, and especially high-profile lawyers, I gave in because I believed a man like Dershowitz, who's supposedly so passionate about constitutional rights, would slam-dunk the appeal of my case. I also believed time was critical in presenting the appeal, because Morgenthau and his hacks in the press were already at work covering up his abuses. In fact, the rewriting of history began just one day after my sentencing when *The New York Times,* clearing up Morgenthau's biggest blunder, reported the remarks of "*Charise* Stahl," not "*Genese* Stahl," as the impostor had called herself—a blatant journalistic fraud.

What's more, as time unwound, even Dershowitz seemed somewhat diffident, no doubt because I was telling him what to do and how to proceed. I found him to be insufferably vain and distant, as if he believed he could walk on water. He bristled when I laid down the ground rules: he would prepare the legal documents, but I would make all the decisions and represent myself in court if I so chose. "That's fine, Abe," he said, especially as I was handing him his checks, but not once did he listen to me.

The prime example was my desire to immediately request that I return to Supreme Court for an emergency hearing regarding the illegality of the fake "Mrs. Stahl." That had been an egregious miscarriage of justice and, by itself, an open and shut cause for reversal of the verdict.

However, Dershowitz was oddly reticent, and when he refused to file the motion, I realized what a phony he was and wasted no time in firing the bastard.

"And return the $150,000 I gave you," I told him.

He agreed. Of course, I'm still waiting for the check. Think of that the next time this two-bit "crusader" for justice goes on TV and professes his high and mighty liberal claptrap about protecting people's civil liberties. Remember, too, that he sat like a lump of sludge as every one of my constitutional rights was spat upon.

The appeal did go ahead, with lesser-known and equally ineffectual lawyers also relegating the issue of the fake Mrs. Stahl to the more traditional and easily ignored constitutional violation argument, namely Judge Beal's illegal refusal to permit me to defend myself and his later refusal to apply the Huntley Law to Rosemary Singer's illegal wiretaps. And, in the end, each succeeding appeals court—relieved of the land mine of the fake Mrs. Stahl, which they did not even need to address—predictably rejected the appeal.

The state, of course, made it impossible for me to prevail in any case by sending in the clowns in robes, first on April 19, 2001 in the Appellate Court, then August 3 in the Court of Appeals. In 2002, the U.S. Supreme Court declined to hear the appeal.

By then, of course, my address had changed a few times. The first weeks of my one-to-three-year sentence were spent within the New York City borders so I could appear at the retrial of the tax fraud case. From the Tombs I was dumped like a laboratory rat into Bellevue Prison Hospital, the place synonymous for generations as a "nuthouse." I suppose my enemies wanted to have me declared criminally insane so that I would become "lost" in a Cuckoo's Nest, never again to be seen or heard. Again, they severely underestimated me.

It was that judicial rat in robes, Judge Harold Beeler, who first thought of the "Bellevue Solution" for me. During my earlier incarceration for contempt of court, he ordered me to be taken to Bellevue for "observation"—not by coincidence, just as the Passover holiday began. I had not missed spending Passover with family for eighty years. But now, rather than allowing me to be with Zipora, who was so sick, my lawyers pleaded with him to tack on the eight days I'd be home to the end of my jail term, but he all but said, "No, I won't do that, but I will let you spend Passover in the nut house."

This unimaginable religious slight did not surprise me. Beeler had, you will recall, ordered me to remove my *yarmulke* and prayer shawl or else be thrown in jail for contempt. Though he was Jewish, he was absolutely contemptuous, no pun intended, of Jewish law and tradition. During the trial, I had asked him one day if he was in fact a Jew.

"I am a symbolic Jew," he said, which I suppose meant he could not care less that he had been born a Jew. And he carried his contempt for anyone else who was a Jew into "symbolic" anti-Semitism.

On the third day of Passover, Zipora, who could not understand why I wasn't at the Seder table leading the prayers in our apartment, left the building in a daze and began roaming the streets alone. She fell and broke her leg and was taken to Lenox Hill Hospital. When I heard of this, I sent word through my lawyer to Beeler begging him to allow me just one hour to visit Zipora, who needed desperately to see and hear me to put her mind at ease. He, in effect, told me and Zipora to drop dead.

And yet, Beeler probably would have been terribly upset that the people who ran Bellevue were doing everything they could to respect my religion and to make my holiday as comfortable as possible. On the first night of Passover, they brought in my rabbi, Arthur Schneider, to say the prayer with me. On later nights came Gilbert Rosenthal, the president of the New York Board of Rabbis and my good friend Yigal Tzarfati of the Israeli consulate. Yigal even offered to stay in jail in my stead so I could go home for the Seder.

All of these fine men wrote letters to Beeler imploring him to let me spend the holiday at home. Rabbi Shiya Hecht, who was on

Rudy Giuliani's commission on human rights, came forward for me. So did Rabbi Pesich Lerner, executive vice-president of the National Council of Young Israel. All were met with deaf ears by Beeler.

And so, when I returned to Bellevue, the powers that be had learned nothing. Plainly, Bellevue was a sanctuary for me. The doctors would not hear of me being mistreated, and they gave me carte blanche in my desire to remain in the public eye. The lifeline of any prisoner is the telephone, and I all but lived with a phone surgically implanted in my hand and ear. For hours on end I made calls to the newspapers assuring the New York literati that while my senate race had been pulled out from under me by Morgenthau, my quest for peace in the Middle East and my simple, practical solutions to society's biggest problems were even more of a mission for me.

Mostly, I wanted the outside world to know that prison was a godsend, not Purgatory. In fact, I myself was shocked that I was experiencing something remarkably life-affirming and enlightening behind these walls. Never before had I spent any appreciable time in the company of mostly poor African-American and Hispanic people, and I had worried about how a wealthy white Jew would be received by these hard-bitten men.

Yet, from day one at the Tombs and at Bellevue, and all through my sentence, they took to me as though I were a kind of Biblical figure come alive, even a Messiah—maybe the long white beard that burgeoned on my face had something to do with it. Almost at once, I wasn't "Abe," I was "Abraham," "Joseph," or, dare I say it, "Moses." Of course, to others not so Biblically inclined, I was simply "Pops" or "Santa Claus." And at Bellevue, they even call me "President"—after electing me president of my entire ward to work with the prison's officials to improve conditions.

This was a real epiphany for me, firstly that the assumptions about blacks and Jews being mutually hateful and distrustful of each other is sheer folly; placed within the confines of the same walls, our historic bonds as society's favorite pariahs were reestablished. I shall always remember how these young men who had been forced by society into becoming criminals would sit with me as I recited Bible stories and pearls of wisdom about life, their eyes widening in fascination. I was the first Jew in their lives who had bothered to befriend them and point out how our cultures interlocked.

400

As for myself, I, too, learned from them, about their lives, dreams, and positive desires to excel in life if given a chance. These so-called "career criminals" had been kept from making a good living and had turned in desperation to drug dealing and stealing. Thus, I began developing another simple and practical solution to one of our biggest problems: recidivist crime. The fact is, prisons do not rehabilitate; no one would even claim that any longer. Instead, they are merely crime factories breeding more and more crime once these men return to the streets. Our short-sighted "leaders" are content with this treadmill. They want nothing more than to lock up these men, and then lock them up again and again, and damn the consequences. The solution is very easy, and I will tell you about it in a minute.

Bellevue itself was a small lesson to me that the old-world assumptions about how to run a prison are dying. It was hardly the "Cuckoo's Nest" it has been called. There are no rubber rooms or strait-jacketed loonies sitting around drooling on themselves. I was placed in detention ward 19541A, on the nineteenth floor, and my "cell" was actually a large room with a bathroom and a sweeping view of the East River and the FDR Drive. As a landlord, I could have rented it for $5,000 a month or sold it for $1 million.

The delicious irony was that the Beelers and the Beals of the world wanted to hurt me by putting me here—yet, it was the most relaxation I'd had in years, away from squealing DAs, evil-eyed judges, and greedy lawyers. I received wonderful care from the doctors—six of them would examine me every morning. And I found myself sleeping like a baby, relieved of the worries of the business wars.

I also ate better, healthier food than I normally do at five-star restaurants where they mottle everything with salt, sugar, and fat. They fed me five times a day, and they even gave me a night snack, usually melon. I found myself enjoying cantaloupe and honeydew so much that it made up the bulk of my diet—and as a result, I had stumbled upon the most effective diet in the world, one no one knew about but which makes weight loss incredibly easy. The secret is that melon, unlike fruit, has little fructose, or fruit sugar, and more fiber, so you can eat a lot of it. I myself was the guinea pig. Eating melon at every meal, I shrunk from over 200 sloppy pounds to 160 lean pounds, in all of six weeks.

When I arrived at Bellevue, my blood pressure was 200/100. Within weeks, it had fallen to 130/70. My blood sugar went from a borderline-diabetic 200 to 100. My skin went from pasty to ruddy. My skin cancer and my arthritis vanished. And, amazingly, my hair, which had quickly turned gray and then snow-white, began turning back to its original brown color!

I had found the fountain of youth in a prison! Courtesy of the very people who wanted my life to end. Go figure.

Another irony was that while many prisoners asked me for legal advice on how to fight the system, I believed in the innate wisdom of my fellow inmates to the point of taking the advice of one prisoner when my tax fraud case was retried, although I probably should not have. I should have followed my routine advice when someone would ask me if I could get them a good lawyer.

"A good lawyer," I would say, "you will only find in hell."

Instead, I put too much faith in someone's advice to see a particular lawyer. I suppose I did this because I was simply so tired of fighting in court, of getting up at 4 A.M. so I could be in court. Accordingly, I forgot my own best instincts and failed to understand that my enemies were extended all the way into the prisons, that the state's Corrections Department would bribe inmates to become rats. They'll tell a guy who's doing twenty-five years that they'll cut it to ten years if they provide information about a target of the state, like I was.

That's what happened after this fellow's lawyer suddenly showed up; he came to see me and wove his way into my good graces.

"They tell me you have a problem and that you need a lawyer," he told me.

Over the next few days, I let my guard down. I told him of all of my plans to beat the bogus tax charges. And as a result, so did Morgenthau. As with the criminal solicitation retrial, my conviction would be arranged in advance.

However, there was a critical difference this time. Judge Bruce Allen actually came to my rescue. Allen seemed as sick and tired of the whole nonsensical case as I was and wanted to head off another long, tedious show trial full of Morgenthau's lies. His solution was for me to cop a plea—that is, to accept what is called an Alford Plea, meaning you agree to a monetary penalty without a plea of guilt. The penalty was $1 million.

I figured that since I still had the Paula Jones check, I would still come out even. It was hardly a completely satisfying, or fair, denouement but, again, I was tired and so was Allen. And so on the morning of August 28, 2000, I came once again to 110 Centre Street—actually, I was most eager to be there that day since I would be seeing Zipora for the first time since I'd been sent away. When Allen convened the session, I took the plea and agreed to sign over the $1 million cash bail I had posted after the indictment.

Of course, Gilda Mariani, Morgenthau's courtroom stooge, was in no mood to call a truce with me.

"Your Honor, the People are opposed to this, opposed to the plea," she stammered, red-faced. "We are opposed because [Mr. Hirschfeld] has not shown the slightest bit of remorse [and has practiced] deception and concealment."

As she yammered on and on, continuing to retry a case that was now officially over, everyone in the courtroom tried hard to stay awake, Allen included.

When Mariani had finally shut up, the judge didn't even respond to her bizarre demands for jail time and additional monetary fines. Instead, this man who had been so hostile to me during the original trial couldn't wait to say nice things to me.

"You are a unique individual," he told me. "You have your own special way of looking at things. And you obviously have a brilliant mind."

He went on: "You see things from a different angle and...after you finish up with [your] sentence on the other case, you may come to some conclusion about our prison system. You might have some ideas there.

"It seems to me that your mind is always at work. Even though your body may be failing you, your mind hasn't stopped yet.....[T]here are those who have fallen just as far and have managed to make something out of the rest of their lives. Based upon what I have seen, if anybody can do it, you probably can. Good luck to you, Mr. Hirschfeld."

That man, I must admit, must have been psychic. It was as if he had been reading my mind. And he was right. I *was* going to have revolutionary ideas about the prison system. And I *was* going to have a life rebirth.

Seeing Bruce Allen's conversion to an Abe Hirschfeld fan, I was a little sad to leave.

"I have to come here more often," I quipped.

"Well, you're welcome any time," he quipped back.

Both of us, of course, were lying through our teeth.

Unfortunately, when I walked out of the courthouse that day, freedom still wasn't mine. I had to serve out my sentence, and while I was out of the loop, Judge Ira Gammerman—who would only grow more and more irrational about me—let my unholy trinity of illicit "business partners," Richard Czaja, Greg Wolpert, and James Matera, virtually erase me from my own companies.

In the spring of 2001, Gammerman committed his worst act of infamy; incredibly, he named Matera the *sole* Managing Partner of Hirstan Associates—my own company, the one I'd managed from the start and held the majority stock interest in. (Czaja and Wolpert, you will recall, had already been given complete control of Stahl Associates, despite the same injunction stated in the original partnership agreement that only blood relatives could succeed either Stanley or myself.) Gammerman did this without a single hearing and a single argument allowed to me. And there would be even more of this concerted effort to literally expunge me from existence in the months to come.

Being locked up certainly made it difficult for me to challenge such illegal and scummy acts. And yet, seeing me keep filing appropriate motions made my enemies uncomfortable. Clearly, putting me in the can was not silencing me. And so their reaction was predictable: they would put me in more insidious "hell holes." First, they had me moved in early 2001 to Riker's Island, the maximum-security jail sometimes called "New York's sixth borough" because, sitting in the East River between Queens and The Bronx, it teems with around 15,000 prisoners strewn over different buildings.

The main facility at Riker's was so degrading and jammed so many people into so little space that in 1980, a Federal court order capped its main jail at 1,200 prisoners, and then later closed it down. For these reasons, as well as for the numerous prison riots (in 1990, over 100 prisoners and guards were injured in one melee), mysterious deaths, understaffed security, and other such charms, New York is so sensitive about the place that the island cannot be found on the city's subway map. It is obliterated, as if it doesn't exist.

Riker's is generally used as a gateway. People who can't afford bail are stockpiled while they await their court dates, and those convicted are put up awaiting transfers to other prisons. However, many black and Puerto Rican prisoners are dumped there to be "scared straight," as are many whites convicted of "white glove" crimes to be "taught a good lesson" by vindictive prosecutors. The latter crowd has included Leona Helmsley, corporate crooks, and me, as prisoner number 00A5187.

Fortunately for me, once more the doctors upon my arrival simply would not allow me to be plopped into a "Midnight Express" hellhole. Instead, I was kept in the North Infirmary Command, or NIC, in a nice, dormitory-style room in one of the newer facilities. There were twenty-seven inmates there, of which I was the only Caucasian—and certainly the only Jew.

Still, no one would mistake my accommodations for the Ritz. Not unless the Ritz takes everything its guests arrive with, including their shirts, pants, jackets, shoes, and sneakers. All of these items are confiscated by the scavengers—the guards who conduct periodic raids looking for nice clothing to keep for themselves. Once taken, they will never be returned. I saw men walking around in nothing but prison pajama bottoms. And my own designer suit that I wore to my court appearances was taken as well. I imagine it is adorning some 38-short guard's closet right now.

Worse, two or three times a week, a mob of guards clad in riot gear, plastic helmets, and wielding billy clubs burst into a dorm or cellblock to conduct a kind of prison *pogrom,* or "shakedown," as the inmates called it. The object was ostensibly to seek out contraband, drugs, cigarettes, and other means of intra-prison barter, but again, any such things would not be confiscated but rather kept by the cops themselves. They would rip up bed sheets, clothes, books, the legal paperwork of inmates, anything they wanted to trash, and all of it would be tossed in a big pile. The inmates would be forced to stand and watch, and some were ordered to lower their pants and bend over for a humiliating strip search.

Of course, even with these raids, one can pretty much get his hands on any drug. I was told there is a thriving drug market within those walls. Even heroin could be purchased, either from other inmates or from the *guards*.

Just as on the outside, there is an economic caste system in prison. Many inmates have amassed a wad of money from these dealings, and they pay off the guards to leave them alone. Another way of doing business is to have an associate or relative on the outside send money to the drug-seller's own associates or relatives, or to a guard's bank account. I heard of one prisoner at Riker's who bribed a guard to smuggle them knives, even *guns*. Another supposedly purchased an officer's jacket so the guy could try to walk out of the front gate disguised as a cop.

I don't know if that plan worked. I found it was in my best interests not to ask too many questions. I had enough trouble with the law to be "the man who knew too much."

Not that I was ever threatened or warned to keep my mouth shut. As in my previous prison tenures, I was treated with great respect and sympathy, by inmates and guards alike, for what had been done to me and for my endless homilies on life. Many hard-bitten "criminals" were in fact very nice young men with good hearts and not half as malevolent as so-called "respectable" men like, say, David Rosenberg or Harold Beeler. They had an honest desire to better themselves and to love their families. Just as in the Tombs and Bellevue, I would enjoy immensely sitting with them, playing casino, and learning what made them tick. I was "Brother Abe" to them, and they were "boychiks" to me.

About the only uncomfortable moments I had were in the TV room when they had me watch rap videos with all that "gangsta" stuff. At first, I couldn't make sense out of it. But even this had a benefit. Remember my plans to produce a hip-hop *Phantom of the Opera* movie? The idea came to me right there in that room. I had the same conversion that I did in the 1950s when a business friend of mine who loved Elvis Presley wangled an invitation for me to come to Graceland, and I spent several hours talking to this very gracious and shy young man who had met so few Jews and was fascinated by my vast store of knowledge and wisdom. And I, in return, sat transfixed listening to him talk about his love for black blues music. That is how I learned to love rock and roll. And I'm not too ashamed to say that, today, hip-hop is my favorite music.

I'm also not ashamed to say that I dipped into my pocket to make things a little better for my prison friends. No, I wasn't played as an easy mark by these men. No one ever came to me for money; it was all my idea. Ten dollars goes a long way in jail. For me, it got my bed made and my clothes washed, and extra food, while at the same time making the guys feel they were earning something. Yet, for them, the money was secondary to wanting to help me out.

Indeed, I was extraordinarily moved by a wonderful letter written by one of my new friends on Riker's Island, an inmate named Juan Sainz, which appeared on a web site called 15minutes.com. Juan was so inspired by me that he wanted to express his feelings. He wrote:

> It is truly without sense to endure any time in jail. But it is really a nightmare when the reasons for being there are unjust. As Montesquieu wrote in 1742: "There is no crueler tyranny than that which is perpetrated under the shield of law and in the name of justice."

> I read many reports and saw many of his works, but to finally meet Abe Hirschfeld was truly an honor.

> He said some time ago, "This country is full of politicians. What is needed are builders."

> These are not the words of a man who has no value for life, freedom, and the American way. Instead, these are the words of a man who was destined to change New York City by giving a chance to its people to build this great city.

> Yes, there have been many changes and many good people to make them. But not all changes were made with the utmost regards towards the lower and middle class citizens of New York.

> In and out of jail, Abraham Hirschfeld has been an inspiration to us all. He's a man whose views of political change has made him a target for our politicians and lawmakers, men of change who in turn have become progress stoppers....

> Compassionate, intelligent, a peacemaker, a good listener and advisor, even a teacher to some...Abe, or Pops, has touched many lives with his work and witty charm....

By perpetrating this tyranny against Abe, the lawmakers/politicians have been exposed for what they really are. [He] is the kind of man whose only fault is to say it like it is and whose voice has been kept mute by the top dogs, violating each and every one of his constitutional rights. And to think all this has been done in the name of justice!

Don't think you have heard the last of him. The best is yet to come!

Since I was saving so much money in jail—imagine how many $400 dinners I didn't have to buy, and I was eating better food for free!—I decided to spend some of it to let my friends on the outside know that I was doing so well. I purchased ads in several newspapers. One was a full-page ad in the *Miami Herald* that cost thousands of dollars. To me, it was well worth it to reveal my feelings about the prison treadmill.

"These men," I wrote in the ad, "are dumped in here by the legal system. That's a social problem I will be looking into when I get out."

In fact, I had already formulated the solution. This is how it works: When prisoners are released from prison, the government should make sure they have enough money in their pockets to see them through so that they can find a job and have a nice place to live. A workable figure? I would mandate $100,000 for each prisoner. Outrageous, you say? Abe, how can you spend the taxpayers' money on these reprobates? Well, the truth is that this is a small price to pay to make our society better and to prevent these men from being trapped on the treadmill that will keep sending them back to overcrowded and disgusting prisons.

Consider that to keep a man prisoner costs many times more than $100,000. Prisons are the biggest money pit of all. Imagine the upside if there were half as many men in these jails, and if each one who does not return contributes to society through taxes and productive lives—the kind of thing the politicians and city planners pay lip service to but have no desire, or brains, to fulfill. If you do the math, you will see that the savings would be enormous. They would more than wipe out the national debt the politicians, in their wisdom, have given us.

I have no doubt that within two decades, this plan will one day be the law of the land, at which time prisons will be closing all over America and converted into the housing so many of our people need. Mark my words. It will happen. Again, I might not be around to see it happen, so I will take yet another bow in advance.

My problem was in getting around and presenting these ideas to the public, either on the campaign trail (with my status as a convicted criminal, Morgenthau and the Stahl mob had made sure I could never again run for office) or as a spirited citizen—because the prison system was not through dumping on me. Once again, the state saw fit to move me, this time far from New York City, as if to further erase me from sight. Not by coincidence, this happened after my fighting spirit had begun to unravel my old foil, the contemptible Judge Ira Gammerman.

I had reached my boiling point with Gammerman's subterranean rulings that illegally displaced me as the managing partner of my own companies in favor of Stanley Stahl's non-blood relative lackeys. So, I wrote Gammerman a letter that I included in another ad that I placed in the *Daily News*. In the letter, I asked why he had "ordered me to transfer the books and operational responsibilities of Stahl Associates to David Rosenberg, the attorney for the estate of my late partner Stanley Stahl."

I asked a simple question: "What right do you have to overrule [my] legally binding contract agreement by making James Matera sole managing partner [in Hirstan Associates]?"

With Gammerman having done so, I concluded he had compromised his role as an impartial judge and should recuse himself immediately.

Well, Gammerman flipped his lid that his dirty laundry had been made public. He became even more unfair, and he began to punish me and to reward Rosenberg in ways that even Rosenberg hadn't asked for.

For instance, Rosenberg had filed a motion for injunctive relief—meaning money—that he later withdrew because he knew it was frivolous. Yet, on April 20, 2001, during a bench conference with Rosenberg and my lawyer, Gammerman actually *suggested* that the withdrawn motion be replaced with a *contempt* motion against me, and he *instructed* Rosenberg on how to file the motion!

Gammerman then completely lost his mind. Rambling incoherently, he said that if I violated any of his orders, he would hold me in contempt and keep me *"in jail forever."*

You read that right. The man promised to lock me up *forever* on a contempt of court charge!

This outrageous and bizarre threat was so prejudicial and onerous that my lawyer in the case, Chris Lynn, was compelled to fire off a letter—which I also ran in an ad in the *Daily News*—to Gammerman. It read:

> I am at a loss to understand [this] statement coming from [an] experienced jurist. In any criminal proceeding, there is a presumption of innocence. [Your] statement unconstitutionally shifted that burden to the accused [and] could easily [have] prejudiced this matter. Accordingly, I would respectfully request a recusal by Your Honor on any further matters involving Abraham Hirschfeld.

Gammerman, however, was beyond shame. Petulantly, and no doubt backed by Morgenthau, he remained on the case, making more legal mayhem, such as refusing to reprimand Rosenberg for claiming he had represented both Hirstan and Stahl Associates. Yet, in a delightful twist of fate, it would be another Big Lie by Morgenthau that would force Gammerman off the bench for the duration of the case.

That happened, as you will see, after my move to another "badass" prison, the Sullivan County Penitentiary in upstate New York. Sullivan County was in the beautiful Catskill Mountains, in the heart of the old "Borscht Belt" where I had often spent many a summer at grand hotels like Grossingers, The Concord, Browns, the Neville, and Kutchers, eating myself sick on corned beef and sour cream and watching budding comics like Jerry Lewis and Dean Martin, Alan King, and Jackie Mason develop their hilarious routines (which happened faster when I provided them with their best jokes).

This wasn't exactly the way I would have chosen to return to the Catskills. And as much as I enjoyed being back in this beautiful former centerpiece of Jewish culture, it was while I was here that all efforts were made to destroy me once and for all.

You already know the ending to that story. And the moral: Abe Hirschfeld wasn't born to be a martyr.

Abraham (Abe) Hirschfeld

CHAPTER THIRTY-THREE: RESURRECTION AND VINDICATION

I will say it flat out: I was supposed to die in the Sullivan County Correctional Facility.

From the moment I was driven through the front gate on March 11, 2001, and given prisoner number 00A5187 to wear on my back and chest, my legion of enemies waited eagerly for word to come that Abe Hirschfeld had died in prison of natural or "unnatural" causes. Whether it was from a heart attack or another prisoner wrapping a barbell around my head, it would have suited them just fine.

During the coming months, I would be moved again, like a pea in a shell game. I would be taken to the Downstate Prison in Fishkill, New York, and to the most notorious prison in the world, the Attica Correctional Facility, thirty miles east of Buffalo. It was there, on September 13, 1971, that the bloodiest one-day encounter between Americans since the Civil War occurred when Governor Nelson Rockefeller sent 1,500 state and National Guardsmen to storm the place to free guards held hostage by prisoners, an act of barbarity that left forty-two people dead including ten hostages. For a brief time, I was in the same prison population there with Godfather John Gotti and John Lennon's killer Mark David Chapman.

I would also be dropped into the Queens House of Detention in March 2002 during another bogus court case when a liar claimed I swindled a coop building in Queens out of $4 million. The only way I could get out of that mess was to settle by divesting fifty-six apartments worth $2 million. At least that rigged trial gave me a chance to blow off some steam, in the best way I know how—cursing out a crooked judge. This one was named Joseph Lisa, and he was as inept and intolerable as the damnable duo of Harold Beeler and Ira Beal. During the proceedings, he enraged me so much that I screamed at him, "Liar! Liar!" That earned me a forced ejection from the court, which seemed more like a reward.

Still, wherever else they ferried me, I always wound up back in Sullivan County. Clearly, my enemies determined that they could put me through the ringer here and squeeze me the hardest. Even my driver of twenty-five years at the time, Victor Ocampo, was convinced I would never come out of the place alive.

413

"He's a man of steel," Victor told *Gotham* magazine when they did a big article about me in the summer of 2001, "but he'll go crazy. I can see it. He'll die in that place. They [will] really destroy him there."

Well, they tried. Hard. Even that *Gotham* story was designed to hurt me. It was called "Not-So-Honest Abe" and adorned with the old *New York Post* slurs against me, such as Pete Hamill's headlines calling me "a nut" and a "force for evil." In fact, I suspected Victor was in on this effort to undercut me and was providing false information to the author. For example, he said that prison made me lose reality and that it turned me hard-hearted and spiteful.

"He's a totally different person now," Victor said. "He doesn't care about anything but himself. In his mind, he's number one. He still thinks his money gives him power."

There was only one thing I could think of that could have made a loyal ally of mine say such hurtful falsehoods: the Stahl spigot of bribes.

I had cooperated with the magazine, naively, again having let down my guard about the reach and power of the Stahl mob. I would not make that mistake again. Immediately, I fired Victor and took the preventive step of firing everyone who worked for me in my office, excluding Elie. I allowed no business to be conducted there; instead, I rented the space to Mike Bloomberg to use as his campaign headquarters while he ran for mayor. (I thought this was only appropriate, given that he was following my lead in running for office using his own stockpile of money.)

When I got out of jail, I resolved I would hire only relatives of the inmates with whom I had made friends. That would be a small part of my overall plan to rehabilitate prisoners by helping them and their families.

Indeed, I continued the compensation arrangements with my fellow inmates who did me favors, having their families sent twenty-five or fifty dollars every week. For one very nice fellow who cleaned my cell for me, I sent his wife $200—although, here again, Victor attempted to make this seem much more melodramatic than it was. He told *Gotham* such payouts were "eye-keeper money," that if I didn't pay, I "might break a leg, who knows? These [men] are all lifers."

That last sentence is the only true one. They were lifers, yes, but on the whole, I was made to feel just as comfortable in Sullivan

County as I had been in Rikers. In fact, I made one of the closest friendships in my life there with an inmate named, appropriately, Joe Sullivan. He was a *real* hit man, for the Mafia, and he was serving life without a chance of parole. In all, he told, he had killed forty-four people. I asked him one day why he had done such a terrible thing.

"Abe," he said matter of factly, "that was my job."

Yet, Joe was one of the gentlest souls I've ever met, a very strict Catholic who had married a nice Jewish girl. His intelligence never failed to amaze me. A man like this ruins the all-too-easy equations of the social scientists who claim that crime is bred by environmental factors, which would seem to explain why so many blacks and Hispanics gravitate to crime.

Those scientists, typical intellectuals that they are, could not be more wrong. There is a kind of genius in the criminal mind. I've often believed that some of the worst criminals would make the best leaders, the best educators, the best doctors, if they hadn't turned to the seductions of crime. Their minds are incredibly sharp; they can figure out any problem. They are smarter than the intellectuals because they can channel intelligence into something workable— albeit illegal. This would certainly explain the actions of one of my cellmates in the Sullivan County jail, David Berkowitz, the infamous "Son of Sam" killer, of whom I will speak momentarily.

For men like these, crime isn't environmental; it is a psychological defect deep within their minds. And if I may say so, it is usually white men who have this defect. With black and Hispanic criminals, I believe the line between crime and productive lives is extremely thin, and we as a society can ensure the latter condition.

I found, too, that in jail, one's mind is forced to be active and sharp. The absence of diversions galvanizes the mind to think. I had, in a sense, been prepared for this form of asceticism because for years I have practiced a solitary routine that has kept my mind sharp. I honestly believe I have spoken with God during these moments— usually when I have sat by myself and played solitaire at three in the morning, with the lights of the New York skyline twinkling through my picture window nine floors above Fifth Avenue. If I win three or four times in a row, I know God is telling me that what I am thinking is correct. I have come upon some of the most ingenious of my inventions in just this manner.

Abraham (Abe) Hirschfeld

Well, it's always 3 A.M. in prison. Especially when you are put in solitary confinement for twenty-three hours a day. That is what happened to me, right from the start, at Sullivan County. Again, remember, here was an eighty-one-year-old man doing a one-to-three-year term put into a maximum-security prison with killers, rapists, bank robbers, and so on. And I was the one they threw into "the hole" faster than anyone else. And why? Because I committed the heinous act of talking on the telephone longer than they wanted me to. Talk about your threats to society!

In the parlance of "the slammer," this meant I had "refused a direct order." And so, I would be locked away and forgotten about for twenty-three hours, two days at a time, three days, however long they wanted. And every time they put me in solitary, I would get out a deck of cards and begin thinking. I don't know if this was how Ghandi did it, but the result would be another way to change the world.

One night, for instance, it came into my mind how to eliminate friction between the religions. Because if you think about it, for three days every week you have a disconnect between religions—Friday, Saturday and Sunday. The Catholics, Jews, and Muslims observe their Sabbath on these respective days. This causes a friction that must be eliminated.

How? Simple. All religions should decide on the same Sabbath day. This is only logical, isn't it? Isn't every holiday on the same day for everybody? Are there different Christmas Days, or Easter Sundays? Thus, I propose the universal Sabbath day be on Saturday, since Sunday is the Biblical seventh day, the day of rest.

At Sullivan County, I took my own poll about this. I asked probably 600 people, and every one of them, be they Christians, Jews, Protestants, Seventh-Day Adventists, Jehovah's Witnesses, everyone, loved the idea. Only Joe Sullivan hedged. "Abe," he said, "I need to think about it." The next morning, he rushed over to me and said, "Abe, I'm with you one hundred percent."

I surely must be an instrument of God on matters such as these. Because only two weeks later, Pope John Paul II, my old third grade classmate, announced that his greatest goal was to "eliminate the friction between the religions." Then, a week after that, Prince Charles, with whom I have been friends with for many years, gave a

416

speech in which he said his mission was to "eliminate the friction between the religions."

My friends in prison must have thought they were blessed to be able to hear these divine solutions first, and they would always want more information about them, such as my theory for raising perfect children. They didn't need the endorsements of Harvard and Yale professors—though the theory has won the backing of some of the country's finest educators. Even the guards would sit with me, listening raptly. Later, after my release, my parole officer, a wonderful lady who had many problems with her son, would beg me for the answer to bringing him back to the family. One day, she came to me crying, thanking me. No one, she said, not dozens of child psychiatrists, had done a thing. But I, with just a few words, had solved the problem.

At moments like these, I felt like Aristotle in the pit of the Forum, dispensing wisdom for the ages.

And yet, I was learning much, too, about myself and how closely I paralleled the life of Moses. For years, I had read The Five Books of Moses, which are the first books of the Old Testament, nearly every day. And while they deeply moved and inspired me, I never saw myself in those magnificent pages. Now, I did. Who else better personified the warning on one of those pages that "they will come at you on seven different roads"?

The Books also brought me closer, spiritually, to Israel, the meaning of being a Jew, and why Jews were chosen. This told me to redouble my efforts to bring peace to the Middle East—and crystallized that I had the only vehicle to make that happen, my Middle East peace treaty so long in abeyance since Dr. M.T. Mehdi had endorsed it in 1974 with the assent of Yasser Arafat. The treaty still contained the answer: a shared Israel-Palestine state, with shared interests and mutual respect.

I saw that state in the Five Books, in the earliest words of the Torah. As always, a story will make you appreciate my plan. The first great student of the Torah and interpreting the laws of Moses was Rabbi Hillel, who could recite any part of the Penateuch, or Book of Genesis, on command and at great length. One day, a gentile who had heard of Hillel tested him.

"Reb Hillel," he said, "I want to learn the Torah, but I am a very busy man. Can you tell me its wisdom only for as long as I can stand on one leg?"

Hillel responded, "Raise your foot." Then he said this: "Love your neighbor as you love yourself. The rest is explanation."

That was all the time he needed. Two sentences. The Bible says it like this: God grants your prayers soonest if we first pray to Him on behalf of others for the same thing. God commanded the children of Israel that they bring to Him pure olive oil beaten for the light, to cause a lamp to burn continually to be a statue forever.

I saw that light. And I believe God has chosen me as his messenger. I also believe that, like Moses, I will live 120 years and die with my eyes still sharp and with a spring in my step.

If I sound a bit evangelical, it's because I often had these types of discussions with my jail mates. Which brings me back to David Berkowitz. This is one of the most despised men on earth for having gunned down eleven young women in parked cars during his horrible killing spree in the mid-1970s. I never would have thought I would get any closer to him than the times I saw his weird grinning face the day the cops finally caught him. And then there he was, right before my eyes, sitting two tables from me in the cafeteria.

His appearance shocked me. The youthful psychopath had given way to a paunchy, graying, middle-aged man trying desperately to find some semblance of inner peace, though he is unlikely to ever find it. Few inmates wanted anything to do with him—in prison, there is an unwritten code of criminal "ethics," and killing women and children are taboo to even the most bloodthirsty of these men. The most anyone would say of him was, "There's that sonofabitch Berkowitz." He always sat alone, lost in thought in a silent trance.

Being me, however, I had a gnawing desire to at least make conversation with him and find out what made him tick. No, I'm not a saint, and I had no intention of "saving" him from hell. It was merely my natural curiosity and my habit of being civil with any man. And so, I sat down next to him one day. To my astonishment, he knew who I was and much of my history. And he immediately opened up to me about his past and his latter-day epiphanies. It seems he still hears the same "voices" he used to in his head, and as a fortress against them, he invented some bastardized form of Judaism in which he believes in Jesus to screen out the voices. It's not Jews For Jesus, which is a legitimate offshoot of Judaism; it's entirely different. He's still a Jew but with the perspective of a non-Jew. Or something like that.

I made little sense of any of this. I spent many hours trying to reassure him that the religion he was born with was his best refuge, but it was clear Berkowitz was far removed from reality. Indeed, at one point he presented me with a cockamamie idea that we should write a book together of our experiences. Needless to say, I reeled from the thought and said thank you no, that we had nothing at all in common, and let it drop.

Still, Berkowitz may have found some peace. When we spoke of his crimes, he expressed what seemed like genuine regret and shame, and he spoke movingly of his conversations with his victims' mothers over the years. I could only hope he realized how much he had taken from those mothers. I'm still not sure he has, or ever will.

But at least I saw a trace of belated humanity in Berkowitz. Not so for another infamous killer I encountered at Sullivan County, Larry Davis, who in 1986 became a perverse folk hero of sorts among sick cop-haters when he wounded six cops in a shootout in the Bronx, then was found not guilty of attempted murder by an all-black jury after his lawyer, the radical leftist William Kunstler, used the pernicious "black rage" defense. Davis wound up in Sullivan County anyway, when he was convicted of killing a rival drug dealer in 1999. When he was sentenced to life, he snarled at the judge, "I ain't afraid of you" over and over. I may have hurled a well-deserved epithet or two at a judge in my time, but Davis would actually have killed that judge if he could have.

Jail had not mellowed Davis when I met him in the yard. He was identifiable by his Black Power skull cap, thick glasses, and baleful stare, and if I had nothing in common with Berkowitz, I had even less in common with Davis.

I did find it odd that Davis took an interest in me, however. He sought me out and asked me frequently for legal advice, though not even Clarence Darrow could have done anything for him. What I did not know at the time was that Davis was being used as a tool by my enemies to befriend me.

The fact is, the state's Department of Corrections lives in an uneasy symbiosis with some of the hardest prisoners in its system. It is another dirty little secret that the state will bribe people like Larry

Davis all the time because of what they can deliver about other prisoners. In my case, I am convinced Davis was bribed to set me up in another loony "murder for hire" scenario that would be unleashed on the public on the day I'd be released from prison, as a last resort after I had beaten the odds and survived my sentence.

Stay tuned. That story is coming up.

The bottom line was that it wasn't criminals like Berkowitz or Davis or anyone else who posed the biggest threat to my health in prison. It was the doctors in the Sullivan County jail. Apparently, this was the state's preferred method of destroying me. It began one morning when I woke up not feeling well and didn't want breakfast. So, they dragged me to the infirmary—which, unlike those at Rikers Island and Bellevue, was more like Dr. Mengele's chamber of horrors.

Once there, I was drugged up like a circus bear. I was forced to take pills and shots I didn't need, maybe twelve to fifteen every day. I didn't know what they were putting into me, but whatever it was made me sick to the point that I felt as if I were on the edge of death.

This form of incarceration is far more insidious than being in solitary. You lie flat on your back, not knowing if you are breathing your last, without access to books or paper to write on. When I would try to stand up, my legs were swollen and useless. For the first time in my life, I felt like an invalid.

Were they trying to poison me to death? What does it sound like to you?

This, then, was my condition as 2001 fused into 2002: barely alive, pinballed from solitary confinement to the infirmary and back. Not for a moment did the prison hierarchy give me a break or even a modicum of respect. In January 2001, when I was in the Downstate Detention Center, I received an invitation to attend George W. Bush's inauguration. I assumed, naively, that being the invited guest of the President of the United States would persuade the superintendent of the state's jails to allow me a furlough to travel to Washington. I suggested to *The New York Times* that I be accompanied by two guards. Not only was I denied but the warden of the prison made light of the request. "We don't do inaugurations," he told the *Times*. There is nothing worse than an idiot who thinks he is clever.

The same attitude was present when I had my first parole hearing in June 2001. I believed it would be a serious hearing, but it was merely a formality and excuse for the parole board to throw mud on my good name. All they kept asking me to do was say I was sorry.

"I will," I told them, "if you can first tell me what I'm supposed to be sorry for. Am I supposed to admit guilt for something I never did, for something only a rigged trial put me in here for?

"There is nothing on God's green earth," I said, "that would make me turn Robert Morgenthau from a buffoon into a genius."

And so, it concluded that early release would "deprecate the seriousness of your offenses and demonstrate disrespect for the law." In truth, it is the corrupt, bribe-riddled system these stooges perpetuate that does exactly that. I guess they didn't want to hear that.

Another bit of extortion they attempted was to try to have me promise not to speak badly of George Pataki and Carl McCall, who apparently had become scared rats in Albany, knowing what I did of their underhandedness. I told the parole board to go to hell. Incredibly, Pataki and McCall would actually go to court and get an *order of protection* against me, an eighty-two-year-old man with swollen legs and a long white beard.

Does this sound familiar? Obviously, the old strategy of tarring me with the stigma of being "dangerous" to anyone in high office was still on the table, now as a last-ditch effort to subdue me.

Last-ditch because as my sentence wound down—my release date was now set for July 28, 2002—I had not only survived in prison but in court as well. I mentioned before how the legal tide began to turn in 2001 when Ira Gammerman overplayed his hand, leaving his insane rulings in jeopardy and his favoritism to Stahl's courtroom henchman David Rosenberg all too exposed.

I have told you how Rosenberg had for years misrepresented himself as the attorney for Stahl Associates and even Hirstan, my own company! But he blew it when he carried this lie into another case before an honest judge. This happened when I refused to accept Gammerman's absurd order to keep all Stahl Associates mail from being delivered to my office after Stanley had died. My recourse showed how sharp my senses still were; instead of suing the Stahl mob to press for the overturn of the ruling, I sued the United States Postal Service, asking that the U.S. District Court for the Eastern

District of New York direct the Postal Service to deliver that mail to me.

I knew I had Rosenberg by the balls because the Postal Operations Manual states that if disagreement arises about where such mail should be delivered, "it must be delivered according to the order of the organization's president or equivalent official." That was me—Gammerman's comical rulings notwithstanding.

But here's the really comical part. With the height of gall, Rosenberg thought he could butt into my suit. First, he wrote to the Postal Service, saying that he had represented Stahl Associates for the last *five* years. Then he filed papers listing the "Disputant" in my case not as the Postal Service but rather as *himself!* This so confused the judge, Norman Menegat, that he put *Rosenberg* on the stand so that my lawyer, Mark Zauderer, could put it to him.

"You do not represent the partnership called Stahl Associates, do you?" he asked.

Rosenberg, under oath, finally 'fessed up.

"No," he said, "I do not."

Judge Menegat had little time or patience for this fool and his lies and issued a stinging defeat to Rosenberg and his mob of jackals by confirming that I was the "president or equivalent official" of the partnership and "[a]s such, Mr. Hirschfeld is entitled to control delivery of the partnership's mail." Rosenberg, he added, "has no personal claim to the mail in dispute."

That victory was as sweet as tasting champagne. And yet such is the venal influence of the Stahl mob that not only was Rosenberg not censured for his lies but the mob ignored Judge Menegat's order and continued keeping my mail from me.

Still, at least I had broken through the outer wall of a corrupt legal system, and my enemies knew it. With my release growing closer, and knowing I would be taking aim at the inner wall, Morgenthau re-entered the stage, though at first I was too happy to have even considered what that man would do.

By the day I walked out of the Sullivan County jail, his plan was underway. On that brilliantly sunny and warm July day, the upstate media crowded outside the prison gate, in what was the biggest event seen in the Catskills probably since Frank Sinatra sang there. And for the good people of that area, I had my own plans—to someday bring *Phantom II of the Opera* to the mountains and rekindle the long-dead hotel scene.

"One seed built the forest," I explained to the media crowd. "Same thing with the Catskills."

Mark my words: I will rebuild and restore the glory of the Catskills. Because only I can.

I then celebrated my release by hosting a "get out of jail" lunch at the Villa Roma Resort. For weeks, I had advertised in the local papers and on radio stations that anyone could come and eat for free. And at noon, around eighty people came in, including a busload of my friends from New York City. I believe I outdid them all in devouring pickled herring. You can imagine how difficult it is for a Jew to sacrifice pickled herring for two years.

The first thing I did after my new limo driver, John Armstrong, had taken me back home to the city, was to finally be able to see my beloved wife, who by now was permanently confined to an assisted-living facility on the Upper East Side. Only then did I begin to think again of Morgenthau and how his lies and heavy-handed ways had driven Zipora into a condition from which she would not recover. Nonetheless, I was overwhelmed with relief to be back home in my Fifth Avenue apartment, and—hallelujah—sleeping in my own bed.

Then, on August 2, only five days after completing my sentence, Morgenthau's venality struck again. That day, in a fetid echo of the Mark Kriegel column seven years before, the *Daily News* carried another "exclusive" story, with the headline emblazoned in big letters, "MURDER IN MIND? Abe is sought in hit list probe."

I thought, "Here we go again" as I read in complete disbelief the first sentence:

"Abe Hirschfeld is out of jail, but authorities fear he still has murder on his mind."

The story went on to weave yet another ludicrous "plot"—in which I was supposed to have paid $100,000 to none other than *Larry Davis* to hire hit men to kill no less than *seven* people, including Judge Ira Gammerman and *my own daughter Rachel!*

The lies in this burlesque of a tale were breathtaking—and breathtakingly stupid. Among the details that the story said "the *Daily News* has learned" was that Davis was my "protector" in jail—which

I'm sure was news to Davis—and that prison authorities had intercepted a check they said I had somehow sent to Davis.

How ridiculous was this? Consider for one thing that prisoners hardly have private mailboxes and that any mail they get is routinely opened. And yet here I was to have written Davis a check—not that prisoners have any of those in jail, either—and sent it to him not expecting to be caught! That is how ridiculous it was.

Indeed, I didn't have to wait long for the red "herrings" in the scenario to consume it in derision. For one thing, the check was not signed. For another, it was not quite explained how Larry Davis was supposed to dispense all that money to his hit men.

Obviously, Morgenthau hadn't hired any better scriptwriters in the last two years.

The whole thing of course reeked of Morgenthau's mendacity and was pitifully clumsy even by Morgenthau's standards—including the fact that, in seeking a conduit for his lies, he chose a reporter named Michelle McPhee, who had been one of the *Miami Herald*'s cabal of liars during my Castle Hotel days. I need not even tell you that Morgenthau never found enough crooked judges and prosecutors to bring charges against me—if there was a kernel of truth to any of it, I would have been back behind bars in a heartbeat—and nothing ever came of this tomfoolery.

Well, one thing did—a very good thing that was doused in delicious irony. How perfect is it that by including Ira Gammerman on my "hit list," Morgenthau ensured Gammerman's blessed departure from hearing my case, since he was now considered a "target" of mine and couldn't possibly rule even-handedly (not that he ever did anyway). Before the summer was out, Gammerman finally recused himself, crying crocodile tears reminiscent of the fake Mrs. Stanley Stahl and whining about how terrible it was to be marked for "assassination." I nearly cried myself, from laughing so hard at his insincerity.

The truth of his recusal was quite the opposite from this tale of woe. It was that Gammerman, quite plainly, turned tail and ran from the bench before he could be removed once his illegal ruling were scrutinized by higher courts. The "hit man" story gave him the cover he needed to run.

I always believed Morgenthau's stupidity would be my ace in the hole, and it was.

And, now, geared up after having beaten all the odds against me, I was good and ready to run the table.

Abraham (Abe) Hirschfeld

CHAPTER THIRTY-FOUR: MY NEXT 85 YEARS

Having kept tabs on my business affairs even while behind bars and hundreds of miles away, I made a seamless transition to resuming my daily office routine. Elie and I once again occupied offices side by side in our headquarters on East 61st Street right next door to the Vertical Club, which had been renamed Sports Club/LA a few years earlier when I leased the now-legendary fitness emporium to a nationwide chain of upscale health clubs.

It was at the club, incidentally, at the swimming pool, that Elie met his current and hopefully permanent wife. I take a bow for that, too. After he had been divorced and in a rut of gloomy loneliness, I had all but directed him to go to the pool, which is the city's premier place for meeting beautiful girls looking for husbands (a quality I had envisioned when I created the Vertical Club in the first place). He went, and within weeks, he was hopelessly in love.

If I had changed for the better while in prison, however, New York city hadn't. In fact, when I returned home and saw the empty space in the magnificent skyline I had come to love so much, I cried just as I had on that terrible morning of September 11, 2001 when I watched on the TV in the Sullivan County Correctional Facility as the World Trade Center towers came crashing to earth with nearly 3,000 innocent men and women entombed in the ashes.

For me, as horrifying as it was, the tragedy and outrage once again crystallized all my old fears about those towers being a sitting duck for terrorists. It also rekindled all of the anger I had felt in 1993 when the WTC was battered by a car bomb left in the garage, only to be rebuilt as if terrorists simply did not exist and there were no lessons to be learned. Was I the only one to foresee that such a dastardly attack could happen again, only with far worse consequences? Apparently, I was.

What's more, I understood that the events of 9/11 could happen yet *again,* since it was clear that the city's planners still had no concept of the disaster they themselves had courted by failing to build the most secure buildings. But then, it seemed, I was the only one who could even conceive of putting up a grand and secure building like that.

And so, I took it upon myself to immediately design a workable plan for a terrorist-proof and airplane-proof WTC. While an army of architects vied for the eventual right to design a new WTC for billions of dollars, I mapped out a blueprint that was typical for an Abe Hirschfeld project—to be completed in half the time and at one-third of the cost of anyone else's plans.

I explained the concept, though not the precise details, which will only be revealed should the city give me the right to build. Put simply, by not giving me the project, the city will only hurt itself. And as much as the Trade Center needs to be built in only the way I suggest, I cannot allow the plans to be stolen from me, and I am not in business to enrich less talented and inspired builders. It is about time New York City drops its grudge against me, for the betterment of everyone who lives there.

I laid out the beauty and ingenious simplicity of my plan first as the featured guest at the National Press Club in Washington, D.C.—the same venue as my tete-a-tete with Paula Jones—on August 18, 2002. Because my parole office refused to let me travel to D.C., I spoke via a video feed, yet it was an important enough event to make the *Washington Post* sit up and take notice.

"Abe Hirschfeld is a legend of sorts in New York real estate circles and beyond," the *Post* reporter wrote the next day. "Hirschfeld's basic argument is that constructing buildings of concrete and masonry makes them too brittle to withstand an airplane collision, but that steel-and-glass buildings with removable walls would hold up much better."

I went into greater detail on my web site, Abehirschfeld.com, which I began in late 2002 to crack through the media embargo on me in New York. (I must admit that the notion of the Internet as an information "superhighway" is one I cannot even fathom much less grasp, given that for me, growing up in Tarnow, our superhighway was a dirt road traversed by horse-drawn carriages. Still, I have come a very long way on that road, and modern technology is surely a wonder of wonders if it can make Abe Hirschfeld a "columnist," just like Pete Hamill, on an even playing field with all those "professional journalists" who believe it's their right to ridicule me. Now, I have a forum, and I intend to use it. The only difference between the "real" writers and me is that I'm the one telling the truth.)

My column entitled "How I Will Rebuild the World Trade Center," went like this:

[W]hy am I the best builder there has ever been? Because what I build is based on vision and genius, the kind possessed by no other builder. Why is this? It's simple. Most builders are no more than architects whose vision is covered by blinders and a herd mentality. I will prove my point with three words: Frank Lloyd Wright. Along with Robert Moses, the man who built New York in the 1940s and 1950s, Frank Lloyd Wright, is my hero. He is regarded as the most famous architect in history, but he was no more an architect than I am. Ironically, he started his adult life working in a garage, and like me never went to any fancy-shmancy schools. But like me, he knew how to design buildings by instinct and innate genius—and by thinking "out of the box."

Today, that is not possible anymore, with all the architects coming out of colleges with full heads of impractical knowledge. They think they can do it all but usually mess up everything. I realized this reality yet again watching the *mishigas* about rebuilding the World Trade Center. I assume you've seen the various monstrosity designs submitted by some of the world's greatest architects—and, like me, I assume you hated them all. They are, of course, eyesores all, and they are not only insults to the 3,000 people who perished in the unspeakable tragedy of 9/11 but also completely impractical, stratospherically over-priced, and unable to withstand a stiff wind, much less a 737 crashing into them.

Now let me tell you why my plan for rebuilding the WTC is the only one that will work.

It starts exactly where any building does—with the foundation. If you have a good foundation, whatever you build will remain strong. A bad foundation and everything will fall. And the best foundation of all is an Abe Hirschfeld garage. In fact, I take not pride but great sadness in saying that the WTC would still be standing today if I'd built the garage under it. I believe the WTC was not destroyed by happenstance. The terrorists learned that it was not impregnable because of the garage bombing there a decade ago. If you succeed once, you go in again.

With my garage, they couldn't have gone in once. There are over 5,000 garages across the world designed from my original "open-air" plan—one which was laughed at in the 1950s when I calmly and rationally pointed out that "cars don't catch cold." Building them as I do, in a vertical plane with a "breathing" exterior,

429

not only gets it done with half the cost and in one-third of the time— but also makes for the safest building you can find....

[In] my WTC design, on the first floor will be a museum and memorial to the victims of 9/11, with their names and pictures displayed on the walls. In the museum will be an affordable restaurant for the masses who come to this shrine. The first ten floors of the building would house the New York Stock Exchange, which needs the space badly. And the rest—at least ten floors but as high as the eye can see if necessary—will be a completely new kind of apartment. And all these floors from top to bottom will be built in my vertical, open-air design.

You will say to yourself, "Open-air? Abe, you're *meshuga*. Why wouldn't that make the building as flimsy and vulnerable as a child's erector set?" That is what the architects say, too—because of their usual stupidity and blindness to simple ideas that work. In truth, no building could be safer. Because it will be built only with structural steel and glass, without any bricks.

Here's a little secret you should know: bricks are the most dangerous things you can build with. When a plane flies into a brick building, those brick walls—which cost a fortune—crumble into sawdust, and the fuel that spills and catches fire is further ignited by the bricks and will keep burning forever.

Now, look at what would happen with a steel and glass building. The plane flies through the glass, gets caught in the steel columns, which act like pincers and shear the wings off. The plane falls straight down to the ground, before the gas tanks can go into the building and explode. All that happens is that a few windows will be broken. Imagine how many lives would have been spared on 9/11 if this had been the case.

Not only is my open-air design safe, it makes for a wonderful, aesthetically-pleasing, modernistic look. There will be open space for 300 people on each floor, with floor-to-ceiling windows offering breathtaking views in every direction. In the winter, the glass walls are closed; in the summer, you can open them and not be trapped in an air-condition prison.

Once more, I'll point out that I am the only one in the world who can build a safe and beautiful WTC . . . I can put up a building in the time it takes the "architects" to bring in all their bricks.

Unfortunately, my plan has been lost in the morass of New York City and New York State incompetence and favoritism. Politicians like George Pataki and his footpage Randy Daniels, the Secretary of State, through their absolute control of the Metropolitan Transportation Authority—the bloated bureaucracy that oversees not only the buses, subways, and bridges but also major construction projects such as the WTC—would sooner slit the throats of 3,000 more people than to allow me a low-bid claim to rebuild the Twin Towers with the dignity, respect, and safety this project deserves.

What most distresses me about the closed club of favor-dispensing clubhouse pols is that Randy Daniels so easily compromised his personal integrity to join the club. After I had sent him to work for Pataki, Daniels—whom I'm sure you will recall was the recipient of a $50,000 gift from me after I built the 21 Hudson Street project—promised me he would keep a line of communication open between Albany and me. Instead, he too knifed me in the back.

Remember that terrible, threatening phone call I got from an incensed George Pataki warning me to keep away from rebuilding the old Altman's Department Store? Where was Randy Daniels? Nowhere to be found. As he was when I was on trial for criminal solicitation to commit murder. As my railroading was underway, I called him in desperation, appealing to his sense of loyalty and fair play to come to the courtroom and be a character witness for me.

"Abe," he told me meekly, "I would like to, I really would. But I've been told your case is too high-level for me to get involved."

In other words, too high-level for him to act like a man and not a mouse.

I told you I would return to the subject of the Altman's shuffle. As it happens, the World Trade Center was just a bigger Altman's, a prized piece of property to be allocated to a Pataki crony. Indeed, it is no mere coincidence that the same man who owns the lease on the WTC was also the man to whom Pataki had given the Altman's project: Larry Silverstein, whose brown-nosing of Pataki had killed off my plans for Altman's and enriched Silverstein by many millions of dollars.

This highlights lesson one in the ways and means of the construction industry in New York: It is more than a just a small world; it is an incestuous world in which one can almost always trace the winners and losers along a locus directly back to Pataki, and in

New York City directly to either Rudy Giuliani or his successor and toady, Mike Bloomberg. I, of course, have never been on that locus, nor would I ever have compromised myself or my beliefs to be. Whatever Abe Hirschfeld will build, be it the Rockefeller Center and Yankee Stadium garages, a neighborhood-renovating office or apartment building, or a corner candy store, it will be built not because of any favor-giving or favor-taking. It will be built because I can build it better than anyone else alive.

That is why New York City today could have a domed Yankee Stadium at the epicenter of a Bronx Champs Elysee. It could have thriving hotel casinos in the South Bronx and on Central Park South. It could have a fail-safe World Trade Center.

Instead, it has none of these. And all because George Pataki thinks it's more important to be in the pocket of people who are mean, vindictive, and petty enough to close my bank accounts, keep my mail from me, and introduce impostors in trials.

Not being in the "club" has surely cost me millions of dollars. However, it has cost New York and the U.S. much, much more. It has cost the world, too—no less than peace in the Middle East, which continues to be a raging inferno and offers Israel no hope of survival.

These are the penalties we are all paying for Abe Hirschfeld being "too hot" to handle and on the wrong side of the Stanley Stahl mob in a case about money.

Do not ever believe for a moment, then, that the politicians and their trail of behind-kissing profiteers like Larry Silverstein are part of the solution. They are the entire problem.

To put it bluntly (the only way I know), our country, our culture, our entire civilization is in the process of crumbling and the future of our children and grandchildren put into the breach because our most cherished institutions of government have been subverted and perverted, twisted into knots and turned into a pig's trough of corruption. I have made it a habit of carrying in my pocket for the last two decades a copy of the United States Constitution; today, I can barely recognize the selfless ideals in this wonderful document, buried under layer upon layer of clubhouse politics.

With this as a backdrop, you can now understand why the World Trade Center will, when and if it is ever rebuilt, be a monument not to its victims but to just another bit of slop in that trough—and, accordingly, an ever-inviting target for terrorists yet again.

The design eventually chosen by George Pataki and his nabobs in Albany and New York City, which came off the drawing board of an architect named Daniel Libeskind, was predictably a monstrosity. Its avant-garde, 1,700-foot-high towers were called "world vertical gardens" but more resembled twin piles of jagged, broken glass. Incredibly, Libeskind put a memorial to the victims thirty feet *below* the ground, which strikes me not as a memorial but as a graveyard. Libeskind would divide the towers into six "habitats," alpine, tropical, tundra, and so on, and an upright botanical garden. Is this New York or the Malayan Archipelago?

His design was so out of touch and so un-New York that it drew gasps of horror and tons of ridicule by real estate professionals and editorial writers. One of the latter, in the *New York Post,* described the Libeskind eyesore as having "Kafkaesque angles," which I assume means it looked overly depressing and that it resembled "a banal suburban park." Another called those "vertical gardens" a "ridiculous" idea, and that to build this structure would require "fiasco-prone biosphere technology" for the sake of all the plants in the "habitats." My old friend and student Donald Trump complained that it "would never have the majesty or the importance of the Twin Towers."

There was even talk that Libeskind—who had never before designed an office building—would not get the plan off the ground and would need to partner up with other planners. No one seemed to know who was really in charge of the project. It was a tangled, tragic-comical mess. And while everyone argued and pointed fingers at each other, the Twin Towers remained a hole in the ground.

Why? Because George Pataki and Randy Daniels have holes in their heads.

Just to clarify, I do not mean to infer that all this chaos and affronting to the memories of those who perished on 9/11 resulted only because I was not allowed to rebuild the Towers. The broader blame lies with a philosophy that has become entrenched in real estate over the past several decades and that is the rise of the architects and the decline of the builders. I addressed this disastrous trend in another of my web site columns, within an overall framework of a critical gap we as Americans face: being out-thought by terrorists because of our obsession to exalt elitist intellectuals at the expense of hard-working people of common stock. The latter, I wrote, were far smarter:

The biggest problem by far in the world today is that the intellectuals we are told to trust have never accomplished anything. Nothing. No intellectual ever has.

Ask yourself: Who discovered America? It wasn't the Spanish government or its intellectuals who ruled the thrones. It was Columbus, a common man. Who invented the airplane? Was it the intellectuals, the pointy-headed professors and mathematicians or philosophers or physicists? No, it was the Wright Brothers, who had no formal education. Who built the trains and the infrastructures of the cities? Not one of those who did went to Yale or Harvard.

A few years ago, I was honored by *Time* magazine, which named me one of the top one hundred builders and titans in history. You already know that I am a common man with a vision. I never graduated sixth grade....But on this *Time* list, I am not alone in such meager schooling. Of the hundred names, I don't think there are even two intellectuals.

On the other hand, they are men who had a vision and worked hard to achieve them—in spite of the nay-saying intellectuals who do not understand true genius.

I ask this: Who invented the means of destruction of the world? Albert Einstein. Quite simply, Einstein was too smart for our own good. Without his intellectual formulas, there would be no nuclear weapons in the world, no weapons of mass destruction....As a builder, I have expressed in this space my loathing for the intellectual architects who have become entrusted with designing important buildings but who routinely fail to create anything of lasting value because they have no ties to the common man. Only a builder can build a great building. Only a builder will walk the neighborhood, meet the people, know what the building should represent. Only then will he bring in people to bring his vision to fruition—the plumbers, the engineers, the electricians. And, lastly, the architects.

Remember, Einstein never built a building. If he did, it would have fallen down.

It was common men like Robert Moses, Frank Lloyd Wright, the Rockefellers, and the Fords who built our society. My old friend Steve Ross began his career with me building parking garages and went on to build the AOL empire—before the intellectuals came in and ruined it. The Internet wasn't invented by Al Gore; it was invented by the government, the military, but it went nowhere until a poor schlub who didn't graduate college took it to the next level. That schlub was Bill Gates.

The tragedy is that we give the intellectuals all the credit and all the money, and they do nothing for us. This is why we are sitting ducks for the bin Ladens, the Saddam Husseins. They are, of course, evil men, but they are also men of their people. They have discovered through hard work and fanaticism the loopholes the lazy intellectuals have left for them. And a terrorist with a cellular phone found the loophole to bring down a spaceship. Think of the damage they can do in a war.

We had better catch up to the terrorists in the common-man area. If we don't, World War III will be upon us before we know it, and we'll be prepared only for World War Two-and-a-half.

The villains in this state of affairs are the enablers of such destructive trends. Which is why I believe the years to come will show George Pataki and Rudy Giuliani in the light they deserve. When catastrophe hit our nation, they were good for one thing and one thing only: acting as undertakers. And cheap publicity hounds. They went to funerals, looked for cameras to cry into—and then, when the cameras were turned off and the dead were buried, they went right back to making sweetheart deals with fat-cats who have no understanding or appreciation of the common man, who of course was left not with millions of dollars but with the crumbs of empty promises.

That goes for George W. Bush, too. The man that I elected President has changed, for the worse. Once in office, he unleashed a hidden agenda of far-right-wing lunacy that plunged our country into the recession I had predicted five years earlier. Like everyone else, I, too, was moved when Bush came to the pit of Ground Zero, stood with police and firemen, and yelled through a bullhorn that he would give New York City $20 billion in aid to help rebuild. Three years later, we are still waiting. And one of his administration flunkies even had the gall to suggest that the police and firemen *volunteer* to work overtime in the event of a future terrorist attack. I think it's fair to assume that no one whom George W. Bush knows has ever done anything for free.

This was hardly the "compassionate conservative" of the 2000 campaign. Bush has shown little compassion but a great deal of incompetence in running the country. And, of course, he took us into a war with Iraq built on a tapestry of lies about an imminent threat of an attack by weapons of mass destruction that didn't exist. While I supported whole-heartedly George Bush Sr.'s intervention in 1991, I believed this war to be illegal under international law, immoral by any standard of what America represents, and insane given how the world would see us.

Worse, I saw in these moves dark motives involving the survival of Israel. I was deeply distrustful of Bush's coterie of wild-eyed, right-wing fundamentalists who believe in crackpot Biblical prophesies of an eventual Apocalyptic battle between good and evil to be fought in Jerusalem—a battle these folks truly believe will end with the destruction of Israel as the cue for the return to Earth of Jesus Christ. They masked these beliefs with a smokescreen of unconditional support for Israel, and to my dismay, the leaders of Israel sucked in to an insane policy of war and more war in their desire to see Saddam Hussein, who had done nothing to Israel in over a decade, vanquished. Yet, you need not be a genius or a Cassandra to see beyond the propaganda designed to narcotize the masses to understand that Iraq was marked for invasion for one reason—not for "liberation," not for oil, but to root the forces of Bush's Apocalyptic Gang in close proximity to Israel, for what is their updated Nazis version of a Final Solution: setting Israel in flames. For this, I make no bones about it, use no soothing euphemisms.

When I look at George W. Bush, I see another Hitler.

On the eve of war, I reflected on my growing unease in my column:

> I believe it is the aim of George W. Bush and the band of wild-eyed "Christian conservatives" with their visions of an Apocalypse in Jerusalem to go into Iraq so as to eventually attack Israel. I believe this war on Iraq, therefore, would be a criminally anti-Semitic act.

This outcome is the only plausible explanation for the war. Nothing else about it makes any sense. So, Bush doesn't like Saddam Hussein. I can understand that. I don't either. He's a *meshugena* bastard. So, why doesn't Bush simply get rid of him? Drop a bomb on him, in his palace, wherever he is. Why should you make the Iraqi people suffer because of one man you don't like?

If a man kills somebody, you prosecute him. You kill him. But do you also sentence his wife and children to death? Why should a whole country suffer for one man? And why should our country suffer the losses we will have? If Bush hates Hussein, he knows where he is. Every day Hussein goes on TV. So, knock down the TV station. Hussein isn't like bin Laden, who's unseen and unheard and knows how to hide.

Nobody would say one word if Hussein was killed. They say a country isn't allowed under international law to kill the leader of another country—but you're allowed to kill thousands of innocent people with bombs? That is madness.

I have a greater concern: Who made us policeman of the world? We have a UN. If something is wrong, let the UN go fight. Let them take care of the problem. You don't pay lip service to the UN, then do what you want anyway without it. Then, too, this man Hussein hasn't done a thing or made a move in twelve years. Let him be. I wouldn't waste a single life for him.

Unfortunately, the bombs did begin falling on Baghdad, and our military's rapid obliteration of what was essentially a 19th Century army caused a swell of nationalistic pride that disguised Bush's motives and the reality that the conquest was no more than old-style colonialist imperialism dressed up as a great patriotic venture. The swift victory made many Americans delirious, as it was at least some illusion of payback for 9/11, but it did not change my mind, and as I watched Israel being suckered into Bush's Middle East "road map for peace"—which if it is a road to anywhere leads into the bowels of hell—I became even more frightened of what the future years will bring in terms of blood and tears in the land of my people.

I grieve about this and blame many people. Yet, I also hold Israel itself responsible for its coming doom. In short, they asked for it. How? As I explained in another column, the fly was lured into the web by the promise of American aid, meaning cold hard cash. The day Israel took money from America was the day it lost its historic sense of independence and desire to live in peace with its Arab neighbors. Indeed, any country that has ever taken America's money has wound up being weakened internally and eventually plunged into chaos and ruination. The great mistake I made in trying to get my peace treaty ratified in Israel through the years has been dealing with leaders who were unwilling to step on America's toes. I have told you about how I spent $400,000 on a TV campaign to elect Ehud Barak as Prime Minister. But he turned his back on me thereafter and suffered defeat at the polls after only one term in office. I have since learned that the key to peace is not any elected official but the people themselves.

Politicians are prostitutes; they will take money to say anything, then they will send you floating down the river. Now I realize that it is the people who make the politicians sit up and listen. The people make the changes. Is that not what the Constitution says?

Thus, I have enlisted to the cause of peace the largest and most important grass-roots Jewish organization in the world, Hadassah. This idealistic, noble women's charity includes some of the most prominent Jewish-Americans in the world. Hadassah is the model of peaceful co-existence. Hadassah hospitals in Israel serve both Israelis and Palestinians. No group of people is more respected. And they support my plan one hundred percent.

On Saturday, March 15, 2003, I was the Master of Ceremonies at the Hadassah dinner in Queens, New York. It was a wonderful, joyous, festive occasion, and I am proud to tell you that the president of Hadassah agreed to attend a press conference with several influential Palestinians to endorse the treaty.

Some of you may say, "Abe, what's the point of such peace-making when war and death apparently is the weapon of choice by our leaders?" I say we need to use our weapons of peace now more than ever. We must insist on peace and raise our voices in unmistakable unity and say no to war.

The most inspiring books I have ever read are The Five Books of Moses and the Declaration of Independence. And the latter begins with the immortal words, "We the people." Again, only we the people can make change. A rising tide will lift up all the boats. The politicians are just the boats in the harbor. We are the tide.

Consider this as well, that outside of Saudi Arabia, not one Jew has ever been killed in any Arab country because he is a Jew. No other Arab country prevents people of other religions and races from living their lives in peace. This is the basis of my peace treaty—that all people want nothing more than to live in peace with their neighbors, no matter who they are. That is the instinct of all people. Yet, many thousands of Jews will be killed because of Bush's way. And we must not allow that to happen.

The biggest pity of all is that my peace treaty could have been ratified 100 times by now since 1974 when Yasser Arafat agreed to it. But it's still not too late for peace. I can bring it about within three weeks. Guaranteed. The first step is for Ariel Sharon to listen to his own people and take the first exit off of George W. Bush's road map to hell. He and all Israeli leaders must stop their intransigence to dealing with Arafat, a good and decent man who dearly wants peace. They must ignore Bush's Palestinian puppet, Mahmoud Abbas, whom he ordered to be installed as Prime Minister merely to marginalize Arafat. They must also recognize other good Palestinians such as Ismail Abu Shana, who has rejected Abbas's crude capitulations.

My peace treaty is a remarkably simple document. And I stand ready at a moment's notice to go to Israel and get them to ratify the treaty, not as a delegate of the U.S. but as a private citizen who holds the only key to peace. I am the only man on Earth who can bring about peace. Colin Powell cannot do this. Colin Powell never ate baba ganoush or shish-kabob or kosher food. He doesn't speak Hebrew. I speak not only Hebrew and English but also Arabic. You have to know people to get them to trust you. It took me six months to get Arafat to sign my peace treaty, but he learned he could trust me. At one point, Arafat asked me, "Why doesn't any Jew besides you want to talk to me?" And you see that's the problem. Too many Jews won't talk to him.

I again assure Israel they won't have to give up an acre of land for there to be one beautiful and peaceful country—Israel-Palestine The most important clause reads thusly: *Human needs and the ability of the State to absorb immigrants shall be the grounds for immigration policy.* That says it all in one sentence. Because while they do not admit to it, Israel needs those Arabs who stream into Israel for the promise of prosperity—people who will jump at the chance to be a janitor at a hotel—and that all people will share a common dream and live together in peace.

I feel confident this will happen, because it very nearly did three years ago when I went to Israel to work for the treaty's ratification. But then my enemies at home had me indicted on false criminal charges because they didn't want me to get the credit for bringing world peace. In their narrow selfish interests and greed, all of those crooked district attorneys and judges and lawyers cost the world the peace it could have had right now.

I believe a prerequisite for bringing to fruition this peace is the defeat of George W. Bush in 2004. However, do not believe I have turned off the Republican Party. Ironically, as George W.'s star fell in my eyes, that of his brother Jeb rose. It is Jeb Bush whom I believe will one day be elected President and will become one of the finest we have ever had. I told him that myself when he was kind enough to invite me—as the only invited guest from New York—to attend his inauguration in December 2002, a month after his reelection as governor of Florida. No, it wasn't because I gave him money, for I hadn't given him a cent. It was for my advice and friendship. While other politicians kept their distance from me, as a "convicted felon" (a rather amusing situation given that so many of them are or will end up as convicted felons—and the rest are merely unconvicted felons).

As for my own political aspirations, they alas will not be fulfilled because of the injunction against felons running for office. Not that this has stopped certain influential New Yorkers from urging me to run anyway; for instance, one very highly-placed East Side Democrat who keeps telling me he wants me to run for the city council seat in my election district. (Apparently, he thinks there can be exceptions to the felon rule, and I believe he is right.) I also firmly believe that if I wanted to run for President, I could do it, by amassing enough popular support to change the absurd prohibition in the Constitution against non-American-born people being able to hold the office. I can move mountains, when I put my mind to it.

And I will continue to move them in my next eighty-five years. I can tell you that I have never felt better in my life than I do as I write these words today. This is partly psychological, having survived the hell I have been put through. And indeed, having found so much strength within, I was prepped for a physical transformation once I was free and clear of the Sullivan County prison infirmary.

Not that the state's tentacles were cut when I walked out of that cursed place. They would have me on a leash until my parole was up on July 28, 2002, and they used every inch of that leash to try and choke me. Remember, I was still being medicated by the twelve drugs I was forced to take everyday in prison. Upon my release, I went to my personal doctor so he could check me out. I told him I wanted to end all of these medications save for one, Flomax, for my prostate, and my sleeping pills. The doctor was aghast. "Abe," he said, "you can't just stop taking these medications. If you do, you can die. You must wean yourself off of them gradually."

Instead, fearing that the state had gotten to this doctor, I weaned myself off of *him,* immediately. I went next to the NYU Medical Center but fared little better. I sat in the reception room for twelve hours before a doctor would see me. He looked me over and sent me home with a tube of some kind of cream and told me to wipe my body with it. But when I did, I felt as if my bones were burning and that my scalp was about to crack open. In agony, I called one of the NYU doctors. He listened for a few moments, then impatiently said to come back in, that he wanted to cut off all my hair and see if I had cancer of the scalp!

Such incompetence led me to one last option. Though I was supposed to request permission for any travel I wanted to do from my parole officer, I said the hell with it. I packed a bag and flew to Miami Beach. There, I checked into Mt. Sinai Hospital. At first, however, I was treated no better. The first few doctors who came to see me did not a thing, and I felt like a prisoner once again—the phone in my room was kept shut off. At one point, my old friend, the former mayor of Miami Beach, Alex Daoud, came to visit me. He couldn't understand why the phone was dead.

"Alex," I told him, "if you knew what's been done to me since you last saw me, you'd understand."

Finally, blessedly, I was seen by an honest doctor, and a brilliant one, Dr. Nathan Siegel, the chief doctor at Mt. Sinai. He came to see me and was absolutely shocked at my condition.

"Doctor," I pleaded to him, "if you don't help me I'm going to die in this bed."

Dr. Siegel spent long hours with me. He himself treated me and allowed only the finest doctors in the hospital to tend to me. One by one, he ended the needless medications, agreeing with me that the only one I needed to take was Flomax. Within days, I felt completely rejuvenated. I flew back to New York with a wonderful sense of ease and calm and relief. Now, at last, I was ready to throw myself into the many exciting projects I had been thinking about.

The World Trade Center rebuilding was one. Another would be to address the urgent matter of building a state of the art stadium that could bring the 2012 Olympics to New York City. The city, of course, has never hosted the Olympic Games, and with reason: the physical logistics of staging far-flung events over a two-week period in a teeming metropolis and not disrupting the already-overburdened populace in a town where you must sit in a taxicab for an hour and a half just getting from First Avenue to West End Avenue.

Enter the Hirschfeld Solution.

You have seen by my World Trade Center plan how my open-air concept has beneficial applications that far transcend garages. That same concept governed my blueprint for an Olympic Stadium to be constructed in the West 50s opposite the Jacob Javits Convention Center—the very land I helped develop with Donald Trump when it was called the Penn Railroad Yards, and which Trump could never turn into his dream of a Television City. I presented the plan on August 28, 2002 at the Sports Club/LA, tying the development of the blighted Javits Center neighborhood—still relatively barren since Trump's epic failure—to the stadium project, thus providing a double bang for the buck.

My press release laid out the blueprint of a typically unique Hirschfeld project:

> The lack of hotel accommodations and parking facilities on Manhattan's West Side has been a major deterrent to this area's viability as a vital and vibrant revenue-producing neighborhood. Hirschfeld's plan will not only alleviate but also solve this problem. The project will include:
> * An open-air garage with a 10,000-vehicle capacity.
> * A state-of-the-art Sports Club facility with 73,000 seats.
> * An Olympic-size stadium with a fully retractable domed roof.
> * A 2,000 room hotel complete with above standard amenities.

Of these features, the most important was the one that carried my signature, the garage, which would be built under the stadium, accordion-style. I explained why in one of my web site columns:

> My vertical design, on the other hand, is a magnificent use of space and money. Again, we think out of the box—a 73,000-seat

stadium built on top of a 10,000-car garage, with a fully retractable domed roof and a 2,000-room luxury hotel. New York today remains the only major city without a modern stadium. It should have been built when Rudy Giuliani was mayor.

Unfortunately, Rudy was only good for one thing: He was a great undertaker. He went to a lot of funerals, while the city rotted.

You're asking: "So, Abe, won't this big stadium clog and choke the West Side with traffic?" I assure you it won't. What it will do is completely revitalize the run-down Javits Center area—and do it while routing traffic straight from the Lincoln Tunnel into the garage, as it will from the Midtown Tunnel via 34th Street, which is always empty because it's double the width of most streets.

The trouble is, New York streets are made for moving traffic, but there's usually no place to move it to. The garage is that place. This is the very reason my garages took America out of a deep recession back in the '50s: by moving all the traffic to shopping malls.

Now you're asking (you ask a lot of questions): "How much will the taxpayers pay for this star-spangled stadium?" The answer: not a penny. I never make taxpayers pay for my buildings. I go right to the banks, and because of my track record for building in record, cost-effective times, they arrange the financing, to be repaid from future profits. There was a reason why Mayor John Lindsay named me to the city's Public Development Council in 1972, a high honor for a fifth-grade graduate, but it recognized my genius—later proven by my revitalization of New York, Albany, and Miami Beach.

When the media floated my plan, Mike Bloomberg was gleeful because it captured the fancy of the worldwide Olympic committees. Indeed, for all the expensive dinners Bloomberg threw for the U.S. Olympic Committee and the I-love-New York monologues at the city's presentations by the likes of Billy Crystal and other entertainers, it was my plan that led the Olympic bigwigs to pick New York as the host city for 2012.

Of course, you know the upshot to this story, which is a lot like many other stories. Bloomberg would not—*could not*—allow me the concession to build the stadium. This puppet of a mayor has no power to buck the authority of his overlords, George Pataki and Randy Daniels.

I found this out when I was granted a meeting with Dan Doctoroff, Bloomberg's Deputy Mayor of Urban Development. I sat in Doctoroff's office waiting for him to appear. Finally, after an hour, an assistant told me Doctoroff had been called away and couldn't make it. Another meeting was not scheduled. Later, I was told by someone very high in the mayor's office that Doctoroff stood me up on orders from Bloomberg himself. No one within the administration, this man told me, can speak with me. Abe Hirschfeld, it seems, is *verboten*.

That sounded an awful lot like what that spineless traitor Randy Daniels had told me about decisions about me being made on the uppermost levels of government. Birds of a feather, I have learned, connive together.

I can only hope and pray that by the time the stadium project will begin, Pataki, Bloomberg, and Daniels will be distant memories. (Rumor had it in the summer of 2003 that Daniels will run against Senator Charles Schumer; while I reiterate that I do not like Schumer, I will ensure that he will crush Daniels in a landslide.) I hope, too, that their successors will realize that the way to success and to an overall Renaissance in New York City will not be to build based on my ideas—but to have me build according to my exact plans. Because without me, without my vision and instincts, any such plans will not work.

You cannot copy an original, after all. There can only be one. Besides, I intend to be around for a long, long time to come.

That, of course, means that the worst nightmare of my enemies will come true. For all the shady and illegal machinations I have had to endure in New York City's courtrooms the last dozen years, the simple act of surviving has served me well. The legal tide that began to turn in 2001 has continued turning in the years since.

Yes, my never-ending legal tussle with Stanley Stahl and his crooked henchmen still remains alive and well in the court system. And yet, the delightful irony that removed Ira Gammerman from the case has predictably allowed me to taste the sweet nectar of justice. The judge who replaced him, an honest jurist named Marcy Friedman, rendered nearly all of Gammerman's insidious rulings invalid in one fell swoop on February 18, 2003. In her ruling, she saw through Gammerman's sleight of hand like a thin veneer of cheesecloth.

She particularly took umbrage at a Gammerman ruling that read like this:

"Abraham Hirschfeld and any person acting with him or on his behalf or otherwise in possession of the books, records, bank account records, and other documents and assets of Hirstan Associates are directed to immediately deliver them to Marcus Rosenberg & Diamond LLP, as attorneys for the co-manager of Hirstan Associates, James Matera, at their offices at 488 Madison Avenue, New York, New York, and all banks or other institutions holding funds or assets of Hirstan Associates are ordered to disregard the directions of Abraham Hirschfeld and comply with the directions of James Matera as the duly authorized agent of Hirstan Associates; and any further attempt by Abraham Hirschfeld to interfere with or act in the name of Hirstan Associates, without prior order of this Court, is null and without force or effect."

This order had become the spoke in the wheel for Robert Morgenthau to follow me all the way to Florida to continue harassing me. Denied a bank account for my own company in New York, I had opened an account in Miami Beach with Fidelity Bank. Within weeks, I received a letter from Fidelity's vice-president, Edward Welch, informing me that the bank was closing the account—at the "behest," I learned, of none other than Gilda Mariani. (This was not the first time Morgenthau's stooge had wormed her way into my affairs a thousand miles from her jurisdiction. When my production of *Phantom II of the Opera* opened in West Palm Beach, she brazenly called the Palm Beach newspapers to plant items that I was about to be arrested, disrupting box office business and prompting many ticket buyers to ask for refunds.)

Yet, now, Judge Friedman rightfully found Gammerman's orders deceitful. She wrote that "Contrary to the Stahl representatives' contention, there is a substantial, bona fide issue as to whether [Gammerman's rulings] constitute a final determination designating James Matera as the sole manager of Hirstan Associates."

Moreover, Judge Friedman even hoisted Gammerman on his own petard, for screwing up his own intention of handing Hirstan over to Matera. While Gammerman's ruling "may have had the effect of designating Mr. Matera as the sole manager," she wrote, "it does not contain an express directive to this effect, and stops short of giving Mr. Matera unconditional authority to execute instruments on his sole signature." In other words, Gammerman's stupidity was again my ally.

When I read Judge Friedman's words, all I could do was shout "hallelujah!" I celebrated the ruling in my web site column, adding a few of Judge Friedman's other findings:

Judge Friedman took a long, hard look at the case and upbraided David Rosenberg for trying to pull an "end run" around the law to make James Matera a permanent managing partner and remove me as a partner. Specifically, she ruled that she had been conned by a "misapprehension"—or lie—that Rosenberg merely wanted "clerical" changes instead of axing me. She also ruled I was due all back monies.

This was a signal victory for the little guy fighting an unjust evil system of thieves. And so, I have renewed vigor as I write these words. The biggest casualty of my prison term was peace in the Middle East. That's what the Stahl mob cost the world. Now, I will return to the quest of peace.

The Friedman ruling was a prelude to an even greater exhilaration in May when I received a phone call from one of my appeals lawyers bearing the astonishing news that the U.S. Supreme Court has agreed to hear my appeal on the criminal solicitation conviction. One month later, there came another call with news just as breathtaking: for the first time, James Matera was ordered to testify in court about why he has any claim to be a partner in Hirstan Associates.

Sometimes, when the tide turns, it causes a tidal wave.

I am hardly gloating, or under any delusions, however. My enemies are very powerful men. Among Stanley Stahl's holdings are the Apple Bank and the Bank of New York. Both of these banks have had considerable business dealings with the bin Laden family. I do not know to what extent the banks have secretly financed terrorism. That is something that should, and must, be investigated because it smells like bad fish.

Why, then, should I expect these men will change their ways against me? I no doubt will still be facing their crooked judges and firing their bribed lawyers. It is still a fact that, despite rulings from honest judges, my share of the profits from my own business, as well as documents relating to my own business, are still being withheld from my possession.

But it is inevitable that I will win in the end.

It is written on the wind.

As I write these final words, I am nearing the end of my parole, whereupon I will be free to travel to Israel on my lifelong mission of peace. I make this vow to my old and good friend Jimmy Carter, a man of peace and good intentions: I will give you $1 million to go to the Middle East with me and settle this terrible conflict at long last, on the precepts on my peace treaty.

Together, or alone if need be, I will try to undo the damage done by George W. Bush and his scandalous, barbaric administration. In the end, when all the talking is done and all the posturing has done nothing to stem the shooting and the killing, I will be the last best hope for worldwide peace.

I also will be pursuing all of my ingenious solutions to our greatest problems, which I have grouped under the general program I have named my "33-Nina Solution"—in homage to my great friend Al Hirschfeld. Actually, the full title is "Abe Hirschfeld's 33 Nina Solution for reversing the recession to economic and social prosperity, including full employment," the particulars of which are:

* True reform of the education and prison systems.
* Reorganizing of the Social Security system, which otherwise will run out of money by 2030, to ensure that no elderly American ever need suffer from poverty or anxiety over access to top quality medical care, housing, and cultural enrichment.
* Full employment at a living wage.
* The end of child crime, depression and disaffection, and the raising of children to become moral, respectful, and well-developed adults.
* A plan for gasoline replacement (non-petroleum power) that will eliminate the strong arm that OPEC has over our country.
* A more effective transportation system based on my Bullet Train technology for a fast and efficient urban and inter-city rail network.
* A national urban redevelopment agenda dedicated to eliminating slums everywhere.
* The end of police brutality based on my integration of cops in patrol cars.

* My no-pill, no-exercise, gimmick-free plan that allows a person to eat all they want while losing desired weight.
* A proven solution to substance abuse and crime.
* A plan to revitalize our economy that within two weeks to three months will bring back our economic prosperity. This plan would reverse the recession to full employment, as it did in 1960, 1978, 1993, and 1995.
* Above all, the need for peace. My peace treaty will create peace in the Middle East in a few weeks and relieve friction between the religions.

I guess what all this means is that if there is a windmill left to tilt at, look for Abe Hirschfeld, the man from Tarnow and La Mancha, to be there making a ruckus.

I can hardly wait for the next one. Let the wind begin to blow!

About The Author

A legendary figure for four decades, Abe Hirschfeld was born in Tarnow, Poland in 1919 and raised in Palestine before coming to America in 1950, to become one of the world's best-known real estate entrepreneurs, inventors, theatrical producers, peace advocates, and joke-tellers. His open-air garage concept revolutionized the American economy in the '50s and he was recently named by *Time* magazine as one of the 20th Century's top hundred most influential business geniuses. Perhaps best known for his $1 million offer to Paula Jones to drop her sexual harassment lawsuit against President Bill Clinton, his stormy tenure as publisher of the *New York Post,* and his many political campaigns, he has attracted headlines and controversy – as well as powerful enemies – by refusing to "keep his mouth shut," even after being sent to prison for two years. Always ready with a quip, a quote and a good idea, he claims to have written over 10,000 jokes, and can prove it during any given dinner. Abe Hirschfeld lives in New York City.

Mark Ribowsky is the author of six previous books including *He's a Rebel: Phil Spector –Rock and Roll's Legendary Producer* and *Don't Look Back: Satchel Paige in the Shadows of the Game*, and *A Complete History of the Negro Leagues*. He lives in New York City.

Lozon
1 28 / 16
24.95

Made in the USA
Lexington, KY
24 March 2016